Head Dress of the British Lancers

Head Dress of the British Lancers
1816 - to the Present

David JJ Rowe & William Y. Carman

Schiffer Military History
Atglen, PA

Dedications

Dedicated to my mother Ellen Annie Abbott, for her constant encouragement.
- David Rowe

Dedicated to my daughter Elizabeth Mary Copas, for all her help in production.
- William Carman

Book design by Robert Biondi.

Library of Congress Catalog Number: 2001095194.

Printed in China.
ISBN: 0-7643-1446-7

Published by Schiffer Publishing Ltd.
4880 Lower Valley Road
Atglen, PA 19310
Phone: (610) 593-1777
FAX: (610) 593-2002
E-mail: Schifferbk@aol.com.
Visit our web site at: www.schifferbooks.com
Please write for a free catalog.
This book may be purchased from the publisher.
Please include $3.95 postage.
Try your bookstore first.

In Europe, Schiffer books are distributed by:
Bushwood Books
6 Marksbury Ave.
Kew Gardens
Surrey TW9 4JF
England
Phone: 44 (0)208 392-8585
FAX: 44 (0)208 392-9876
E-mail: Bushwd@aol.com.
Free postage in the UK. Europe: air mail at cost.
Try your bookstore first.

Foreword

By Major (retd.) Roy Wilson, formerly Officer Commanding 300 Squadron, Home Service Force (T.A.).

Anyone who has read and enjoyed David Rowe's book on heavy cavalry helmets, and the many military publications by Bill Carman will need no reminder of their painstaking approach. In this work, intended to compliment the earlier book on heavy cavalry helmets, they not only go on to discuss all the various patterns of the British Army lance cap, covering the Regular Army and the Yeomanry, they also consider each component part in detail, enabling the reader to build up a comprehensive picture of this most striking head-dress.

Most welcome is the authors obvious concern to seek out information by examining original sources, including the lance caps themselves, rather than relying on the simple repetition of the sometimes ill-researched remarks of others.

Every serious student of British military uniform should have this book on their shelves. It will become an essential source of reference, and I am confident that it will remain the standard work on the subject for many years to come.

Contents

Acknowledgements

The author's express their thanks to the following, who in one form or other have contributed to this book, with our very special thanks to Geoffrey (Geoff) Frost M.AMS for providing continuous invaluable assistance by carrying out extensive research on our behalf, and for taking the detailed photographs of the Bedfordshire Yeomanry officers lance cap and the 12th Lancers other ranks lance cap that are illustrated in this publication.

Special thanks also to Christopher Bryant and Meng-Chi Tsen for permitting many of their fine lance caps to be photographed, to Hugh King, President of the Aldershot Militaria Society, for permitting many rare examples of lance cap plates within his collection to be photographed and included amongst the books illustrations. To Jon A. Maguire for dismantling his officers pattern lance cap of the 5th Lancers and for photographing same on our behalf, to Major Ray Wilson for writing the foreword to the book, and for providing finite details relating to the lance cap of the East Riding of Yorkshire Imperial Yeomanry, to the Parker Gallery, Pimlico, London for allowing military paintings and prints from their extensive stock to be reproduced, and to R.J. (Bob) Marrion, Rodney Player, and W.J. (Bill) Younghusband for kindly permitting their work to be illustrated in this book.

We also express our thanks to the following for their valued assistance. The late Leslie Barlow, A. H. Bowling, Tony Bradley, J.M. Brereton, M.D. Brittain Esq, Roy Butler Esq, Sgt A.G.(Andy) Cassidy (The Berkshire Yeomanry), Jack Cassin-Scott, A.R. Cattley, Louis Chalmers, Rene Chartrand, John Cooper A.M.S., Elizabeth Mary Copas, Brian Daly, Eric Dickinson, Alan Fordham, Don and Bryan Fosten, Arthur Fox-Davies, Lt Colonel the Hon E.G. French, the late John Gaylor, Philip Greenaway, Charles Griffin, B.T.A. Griffiths, Doug Hagger, Philip J.Haythornthwaite, Captain J.M. Holtby (Queen's Royal Lancers), K.B. Hook, Walter Lambert Esq, David le Roi, Peter Lewisham, Canon W.M. Lummis M.C., Major General (Rtd) James Lunt (16th/5th The Queen's Royal Lancers), Andrea Martin, Bryan Martin Esq, Erica Marx, David McAlpine Esq, P.J.R. Mileham, Frank Mitchell, John and Boris Mollo, Brian J. Newbury F.R.S.A., Dr P. Newman, Major Parkyn, S.R. Roget M.A., Christopher Rothero, Lynda Margaret Rowe, Richard Scollins, Wendy Skilton, R.J.(Bob) Smith, Ian Sumner, Robert J.Tredwen, Lt Colonel P.S. Walton, Philip Warner, F. Wilkinson Esq, Robert and Christopher Wilkinson-Latham, Russell E. Wood, and Stephen Wood.

We further express our appreciation to the staff of the following establishments and publications, and to the members of the societies listed, for their assistance in one form or other. Adam & Charles Black (Publishers), Argus Specialist Publications, Arms and Armour Press, Art Gallery Beverley, Blandford Press, Blunderbuss Antiques, Bosleys Military Auctioneers and Valuers, Brassey's (UK) Limited, Christie's South Kensington Limited, Colchester Town Libraries Services, Dee & Atkinson (Driffield), Drew's of Aldershot, East Yorkshire Borough of Beverley Council, First National Pictures, Geoff White of Bristol, Her Majesty's Stationery Office, Imperial Tobacco Co Ltd, Leo Cooper Publishing, Lincolnshire Life Magazine, Lyle Publications, Mayger of Hounslow, Military Antiques (Islington), Military Modelling Magazine, Modelworld Magazine, Museum of Lincolnshire Life, the late Anna Pollak O.B.E., Punch Magazine, Raphael Tuck & Sons, Regiment Magazine, Regimentals of Islington, Scottish War Museum, Soldier Magazine (U.S.A.), Sotheby's Auctioneers, Spellmount Publishing Limited, Spink's Auctioneers, London, Sunbury & Co, Middlesex, The Aldershot Militaria Society, The Berkshire Yeomanry, The Anne S.K. Brown Military Collection at Brown University (U.S.A.), The Crown Imperial Society, The Plumery, The Prince Consorts Library, Aldershot, The Queen's Royal Lancers Regimental Museum, The Robert Ogilby Trust, The Victorian Military Society, Tradition (London), Wallis and Wallis of Lewes, Sussex, Warner Bros, and the York Castle Collection.

Finally, we pay tribute to the late R.G. (Ron) Harris, an eminent author on matters military, whose past work includes cavalry mounted bands, drum banners, drum horses, the yeomanry force, its mounted bands and drum banners, the history and uniforms worn by many of the yeomanry regiments, and numerous other short articles on the British Army, published in various diverse military journals and magazines. We also express our respect to the memory of the late Stanley Kretschmer, a dedicated collector of cap badges, cavalry head-dress, military postcards, and contemporary black and white photographs of soldiers, a modest selection of the latter part of this unique collection being reproduced in this book by kind permission of D.P.& G. of Doncaster.

List of Plates

Chapter One

Introduction

It is the common practice for a profile of the author to be included on the rear inner page of the dust cover of a book. This will usually detail some personal information about the author's birthplace, education, career, family, hobbies etc., it will not however usually state why the author became interested in the subject of the book. To correct this anomaly, our joint introduction gives an insight into why the author's were motivated to put pen to paper to write the text for this particular book.

David J.J. Rowe

My serious interest in cavalry uniforms began in 1975, on the day I first visited a militaria shop situated in the West End of London. There on display where items of cavalry head-dress, pouches, sabretache's, swords and uniforms in all their splendid glory, which evoked in me a vision of these former famous cavalry regiments that had once formed part of the famous British Army. I was immediately impressed with the busbies, helmets, and lance caps on display, and purchased my first item of head dress, this being an other ranks 'Albert' pattern helmet of the 1st (King's) Dragoon Guards, complete with plume for the then princely sum of one hundred and twenty pounds.

Several months later, having purchased an officers lance cap of the 9th Lancers, and other ranks example of both the 12th, and 21st Lancers, they forming the basis of my collection, I now turned my attention to attempting to find out as much information as possible about each item. Living at that time quite close to the National Army Museum at Chelsea, London, I made use of the facilities available within the museum's reading room. However, upon commencing my research at this establishment, I quickly realised that whilst the museum's bin-book albums contained many coloured illustrations and photographs of various types of cavalry head-dress, there existed an almost total lack of reference books on this specialised subject, not that this was in any way the fault of the museum's staff.

There were of course available to readers, three most notable exceptions, these being R.H. Rankin's book entitled *A Pictorial History of Military Head-Dress 1660-1914*, and W.Y. Carman's, books entitled *Headdresses of the British Army - Cavalry*, and *Yeomanry*, all of which are regrettably now out of print.

In addition to the three books referred to above, the only other sources of reference known to the author are the official publications *Dress Regulations for the Army* covering the period 1822 to 1900, and 1911 and 1934. These authoritative publications gave details of the pattern of uniform to be worn by the officers of the various branches of the army at the period concerned, including details relating to the officers pattern lance cap, fuller details of which are given in chapter six. Never the less, until the publication of the 1900 Dress Regulations, the lance cap plate was merely described as being *'a gilt plate in front, with silver badge of regimental pattern'*.

There was at least an improvement in the level of information provided in the Dress Regulations of 1900, which gave details of the design for each of the regiments lance cap plate. The Dress Regulations of 1934 were hardly more informative, but did give information on the pattern of lance cap to be worn by the 9th Lancers, the 12th Lancers, and the amalgamated 16th/5th, and 17th/21st Lancers, together with details of the lance cap plates worn to be worn on these caps, but again minus battle honour details.

In the recent past, the occasional article on cavalry uniforms has been published in one or other of the various militaria journals/magazines, included in which would have been some information on cavalry head-dress. In general however, when describing the lance cap, these articles usually covered the most commonly known 1856 pattern of cap and did not go into any great detail, particularly with regard to the various differing pattern of lance cap plate fitted to these caps, nor the colours pertaining to the 'plume' rosette.

Over the years I had amassed a considerable amount of both photographic and written information on cavalry head-dress. However, the sources from which this knowledge was gathered came from many widely differing origins, there being no one book known to the author that would provide all the detailed information required on either heavy cavalry helmets, or lance caps etc. It was for this reason therefore that I decided to put pen to paper in order to remedy this shortcoming. As my ever changing collection of head-dress had over the years tended to consist mainly of heavy cavalry helmets, this was to be the subject of my earlier book *Head Dress of the British Heavy Cavalry* (3) published December 1999, although I had by this time already decided that my second project was to cover the lance caps of the British Army, and had commenced assembling detailed information on this subject.

Having over the years acquired several of the excellent book on military dress written by W.Y. Carman, who kindly not only wrote the foreword to my earlier book, but also contributed to, and proof read the text, I contacted Bill to outline my ideas for the lancer book. Having discussed with him my initial outline plans on this subject, and knowing of Bill's extensive knowledge of lance caps, it became obvious that the most sensible course of action would be for the two of us to pool our resources and to collaborate as 'partners in crime' to co-write this book, this idea happily having borne fruition.

William Y. Carman

As a child my soldier father ensured that I had many toy soldiers with which to play with, and thereby at a young age I gained valuable knowledge of the different pattern of uniform worn by the various branches of the then British Army, this scholarship creating an interest in uniforms that has never ceased to give me great pleasure.

As a young man in 1935, I was at the formation of the British Society of Collectors of Model Soldiers, later to be retitled the British Model Soldier Society, with branches throughout the United Kingdom. My interest in this newly formed society resulted in my undertaking the editorship of the their monthly bulletin, for which I wrote many articles on all types of military uniforms.

My interest in both model soldiers and military uniforms continued unabated, and later in life I became a maker of British historical soldiers, these scale model figures being sold in a shop in London's prestigious Burlington Arcade, and at Hamleys, the most famous toy store in the world.

After military service in the Middle East, I returned to civilian life and carried out research in the Public Records Office at Kew, and at the British Museum in Bloomsbury, London. I was offered, and accepted a position at the Imperial War Museum which was mainly concerned with modern warfare, and it was at this establishment that I continued my professional interest in matters military. I later transferred to the National Army Museum where I was able to pursue my enthusiasm for research on full dress uniforms of the period 1660 to modern times, eventually retiring from the museum whilst holding the post of Deputy Director.

My first book entitled *Naval Uniforms Past and Present*, was published in 1940, followed a few years later by publications on such subjects as the Egyptian Army, firearms, and military uniforms. In 1961, my book *Indian Army Uniforms, Volume One - Cavalry* was published, followed in 1969 by *Indian Army Uniforms, Volume Two - Infantry Etc.*

Earlier in 1968, at my own expense I had published my book *Headdresses of the British Army Volume One - Cavalry*, and following the success of this publication, in 1970 I published the second volume *Headdresses of the British Army - Volume Two - Yeomanry*, each of these volumes containing information relating to lance caps. In 1982 *Uniforms of the British Army - The Cavalry Regiments* was published, followed by the second volume, *Uniforms of the British Army - the Infantry Etc.* in 1985.

In addition to writing books, I have written a great many articles for many military magazines, including *Military Illustrated*, *Military Modelling*, and *Antique Arms and Militaria*, for whom I wrote articles on such subjects as belt plates, lance caps, heavy cavalry helmets, yeomanry head-dress, and the head-dress of the Yorkshire Yeomanry.

I has always been my intention to share my knowledge on matters military, and I have been able to achieve this undertaking by writing a great many articles for the journals of several militaria societies, included amongst which has been the British Model Soldier Society, the Military Historical Society, and the Society for Army Historical Research. I have also carried out uniform research for the films 'Khartoum' and '55 Days in Peking'.

My interest in military uniforms has never diminished, and over the years I have acquired various items of military dress, including items of head-dress and sabretache's, although due to the popularity of such items amongst collectors of militaria, the cost of these items has risen to such an extent that these days my interest is mainly confined to researching the origins of uniforms etc.

With regard to my researching information relating to items of uniform, it is apparent that a great deal has been written in the past without the author's checking the accuracy of the source they have consulted (even some regiments did not know the truth about their dress). This has led to me collecting and compiling my own files on all aspects of military dress, they containing much contemporary information, the files now numbering several hundred.

The opportunity of being able to co-write this current work, which is intended to be definitive, containing as much confirmed information as possible on the subject concerned, was one that I could not resist, for normally publishers prefer pictures to the written word, not that this publication has any lack of illustrations. By presenting new information on such an interesting aspect of military head-dress, it is hoped that others will add their information, thereby contributing to the common good, and increasing our understanding on this subject.

Chapter Two

The Origins of the Lancers and the Lance Cap

The Lancers

It was in the eighteenth century that the concept of equipping British cavalrymen with the lance was raised by Major John Floyd of the 21st Light Dragoons, who in January 1780 wrote to Lord Herbert[1] stating that he had acquired half a dozen lances and was making his rough-riders practice with them, his enthusiasm however led him nowhere (1).

Notwithstanding the above, the British Government had employed lancers as early as 1793, when at that time a large expeditionary force was formed under the command of the Duke of York to go to the Netherlands to fight the forces of the new French Republic (2). It was also decided to recruit fighting troops in Europe, from the many nations who had suffered at the hands of the French, and such a unit was the *Uhlans Brittaniques*[2] or British Uhlans, (*See Fig: 1.*) who were recruited from Polish soldiers in Germany, under the Marquis de Bouille who commanded the regiment from June 1793. In November of that year the regiment was favourably reviewed by the Duke of York, and they were soon engaged in the Flanders campaign. However, by 1796 the troops had left that area and were sent to the West Indies where their role was to be that of infantrymen, the regiment eventually being disbanded by 1798 (2). N.B. Apparently when in the West Indies, their uniform changed, although the lance cap remained in use (1).

In November 1811, Captain J.B. Drouville of an unidentified horse unit sent a proposal for the formation of British Lancers, to H.R.H the Duke of York. The idea behind this plan was to treat the lancers as light cavalry, and to clothe them in an inexpensive uniform comprised of a grass-green jacket, worn with either green overalls or white breeches and boots, their head -dress to be a shako in the German style called Schaws. In the event no satisfaction seems to have occurred[3], and when eventually British Lancers were formed, the suggested uniform was ignored with the Polish style of dress being adopted instead. N.B. It was also proposed that the pennon atop their lance should be the complete Union flag (1).

The effectiveness of the lancers as light cavalry, as used by opposing armies had not however gone unnoticed by Napoleon Bonaparte, and on the 18th June 1811 nine regiments of 'Light Horse Lancers' were formed by converting some existing regiments.[4] The existence of these regiments was however short lived, as one regiment was subsequently disbanded in 1814, the remaining eight regiments being disbanded following the defeat of Napoleon's army at the Battle of Waterloo in 1815 (3). The dashing exploits and successes of Napoleon's Polish Lancers[5] were not overlooked, particularly after the experiences of the British Army in the Peninsular, noticeably at the Battle of Albuhera in May 1811, and later after both the Heavy Brigade, and the Union Brigade had suffered at the hands of the Polish Lancers during the Battle of Waterloo in 1815 (4).

Eventually, the capability of the lance as an effective cavalry weapon dawned upon the British Authorities, and in 1816 it was decided to convert four light cavalry regiments to the role of lancers. The regiments chosen were the 9th, 12th, 16th, and 23rd Light Dragoons, who became armed with the lance, and adopted the lancer style of dress complete with lance cap.

The Formation of British Lancer Regiments

Although an official submission for the formation of lancers was issued on the 19th September 1816, to the effect that the 9th, 12th, 16th and 23rd Regiments of Light Dragoons were to be equipped with the lance, the actual conversion and change of dress took place much later. In fact regimental histories do not quote the change of uniform and so answers are sought elsewhere.

The 9th Lancers are said not to have been equipped with the lance until the 27th May 1817. In the case of the 12th Lancers, the actual submission date of 6th March 1817 states that the 12th Light Dragoons were to be styled the *12th or Prince of Wales's Royal Regiment of Lancers*, and that their facings were to be scarlet instead of yellow and the lace to be gold instead of silver[6], these alterations to take place from the 25th December 1817. Therefore with such a long period of time between the official submission for their formation, their titles and uniform changes, much deliberation might have taken place, with some regiments proceeding with the change from a Light Dragoons to that of Lancers more slowly than others (5).

It is surprising that no confirmed official information has been uncovered regarding the details of the first pattern of lancer uniform, even though such information has been sought by military historians and students of military dress for many years. In fact, details of the officers lancer uniform do not appear in official print until the first issue of the '*Regulations for the Dress of General Staff and Regimental Officers*' from the Adjutant-General's Office, Horse Guards, on the 25th April 1822. N.B. The title of the above publication was several years later changed to 'Dress Regulations for The Army'.

Figure 1: Uhlans Britanniques c.1793-1795. Note the reference to the lancer cap having a black fur turban. Courtesy of the Anne S.K. Brown Military Collection.

The Lance Cap

The origins of the lance cap can be traced backed to Poland, however the cap worn by Napoleon's Polish Lancers was quite unlike the original cap, which can be traced back to the seventeenth century and was of cloth, being edged with fur.

The cap that was to develop into the pattern worn by the aforementioned European lancers, originally had an upright standing bag instead of a 'falling down' bag, however by the middle of the eighteenth century the cap had progressed, and a version having an imposing 'erection' with puckered, or pleated sides was being worn by Polish hetman (6).

It was not until 1770 that a cloth cap with the distinctive 'four-sided top' came into being, this cap being worn with a feather plume rising from its left side. By 1790, most of the Polish National Cavalry had taken into wear this pattern of head-dress known as the czapka (cap), their cap having a dark red top with the feather plume being white in colour (6).

The czapka pattern of cap was originally worn by the pheasants of the Cracow District of Poland, and it is suggested that it was the revolutionary spirit of these pheasants that brought popularity to this pattern of head-dress. However at this period, the cap was still edged with fur, and was without a peak (6). N.B. The original polish cap had a loose cloth top, but when the 'Konfederatka' cap was introduced the four sides became imperative (5).

The head-dress worn by the Uhlans Britanniques was an early form of lance cap, having four sides of fluted white cloth, being without a peak and having a fur band which went all the way round the cap. Additionally there was a fulsome scarlet plume and a festoon of yellow cord.[7] (1).

At the close of the eighteenth century, the Polish troops formed legions in Italy and elsewhere and allied themselves with Napoleon Bonaparte, and it was at this period that the czapka took on a more rigid shape. The now familiar 'square top' was supported by stiff ribbed sides[8], with a front peak having been added and plaited cords adorning the body of the cap. N.B. The wearing of the czapka was not restricted to being worn by the mounted troops (lancers), it being known that the cap was worn by members of both the Polish artillery and infantry (6).

Figure 2: 'An unofficial, but proficuous use of the Lance.' The reply by Mr. Fish probably refers to a debate regarding the future use of the lance as an effective weapon. David Rowe collection. Previously published in the Regiment Journal 20th February 1897.

NOTES

1. Lord Herbert had formerly served in the 1st (Royal) Dragoons, and later possibly held an appointment in the Adjutant-General's Department.

2. The Uhlans Britanniques wore a form of lance cap, a short red jacket with yellow cord across the chest, with green collar, cuffs, turn-back, waistcoat and breeches. Trousers were worn with black boots (1).

3. Having received no satisfaction, Captain Drouville published a detailed work of some fifteen pages and six plates on the subject of British Lancers, detailing troopers dress and also his horse. N.B. From about 1812 to 1822 'Military Costume of Europe' by Goddard & Booth was published (in parts), which included a colour plate seemingly based on the Drouville prints, but with the addition of a white and red plume on the shako, and with a red and yellow pennon on the lance (1).

4. Of the nine regiments of French 'Light Horse Lancers' formed in 1811, six regiments were composed of French soldiers (the 1st, 3rd, 8th, 9th, 10th and 29th Dragoons), there were two regiments of Polish soldiers from the Vistula Legion (the 7th and 8th), with one regiment (the 9th) being a mixture of German and Polish soldiers of the 30th Chasseurs a Cheval (3).

5. The lance cap (czapka) worn by members of the Polish Light Horse Lancers, had a blue 'crown', the piping and band in the regimental facing colour. Black leather skull and front peak, with to the front of the cap a brass rayed plate, brass chain with lion's head bosses, and a red pointed pompon (3). N.B. The officers cap had a white upright plume.

6. As the 12th Light Dragoons, the regiment wore a broad topped shako having silver lace around the top, a blue jacket with primrose yellow facings and silver lace, together with white breeches and knee-boots (12).

7. The yellow cord was used to rescue the cap if it fell off, and is said to have been so long that it was also used at a picketing rope for tethering the horse (1).

8. On actual contemporary examples on display in Cracow Museum, the ribbed body of the cap is kept rigid by means of half-round pieces of cane sewn inside the head-dress (6).

Chapter Three

The Lancer Regiments

Regimental Histories

Before proceeding onwards to the development of the lance cap, the following are 'thumbnail' histories relating to the raising of each of these line regiments[1], which includes their battle honours (with dates) up to 1914, famous mounted charges, some associated nicknames, regimental personalities, and amalgamation details for each regiment, together with other information which it is hoped will be of relevance to collectors of lance caps, and to readers interested in the lancer regiments. N.B. The date given for each battle honour is the date the honour was granted which may not always be the same date as the actual battle or campaign concerned, as honours were frequently awarded retrospectively.

Also included in this chapter is an account of the officers full dress uniform (c.1911-1912), including known details of the lance cap for both the 19th and the 23rd Lancers as worn prior to disbandment. Likewise there is a description of the full dress uniform worn for mounted duties, for the 5th, 9th, 12th, 16th, 17th, and 21st Lancers, the particulars being based on an approximation of the details given in the Dress Regulations of 1900 (this being the last pattern of full dress uniform), with regimental variations being given in bold text. N.B. In 1900, the officers of the six regular lancer regiments were still wearing the black patent leather sabretache having gilt metal regimental devices upon the flap, although c.1902 the wearing of this item of equipment was finally abolished.

Colonel/Lt Colonel's

It had been noted by the author's, that within many of the sources of reference consulted, that the term Colonel is loosely used to describe both a Lieutenant Colonel and a full Colonel, and this should be borne in mind when reading the following text.

Continuing on with the subject of Colonel's, it is of interest that prior to the outbreak of the First World War it was not unusual for the ruler of a continental power to be appointed Col-in-Chief (CIC) of a British Army regiment. In this respect it is recorded that on the 25th March 1896 his Imperial and Royal Apostolic Majesty Francis Joseph I, K.G. Emperor of Austria and Hungary was appointed CIC of the 1st (King's) Dragoon Guards, an appointment he retained until the outbreak of the war in August 1914. For the 1st (Royal) Dragoons, H.I.M. William II, German Emperor and King of Prussia held a similar appointment from the 5th May 1896 until 1914, and in the 2nd Dragoons (Royal Scots Greys), the position of CIC was held by H.I.M. Nicholas II Emperor of Russia from the 8th December 1894 until his untimely death (7).

If certain of the heavy cavalry regiments could have the prestige of having a ruler of a foreign country as their Col-in Chief, then so too could the lancers. On the 8th June 1902 (7), H.M. King Alfonso XIII of Spain was appointed CIC of the 16th (Queen's) Lancers, and following their amalgamation with the 5th Royal Irish Lancers in April 1922, His Majesty continued his connection with the regiment by becoming the CIC of the newly formed 16th/5th Lancers, an appointment he held until 1941 (7). N.B. In a regimental history of the regiment by James Lunt (a former Colonel of the 16th/5th Lancers), the date of the King's appointment as Colonel-in-Chief is given as 1905.

5th (Royal Irish) Lancers

On the 9th January 1858, an order from Horse Guards announced the Queens command that the former Adjutant General's letter dated the 8th April 1799 relating to the disbandment of the *5th Royal Irish Regiment of Dragoons* be cancelled, and that this regiment be restored.

The new regiment was raised at Newbridge, Ireland in 1858 (16), the original title being the *5th or Royal Irish (Light) Dragoons (Lancers)*, they being authorised to adopt the battle honours awarded to their predecessors the 5th or Royal Irish Dragoons (4). It is of interest that the formation of this regiment completed a quartet of 'Irish' line cavalry regiments[1], they being the 4th (Royal Irish) Dragoon Guards, 6th (Inniskilling) Dragoons, 8th (King's Royal Irish) Hussars, and 5th or Royal Irish (Light) Dragoons (Lancers). N.B. J.M. Brereton in his book on the regiments and corps of the British Army (9) gives the title of the reformed regiment as '*5th (Royal Irish) Dragoons*'.

In 1861 the regiments title was shortened to the *5th (Royal Irish) Lancers*, and two years later it began its first overseas service when it began an eleven year tour of India. Two squadrons of the regiment saw active service during the Suakin Campaign, joining the force sent to relieve the besieged General Gordon. These squadrons were in action at both Hasheen and at Tamai, where the 'Fuzzie Wuzzies' nearly managed to penetrate a British square. During this action the losses to the 5th Lancers included their Commanding Officer and eight other ranks killed in action. For their participation in these engagements the regiment was awarded the battle honour 'Suakin 1885' (8). The regiment also saw service during the South African War of 1899-1902 where during the Defence of Ladysmith they made their famous mounted charge against the Boer guerrillas at Elandslaagte. It was in the course of this war that the first Victoria Cross to be bestowed upon an officer of the regiment, was awarded to Lieutenant Frederick Brooks Dugdale for his gallantry on the 3rd March 1901 (16).

Following their service during the Boer War, the regiment returned to England in 1902, being stationed at Colchester Garrison in Essex. The year 1905 saw the 5th Lancers taking over the West Cavalry Barracks at Aldershot, Hampshire, remaining there for some three years, before being posted in 1908 to York Barracks in the north of England. The regiment was moved to Marlborough Barracks, Dublin in 1910, where in 1911 their mounted band took part in the Coronation procession held in the City in honour of King George the Fifth, with a detachment also being sent to London to perform Coronation duties (10).

Perhaps the most distinguished officer ever to wear the regiments green swan feather plume, was Edmund Hynman Allenby[2], nicknamed The Bull" who served with great distinction with the 6th (Inniskilling) Dragoons during the Boer War, and on returning to England was promoted to command of the 5th Lancers. In 1915 he was given command of the Egyptian Expeditionary Force, which under his command defeated the Turkish forces at Megiddo in September 1918 (4).

Prior two their disbandment the four battle honours awarded to the former 5th Royal Irish Regiment of Dragoons were Blenheim, Oudenarde, Ramillies, and Malplaquet, with the honours awarded to the reformed (lancer) regiment up the outbreak of the First World War being Suakin, South Africa 1899-1902, and Defence of Ladysmith.

The regiment had various nicknames amongst them being: '*The Redbreasts*', and '*The Daily Advertiser*' (11), and '*The Irish Lancers*' (8). In 1920/21 the regiments title was shortened to the *5th Royal Irish Lancers* (12), and in April 1922 the 5th Royal Irish Lancers amalgamated with the 16th The Queen's Lancers to become known as *The 16th/5th Lancers*, redesignated the *16th/5th The Queen's Royal Lancers* on 16th June 1954. The regiment later merged with the 17th/21st Lancers on the 25th June 1993 to form *The Queen's Royal Lancers.*

Figure 3: 'A dismounted officer of the 5th Lancers.' Captain F.J.R. Thackwell in dismounted review order though to be c.1863, in which can clearly be seen the horsehair plume. The Dress Regulation of 1857 state that the plume was to be of cocktail feathers, although contemporary photographs often shown the hair plume being worn in an officers cap. F.J.R. Thackwell commissioned Cornet 1860: 5th Lancers. Captain 1863: 5th Lancers. Killed by a tiger whilst in India c.1869. Copyright D.P.& G.

The Officers Full Dress Uniform

The Head-Dress

The full dress head-dress for the officers was the 1856 pattern lance cap, with a green plume of either swan feathers or horsehair, complete with gold gimp and orris cord cap-lines, further details of which are given in chapter seven.

The Tunic, Overalls and Accoutrements

The tunic of dark blue cloth, the plastron, piping to the outer seam of the sleeves and to the rear seams, were all in the regimental facing colour of scarlet, with gilt buttons of regimental pattern. Regimental pattern collar badges were worn, the collar and cuffs also in scarlet and adorned with gold lace. Gold wire shoulder cords. The waist girdle was of gold lace with two crimson stripes, with the sword slings also of gold lace, having a scarlet silk stripe to the centre, and being backed with leather. Pantaloons of blue cloth with two yellow stripes down each outer seam, with black knee boots with steel spurs being worn in this order of dress.

Shoulder belt of gold lace, with a scarlet silk stripe to the centre, being backed with scarlet morocco leather, the ornament, buckle, tip, and slide, and the chains and prickers were all in silver. The pouch of scarlet leather having a silver flap, bearing either the 'ER VII' or 'GRV' Royal Cypher beneath a crown all in gilt metal. White leather gauntlets, and the 1896 pattern cavalry officers sword with gold and crimson cord sword knot, with steel scabbard completed the uniform.

9th (Queen's Royal) Lancers

Originally raised in 1715 as *Wynne's Dragoons*, their title changed to the *9th Regiment of Dragoons* in 1751, and again in 1783 when they became known as the *9th Light Dragoons*. In this role they participated in the Peninsular War, the battle honour '*Peninsula*' having been subsequently awarded to the regiment by 1815. The year 1816 saw the regiment being selected as one of the four light dragoon regiments to be converted to lancers, their title changing to the *9th Light Dragoons (Lancers)* (12). To enable the regiment to become proficient in their new role, a detachment of the 9th was sent to London to train in the use of the lance under the supervision of Major R.H. deMontmorency[3] of their regiment (13). The year 1830 saw a further change of title, this time to the *9th (The Queen's Royal) Light Dragoons (Lancers)* (12).

Some fourteen years later, in their new role, and under the command of Major Hope Grant[4] they saw action at Sobraon during the first Sikh War of 1845-1846, and the second Sikh War of 1848 - 1849, taking part in the actions at Chillianwallah, and Gujerat (Goojerat). It was during the latter battle, that the regiment, together with their comrades in arms, the Scinde Horse, successfully charged a body of some 1,500 Afghanistan cavalry who were allied to the Sikh army. They later took part in the suppression of the Indian Mutiny where they were engaged in the fighting that ensued during the capture of Delhi, it being there that they earned the nickname of the *Delhi Spearmen*', with the regiment also taking part in the Relief of Lucknow (4). For their bravery during the mutiny, thirteen members of the regiment were awarded the Victoria Cross (14).

In 1861 another change of title occurred, this time to the *9th (Queen's Royal) Lancers* (12).

Whilst engaged in the operations in Afghanistan of 1878 -1880, the 9th accompanied Sir Frederick Roberts on his memorable march from Kabul to Kandahar. During the South African War of 1899-1902 they took part in the actions at Belmont, Enslin, Modder River, and Magersfontein, participating in the Relief of Kimberely and the fighting at Paardeberg, Poplar Grove and Karee Siding. The members of the regiment who served throughout the Boer War were awarded as many as nine clasps to the two medals, they being seven clasps to the Queen's medal and two clasps to the King's medal (4). N.B. Earlier, in 1879 during the Zulu War, the Victoria Cross was awarded to Lieutenant Lord William Beresford of the 9th Lancers (14), who assumedly must have been on detached duty from his regiment at that time.

On the 30th January 1889 H.S.H. Prince Francis of Teck[5] joined the regiment as a 2nd Lieutenant, however his time with the regiment was short lived, as on the 17th April 1889 he transferred to the 1st Battalion of the Kings Royal Rifle Corps (7).

The battle honours awarded to the regiment up until 1914 are as follows. Punniar, Sobraon, Chillianwallah, Goojerat, Punjaub, Delhi, Lucknow, Kabul, Afghanistan 1878-80, Charasiah, Kandahar, Modder River, Relief of Kimberley, Paardeberg, and South Africa 1899-1902.

The regimental nicknames were: '*Delhi Spearmen*', '*The Queen's*', and '*Wynne's Dragoons*' (11). Yet another change of title occurred in 1920 when the regiment became the *9th Queen's Royal Lancers* (12). Having been unaffected by the amalgamations that occurred in 1922 and bearing this title, the regiment subsequently amalgamated with the 12th (Prince of Wales's Royal) Lancers in September 1960 to form the *9th/12th Royal Lancers (Prince of Wales's).*

The Officers Full Dress Uniform (*See Fig: 4.*)

The Head-Dress

For the officers, the full dress head-dress was the 1856 pattern lance cap, having a black and white plume of either swan feather or horsehair, complete with gold cord cap-lines.

The Tunic, Overalls and Accoutrements

The tunic of blue cloth, the plastron, piping to the outer seam of the sleeves and to the rear seams, all in the regimental facing colour of scarlet, with regimental pattern gilt buttons. Collar badges of regimental pattern, the collar and cuffs also in scarlet, and adorned with gold lace. Shoulder cords of gold wire.

The girdle was of gold lace with two crimson stripes, the sword slings also in gold lace, but not having a silk stripe to the centre, being backed with leather. Pantaloons of blue cloth with a double yellow stripe down each outer seam, worn with black knee boots with steel spurs.

Shoulder belt of gold lace, but without a silk stripe to the centre, backed with morocco leather, the breast-ornament, buckle, tip, and slide, and the chains and prickers were all in gilt metal. The pouch of scarlet leather, having a silver flap bearing A R reversed and intertwined with a crown above, all in gilt metal. N.B. This was the only lancer regiment at this period not to bear the Royal Cypher on the flap of the officers pouch. The 1896 pattern cavalry officers sword with gold and crimson cord sword knot, with a steel scabbard, together with white leather gauntlets completed the uniform.

Figure 4: 'Officers of the 9th Lancers.' A group of officers of the regiment in dismounted review order c.1894. It is of interest that on only one officers cap are the white feathers of the plume visible. Copyright D.P.& G.

12th (Prince of Wales's Royal) Lancers

The regiment was raised in July 1715 in the neighbourhood of Reading, by Brigadier-General Phineas Bowles, they being known by the name of their colonel. Some three years later, the regiment was sent to Ireland, where it remained for 75 years, during which period Lieutenant Arthur Wellesley (later to become the Duke of Wellington) served with the regiment for two years, the regiments title having been changed to the *12th Dragoons* in 1751. The year 1768 saw another change of title to *12th (or Prince of Wales's) Regiment of (Light) Dragoons* (12).

The 12th then serviced in Corsica, Italy, England, Portugal and Egypt, and in 1802 on its return from the operations against Napoleon's army in Egypt, authority was granted for the regiment to bear a Sphinx, and the word 'Egypt' on it guidon's and appointments.

In 1811 the regiment joined Wellington's army in the Peninsular, and some four years later, on the 15th June 1815 was present at the Battle of Waterloo under the overall command of Major General Sir John Vandeleur, being brigaded with the 11th and 16th Light Dragoons. During this most famous battle, the 12th Light Dragoons under the command of Lt Colonel Ponsonby[6], made a most successful charge against the right flank of the French army. Regrettably fortunes changed, and the regiment was then itself charged by some of Napoleon's Polish Lancers, the 12th being obliged to withdraw, leaving on the field of battle their commanding officer Lt Colonel Ponsonby, who being severely wounded was left for dead (15).

In 1816 the regiment was selected to be converted to lancers, their new title being the *12th (The Prince of Wales's) Lancers,* being changed the following year to *12th or Prince of Wales's Royal Lancers* (12), and in 1839 a royal connection with the regiment arose when H.R.H. George, 2nd Duke of Cambridge[7] was attached to the regiment for a period of some two years (7).

The regiment saw active service during the Kaffir War of 1851, and later in the Crimea, and completed three tours of India before becoming the first cavalry regiment to reach Cape town at the commencement of the Boer War. Here the regiment formed part of the Cavalry Brigade and took part in the famous ride to, and the relief of the besieged town of Kimberley on the 17th February 1900. They were also in action in the engagements at Paardeberg where the famous Boer Commander, General Cronje surrendered, and at the actions at Poplar Grove, Dreifontein, Karee Siding, Houtnek, Vet

River, Zand River, and at Diamond Hill, where their Commanding Officer Lord Airlie was killed whilst leading his regiment in a splendid charge against the enemy (4) (details relating to Lt Colonel Lord Airlie are given in endnote four, of chapter four). N.B. By 1900, according to the dress regulations of that year, the regiments title had changed to the *12th(Prince of Wales's Royal) Lancers.*

A further royal connection occurred when H.R.H Edward, Prince of Wales (later King Edward V111) was appointed Colonel-in -Chief of the regiment on 12th April 1919 (7).

Prior to the outbreak of the First World War the regiments battle honours were as follows: the Sphinx for Egypt, Peninsula, Waterloo, South Africa 1851.2.3., Sevastopol, Central India, Paardeberg, Relief of Kimberley, and South Africa 1899-1902. The regimental nickname: '*The Supple Twelfth*' (11). In 1920 the title changed yet again, this time to the *12th Royal Lancers (Prince of Wales's)* (12), and in September 1960 the regiment amalgamated with the 9th Queen's Royal Lancers to form the *9th/12th Royal Lancers (Prince of Wales's).*

The Officers Full Dress Uniform (*See Fig: 5.*)

The Head-Dress

Full dress head-dress for the officers was the 1856 pattern lance cap, with the plume being scarlet in colour and of either swan feathers or horsehair, complete with gold gimp and orris cap-lines.

The Tunic, Overalls and Accoutrements

A blue cloth tunic, the plastron, piping to the outer seam of the sleeves and to the rear seams, all being in the facing colour of scarlet, with gilt buttons of regimental pattern. Regimental pattern collar badges were worn, with the collar and cuffs also in scarlet, and being adorned with gold lace.

The waist girdle of gold lace with two crimson stripes, the sword slings also in gold lace, having a central scarlet silk stripe and being backed with leather. Blue cloth pantaloons with a double yellow stripe to each outer seam, worn with black knee boots and steel spurs. Shoulder belt of gold lace, with a central scarlet silk stripe, being backed with morocco leather, with the breast ornament, buckle, tip, and slide, and the prickers and chains all in silver. The pouch of scarlet leather, having a silver flap bearing a gilt crown above the Royal Cypher of 'GRV'. White leather gauntlets, and the 1896 pattern cavalry officers sword with gold and crimson cord sword knot, and steel scabbard, completed the uniform.

16th (Queen's) Lancers

The regiment was raised in 1759 as the *16th Light Dragoons* under the command of Lt Colonel John Burgoyne (later Major General J. Burgoyne), who had previously served with the 2nd Foot Guards (Coldstream Guards). N.B. As with several cavalry regiments at that time, the commanding officers name was associated with the regiment, their nickname becoming '*Burgoyne's Light Horse*' (8). N.B. For a few years the regiment was also known as the 2nd Light Dragoons (12).

The regiment first saw action in 1761 when two troops of the regiment took part in an expedition to capture Belle lle (Bell Isle), situated off the Brittany coast. The following year saw the regiment sailing for Portugal, where they, together with their Portuguese allies did battle against the armies of France and Spain.

Back home in 1766, the 16th Light Dragoons were reviewed by H.M. King George III, who commanded that henceforth the regiment should be styled as *'16th the Queen's Light Dragoons'* (8).

In 1775 the regiment sailed for New England to fight against the forces of General George Washington, arriving in New York in March of that year. Whilst in New Jersey the regiment captured General Charles Lee, and later took part in the battles at Brandywine Creek and Germantown, returning to England in 1779. The year 1793 saw the 16th engaged in a campaign against the armies of Revolutionary France, the regiment earning its first battle honour at Beaumont, near Le Cateau on the 26th April 1794 (8).

The year 1809 saw the regiment again fighting against the French forces, they seeing action at Fuentes d'Onor, Salamanca, Nive, and Vittoria. Some six years later the 16th were in action at the Battle of Waterloo, where they formed part of Major General Sir John Vandeleur's Cavalry Brigade, along with the 11th, and 12th Light Dragoons.

Ireland was to be the regiments station in 1816, and it was whilst there that they were converted to a lancer regiment, there title being changed to the *16th (The Queen's) Light Dragoons (Lancers)* (12). At first the regiments lancer uniform was blue, although in 1830 the colour was changed to scarlet, a colour they managed to retain when in 1846 all the other Lancer regiments were ordered to wear blue uniforms (8). The 16th became the first British regiment to use the lance in action, which they did with success at the capture of Bhurtpore on the 10th December 1826. The regiment later took part in the First Afghan War of 1841, and the First Sikh War of 1843-1846, where on the 28th January 1846 at the Battle of Aliwal[8], under the command of Major J. Rowland Smyth, they made a most successful mounted charge against the Sikh forces (16). In 1861 the regiments title was altered to the *16th (The Queen's) Lancers* (12).

Following service in Ireland, and England, the 16th were posted to India, and it was whilst stationed there that they were ordered to proceed to South Africa, where they saw action at both Kimberley and Paardeberg (16). N.B. Lieutenant The Viscount Fincastle (later the Earl of Dunmore) had by this time already been awarded the Victoria Cross for his actions during the Tirah Expedition of 1897. By 1900, according to the dress regulations of that year, the title was *16th (Queen's) Lancers* (12).

A celebrated officer who served with the regiment in 1899 and who later went on to attain high rank was General Hubert de la Poer Gough[9], however pride of place within the regiments 'Hall of Fame' must surely go to William Robertson.[10] He enlisted in the 16th Lancers in 1877, was commissioned into the 3rd Dragoon Guards in 1888, and rose to the rank of Field Marshal of the British

Figure 5: '12th Lancers.' A fine study of a mounted officer of the regiment of the late pre 1900 period. Note the elaborate device to the flap of the sabretache. Copyright D.P.& G.

Army (17). This achievement must surely be a fine example of the old saying *'A Field Marshal's baton in every private's knapsack'.*

As stated previously, H.M. King Alfonso XIII of Spain[11] was appointed Colonel-in-Chief of the regiment shortly after the commencement of the twentieth century, and in 1935 a further royal connection arose on the 6th July of that year when H.R.H. Henry, Duke of Gloucester, a serving officer with the 10th Royal Hussars, who at that time was attached to the 11th Hussars in the rank of Captain, was appointed Major and seconded to the 16th/5th Lancers (7).

By 1909 the regiment had been awarded more battle honours than any other British cavalry regiment (16), they being as follows. Beaumont, Willems, Peninsula, Waterloo, Bhurtpore, Afghanistan, Ghuznee, Maharajpore, Sobraon, Talavera, Fuentes D' Onor, Salamanca, Vittoria, Nive, Paardeberg, Relief of Kimberley, and South Africa 1900-02.

The regimental nicknames include. *'The Red Lancers'*, *'The Scarlet Lancers'*, and *'The Queen's'* (11). In 1920 the title was simplified to the *16th The Queen's Lancers* (12), and in April 1922 the regiment amalgamated with the 5th Royal Irish Lancers to become known as the *16th/5th Lancers*, redesignated as the *16th/5th The Queen's Royal Lancers* on 16th June 1954, they merging almost forty years later with the 17th/21st Lancers on the 25th June 1993 to form *The Queen's Royal Lancers* (16). N.B. The date given for the amalgamation of the 16th, and 5th Lancers is the 29th September 1922 (121).

The Officers Full Dress Uniform

The Head-Dress

The officers full dress head-dress was the 1856 pattern lance cap worn with a black plume of either swan feathers or horsehair, complete with gold gimp and orris cord cap-lines.

The Tunic, Overalls and Accoutrements

A scarlet cloth tunic, the plastron, piping to the outer seam of the sleeves and to the rear seams, all in the facing colour of blue, with regimental pattern gilt buttons. Collar badges of regimental pattern, the collar and cuffs also in blue, and being adorned with gold lace. Shoulder cords of gold wire. N.B. In 1846 the lancer regiments were ordered to change their jackets from scarlet to blue, the 16th however appear to have disregarded this instruction, and retained their distinctive jackets thereby earning the nickname 'The Scarlet Lancers' (8). The waist girdle was of gold lace with two crimson stripes, the sword slings also being in gold lace, having a blue silk stripe to the centre, backed with leather. The pantaloons were of blue cloth with a double yellow stripe down each outer seam, worn with black knee boots and steel spurs.

The shoulder belt of gold lace, having a central silk stripe in the facing colour of blue, being backed with morocco leather, the breast-ornament, buckle, tip, and slide, and the chain and prickers were all in silver. The pouch of scarlet leather, having a silver flap upon which was the 'GRV' Royal Cypher surmounted by a crown, all in gilt metal. The 1896 pattern cavalry officers sword with gold and crimson cord sword knot, with a steel scabbard, together with white leather gauntlets completed the uniform.

17th (Duke of Cambridge's Own) Lancers

The task of raising the forerunners of the 17th (Duke of Cambridge's Own) Lancers, the regiment with which the chapter is concerned, was entrusted to Colonel John Hale[12], whose commission was dated November 1759. Colonel Hale undertook the commission by raising four troops of light cavalry at Watford, and at Rickmansworth. Originally Hale's regiment was to have been numbered the 18th, but due to the failure of Lord Aberdour to recruit a sufficient number of men when raising a regiment in Scotland, Lord Aberdour's regiment was disbanded, with the result that in 1863 Colonel Hale's regiment was moved from eighteenth place to become the *17th Light Dragoons* (12).

For short period in their history the regiment was titled the *3rd Light Dragoons* (1765 to 1769), however it was as the *17th Light Dragoons* that the regiment was known, when in 1822 it was declared that they were to be converted to a lancer regiment. However, as at this time the regiment was on 'foreign' service, in India (12), they continued to wear the light dragoon uniform, sailing for home in January 1823. N.B. The actual date of their conversion is given as the 20th August 1822 (WO 3/72) (5).

Just over thirty years later the regiment was on active service in the Crimea, where together with the 4th Light Dragoons, the 8th Hussars, the 11th Hussars, and the 13th Light Dragoons they formed the Light Brigade under the command of Lord Cardigan (James Thomas Brudenell 7th Earl of Cardigan). Overall command of the cavalry, both the heavy, and light brigade during the Crimean campaign was given to Major General Lord Lucan. N.B. Lt Colonel George Charles Bingham (later the 3rd Earl of Lucan), commanded the 17th Lancers from 1826 to C.1838 (16).

On the morning of the 25th October 1854, the regiment was led by Captain William Morris[13], who due to either the death or sickness of his superior officers had assumed command of the regiment. Together with the other four regiments that made up the Light Brigade they rode into the North Valley at Balaclava, where they charged the Russian guns thereby creating a military legend. N.B. Some 147 men of the 17th Lancers entered the 'Valley of Death', of which only seventy members of the regiment returned, included amongst which was Captain Morris (19).

In recognition of their extreme courage, three members of the 17th were awarded their nation's highest honour the Victoria Cross. This most famous award was presented to Sergeants John Berryman, John Farrell and Charles Wooden. N.B. Both Sergeant Berryman, and Sergeant Wooden later received honorary commissions in the rank of Lieutenant (Quartermaster) (20).

On leaving the Crimea, the regiment returned to England, and in 1856, where after only some nine months of home service, they were posted to India, where they saw action during the Indian Mu-

Figure 6: 'A mounted officer of the 17th Lancers.' Captain McGhee the Riding Master of the regiment in mounted review order, probably taken at Hounslow Barracks c.1896. N.B. He was commissioned Riding Master (with honorary rank of Captain on the 13th November 1882 (34). Copyright D.P.& G.

tiny. It was not until 1864 that the 17th again returned to England, remaining there until 1879, when they were then posted to South Africa, the regiments title meanwhile having been changed in 1876 to the *17th (Duke of Cambridge's Own) Lancers* (12). It was in South Africa, on the 4th July 1879, that they distinguished themselves in a most successful mounted charge against the Zulus at the Battle of Ulundi (16).

It is worthy of note, that a royal connection with the regiment had occurred on the 25th April 1842 when H.R.H. George, 2nd Duke of Cambridge was appointed Lt Colonel of the 17th Light Dragoons (Lancers), an appointed he held until the 23rd September 1852. In 1870 the regiment was granted the addition of '*Duke of Cambridge's Own*' to its title, with a further royal association occurring some twenty-three years later on the 11th January 1893, when H.S.H. Prince Adolphus, Duke of Teck14. was appointed 2nd Lieutenant, serving with the regiment for some seven years before transferring to the 1st Life Guards in 1895 (7).

Came the year 1900, and the regiment was once again on active service, this time their foe being the Boer commandos in South Africa. It was during this conflict on the 7th August 1900, that the Victoria Cross was won by Sergeant Brian Turner Thomas Lawrence[15] for his actions at Essenbosch Farm (21). Also during that same year on a September day, 'C' squadron of the regiment proved their mettle when close to Modderfontein Farm, and against hopeless odds, they fought valiantly against a Boer attack. The Boer guerrillas were led by Jan Christian Smuts (later Field Marshal Rt Hon J.C. Smuts) (22), and after the 17th Lancers had lost thirty men killed and many more wounded, the lancers were ultimately forced to surrender (23).

Of all the many distinguished officers who at one time served with the regiment and who later went on to achieve high rank, perhaps three of the most famous were Lt Colonel D.C. Drury-Lowe (later Lt General Sir D.C. Drury-Lowe G.C.B.) (24), who commanded the regiment at Ulundi in 1879, Lt Colonel Douglas Haig[16] (later Field Marshal Viscount Dawick O.M. K.T. G.C.B. K.C.B. K.C.I.E. G.C.V.O. K.C.V.O. C.B. A.D.C.) (See Fig: 14.), and Lieutenant Henry Evelyn Wood V.C. (later Field Marshal H.E. Wood V.C. G.C.B. G.C.M.G. K.C.B. D.L. D.C.L. (25), who first served in the Royal Navy, before transferring as a Cornet into the 13th Light Dragoons where he saw service during the Crimean campaign (20). His Victoria Cross was awarded for actions at Sindwaho on the 19th October 1858, and subsequently at Sindhora during the Indian Mutiny (21).

The battle honours awarded to the regiment prior to the outbreak of the First World War are as follows. Alma, Inkerman, Balaclava, Sevastopol, Central India, South Africa 1879, and South Africa 1900-02.

The regimental nicknames include. '*Bingham's Dandies*', '*Skull and Crossbones*', '*The Death or Glory Boys*', (11), '*The Horse Marines*' and '*The Tots*' (16).

Figure 7: 'The Officers of the 17th Lancers.' General, the Rt. Hon. Sir R.H. Buller G.C.B. K.C.M.G. (34) with the officers of the regiment in dismounted review order. Copyright D.P.& G.

In 1920 the regiments title was altered to the *17th Lancers (Duke of Cambridge's Own)*, and in April 1922 the regiment amalgamated with the 21st Lancers (Empress of India's) to be known as the *17th/21st Lancers*, they merging on the 25th June 1993 with the 16th/5th The Queen's Royal Lancers to form *The Queen's Royal Lancers* (16). N.B. There are at least two known dates given for the amalgamation of the 17th, and the 21st Lancers, these being the 25th June 1922 (122), and August 1922 (the date given for the completion of the amalgamation) (115).

The Officers Full Dress Uniform (*See Figs: 6. and 7.*)

The Head-Dress

The 1856 pattern lance cap was the full dress head-dress for the officers, worn complete with a white plume of either swan feathers or horsehair, together with gold gimp and orris cap -lines.

The Tunic, Overalls and Accoutrements

The tunic of blue cloth, the plastron, piping to the outer seam of the sleeves, and to the rear seams, all in the facing colour of white, with regimental pattern gilt buttons. Collar badges of regimental pattern were worn, with the collar and cuffs also in white, and being adorned with gold lace. Gold wire shoulder cords.

The waist girdle of gold lace with two crimson stripes, the sword slings also in gold lace, having a white silk stripe to the centre, and being backed with leather. Pantaloons of blue cloth, having double white stripes to each outer seam, worn with black knee boots and steel spurs.

The shoulder belt of gold lace, having a central white silk stripe, being backed with morocco leather, the breast-ornament, buckle, tip, and slide, and the prickers and chains all in silver. The pouch of blue leather, having a silver flap bearing the Royal Cypher of 'GRV' beneath a crown, all in gilt metal. White leather gauntlets, and the 1896 pattern cavalry officers sword with gold and crimson cord sword knot, together with a steel scabbard, completed the uniform.

19th Lancers

The first cavalry regiment to be numbered the 19th was raised in 1759, although after only four years, they became the *18th Regiment of Light Dragoons* as a result of the then 17th Light Dragoons being disbanded and the number "17" being taken by the then 18th Light Dragoons. The year 1779 saw the 'new' *19th Light Dragoons* being raised by Major General Russell Manners on the authorization of King George III, this regiment being disbanded some four years later in 1783 having seen no active service.

The regiment with which this book is concerned was raised in 1781 its original title being the 23rd Light Dragoons, however resulting from the disbandment of several lower numbered regiments of light dragoons, the regiment was, on the 26th April 1786 retitled the 19th Light Dragoons (14). The regiment served for a great many years in India, where they distinguished themselves in the battle of Seringapatam[17] in 1792, during which period it was engaged against the forces of Tippoo Sahib, the French and their allies, and the Mahratta Confederacy, it being during the latter conflict that they were engaged in action at the battle of Assaye on the 23rd September 1803. In October 1806 the regiments spell of duty in India came to an end and the regiment left Madras to sail for Britain, arriving back at Tilbury, England in April 1807. The 19th were subsequently posted to Ireland in December 1809 where they remained until c.1813, their first battle honour "Assaye" having been awarded in April 1807. Upon America's declaration of war, three squadrons of the regiment were sent to Canada, arriving in Quebec in May 1813 (12), where after conspicuous work on the frontier, notably at Fort Niagara and at Lundy's Lane, the regiment was awarded its second battle honour "Niagara", being granted permission to bear this honour on its appointments and standards (4). N.B. Notification of the battle honour "Niagara" dates from a letter from Horse Guards dated 19th May 1815 (14).

Having returned from Canada, a submission was made on the 23rd October 1817 that the 19th Light Dragoons should be appointed to be lancers, and the order confirming this was made on the 28th October of that year (27). Their time in their new role was however to be short lived, as upon the general reduction of cavalry units that took place in 1821, and following the issue of a Warrant of the 23rd August 1821 (14), the 19th Lancers were disbanded in September of that year (12).

The battle honours awarded to the regiment as Light Dragoons were Seringapatam, Assaye, and Niagara.

The Officers Full Dress Uniform

The Head-Dress (*See Fig: 8.*)

The Skull, Sides and Top

The lance cap had the upper ribbed section in yellow cloth[18], with gold gimp and orris cord running up the angles and across the ten inch square patent leather trencher top, with to the upper left front of the ribbed cloth section a gold bullion rosette, to the centre of which was the 'GR' Royal Cypher. Attached to the gold cord of the centre angle was a small gold coloured lion's head having a gilt metal ring within its mouth, onto which could be attached the ribbon joined to the 'loose ends' of the chinscales.

Positioned to the top right hand corner of the cap was either a gilt metal hook, or a loop onto which could be attached the loose end of the cap-lines, with located midway to the gold cord running up the left hand angle was what appears to be a small gilt 'button' onto which could be secured the loop attached to the flounders of the cap-line (*See Fig: 8.*).

The skull was covered with black patent leather, having a band of three inch wide gold lace with a blue stripe around the waist, below which was further gold lace, again with blue stripes.[19] The front peak of black patent leather decorated with three differing width stripes of gold embroidery, the widest stripe being to the centre, with to the rear of the cap a very large false peak (constantly turned up) embroidered with gold braid.

The Lance Cap Plate

The large silvered angular rayed plate bore a large gilt metal Royal Arms with supporters, immediately beneath which was a long gilt scroll bearing the battle honour '*Seringapatam*', below which was a gilt elephant on a mount. To either side of this mammal a scroll bearing a battle honour, '*Niagara*' to the right, and '*Assaye*' to the left (when facing the cap), both honours being in gilt metal. N.B. It is suggested that there was a previous pattern plate[20] that lacked the pre 1818 scroll bearing '*Seringapatam*', which was at a later date altered to carry this particular battle honour (27).

The Ear Bosses, Chinscales, and Cap-Lines

The ear bosses were most unusual as they appear to have consisted of what can best be described as being a medium sized gilt metal recessed 'button' with a raised centre dome, attached to which were the gilt metal chinscales (*See Fig: 8.*).

Gold plaited cord cap-lines measuring some four and a quarter inches in length[21] complete with bullion tassels and flounders, the cap being worn with a white over feather plume. N.B. Some photographs exist that show this head dress with the plaited cord wound around the cap just below the yellow cloth section, with an end looped to the right hand corner of the trencher top (27).

Of interest are illustrations of two slightly differing pattern lance caps that appear in *Regiment Magazine* issue No.47. The first is a coloured line drawing, said to be of an officers cap worn c.1816, this cap being described as above.

The second cap is illustrated in three black and white photographs, front, rear and side views, and differs in that the top of the cap is of yellow cloth, the plate is devoid of any battle honours, and the chinscales are joined at the centre by a small lion's head catch. The text accompanying these three photographs states that this 'later lance cap of the officers which was more straight sided and with a markedly different plate,' and continues 'the front plate and ornaments were all gilt'. The reference to this cap being a 'later lance cap' is open to speculation, for the lack of battle honours to this plate would suggest that if indeed this is a cap of the 19th, then it is an earlier version than the cap having the plate displaying honours as described above. N.B. See chapter fourteen for the description of a similar pattern lance cap.

The Jacket (Coatee), Overalls and Accoutrements

The following limited information relating the officers full dress uniform has been based on a coloured painting by the highly accomplished military artist Richard Simkin, together with the brief text that accompanied this illustration in the book 'Uniforms of the British Army - The Cavalry Regiments' (12).

A jacket of blue cloth, the plastron, piping to the outer seams of the sleeves and to the rear seams, in the regimental facing colour of light yellow, with regimental pattern gilt buttons. The collar and

Figure 8: 19th Lancers. Offset view of the officers pattern cap. Note the gilt metal battle honours 'Seringapatam' and 'Assaye' to the plate. Of interest are the early pattern cap lines, and the method by which the chinscales are attached to the cap which possibly may not be an original fitting. Courtesy of Colin Griffin.

Figure 8A: 19th Lancers. Rear view of the officers pattern cap illustrating the constantly turned up rear peak.

cuffs were in the same colour, having the additional adornment of gold lace. To the rear of the jacket, the pleated skirts had two ornaments of hanging bullion. Epaulettes of gold bullion, and gold aiguillettes completed the upper wear.

The girdle was of gold lace with two crimson/red stripes, with the sword slings being of gold lace, backed with leather. The overalls/trousers were originally of grey cloth (blue grey) with a double gold stripe down each outer seam, the colour of the overalls being changed to blue sometime before the regiment was disbanded. Black Wellington boots with yellow metal spurs were worn.

The shoulder belt was of gold lace backed with leather, having prickers and chains, the shoulder pouch being of black patent leather with gilt mounts. White wrist gloves, and the 1796 pattern officers light cavalry sword with gold sword knot, and a steel scabbard. The officers pattern sabretache had gold lace with dark blue cloth to the centre, being adorned with a gold embroidered crown, G.R. cypher, battle honours, and a silver elephant.

21st (Empress of India's) Lancers

There had been four regiments of Light Dragoons numbered the '21st', the first being the 21st (Granby's) Light Dragoons, or Royal Foresters raised in 1760, and disbanded in 1763, the second regiment numbered the 21st Light Dragoons was formed in 1779, being disbanded in 1783. The third regiment of 21st Light Dragoons was raised in 1794 and disbanded in 1819, the fourth regiment being the one with which this chapter is concerned. This regiment can trace its origins back to the former *3rd European Light Cavalry of Bengal* who were transferred from the East India Company to the British Army in 1861, their new title at first being the *21st Light Dragoons*, they being renamed the *21st Hussars* within a short period of time (12).

The year 1897 saw the regiment being the last hussar regiment to be converted to the role of lancers[22], this being sanctioned under Army Order A.O.162 of 1898 (28). The regiments new title at this time was the *21st Lancers*, they wearing blue tunics, with scarlet facings, with a white plume for the lance cap.

It was not long, before this, the youngest of the lancer regiments won its spurs, for on the 2nd September 1898, the 21st Lancers numbering a little over some three hundred and twenty officers[23]. and men, under the command of Lieutenant Colonel R.H. Martin carried out a spectacular charge against an enemy force estimated to have exceeded some 1,500 Dervish warriors of the Khalifa at Omdurman (29).

For their gallantry, three members of the regiment were honoured by being awarded the Victoria Cross, they being Captain Kenna,[24] Lieutenant de Montmorency, and Private Byrne (30). An officer temporarily attached to the regiment who took part in this charge and later went on to achieve fame and very high office in the service of his country was Lt Winston Churchill[25] of the 4th Hussars). In October 1898 following the above action, the regiment was renamed the *21st (Empress of India's) Lancers* (28).

In 1899, the regiment returned home from Egypt only to be almost immediately sent to the Curragh, in Ireland, then on to Dublin where they remained for four years. The following three years were spent at home, first at Hounslow near London, c.1904, then to Aldershot in Hampshire, c.1906, onwards to Canterbury in Kent, c.1909, before once more returning to Egypt in 1911, then to India c.1912/13 (30).

The sole battle honour awarded to the regiment at this period was Khartoum. The nickname of the regiment was '*The Dumpies*' (16).

In 1920 the regiments title was altered to the *21st Lancers (Empress of India's)* (12), and in April 1922 they amalgamated with the 17th Lancers (Duke of Cambridge's Own) to become known as the *17th/21st Lancers*. This regiment merged with the 16th/5th The Queen's Royal Lancers in 1993 to form *The Queen's Royal Lancers*.

The Officers Full Dress Uniform (*See Fig: 9.*)

The Head-Dress

The 1856 pattern lance cap was the full dress uniform head- dress for the officers, worn with a white plume of either swan feathers or horsehair, complete with gold gimp and orris cord cap-lines.

The Tunic, Overalls and Accoutrements

The blue cloth tunic had the plastron, the piping to the outer seam of the sleeves and the rear seams, all in the facing colour of French grey, with regimental pattern gilt buttons. Collar badges of regimental pattern, the collar and cuffs also in French grey, and adorned with gold lace. Shoulder cords of gold wire.

The girdle of gold lace with two crimson stripes, the sword slings also of gold lace, having a white silk stripe to the centre, being backed with leather. Pantaloons of blue cloth with a double yellow stripe down each outer seam, worn with black knee boots and steel spurs.

The shoulder belt (said to be of Hussar pattern)[26] of gold lace, having a central French grey stripe, being backed with blue leather, the breast-ornament, buckle, tip, and slide, and the chains and prickers were all in silver. The pouch was of black leather having a silver flap bearing a crown with the Royal Cypher of 'GRV' beneath, all in gilt metal. The 1896 pattern cavalry officer sword with gold and crimson cord sword knot, and steel scabbard, together with white leather gauntlets completed the uniform.

23rd Lancers

As was frequently the case, those regiments having a high regimental number had several lives and deaths, there having been three regiments numbered '23' ranking as light dragoons in the British Army. The first regiment so numbered was raised in 1781, being formed from drafts of men from the 7th Light Dragoons, the 17th being re-numbered in 1786 as the 19th Light Dragoons. Then in

1794, Colonel William Fullerton raised six troops in Ireland, the regiment being numbered the 23rd and serving until 1802 when it was reduced (31).

In 1796 the regiment was posted to the West Indies, and served at St. Vincent and Porto Rico until being sent to Portugal in 1798 where it remained until 1800. The following year (1801) saw the regiment in Egypt, where they formed part of the expedition to oppose Napoleon Bonaparte's scheme for the annexation of Egypt. For its services at Alexandria during this campaign, the 26th were awarded the battle honour *"Egypt"*, and were permitted to adopt the Sphinx as a badge of honour (14).

In 1803, upon the disbandment of several senior regiments, the 26th were, on the 31st March of that year redesignated the 23rd Light Dragoons, they seeing service in the Peninsula where they were engaged at the battle of Talavera on the 27th and 28th July 1803, being awarded the further battle honours *"Peninsula"* and *"Talavera"*[27] for their services (14).

In 1816, they, together with the ninth, twelfth, and sixteenth Light Dragoons were selected to be armed, dressed, and equipped as a regiment of lancers, albeit in the case of the twenty-third their time in their new role was short lived, with the regiment being disbanded in October 1817.

The battle honours awarded to the regiment as Light Dragoons were as follows. The Sphinx for Egypt, Talavera, Peninsula, and Waterloo.

Figure 10: 'The 21st (Empress of India's) Lancers.' Officers and men of the 21st (Empress of India's) Lancers in review order, and in 'Fighting Kit as at Omdurman' after W.T. Maud, published as a supplement to 'The Graphic' in 1897. N.B. The original of this fine painting hangs in the officers mess of the Queen's Royal Lancers. By courtesy of the Parker Gallery.

The Officers Full Dress Uniform (*See Fig: 11.*)

The Head-Dress

The Skull, Sides and Top

The official description of the officers pattern lance cap quotes a cloth trencher top ten inches square, which is fully ten inches across from corner to corner, but curving in the centres to nine inches. The front angle was to be in a direct line with the centre of the peak, which means that the top projects about two inches further forward than the peak. The fluted sides were to be three and a half inches deep[28], with the rosette (boss) of crimson with an embroidered 'GR' within the many turns of the silver bullion. N.B. Both the ribbed cloth top, and the velvet backing to the 'GR' on the rosette were crimson.

The lace in the regulations is given as gold and crimson, and being three-quarters of an inch wide, but in fact the lace is a full one inch on an actual cap (as also given in Messrs Hawks & Co's specification), with the metal lace being of silver and crimson.[29] The lower part of the cap had much red-striped silver lace leading down to a narrow band of lace edged with blue stripes (31). N.B. Details of the lance cap plate are given in chapter six.

OPPOSITE
Figure 9: 'An Officer of the 21st Lancers.' A fine study of an officer of the regiment in mounted review order. N.B. It is thought that this photograph was taken c.1898-1901 as the officer is equipped with a sabretache. Copyright D.P.& G.

To the rear of the cap a very large false peak edged all round with silver braid, which as the regulations state is *'constantly turned up behind'*. The front peak was also adorned with silver lace, with the chin-scales and lion's head bosses being of silver coloured metal (31).

The lance cap was complete with a crimson and white feather plume for the officers, horse hair for the other ranks, and was worn together with gold cap-lines for the officers, yellow for the rank and file.

The Jacket (Coatee), Overalls and Accoutrements (*See Fig: 11*).
A dark blue jacket having the collar, cuffs, plastron, turn-backs, and piping in the facing colour of crimson (31). To the rear of the jacket, the pleated skirts had two ornaments of silver bullion, with large silver bullion epaulettes completing the upper wear (14).

The waist girdle was of gold lace having a double crimson stripe, which when 'mixed' with the silver lace of the tunic does seem somewhat peculiar. The overalls/trousers were crimson with silver lace down the outward seams. No information was available to the authors regarding the boots or spurs worn.

The shoulder belt was of silver lace having crimson central stripe, complete with prickers and chains, the pouch of black leather having a silver flap bearing a gilt crown and double 'G.R' cypher.

The sabretache had a crimson cloth face bearing a crown, 'GR' reversed and intertwined, the battle honours in gold embroidery, with the Sphinx in silver, the whole bordered with silver lace (14). The sword carried was the Mameluke pattern with ivory hilt, complete with a crimson velvet and gilt metal scabbard (31).

Figure 11: A fine example of the officers full dress uniform of the 23rd Lancers. Note the fine gilt metal Hanoverian arms to the centre of the plate. Copyright W.Y. Carman.

NOTES

1. Line cavalry regiments consisted of the Dragoon Guards, Dragoon, Hussar, and Lancers regiments. it did not include the 1st Life Guards, 2nd Life Guards, or Royal Horse Guards who are Household Troops and take/took precedence over the line cavalry regiments.

2. Edmund Henry Hynman Allenby, later Field Marshal Sir E.H.H. Allenby, 1st Viscount of Megiddo and Felixstowe G.C.B. G.C.M.G. G.C.V.O. K.C.B. C.B. Lieutenant 10th May 1882: 6th Dragoons. Captain 10th Jan 1888: 6th Dragoons. Major 19th May 1897: 6th Dragoons. Lt Colonel 2nd Aug. 1902: 5th Lancers (32). Half-pay 1905, then to 4th Cavalry Brigade. Major-General 1910: Inspector of Cavalry. Commanded 5th Army Corps 1915, then to 3rd Army Corps. Commander-in-Chief, Egyptian Expeditionary Force 1917-1919. Colonel of The Life Guards, and Colonel of the 16th/5th Lancers (33).

3. R.H. de Montmorency was taken prisoner whilst serving with the 13th Light Dragoons during the Peninsula Campaign. He spent some three years in Paris, where, whilst on parole he was able to observe the methods used by Napoleons Polish Lancers. He later wrote and published the first training manual on the use of the lance (13).

4. Major Hope Grant (later General Sir H. Grant G.C.B. K.C.B.). Cornet C.1826: 9th Lancers. Command of troop 1835: 9th Lancers. Served during the China War of 1841-42, Major 1842: 9th Lancers. Served at Sobraon during the first Sikh War of 1846, at Chillianwallah and Gujerat during the second Sikh War of 1848-49, the Relief of Lucknow and the Battle of Cawnpore during the Sepoy War 1857-58. Major-General K.C.B. Lt General (local rank) served the China War 1860. Awarded G.C.B. Adjutant-General at Horse Guards 1865. Commanded at Aldershot 1870-74 (4).

5. H.S.H. Prince Francis of Teck was promoted as follows. 2nd Lt 30th January 1889: 9th Lancers. 2nd Lt 17th April 1889: Kings Royal Rifle Corps. Lieutenant 26th August 1891: 1st Royal Dragoons. Captain 25th July 1894: 1st Royal Dragoons. Major 16th November 1901: The Reserve (7).

6. Colonel Ponsonby (later Major-General Ponsonby) was already badly wounded when a Polish Lancer drove his lance into Ponsonby's back. He was then ridden over by two squadrons of Prussian cavalry, and his apparently lifeless body plundered by two French soldiers. He was however made of stern stuff, and survived these terrible wounds, eventually dying in 1837 (15).

7. H.R.H. George, 2nd Duke of Cambridge later became Field Marshal H.R.H. G W F C Duke of Cambridge, K.G. K.T. K.P. G.C.B. G.C.S.I. G.C.M.G. G.C.I.E. G.C.V.O. A.D.C. (34).

8. When the Battle of Aliwal was over, the lance pennons of the regiment were so crumpled and blood stained that they had the appearance of having been starched and crimped. To this day, the lance pennons that hang from the lances positioned outside the Regimental Guard Room are crimped and starched (8).

9. Hubert de la Poer Gough (later General Sir H. de la Poer Gough G.C.B. K.C.B. G.C.M.G. K.C.V.O.). Lieutenant 23 July 1890: 16th Lancers. Captain 22nd Dec. 1894: 16th Lnrs. Major 22nd Oct. 1902: 16th Lnrs. Lt Colonel 19th Dec. 1906: 16th Lnrs (35). Served on the Tirah Expedition 1897-98, South Africa 1899-1902. Brevet Lt Colonel 1904-06: Staff College. Commanded 16th Lancers 1907-11. 3rd Cavalry Brigade 1914. 2nd Cavalry Division, and then the 7th Division 1915. 1st Army Corps 1916. 5th Army 1916-18. Colonel of the 16th/5th Lancers 1936-1943 (36). There is an excellent black and white illustration of Lt Col de la Poer Gough in the full dress uniform of the 16th Lancers in *Regiment Magazine* issue No.47, page 39. N.B. Both General Gough's father and his uncle were decorated with the Victoria Cross for their actions during the Indian Mutiny, and years later his brother was also awarded the V.C.(8).

10. William Robertson, the son of a village Postmaster and Tailor, enlisted into the 16th Lancers on the 13th November 1877. By 1885 he had been promoted to the rank of Troop Sergeant Major (8), and went on to become Field Marshal W. Robertson Bart, G.C.B. G.C.M.G. G.C.V.O. D.S.O. D.C.L. L.L.D. He was Colonel of the 2nd Dragoons (Royal Scots Greys) from 1916 until 1925, Colonel of the 3rd Carabiniers from 1925 to 1929, and Colonel of the Royal Horse Guards from 1929 until his death in 1933 (17).

11. It is the custom in The Queen's Royal Lancers for the cross-strap of the officers Sam Browne belt to be worn in reverse, i.e. fastened at the back. This tradition apparently dates back to the early 1920s when as Col-in-Chief of the former 16th Lancers, King Alfonso XIII of Spain was due to inspect the regiment at Tidworth. It was observed by the then Commanding Officer of the regiment, Lt Colonel Geoffrey Brooke (later Major General G. Brooke) that the King was wearing his 'Sam Browne' belt back to front. Colonel Brooke felt it inappropriate to bring this 'mistake' to the King's attention, and therefore ordered all the officers of the regiment to reverse their 'Same Browne' belts, a tradition maintained to this day (8).

12. Colonel John Hale served under the command of General James Wolfe, who in 1759 was mortally wounded at Quebec. In order to retain the memory of his distinguished General, Hale chose a death's head and crossbones at the regiments badge, with 'Or Glory' as their motto. N.B. The skull and crossbones badge is similar in appearance to the one that was worn by the Black Brunswickers (11).

13. Captain William Morris entered the 16th Lancers as a Cornet on 18th June 1842. Lieutenant 14th May 1845: 16th Lnrs. Captain 25th April 1851: 17th Lancers. Brevet Major 12th Dec 1854. Major 1857: 17th Lnrs. Died at Poona, India on the 11th July 1858. N.B. At Balaclava this officer received two sabre cuts to his head, a lance thrust to his forehead, a sabre cut to his left arm, and two broken ribs (20).

14. H.S.H. Prince Adolphus, Duke of Teck (later Marquess of Cambridge) was appointed 2nd Lieutenant 11th April 1888: 17th Lancers. Lieutenant 11th Jan 1893: 17th Lancers. Captain 26th June 1895: 1st Life Guards. Major 29th November 1900: 1st Life Guards. Brevet Lt Colonel 11th November 1910. Hon Colonel 19th July 1912: 8th Battalion, The London Regiment (7).

15. Sergeant Brian Turner Thomas Lawrence (Army Number 3934) was born at Lower Park House, Bewdley, Worcestershire in 1873. He was decorated with the Victoria Cross by His Majesty King Edward VII on 12th August 1902. He died in Kenya, East Africa on the 7th June 1949 (21).

16. Lt Colonel Douglas Haig (later Field Marshal the 1st Viscount Dawick O.M. K.T. G.C.B. K.C.B. K.C.I.E. G.C.V.O. K.C.V.O. C.B. A.D.C.). Commissioned 1885: 7th Hussars. Served Sudan (Soudan) 1898, South Africa 1899-1902. Lt Colonel 1901-1903: 17th Lancers. Major-General 1904. Lt-General 1910. General 1914. Field Marshal 1917. Commander-in-Chief, Expeditionary Forces in France and Flanders 1915-19. Field Marshal, Commander-in-Chief, The Forces in Great Britain 1919-20. Colonel of the Royal Horse Guards. Colonel of the 17th Lancers (25).

17. After a delay of some twenty-six years, the battle honour 'Seringapatam' was finally granted to the regiment on the 28th March 1818 (27).

18. It should be mentioned that several lance caps having a yellow cloth top and sides exist, that lack the proper lance cap plate. These caps appear to have come from Messrs Hawkes, military tailor and outfitter, and it has been suggested that these caps did at one time have a front plate, however it is not known what distinctions were borne on the plate (27).

19. The following details, recorded by Messrs Herbert on an old piece of paper water-marked 1815, relate to the cap of the 19th Lancers and are reproduced as written:

> 'Dress Cap
> 21 ins. blue and gold 3 inch new wave lace
> 22 ins. blue and gold 1 inch new wave lace
> 1 yard 20 ins. gold 5/8 in. braid
> 2 yards gold 3/16 in. braid
> 14 ins. engine Royal cord
> 9 ins. Russia braid
> 1.1/4 yds. gold round lancer cord
> Extremely rich large dotted bullion boss with GR in centre on scarlet'.

N.B. Messrs Herbert & Co published five volumes of uniform detail ranging from c.1807 to late Victorian times (27).

20. When in 1818 the honour '*Seringapatam*' was awarded, the old lance cap plates had the 'mounts' removed and then replaced to include this latest honour. This apparently resulted in the Royal Arms being positioned so high up on the plate that the top of the arms (the lion surmounting a crown) was nearly off the edge of the plate. N.B. If Messrs Hawkes had to make the change to the plate, it is possible that they could have had spare caps available to which they merely added the amended plates (27).

21. Details in Messrs Herbert's book state that the cap-line was 4.1/4 yards long of gold lancer cord chain in front, and a pattern of the facing which was pale yellow (27).

22. It appears that in 1896, the War Office decided to create three brigades of lancers, and as at that time only five lancer regiments existed, it was decided to convert the most junior light cavalry regiment, this being the 21st Hussars (14).

23. Officers known to have been attached to the 21st Lancers and taken part in the charge at Omdurman are, Lt J.C. Brinton: 2nd Life Guards, Lt W.L.S. Churchill: 4th Hussars, Lt R. Grenfell: 12th Lancers (killed in the charge), Lt the Hon R.F. Molyneux: Royal Horse Guards, and Lt F.W. Wormald: 7th Hussars.

24. Captain Paul Aloysius Kenna V.C. (later Brigadier P.A. Kenna), mortally wounded at Gallipoli on the 30th August 1915 (30). Lt the Hon Raymond Hannay Lodge Joseph de Montmorency V.C., 2nd Lieutenant Sept. 1887: 21st Hussars. Lieutenant 6th Nov. 1889 (34), killed in action as a Captain, commanding Montmorency's Scouts during the Boer war (30). Private Thomas Byrne V.C. served for a year in the 8th Hussars before transferring to the 21st Hussars. He left the army in 1908, and died at Canterbury in 1945 (30).

25. Winston L.S. Churchill, (later Sir W.L.S. Churchill), 2nd Lieutenant 1895: 4th Hussars. Lieutenant 1896: 4th Hussars. Lieutenant 1899: South African Light Horse. Major 1915: Oxfordshire Hussars. Lt Colonel 1915: 6th Battalion, Royal Scots Fusiliers. Minister of Munitions: 1917. Elected Prime Minister of Great Britain 1940 and 1951. Knighted: 1953 (37).

26. In the 1970s it was not unusual for an hussar/lancer officers shoulder belt to be offered for sale with the silver breast ornament, prickers and chains, and in the case of the 13th, and 19th Hussars. the battle honour scrolls all missing. These fittings would have been removed from the shoulder belt and sold for their scrap silver value, due to the price of silver having risen to an unprecedented price. This foolish act of 'vandalism' cost the seller dearly, for the belt then became almost worthless, whereas if sold complete it would have been worth more that the scrap silver value.

27. Whilst the battle of Talavera took place on the 28th July 1809, the battle honour "*Talavera*" was not awarded to the regiment until the 28th May 1816 (14). N.B. An interesting feature of the uniform worn by the members of the regiment during this battle was the light dragoon helmet. The regiment lost many men and their helmets, the latter being acquired by their enemy the 3rd Baden Infantry, who were fighting on the side of the French. For four years after the battle the Baden Infantry band members wore these 'captured' helmets, which they said carried 'sirens' on the side of the head-dress (31).

28. On an existing example of this pattern of cap, the cloth is only three inches, and as this is curving, only two and a half inches high (31).

29. A contemporary note of Messrs Hawkes Moseley & Co (Cap makers to their Majesties H.R.H. the Prince of Wales and Royal Family) lists the following for the 23rd Lancers:

> '21 ins crimson & silver new pattern lace, 3 inches.
> 22 ins crimson & silver new pattern lace, 1 inch.
> 1 2/3 yds silver 5/8 in French braid.
> 1 2/3 yds silver 1/8 in French braid.
> 1/2 yd silver engine Royal Cord.
> 1 1/3 yd silver round engine cord.
> A silver No. 2.1/2 twisted bullion rose with silver embroidered GR in centre on crimson cloth' (31).

Chapter Four

Purchase and Supply of the Lance Cap

Officers

During the period with which this book is primarily concerned, a commissioned officer was responsible for the ordering and purchase of his own accoutrements, head-dress, sword, and uniform, and in the case of a cavalry officer for the supply and purchase of his changer, saddlery etc. The accoutrements, head-dress, sword, and uniform were obtained from the outfitter or military tailor appointed to the particular regiment in which the officer was to serve, they maintaining pattern books showing the relevant uniform details, including those unique to the particular regiment concerned.

As with most things in life, very little remains unchanged, and many of these fine establishments have over the years either merged to form a larger organisation or ceased trading altogether. At the turn of the nineteenth century, there would have been one or more military outfitter/tailors premises situated in any city/town having a military garrison within its boundary. A few such cities/towns are Aldershot, the 'Home of the British Army', and Canterbury in the south of England, Colchester in the east, York in the north, Glasgow in Scotland, and Cork in Ireland, with many of the more established suppliers of military dress also having additional premises in London.

Below are listed some of the better known military outfitters/tailors, recorded as having supplied uniforms to officers of the six regular lancer regiments, and to one yeomanry (lancer) regiment over the past one hundred or so years, together with the title of the regiment/s they are known to have supplied being given alongside each 'outfitters' name:

Cater & Co., London	City of London Yeomanry
Hamburger and Company of Covent Garden, London	5th, 9th, and 17th Lancers
Hamburger, Rogers & Co., of 30 King Street, Covent Garden, London	Lincolnshire Imperial Yeomanry
Hawkes and Company[1] of Piccadilly, London	5th, 9th, 16th, 21st, and 23rd Lancers, East Riding of Yorkshire Imperial Yeomanry
John Jones Ltd., London	17th/21st Lancers
H. Poole & Co. of Savile Row, London W.1.	East Riding of Yorkshire Imperial Yeomanry
Rogers & Co., London	16th/5th Lancers
Rumsey Wells (G & S Wells), Norwich	16th Lancers
F.A. Stone & Sons	16th Lancers
Sandilands & Son, Conduit St., London	21st Lancers

At the turn of the nineteenth century for an officer in one of Queen Victoria's elite regiments of cavalry, the cost of providing a complete uniform, including head-dress, sword, charger and saddlery, was to say the least most expensive. In spite of having purchased all the above items for his present regiment, an officer could also incur additional financial outlay upon either exchanging regiments, or upon being gazetted to a new regiment as a result of promotion.[2] In either instance the officer would be required to purchase a new head-dress, uniform, sword, saddlery, and possibly a replacement charger, if say the officer concerned was transferring from a light to a heavy cavalry regiment, or the reverse.

In view of the above, the cost of his commission[3], and the mess bills likely to be incurred by a commissioned officer, few, if any Victorian cavalry officers could afford to live on their army pay. However as a great many came from either titled or 'well to do' English 'country seat' families, this financial outlay was probably not too great a hardship. A example of the 'officer class' serving in a cavalry regiment at the close of the late 1890's is typified by the following named officers, who were all serving in one of the six regular lancers regiments at that time (34).

5th (Royal Irish) Lancers
Lieutenant R.C. Browne-Clayton
Lieutenant W.M.C. Du Q. Caillard

9th (Queen's Royal) Lancers
Captain Lord D.J.C. Compton
Captain H.E. Twisleton-Wykeham-Fiennes
Captain Hon. C.H.C. Willoughby
2nd Lieutenant F.T.T. Hamilton-Blackwood

12th (Prince of Wales's Royal) Lancers
Lt Colonel Earl D.S.W. Airlie[4]
Captain Hon. H.G. Heneage

16th (Queen's) Lancers
Lieutenant Viscount A.E. Fincastle (later awarded the V.C.)
2nd Lieutenant Hon. C.M. Evans-Freke

17th (Duke of Cambridge's Own) Lancers
Major Hon. L.H.D. Fortescue
Captain Hon. H.A. Lawrence
Lieutenant Lord O. de V. Beauclerk

21st Lancers
Lieutenant Hon. R.H.L.J. de Montmorency

Figure 12: Studies of the 16th (The Queen's) Lancers. The regimental Christmas card of the 16th/5th The Queen's Royal Lancers c.1982. Author's collection.

With such an array of titled officers as listed above, all of which served in just one branch of the cavalry, it is hardly surprising that there appears to have been a saying amongst Victorian cavalry officers to the effect that '*The main purpose of cavalry is to give tone to what otherwise would simply be a mere vulgar brawl*'.

With the outbreak of the First World War, the wearing of the full dress uniform by the rank and file was discontinued, with their uniforms being returned to the quartermasters stores, this order of dress never to be officially restored. For the commissioned officers however, as they owned their uniforms, they naturally retained them, and when hostilities ceased and peacetime soldiering returned, there occurred occasions when the full dress/review order uniform was once again to be seen at military events such as levees, the presentation of a new standard, and reviews etc.

Warrant Officers

Dress Regulation relating to the uniform of Warrant Officers were not produced, and our research has identified that there seems to be little uniformity with regards to the full dress uniform worn by soldiers holding this rank, such as the Regimental Sergeant Major and the Bandmaster, the quality of their uniform appearing to vary from regiment to regiment.

Bandmaster

During the Georgian period the Bandmasters uniform was provided at the expenses of the regimental officers, and originally this high profile position would have been held by a civilian, or an N.C.O. of the regiment concerned. Whilst late into Queen Victoria's reign the appointment of Bandmaster would have been held by a commissioned officer, it is with the Warrant Officer rank that we are concerned. However, very little information was available to the author's regarding the pattern of uniform worn by Warrant Officers holding the post of Bandmaster within the lancer regiments for the period immediately prior to, and during the early days of the twentieth century. Nevertheless, it is reasonable to expect that such a prominent post would entitle the Warrant Officer concerned to be attired in a uniform that was not unlike that of a commissioned officer, as was the case in many of the heavy cavalry regiments.

There is however, in the excellent issue of *Regiment Magazine* devoted to The Queen's Royal Lancers (14), a photograph of the mounted band of the 5th (Royal Irish) Lancers in full dress uniform c.1898, in which can be seen what appears to be the Bandmaster wearing an officers style uniform complete with a swan's feather plume in his lance cap. N.B. As this photograph was apparently

Figure 13: 'An Officer of the 17th Lancers.' A fine study of the 'officer class' this officer serving in a crack cavalry regiment, and thought to be Sir Francis Burdett Bt A.D.C. D.L. J.P. (1869-1951), in mounted review order pre 1901. N.B. This officer served in South Africa 1900 (wounded, medal and four clasps), and in the European War (117). Copyright D.P.& G.

Figure 14: Field Marshall Earl Haig O.M. K.T. G.C.B. K.C.I.E. G.C.V.O. K.C.V.O. C.B. A.D.C. in his full dress uniform as Colonel of the 17th (Duke of Cambridge's Own) Lancers. Author's collection.

taken c.1898, it is possible that the Bandmaster concerned was in fact a commissioned officer. Jumping some 100 or so years, it is recorded that at the Royal Tournament held in July 1991, that the Bandmaster of both the 9th/12th Lancers, and the 16th/5th Lancers each wore a uniform of officers quality complete with officers pattern lance cap. Also present at that event was the Bandmaster of the 17th/21st Lancers who wore a similar style uniform, but with a modern, special pattern cap, fuller details of which are given later in chapter nine.

Regimental Sergeant Major

A photograph in the authors collection illustrates an R.S.M. of the 4th Dragoon Guards c.1881, in which it can be seen that his helmet bears the officers helmet plate, whilst his tunic appears to be in the style of a Senior N.C.O's pattern. Conversely, a similar photograph of the R.S.M of the 1st Dragoon Guards c.1897, clearly shows that his helmet is the other ranks pattern, whilst his tunic resembles that of a junior commissioned officer. To confuse this matter still further, a photograph of the Bandmaster of the 3rd Dragoon Guards taken c.1927, shows him wearing his full dress tunic and holding his helmet, both of which are of the officers pattern (38).

Whilst the above photographic information relating to the pattern of uniform worn by cavalry Warrant Officers is of interest, it is relevant to the heavy cavalry regiments, and not to the lancer regiments with which the book is primarily concerned. It does however serve to illustrate the variations in the style of dress worn by a Regimental Sergeant Major of a cavalry regiment during a time span of some forty-six years.

Fortunately however, there appeared in a 1973 edition of *Modelworld Magazine*, a most informative article on the 17th Lancers c.1904 written by A. H. Bowling (39). In this article mention is made of there being three classes of dress for men below the rank of commissioned officer, these being divided into Warrant Officer and Staff Sergeant, Sergeants, and other ranks. The article also mentions a War Office Publication 'Clothing and Necessities' issued in 1907 which gives three grades of lance cap for the 17th Lancers, together with the difference in price and quality'. The article continues by giving the following information relating to the cap. 'For Warrant Officers & Staff Sergeants the cost was £1 12s 4d, for Sergeants £1 1s 9d and for lower ranks £0 14s 2d.'. It further states that 'the cap-lines for Warrant Officers and Staff Sergeants were made of gold cord and cost £1 11 0d, all ranks below having yellow worsted cord lines at a cost of only £0 1s 1d'. N.B. In addition to the above, it is known that the lance cap worn by Warrant Officers and Staff Sergeants had a gold lace band around the waist, in place of yellow cotton braid, and that the plume boss was of gold coloured cord, as opposed to the cotton boss fitted to the private soldiers cap.

In a copy of *The Journal of the Crown Imperial Society* of 1982 (40), there appeared a most interesting photograph of R.S.M Praeger of the 9th Lancers c.1899, in which it appears that he is wearing the Warrant Officers pattern lance cap, whilst his plume is the officers pattern of swan feathers. Also in this photograph it may be seen that his tunic follows the officers pattern, having gold lace edging to the collar but being without the officers pattern gold wire shoulder cords, and that the waist girdle appears to be the officers gold lace pattern.

Figure 15: 'Late Again.' A Victorian caricature of a dismounted officer of the 17th Lancers in mounted review order of dress. David Rowe collection. Previously published in the Regiment Journal 1897.

At the dawn of the twentieth century, the wearing of an officers style uniform by the R.S.M. also appears to have been the practice in the 16th Lancers, as may be seen in a photographic illustration of Regimental Sergeant Major Thomas Walter James D.C.M. c.1906, that appeared in *Regiment Magazine*, issue Forty-Seven, in which it can be seen that his uniform very closely resembles the officer pattern (lance cap not visible).[5] However, in the same excellent magazine there is a photographic illustration c.1891 of Regimental Sergeant Major Charles Clarke of the 17th Lancers, whose uniform bears little, if any, resemblance to the officers pattern, with his lance cap being of Warrant Officers pattern with hair plume.

Further information on this interesting subject came to light when examining a photograph of the '21st Lancers on the march c.1901/04', that accompanied an extremely well documented article on this regiment by Bob Marrion that appeared in a 1994 edition of *Military Modelling Magazine* (30). What is of particular interest about this photograph, is that slightly behind the group of officers rides the Regimental Sergeant Major, and it can clearly be seen that his lance cap has an officers pattern feather plume.

When seeking information relating to the provision of the full dress uniform for a soldier holding the appointment of Regimental Sergeant Major[6], it has been stated upon good authority, that during the late 'Victorian' period and the 'Edwardian' era, and possibly even later, that when a R.S.M. was newly appointed, the officers of his regiment contributed financially towards the cost of his full dress uniform. This gesture by the officers, would possibly also include the purchase of the swan feathers plume, and if this explanation is borne of truth it would help explain much of the 'mix and match' of the Warrant Officers uniform as described above. N.B. Refer to endnote No.5 for further information regarding this matter.

A final word regarding the head-dress of the Warrant Officer relates to a photographic type Christmas card (believed to have been obtained at York Castle Museum), that was sent to David Rowe in 1978. The coloured picture on the cover of this card re-enacted a scene of ladies and gentlemen in period dress meeting outside an apothecary and druggist at Christmas time. This staged piece includes three men in military uniform, one of which is wearing the full dress uniform of the East Riding of Yorkshire Imperial Yeomanry of the period c.1906/07. In the illustration it can be clearly seen that the 'soldier' concerned has a crown above four inverted chevrons to his right sleeve indicating that he is a Sergeant Major, however, for some reason his head-dress is the lance cap with swan feathers plume, normally only worn by the commissioned officers of this regiment. Although the author's have no confirmed information as to whether or not this pattern of head-dress was worn by sergeant majors of this particular regiment, it is thought possible that in this instance the lance cap was used merely to complete the full dress uniform worn by the gentleman concerned, although this has not been verified.

Other Ranks

For the rank and file, the accoutrements, uniform, sword and head-dress were all issue items. The Royal Warrant and Regulations Regarding Army Services published on the 1st July 1848 divided the items issued to the rank and file into clothing, necessaries and accoutrements[7], and for members of a lancer regiment the lance cap with plume was replaced once every four years (19).

It is recorded that prior to the conflict of 1914-1918, that most of the uniforms for the other ranks were made at the Army Clothing Factory at Pimlico London[8], these premises being situated on the north embankment close to the River Thames. The uniforms were usually sent out to the regiment ready made, and were then 'altered to fit' the wearer by the regimental tailors.

Figure 16: An unissued troopers tunic of the 9th Lancers. N.B. There is a makers paper label within the tunic, which gives the date of manufacture as being March 1914. David Rowe collection.

The uniform and necessaries[9] issued to the soldier shortly after joining his regiment was comprised of numerous items, and was worth a considerable amount of money. This cost tended to vary according to the particular regiment in which the soldier was to serve, the most costly being the provision of a uniform in the Household Cavalry, for in these three prestigious regiments, the approximate cost to outfit[10] a private (trooper) early in the 1900's, was in the region of £27 0s 0d, which included such items of uniform as the tunic at £2 4s 10d; buckskin breeches at £5 16s 0d; and jack boots at £3 9s 0d (41).

For the lancer regiments the cost of providing a private soldiers uniform was somewhat less expensive, being in the region of £14 0s 0d., included in which was £0 15s 3d[11] for the lance cap and cap lines, and £1 7s 0d for a tunic similar to the example illustrated in Fig: 16. (41). However, for Warrant Officers and senior non commissioned officers, this cost was slightly higher due to the addition of gold braid/lace etc. N.B. For detailed information relating to the price of the component parts that made up the warrant officers, sergeants, and the other ranks pattern lance cap c.1911, kindly refer to appendix two.

NOTES

1. Hawkes & Company, now trading as Gieves & Hawkes, No.1 Savile Row, London W.1.

2. A few examples of cavalry officers either exchanging or being promoted into a different regiment during the period 1880 to 1900 are given below. 17th April 1880: Captain R.G. Godson from the 1st Dragoon Guards to the 3rd Hussars. 4th May 1882: Captain M. McNeill from 4th Hussars to the 4th Dragoon Guards. 6th September 1882: Lieutenant Arthur Hughes from 5th Lancers to the 10th Royal Hussars. 15th September 1897: Captain C.G. Morris from 5th Dragoon Guards to the 1st (Royal) Dragoons. 4th July 1900: Captain E.A. Williams from 18th Hussars to the 1st Dragoon Guards.

3. Prior to the abolition of the Commission Purchase System in 1871, a commission was purchased from either an exchanging, promoted, or retiring officer, the cost of the commission concerned being dependent upon the rank that the purchaser was eligible to buy. Below is an example of both the 'regulation' and 'over regulation price' for each commissioned rank.

Regulation Price (The Cavalry)		Over Regulation Price (The 5th Lancers)	
Lt Colonel	£4500	Lt Colonel	£8700
Major	£3200	Major	£6400
Captain	£1800	Troop Captain	£4200
Lieutenant	£700	Lieutenant	£750
Cornet	£450	Cornet	not applicable (8).

4. David William Stanley Ogilvy, 8th Earl of Airlie. Lieutenant 13th June 1875: 10th Hussars. Captain 28th Feb. 1884: 10th Hussars. Major 3rd Aug 1892: 10th Hussars (24). Major 2nd Jan 1897: 2nd Dragoon Guards. Lt Colonel Dec 1897: 12th Lancers. Hon Colonel 27th Nov. 1895: 3rd (Dundee Highland) Volunteer Battalion (34). Killed in action whilst in command of the 12th Lancers during the Boer War on the 11th June 1900 (24).

5. The text accompanying the photographic illustration of R.S.M. T.W. James advises that 'his cap was also of officers pattern, except that the visor (peak) was of plain undecorated leather. It also states 'it was customary in the 16th for the regimental officers to collectively pay for the R.S.M.'s uniform' (14).

6. The Regimental Sergeant Major of The Queen's Royal Lancers (formed in 1993 by the amalgamation of the 16th/5th and 17th/21st Lancers) wears an officers pattern dress cap, shoulder belt and pouch when in Number One Dress. N.B. The shoulder belt is complete with prickers and chains etc. (16).

7. Accoutrements included such items as cloak, pouch, pouch belt, sabretache, sword, sword knot, sword scabbard, and waist belt (19).

8. Three known suppliers of the actual lance cap for the rank and file were G. & W. Almond, Army Contractor, 67 Willow Works, London S.E., Hobson & Sons, and James Lock (Hatter) of London.

9. Necessaries would include such items as brushes, cutlery, razor, shirts, socks, and towels etc. (41).

10. Apart from the items of full dress issued to the rank and file, there was also an issue of working dress (a plain canvas suit), and an issue of service dress (of drab or khaki colour) (41).

11. The cost of £0 15s 3d for a lancer chapka c.1904 was, to say the least quite costly, especially when one considers that in 1900 the average pay for a manual worker, say a labourer was only £1 18s 6d per week.

Chapter Five

Component Parts that Make up a Lance Cap

In order to minimise repetition when relating details of the particular item of head-dress with which this book is concerned, the words chapka and cap have also been used when describing, or referring to the lance cap. Additionally, for ease of reference and identification the chapka has been broken down into its various component parts, and throughout this book, listed below, is the sequence in which each lance cap will be described.

As with any manufactured item there will always be slight variations in design, dimensions and quality, and the fact that there might exist an officers pattern cap where the colour of the silk head lining, or the chinchain backing differs slightly from the colour described in this book does not in any way imply the item concerned is 'wrong', but more probably that the difference is simply due to a manufacturers variation in the materials used.

1. The Top and Upper Section.
2. The Rosette.
3. The Skull and Peak.
4. The Lance Cap Plate
5. The Chinchain and Ear Bosses
6. The Head Lining.
7. The Plume and Plume Socket.
8. The Cap-Lines.

N.B It is not intended to imply that the descriptions used, nor the order in which the component parts have been listed above, would in any way have been those utilized by the original manufacturers of the lance cap.

Originally, it had been thought that very little else that could be added to the above, however we had reckoned without our friend Jon Maguire of Oklahoma City, who most generously disassembled his superb example of a post 1902 officers pattern cap of the 5th (Royal Irish) Lancers, in order that many of the individual component parts that make up the cap may be photographed for inclusion within this book.

The Top and Upper Section
The cloth top and ribbed sides of the cap was covered in cloth of the regimental facing colour, being supported on the inside by a metal framework made of thin metal 'rods' as illustrated in *Figs: 17B* and *17E*. Gold gimp and orris cord extended across the top of the cap and down the four angles (*See Fig: 17F.*).

The Rosette
The gold bullion rosette as illustrated in *Fig: 17C.* was attached to the upper left front of the cap by means of two small threaded studs to the reverse of the rosette as illustrated in *Figs: 17D.* and *17E.*, which passed through corresponding holes in the plume socket (See *Fig: 17F.*), then on through the ribbed cloth where it was secured by two small brass nuts.

The Skull and Peak
The skull was of black patent leather, with around the waist there being gold lace, with gold braid below, as illustrated in *Fig: 17G.*, fuller details of which are given in chapter seven. To the rear of the waist, a gilt metal ring and hook upon a gilt metal four-petalled leaf (*See Fig: 17H.*). The front peak of black patent leather, being adorned with three stripes of gold purl, as may be seen in *Fig: 17A.*

The Lance Cap Plate
The gilt metal rayed plate was adorned with a silver plated overlay, to the reverse of which were several very thin short 'pins', which were passed through corresponding holes in the gilt metal rayed 'back plate' as illustrated in *Fig: 17J.*, then bent flat to secure the overlay in place. The number of 'pins' used was usually dependent upon the size of the overlay concerned, or as in the case of the overlay for the 5th Lancers, upon the number of component parts that made up the overlay.

For the 5th Lancers the silvered overlay was comprised of five separate pieces, these being (1) the post 1902 Royal Arms, as illustrated in *Fig: 17K.*, (2) the battle honour 'Suakin' (3) the honour date of '1885' (*See Fig: 17M.*), (4) the 'angel harp', (5) the title scroll, and the battle honours 'Blenheim', and 'Oudenarde' (the left

INSET *Figure 17:* A superb example of a post 1902 officers lance cap of the 5th (Royal Irish) Lancers, complete with feather plume. *Figure 17A:* The cap with the plume removed.

Figure 17B: Inside view of the skull of the cap, in which may seen part of the metal framework that supports the top and ribbed sides of the cap.

Figure 17C: The gold bullion plume rosette, bearing the embroidered Royal Cypher of ER VII on a green velvet ground.

Figure 17D: Rear view of the bullion rosette, in which can clearly be seen the two brass threaded studs used when securing the rosette to the cap.

Figure 17E: Inside view of the cap, with the bullion rosette in situ showing the method of attaching the rosette to the cap. N.B. The steel 'thumb' screw between the brass studs is not original.

Figure 17F: The plume socket, a part of the cap not normally visible, due to it usually being hidden behind the bullion rosette.

Figure 17G: The skull of the cap with the plate removed, in which may be seen the stitching to the peak/skull. Note the 'saving' on both gold braid, and leather on the section of the skull normally hidden from view.

Figure 17H: Rear view of the waist of the cap, illustrating the gilt metal ring and hook mounted upon a gilt metal four-petalled leaf.

DIEU ET
MON DROIT
1885
OUDENARDE
RAMILLIES
ROYAL
IRISH

side, when facing the lance cap plate) and 'Ramillies' and 'Malplaquet' (right side), all as illustrated in *Figs: 17O.* and *17P.* N.B. On the plate of certain regiments, the battle honours overlay was at one period in gilt metal, and whilst the gilt or silvered battle honours on the overlay were usually die-struck, it is not unknown for the battle honours to have been made in *cast* metal (*See Fig: 17N.*). In fact it is also not unknown for the battle honours on a plate to be comprised of a combination of both cast, and die-stuck honours.

The complete lance cap plate, was attached to the skull of the cap by means of thin wires being passed through the 'sewing' holes located at the outer edge of the rayed plate, as may be seen in *Fig: 17J.*, and then on through corresponding holes in the patent leather skull to secure the plate in place. N.B. It is not unknown for the officers plate to also have two short threaded studs to its reverse as on the other ranks pattern plate.

The Ear Bosses and Chinchain

The two gilt lion's head bosses differed in that the left hand boss (right side, if viewing cap from the front) had a closed ring attached to its chin onto which was attached the end link of the chinchain as illustrated in *Fig: 17S.*, whilst the right hand boss (left side, if viewing cap from the front) had a hook attached to its chin onto which was attached the 'loose' end of the chinchain (*See Fig: 17Q.*). To the reverse of each lion's head boss was a threaded stud (*See Fig: 17S.*), which enabled the boss to be attached to the skull of the cap by the stud being 'screwed' into a threaded socket that protruded through a hole in the side of the cap. This socket formed part of a brass disc, having six small holes around its milled edge, the disc being positioned on the inside of the skull of the cap with the socket passing through a corresponding hole in the patent leather of the skull, and was sewn in place using the six small holes as illustrated in *Fig: 17T.* The chinchain was of plain burnished chain mounted on black patent leather and lined with black velvet (*See Fig: 17S.*).

The Plume and Plume Socket

The swan feathers plume was fitted with a gilt metal ring to the top of the 'crown' of the plume as illustrated in *Fig: 17Y*, said to have been used to pull the plume into its storage tin, or used to hang the plume in a natural position when wet. To the base of the plume a metal stem as illustrated in *Fig: 17X.*, that was passed through the slot in the base of the plume socket as illustrated in *Fig: 17W.*, the officers pattern gilt metal plume holder being as illustrated in *Fig: 17U.*

Regrettably the cap-lines did not accompany this particular lance cap, and therefore no description is included.

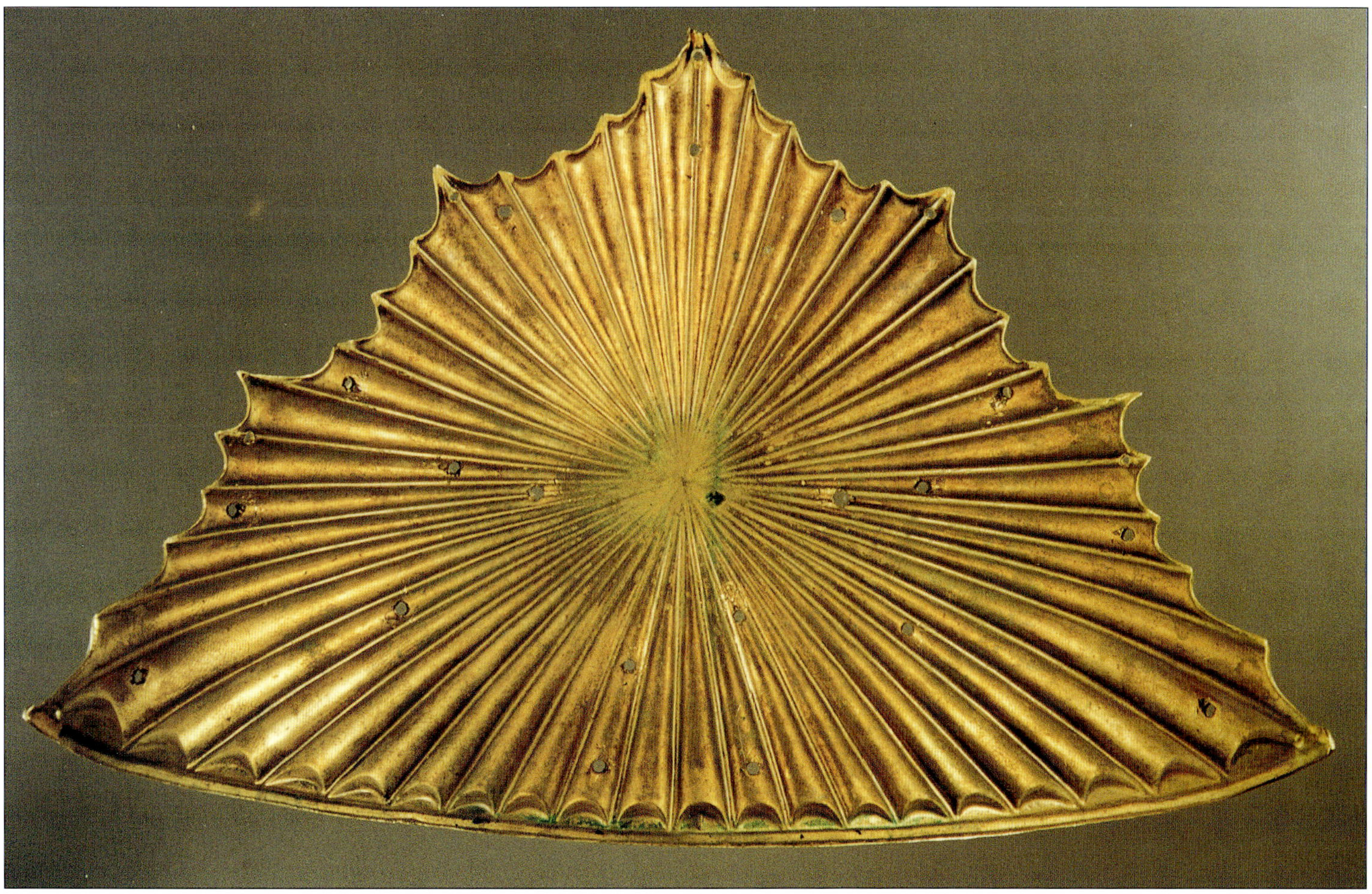

OPPOSITE - *Figure 17I:* Close-up view of the cap with the plate insitu. ABOVE - *Figure 17J:* The gilt metal rayed plate with the silvered overlay removed. N.B. The holes to the outer edge of the plate, are those through which the 'wire' binding was passed to secure the plate to the skull of the cap. The inner holes are for the 'pins' of the overlay.

Figure 17K: Front view of the die-stamped post-1902 Royal Arms.

Figure 17L: The rear view of the die-stamped, post-1902 Royal Arms.

OPPOSITE TOP - *Figure 17M:* The remaining four component parts (Royal Arms excepted) that make up the silvered overlay on this regiments lance cap plate, comprising (1) the battle honour '*Suakin*', (2) the honour date of '*1885*', (3) the battle honours '*Blenheim*', '*Oudernarde*', '*Ramillies*', '*Malplaquet*', together with the title scroll '*Fifth Royal Irish Lancers*', (4) the 'angel harp'.

OPPOSITE BOTTOM - *Figure 17N:* The reverse side of the four-part overlay as described above. N.B. These parts of the overlay are cast items, and not die-struck as was the Royal Arms.

Figure 17O: Close-up view of the left hand side of the overlay (facing the plate), bearing '*Blenheim*', '*Oudernarde*', and '*Fifth Royal*'.

Figure 17P: Close-up view of the right side of the overlay, bearing '*Ramillies*', '*Malplaquet*', and '*Irish Lancers*'.

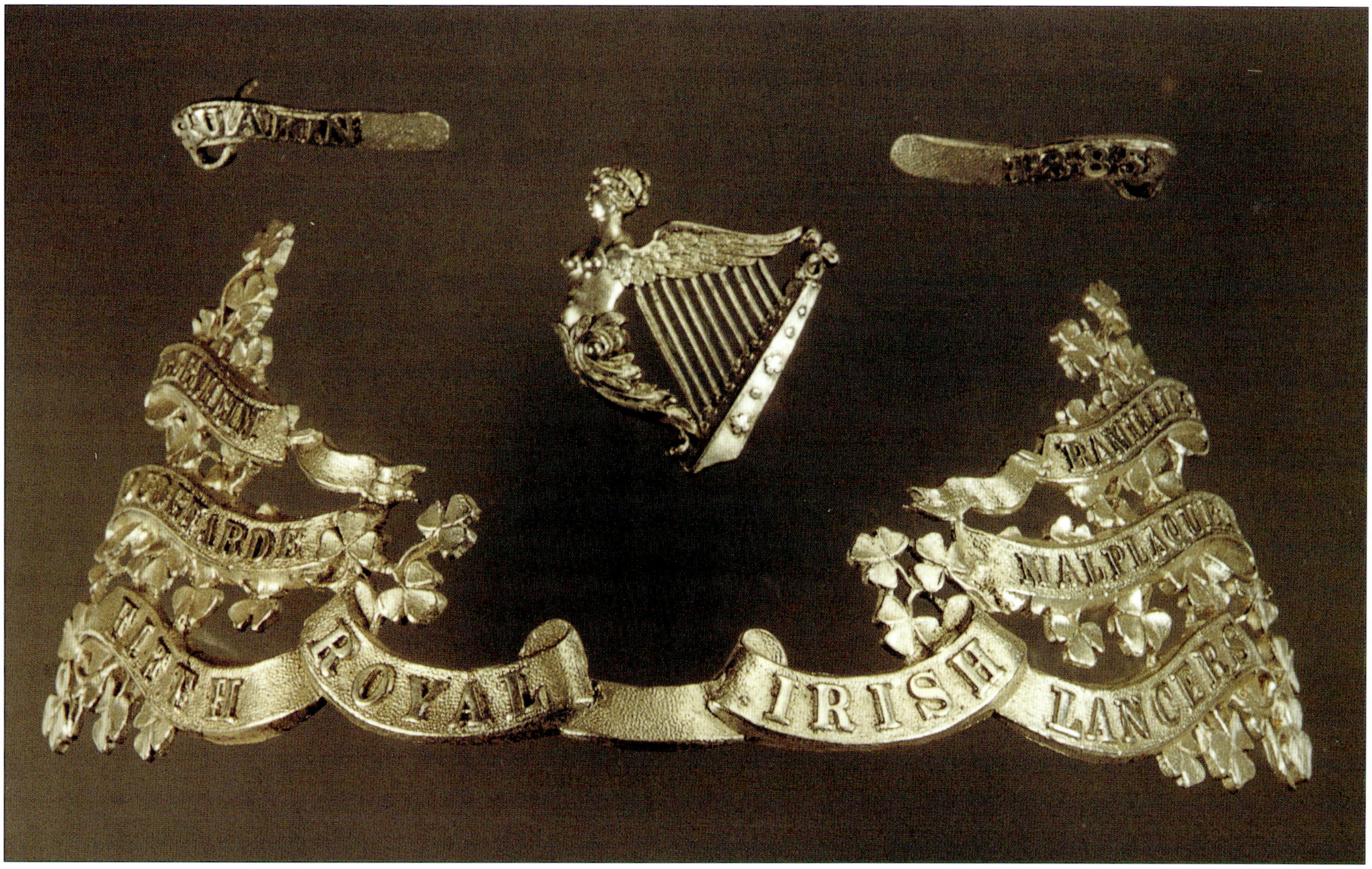
ROYAL
IRISH
LANCERS

Figure 17Q: The right hand lion's head boss (the left side if facing the cap), illustrating the hook to the lion's chin.

Figure 17R: The reverse side of the right hand lion's head boss in which may be seen the 'top' of the hook passing through inside the chin of the lion's head.

Figure 17S: The reverse side of the left hand lion's head boss (the right side if facing the cap), complete with the velvet backed chinchain. Note the threaded stud to the centre of the boss.

Figure 17T: A view of the disc having a milled edge, sewn to the inside of the skull of the cap. N.B. Just able to be seen is the inside of the socket, into which the threaded stud of the boss is screwed.

Figure 17U: The officers pattern gilt metal plume holder.

Figure 17V: The above plume holder as viewed from above.

Figure 17W: The plume holder as seen from its base, illustrating the 'slot' through which the metal stem of the plume was passed.

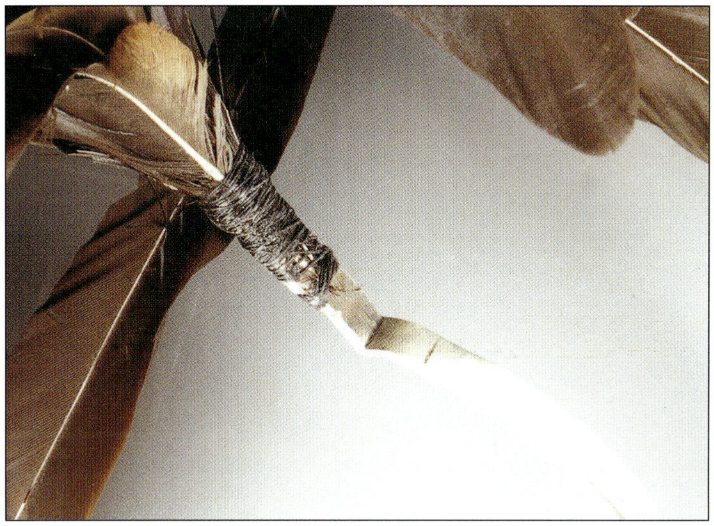

Figure 17X: The metal plume stem. Note how the swan feathers are bound to the stem.

Figure 17Y: The top of the plume illustrating the gilt metal ring to the centre of the 'crown' of the plume.

Chapter Six

The Early Patterns of Lance Cap

Our research into the actual date a specific pattern of cap was introduced, has identified that there appears to be conflicting evidence relating to the exact date that each of the regiments first adopted the pattern of lance cap concerned. A possible influencing factor in this respect may well be whether the regiment concerned was stationed at home (England) or abroad at the time the new pattern of chapka was first introduced.

In view of the above it should be noted that the dates quoted within this book relating to the introduction of a particular pattern of lance cap, are intended to be used as a guide only, and considered as an approximate date, regardless of how respected the source of reference.

Whilst occasionally dated photographs may be useful in identifying a particular uniform, mistakes do occur, therefore a dated photograph should not always be treated as 'proof positive' that the uniform concerned was being worn by a particular regiment at the period indicated on the photograph, unless there is corroborating evidence.

A further source of information relating to uniform identification is from 'so called' contemporary dated paintings. However, once again caution should be exercised, as often a work of art will depict a soldier wearing a uniform known to have been taken into wear by the regiment concerned at some time or other, albeit that this was not the pattern of uniform being worn at the time the commission was actually undertaken.

Additionally, there exist paintings illustrating action scenes in which are depicted actual incidents that occurred many years prior to the painting concerned being undertaken. These paintings occasionally contain slight inaccuracies due to the artist illustrating a particular item of dress being worn in their artwork, whilst in fact it was to be several years before the item of uniform concerned was actually adopted by the regiment.

A particular example of this type of 'error' is the famous painting entitled '*The Charge of the Heavy Brigade during the Battle of Balaclava*' (25th October 1854)[1] by the artist G.D. Giles. In this most spirited action painting, it can clearly be seen that the officers and men of the 5th Dragoon Guards engaged in the charge are wearing the 1871 pattern helmet plate on a helmet that appears to be a mixture of both the 1847 and the 1871 pattern. This anomaly may be the result of the artist making a minor mistake, or it may purely be that he, like a great many other painters was invoking artistic license. Either way it does not detract from what is a most exciting action painting.

THE FIRST PATTERN LANCE CAP

Both actual examples of the early pattern lance cap are extremely scarce indeed, as is documentation relating to this item of headdress, with what little is available often being both confusing and contradictory with regard to the colour of the cloth, lace and metals etc. Photographs of early pattern caps are also very scarce, and in this respect the authors are grateful to Christopher Bryant of the United States of America, for permitting photographs of his special pattern officers cap of the 9th Lancers to be reproduced in this publication (*See Fig: 18.*). We also refer readers to *Regiment Magazine*, issue No.47 where there is a black and white photographic illustration of the first pattern officers cap of the 17th Lancers pre 1830, and a modern coloured drawing of the officers pattern cap c.1816 of the 23rd Lancers.

The first pattern lance cap bore only a superficial resemblance to the instantly recognisable 1856 pattern cap, being both big and heavy, and having almost straight sides rising to a 'splayed out' top. N.B. A distinctive feature of this pattern of cap was the large permanently turned up rear peak of black leather adorned with lace.

The first official description of this pattern of cap was given in a small printed book published on the 25th April 1822 entitled '*Regulations for the Dress of General, Staff and Regimental Officers*' from the Adjutant-General's Office, Horse Guards. This publication was priced at four shillings in boards, and printed and sold by William Clowes, London (5).

Now at last one is able to find firm information on the uniforms worn by army officers during the early part of the nineteenth century, that said, this publication did not attempt to give full de-

Figure 18: 9th Regiment of (Light) Dragoons (Lancers). A superb example of this early pattern lance cap. Note the lion's head mask above the centre of the lance cap plate, onto which are attached the ends of the chinscales. Courtesy of Christopher Bryant. Photo: R. Biondi.

tails on the uniforms concerned. It did however lay down what should be worn by the various sections of the army such as the artillery, heavy cavalry, light dragoons, infantry etc., the regulations quoting information on the senior regiment of each 'group', that being the 9th regiment for the Lancers.

It should be appreciated that these regulations for the officers were long delayed in production, and therefore for a while, the officers, who purchased their own uniforms in the early days, had a free hand in what they wore. The sovereign then ordered that the officers dress should be like that worn by the men of their respective regiment, albeit that the uniform differed in quality and by the amount of decoration. The patterns sealed were made available to be seen at Whitehall, and in this way tailors engaged in making military garments were able to view the sealed pattern concerned to ensure that the regulations were obeyed, this facility being continued into the twentieth century, as may be seen in appendix one. N.B. One reason why some existing relic caps might vary from regulations is that an officer might have continued to wear an out-of-date pattern cap, having perhaps a new bullion rosette or distinction added, the cap thereby having been updated, thus saving the officer the additional cost of having to purchase a completely new cap.

Whilst in time the regulations became more detailed, those first published were made simple and took little account of the fact that there were several regiments within a particular 'group' such as the heavy cavalry, infantry, lancers etc. As a result, the individual regimental distinctions were not quoted, the official description of a particular item of dress being based on the senior regiment within that section, with the variation of embroidery, facing, lace etc. being selected and later checked at a regimental inspection (5).

Dress Regulations 1822

The following extract from the regulations of 1822 is the section devoted to the Lancers and has been reproduced verbatim, complete with original punctuation and spelling:

Dress

'Cap-crimson cloth, trencher top, ten inches square, front angle in a direct line with centre of peak, fluted sides three inches and a half deep, encircled at bottom with gold and crimson three-quarter inch lace, under which originates gold and crimson cords running up all the four corners transversely over crown; on left side a large gold bullion rosette, with embroidered G.R. on crimson velvet in the centre; upper part of scull (skull) *laced round with a three inch gold and crimson lace, terminating under large gilt plate with king's arms, which occupies the front, a black patent leather peak in front, another constantly turned up behind, the former laced on outward edge with a wide between two narrow gold braids, the latter with a wide braid between a narrow one and a gold cord; studded gilt scales and lion's heads, with a lion's head attached to gold cord in front: on right corner of top through which they are fastened, two gold olivets and loops: on right corner for the lines, which are of gold cord with rich flounders, bullion tassels, loops, and sliders; line to fasten to left shoulder, pass round the body, and fasten to cap on right side; space between front plate and back peak occupied by two sets of braid on black leather ground, each consisting of a wide between two narrow gold braids shewing black stripes'.*

'Feather-crimson and white drooping cock-tail'.

'Note. - Regiments not having crimson facing, to substitute their own established regimental facing in lieu of it, in those places described as crimson. The distinction of gold and silver to be preserved as heretofore'.

N.B. Although 'patent' leather is mentioned in the above extract from the Dress Regulations of 1822, it is possible that skived leather was actually used for the early pattern caps.

The First Pattern Cap - Additional Information

The following information relating to the first pattern cap has been gathered from authoritative sources, and is additional to that contained in the above quoted dress regulations.

The Cloth Top and Sides

The ten inch square trencher top of the cap kept its shape because of a 1/8th inch wire skeleton rising from the leather skull. The four-side cloth top was made rigid by many sewn rows or 'pockets', into which could be inserted cane or split ozier, and whilst the top and sides are quoted as being of crimson cloth in the above regulations, it is known that this was not the case for all the lancers regiments of that period, as shown below.

Regiment	Colour of Top and Sides.
9th Lancers	Crimson (*See Fig: 18.*).
12th Lancers	Red.
16th Lancers	Red.
17th Lancers	White (from c.1823).
19th Lancers	Yellow[2] (1817-1821) (*See Fig: 8.*).
23rd Lancers	Crimson[3] (1816-1817) (6).

N.B. It would also appear that the cap makers varied the proportions of the cap to appeal to the officers of the regiment concerned (6).

The Bullion Rosette

With regard to the embroidered Royal Cypher to the centre of the bullion plume rosette[4], it is known that for the 23rd Lancers the GR cypher was doubled and reversed, as illustrated in *Fig: 20*).

The Skull and Peaks

More than one specialist might supply a lance cap and therefore there might be a difference in make between various regiments, but basically they would follow the sealed pattern. Garments might be made in three sizes to fit a soldier, but with regard to head-dress this could be a problem as heads varied in size, and could be oval shaped or round. N.B. Even the head lining inside could not always be adjusted for a comfortable fit. The exterior of the skull was of black leather adorned with lace as described above, but inside the skull, pasteboard or buckram may have been added for strength and shaping. The front peak was as described in regulations, as was the 'constantly turned up' rear peak, which did not in fact serve the purpose of a peak, but gave additional strength to the back of the head-dress which was vulnerable to murderous slashes from enemy swords (5) (*See Fig: 18B.*).

The Lace to the Waist

Below the three inch gold 'lace' referred to in the above regulations, was a narrow band of metal lace, having a coloured stripe to the centre, the colour of the lace adorning the cap being listed below (6). N.B. The lace tended to differ slightly from regiment to regiment, and was not bobbin lace as used on curtains and tablecloths, but a loom weaving together of silver or gold wire, and a cloth base.[5] (5).

Regiment	Colour of Lace
9th Lancers	Gold

12th Lancers	Gold
16th Lancers	Silver[6]
17th Lancers	Silver[7] (from c.1823 as illustrated in *Fig: 21A*.).
19th Lancers	Gold (1817-1821)
23rd Lancers	Silver (1816-1817) (6).

The Lance Cap Plate

An interesting feature of the first (large angular shaped) plate is that it was of flat metal, and not with ribbed rays as on the later pattern plates. The main embossed device was the Royal Arms of the period, being the four quarters of Great Britain and Ireland, with the first and fourth quarters being three lions for England, the second quarter having the Scottish lion in tressure, the third quarter bearing the harp of Ireland, which in an escutcheon was the shield of the Hanoverian arms of King George III. Additionally there was the lion surmounting a crown overall, with the supporters being the lion and unicorn (5).

The gilt plate of the 9th Lancers bore the Royal Arms as described above, being surrounded by a double row of half-balls (to the outer edge of the plate), with between the 'balls' there being nine floral motives, the number being able to denote the regiment. Along the base of the plate a single row of half-balls, to the centre of which was the battle honour '*Peninsula*' as illustrated in *Fig:*

Figure 18A: 9th Lancers. Close-up view of the lance cap plate illustrating the Hanoverian Royal Arms, the single battle honour of 'Peninsula', and colour of the ribbed cloth section. Note. the 'G.R.' Royal Cypher to the centre of the bullion rosette. Courtesy of Christopher Bryant. Photo: R. Biondi.

Figure 18B: 9th Lancers. Side view of this cap, in which can be seen the false peak to the rear of the cap, and the early pattern lion's head bosses. Courtesy of Christopher Bryant. Photo: R. Biondi.

18A. N.B. The honour 'Peninsula' was granted to the regiment on the 6th April 1815 before the 9th had been converted to lancers (5).

The 12th Lancers also had a flat plate gilt metal plate complete with a similar pattern of Hanoverian Royal Arms, however they had already acquired three battle honours by this time and these were displayed thus. To the centre of the plate below the Royal Arms, the *Sphinx*[8], with to the right side within a frame '*Peninsula*', and to the left '*Waterloo*' also within a frame. Additionally there were sprays of laurel leaves on the left and right side of the plate, with only a small 'dotted' border around the scalloped outline. N.B. The Sphinx for Egypt was granted on the 6th July 1802, Peninsula was granted on the 6th April 1815, and Waterloo on the 8th December 1815 (5).

Sadly confirmed evidence is lacking for what might have been borne on the plate of the 16th Lancers, but it is thought that in addition to the Royal Arms they might have had 'Peninsula' and 'Waterloo' although this has yet to be verified.

The 23rd Lancers had gained four battle honours, their plate differing in that it was rayed. As these pattern plates were die-struck, it might have been to much to expect a flat plate to stand up to so much lettering and possibly it was thought that a rayed plate would give better support. To the centre of the plate was the Royal Arms upon a separate rayed star, with the Sphinx immediately below the arms, with stamped into the rayed back plate the honours as follows. To the left side 'Peninsula' above 'Waterloo', with 'Talavera' above 'Egypt' to the right side of the plate as illustrated in *Fig: 20*. N.B. It is not known if this was the original pattern plate for this regiment (5).

Figure 18C: 9th Lancers. Front view of a similar officers pattern cap. Note the 'dowel' attached to the left hand top corner of the cap believed to have been used to secure the cap-lines to the cap. Courtesy of The Parker Gallery.

Figure 18D: 9th Lancers. Rear view of officers pattern cap illustrating the gold braid decoration to the constantly turned up rear peak. Courtesy of the Parker Gallery.

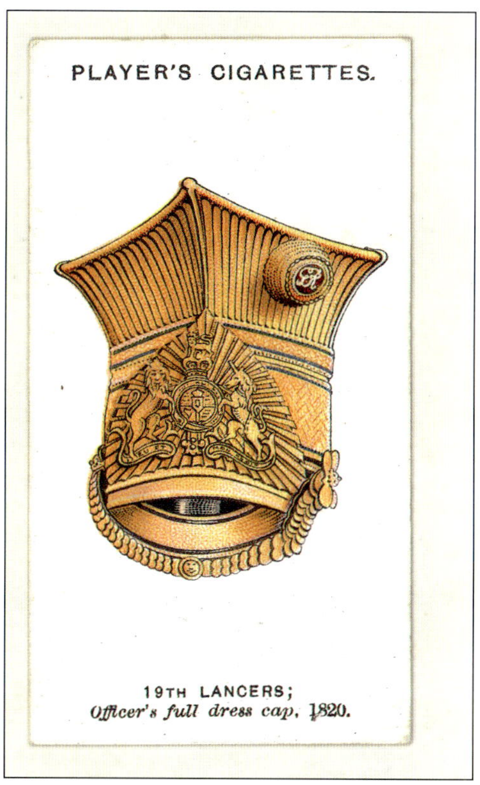

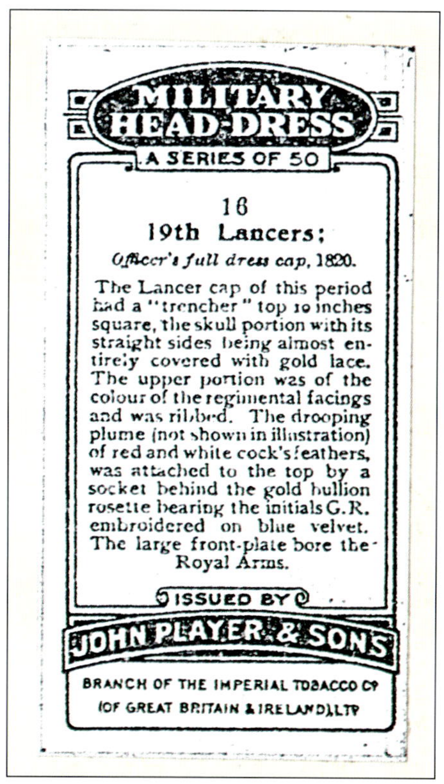

MILITARY HEAD-DRESS

A SERIES OF 50

16

19th Lancers;

Officer's full dress cap, 1820.

The Lancer cap of this period had a "trencher" top 10 inches square, the skull portion with its straight sides being almost entirely covered with gold lace. The upper portion was of the colour of the regimental facings and was ribbed. The drooping plume (not shown in illustration) of red and white cock's feathers, was attached to the top by a socket behind the gold bullion rosette bearing the initials G.R. embroidered on blue velvet. The large front-plate bore the Royal Arms.

ISSUED BY

JOHN PLAYER & SONS

BRANCH OF THE IMPERIAL TOBACCO Cº (OF GREAT BRITAIN & IRELAND) LTD

Figure 19: 19th Lancers. A depiction of the officers pattern cap, stated to be c.1820 (complete with the text to the reverse). This is card No.16 from a series of fifty cards issued by John Player & Sons, March 1931. David Rowe collection.

The Plate of the 17th Lancers (*See Fig: 21B.*)

Having sailed from India in January 1823, the 17th Light Dragoons, having officially been converted to lancers on the 20th August 1822 (WO 3/72) would have taken up their new role and dress sometime after their arrival in England. Their cap was of the regulation pattern having a white cloth top, being adorned with silver lace. The rayed silver back plate was die-struck and carried the Royal Arms in gilt metal, below which in silver was the skull upon crossed bones[9] (the skull facing to the left). Immediately beneath the 'Death's Head', a tripartite silver scroll bearing 'Or' (left scroll), (centre scroll blank), and 'Glory' (right scroll) (5). N.B. All above positions quoted are as for a person looking directly at the plate.

The Chin Scales

The chinscales were made in two sections, each of seventeen graduated convex scalloped scales. The wide end of each of the two sections was attached to the side of the skull by means of the gilt ear bosses, the narrow ends of the scales being tied together in the centre and worn on the chin. It would seem however that the chinscales were frequently worn tied up to the small lion's head hook attached to the gold cord on the front angle of the cloth section (5). In the 9th Lancers the gilt metal scales were embossed on the edges with small half-balls, similar to those on the lance cap plate (*See Fig: 18.*), the chinscales being joined together by red/scarlet 'ribbon', whilst in the 23rd Lancers a buckle and strap was used to join the scales

Figure 20: 23rd Lancers. A fine study of the officers pattern lance cap minus plume. Note the method of securing the ends of the chinscales to the upper front of the cap. Copyright W.Y. Carman.

Figure 21: 17th Lancers. The officers pattern cap of the pre 1830 period, thought to have been worn c.1828-31. Of interest is the double 'GR' Royal Cypher to the centre of the bullion rosette, the colour of the velvet backing, and the shape of the ray ends of the back plate. Note the lace, chinchain and ear bosses were silver at this period. Copyright W.Y. Carman.

Figure 21A: 17th Lancers. Side view of the officers pattern cap illustrating the silver lace to the waist having a central blue stripe, and the lace to the rear peak. Copyright W.Y. Carman.

together. N.B. For those regiments having silver lace to the cap such as the 17th Lancers, the chinscales and ear bosses were of silver coloured metal.

The Cap-Lines

The officers had gold/silver cap-lines, the colour of which was depended upon the regimental lace colour. The lines had tassels and flounders (plaited oval shapes), with the rank and file having cap-lines of yellow or white cotton, again dependent upon the regimental lace colour (6).

The Other Ranks Pattern Cap

It was not possible to present a detailed description of the cap worn by the rank and file due to the authors not having had the opportunity of examining an example of this cap, and there being little information available from either contemporary paintings or prints. However from one picture seen, it appears that the front peak of the cap was of plain unadorned leather, the lance cap plate being simpler, with yellow or white embroidery replacing the gold and silver lace used on the officers pattern caps, all of which is as would be expected. (6).

Figure 21B: 17th Lancers. Close-up view of the officers pattern lance cap plate illustrating the Hanoverian arms. Copyright W.Y. Carman.

Some four years later the 1826 Dress Regulations were published, which although very similar to the above in content, did contain some important additional measurements. Therefore the later official description of the cap is reproduced below, with the additions and amendments being given in bold text.

Dress Regulations 1826

'Cap-crimson cloth, trencher top, ten inches square, front angle in a direct line with centre of peak, fluted sides four inches deep, encircled at bottom with gold and crimson three-quarter inch lace; the waist of the cap fourteen inches in girth; under which originate gold and crimson cords running up all the four corners transversely over crown; on left side a large gold bullion rosette with embroidered G.R. on crimson velvet in the centre; upper part of scull laced round with a three inch gold and crimson lace, terminating under large gilt plate with king's arms, which occupies the front, a black patent leather peak in front, another constantly turned up behind, the former laced on outward edge with a wide, between two narrow gold braids, the latter with a wide braid between a narrow one and a gold cord; studded gilt scales and lion's heads, with a lion's head attached to gold cord in front: on right corner of top through which they are fastened, two gold olivets and loops: on right corner for the lines, which are of gold cord with rich flounders, bullion tassels, loops, and sliders; line to fasten to left shoulder, pass round the body, and fasten to cap on right side; space between front plate and back peak occupied by two sets of braid on black leather ground, each consisting of a wide between two narrow gold braids shewing black stripes: the total depth of the cap from side to the top, eleven inches.'

'Feather-crimson and white drooping swan, twelve inches long'.

Figure 22: 12th Lancers. A superb example of the officers pattern cap, thought to have been worn c.1828-29. Of interest is the numeral '12' affixed to the plate immediately above the honour 'Egypt', and the 'GR' Royal Cypher to the centre of the bullion rosette. N.B. The reflection evident on this photograph is due to the cap having to be photographed whilst in it's glass display cabinet. Courtesy of Charles Griffin.

THE SECOND PATTERN LANCE CAP

In 1828 the announcement that a new pattern cap was forthcoming was contained in a Horse Guards circular that stated that a new pattern lance cap for Lancers had been approved by H.M. King George IV, and on the 14th October 1828 a circular letter stated that the new patterns for officers and men had been sealed. However details of these caps are unknown and it is not known if they ever went into production, this matter seemingly not being settled before the death of King George IV on the 18th June 1830 (5).

Upon the accession to the throne of King William IV, he made sweeping changes throughout the army, one being that he thought that all the fighting men in his army should be clothed in garments of the National colour red (the colour of St. George's Cross), the only exception being the Royal Horse Guards (Blues) who were permitted to retain their blue jackets. This change resulted in those regiments who had previously worn blue jackets now wearing red, and those regiments thus effected having to change their facings. N.B. Additionally those regiments wearing red topped caps were to change to blue (5).

A further great change that effected the uniform of the regular army, was that those regiments having silver lace as a distinction had to discontinue the use of this metal in favour of gold in 1830. Any regiment having a blue central stripe to the lace around the waist of their cap (e.g. 17th Lancers) changed to a red stripe, these modifications appearing in the published regulations of 1831, the three paragraphs relating to the lance cap being reproduced below. N.B. This left the wearing of silver lace for the uniforms of the militia and volunteers.

Dress Regulations 1831

'Cap-blue cloth, trencher top, ten inches square, front angle in line with centre of peak, fluted sides five inches and a half each side at the waist; gold cord running up the four corners transversely over crown; on left side a large gold bullion rosette with embroidered W.R. on blue velvet in the centre; round the waist a gold and scarlet band, two inches wide, terminating under a large gilt plate with king's arms and regimental devices, which occupies the front; a black patent leather peak in front, another constantly turned up behind laced with a broad and two narrow braids; a gilt chain and lion's heads; space between front plate and back peak occupied by two stripes of three-quarter inch gold braid on black leather ground; the depth of the cap from the side to the top nine inches.'

'Cap-Line-plain gold cord, with two bullion tassels two inches deep, to pass round the body, and to be secured to the back of the cap by a loop'.

'Plume-black cocktail, drooping sixteen inches in front, nine inches at back'.

Figure 23: 16th Lancers. An officer of the 16th (The Queen's) Light Dragoons, being a reasonably accurate depiction of an officer of the period c.1835. David Rowe collection.

Additional Information

12th Lancers

On the 12th April 1831 the 12th Lancers were due to change into scarlet jackets, and being a royal regiment they had blue facings as entitled (as published 22nd April 1831 - WO 3/267), which meant that the cloth upper of their cap was to be changed from red to dark blue, the gold lace around the waist of the cap having a central scarlet line. N.B. The regiment regained its scarlet top to the cap in 1842 when the scarlet jacket gave place to blue again, the cap having 1/8 inch tracing, gold Russia braid, with the gold lace to the waist having a blue silk central stripe (5).

16th Lancers

The 16th were expected to have new clothing prior to the 25th December 1830, if their new caps were to arrive in Meerut, India where they were stationed at that time. N.B. On the new cap the silvered metal fittings were replaced with ones of gilt metal.

17th Lancers

The 17th Lancers also had to change to a scarlet jacket, however as their facings remained white, there was no change in colour to the cloth top of the cap, which had gold quarter weltings, gold lace having a red central stripe around the waist, with gilt fittings replacing the former silver ones (5).

The Lance Cap

According to the regulations, it was intended that the second pattern of cap should be two or three inches less in overall height, with the broad band of lace around the middle of the cap to be removed, although it would appear that the military hatters of the day used 'artistic license' in this respect. It was also stated that a chinchain was to replace the former chinscales, all of the above being intended to lessen the cost of producing the cap (6).

The other important differences between the 1st and 2nd pattern of cap may be summarised as follows. Whilst there was no change to the size of the square top of the cap, the colour of the cloth material changed from crimson to blue, with the sides of the cap being increased from four inches to five and a half inches, and the depth from side to top reducing from eleven inches down to nine inches.[10] N.B. The 'lions head in front' was now absent, its presence having become obsolete due to the chin scales having been replaced by a chinchain.

The Royal Cypher to the centre of the bullion rosette changed from that of GR to WR (WRIV), with the colour of the velvet backing changing from crimson to blue, although this change of cypher probably did not take place until other uniform changes took place, such as the change from silver to gold lace. N.B. In the 17th Lancers, the velvet backing to the Royal Cypher later appears to have been red, as may be seen in an excellent photographic illustration of this regiments cap that appeared in *Regiment Magazine*, Issue Twenty, page thirty-four, and on the post 1837 example illustrated in *Fig: 25B*.

Additionally, the lace to the waist of the skull of the cap was reduced from three inches (having a crimson centre stripe), down to two inches with a scarlet central stripe, with the braid adorning the rear upturned peak changing from a wide braid between a narrow one, and a gold cord, to a broad and two narrow bands. N.B. Although not mentioned in the Dress Regulations of 1831, the front peak retained the braid 'on the outward edge with a wide between two narrow gold braids'.

Figure 24: 17th Lancers. An officers post 1830 period cap, the bullion rosette bearing the 'WR' Royal Cypher. Note that the skull faces to the front and is positioned above the crossed bones. Photo: W.Y. Carman.

The Lance Cap Plate

'The new cap plate was die-struck with rounded rays, and a feature of this plate was the broad band at the base, which in the case of the 12th carried the honour 'Egypt' with the regimental number above the honour in arabic figures', the plate also displaying the battle honours 'Waterloo' (left), and 'Peninsula' (right), when facing cap as illustrated in *Fig: 22*. N.B. This pattern of plate is thought to have been worn c.1828 -29.

The 16th Lancers had the battle honour 'Bhurtpore' surmounting the Hanoverian Royal Arms, with the title 'Queens' beneath the arms. To the left of the Royal Arms a rising scroll bearing the honour 'Peninsula', with to the right of the arms a similar scroll bearing the honour 'Waterloo', with the numeral '16' upon the broad band at the base of the plate. N.B This pattern of plate is thought to have been worn c.1828-37.

The rayed back plate on the 17th Lancers changed from silver to gilt metal, and bore their distinctive skull and crossed bones in silver metal, with the panel at the base of the plate being used to carry a scroll bearing 'Or Glory' also in silver. The upper part of their plate carried a small version of the Royal Arms, with the Hanoverian escutcheon all in silver as illustrated in *Fig: 24*., in which it can be seen that the skull faces to the front and is positioned above the bones. N.B. The position of the skull and crossed bones on the plate appears to have changed more than once, there being known versions having the skull looking to the left and upon the bones, (when facing the cap), the skull facing to the centre and above the bones, and the skull upon the bones (skull facing to the centre) as worn on the cap c.1854.

For the rank and file the plate was die-struck and of one piece, however for the officers whilst the back plate was die- struck, the Royal Arms, devices, and battle honours (where appropriate), were often of cast metal.

From Front Plate to Back Peak

The space occupied between the front plate and back peak changed from being described as 'occupied by two stripes of three-quarter inch gold braid on black leather ground' to 'occupied by two sets of braid on black leather ground, each consisting of a wide, between two narrow gold braids' showing 'black stripes'. N.B. The black stripes mentioned, were in fact actually, the black leather of the peak showing through the gold braid.

Dress Regulations 1831

The Special Pattern Cap of the 9th Lancers

A special order of the 24th February 1832 (PRO WO 3/84) described this cap as being, '*black patent leather throughout, the trencher top 9.3/4 inches square with plain strips of metal up the angles, gilt metal waistband 2 inches wide formed of semi-circular rope, each two of which sections are bound together by a double rope in the centre. Gilt metal plate bearing regimental devices, gilt metal mount or boss (below the plume stem) 2.3/4 inches in diameter, made of a rope coiled round a button five times. Gilt chinstrap and lion's head fastenings. Black leather peak, permanently turned up at the back. Front plate, crown over two oval shields, Royal Arms and Queen Adelaide. Lion and Unicorn, two lances behind. Below AR reversed cypher and title 'Royal Lancers*'. This pattern would no doubt be worn up to 1855 or 1856, when the back peak was generally discontinued (45). N.B. There was no mention of the special pattern cap of the 9th Lancers in Dress Regulation either 1831 or 1834 (5).

The 9th Lancers Plate - Additional Information

In 1830 King William decided to closely associate his Queen with this regiment, their new title being the *9th (Queen's Royal) Light Dragoons (Lancers)*, and therefore a plate of some merit was required.

A design made by Messrs Hawkes which still exists, depicts the usual rayed back plate bearing the devices of the Hanoverian Arms, below which was a largish 'IX'. Beneath this roman numeral there was a long curving scroll bearing '*Or Queens Royal Lancers*', and a rectangular label bearing '*Peninsula*'. For some unknown reason this pattern of plate was not accepted, and the design as described below, which incidentally did not appear until February 1832 was taken into use. N.B. The new plate not being accepted until 1832 meant that the earlier pattern continued in use for some time, albeit that it was obviously out-dated (5).

When the new pattern plate was finally introduced it comprised the standard rayed plate bearing a crown above two ovals, the right oval being the arms of Queen Adelaide, the oval to the left the Royal Arms, complete with the Lion and Unicorn supporters. Below the two ovals the Queen's cypher 'A.R.' interlaced and reversed, beneath which was a single long scroll bearing '*Royal Lancers*' finishing with sprays of laurel at either end. For the officers, the plate, ovals and scroll were all in gilt metal, with the cypher being in silver. However for the rank and file the plate was of one piece die-struck brass. N.B. It will be seen that the battle honour '*Peninsula*' is absent from this plate, and did not in fact re-appear until many years later.

THE THIRD PATTERN (PRE 1856 PATTERN LANCE CAP)

Upon the accession to the throne by H.M. Queen Victoria on the 20th June 1837 the lance cap plates and boss centres bearing 'WR' of the late king became obsolete, although they were to remain in service for many months to come.

The embroidered 'WR' to the centre of the bullion boss was to be replace by 'VR', and on the new pattern plates the Hanoverian Arms was to be replaced by the Royal Arms of Great Britain which carried the quarters of three lion's for England (upper left and lower right quarter), a lion for Scotland (upper right quarter), and the harp for Ireland (lower left quarter) all within a garter bearing '*Honi Soit Qui Mal Y Pense*' and surmounted by a crown, except for the 9th Lancers who retained their distinctive crowned device of Queen

OPPOSITE - *Figure 25:* 17th Lancers. A superb example of the officers post 1837 pattern cap complete with feather plume, and gold bullion cap-lines. Courtesy of Christopher Bryant. Photo: R. Biondi.

ABOVE - *Figure 25A:* 17th Lancers. Close-up view of the large lance cap plate. Note the fine quality of the post 1837 pattern Royal Arms surmounting the regimental motto. Courtesy of Christopher Bryant. Photo: R. Biondi.

Adelaide's arms and Royal Arms within ovals etc as illustrated in *Fig: 29B*. N.B. At this period it appears that both the Royal Helmet and Mantling were still included as part of the Royal Arms, as may be seen on the 17th Lancers plate illustrated in *Fig: 25A*.

In 1840 the red/scarlet jacket introduced in 1830 at the behest of King William IV, and worn by the lancer regiments was discontinued and the blue jacket gradually came back into wear (16th lancers excepted), with the inevitably consequence that for some regiments the facings once again changed. The facing colours now became scarlet for the 9th, blue for the 16th (unchanged), and white for the 17th Lancers (unchanged). In the case of the 12th Lancers the facings did not change to scarlet until 1842.

Figure 25B: 17th Lancers. Close-up view of the gold bullion plume rosette. Note the 'V.R.' Royal Cypher to the centre of the rosette. Courtesy of Christopher Bryant. Photo: R. Biondi.

Figure 26: 9th Lancers. A depiction of the officers pattern cap. This is card No.20 from a series of 50 cards issued by John Player & Sons, March 1931. The text of the reverse of the card reads. '9th (Queen's Royal) Lancers; *Officers full dress cap, 1830-40*", followed by a reasonably accurate description of the cap. Note that the upper sides are depicted as being of leather. David Rowe collection.

The Officers Pattern Cap

The first authoritative description of this pattern of cap was not published until 1846, although the cap had been worn for some time before that date, the actual date of adoption being unrecorded.

The official description of this pattern of lance cap as referred to above, appeared on page one hundred and twenty-six of the *Regulations for the Dress of General, Staff, and Regimental Officers of The Army 1846*, being reproduced below as originally written in the above publication. The new description of the cap varies the dimensions from that of the earlier regulations, but whether this indicates a new pattern of cap, or just the loosening of some measurements is not clear.

Dress Regulations 1846

Cap-cloth; colour of the facings, eight inches and three quarters deep in front, nine inches and a half at back, and the top nine inches and a half square; gold cord across the top and down the angles; on left side a gold bullion rosette, with embroidered V.R., on blue velvet; round the waist a band, two inches wide, of gold lace, with a blue stripe; in front a gilt ray plate, with silver Queen's arms and regimental badges; peak and fall of black patent leather, braided with gold; gilt chain, fastening to lion's heads at the sides'.

'The 9th Lancers have permission to wear a cap of the regimental pattern with gilt metal ornaments'.

'Cap-Line-gold cord, with bullion tassels and flounders, to pass round the body, and to be secured to the back of the cap by a loop'.

'Plume-black drooping cocktail feathers, fourteen inches long, and four inches on the mount: in India, black horse-hair of the same length'.

The Officers Cap - Additional Information

The above description of the cap can hardly be described as informative, the description for the 9th Lancers cap even less so, and regrettably, little written additional information was available to the author's regarding this most interesting cap. In spite of the above, the following alternative description has been prepared in which is presented further information on this pattern of cap, with the enhanced details included by the author's, being given in bold text.

The overall dimensions of the cap are as given above[11], with the top and ribbed cloth sides in the regimental facing colour of scarlet in the 12th, blue in the 16th, and white in the 17th Lancers, with gold cord extending across the top of the cap, and down the angles. To the right hand corner of the cloth top, a gilt metal hook for the chinchain, with a similar hook to the rear quarter angle of the cloth top (6).

The bullion plume rosette was similar in appearance to the rosette on the previous pattern cap, although as mentioned above the embroidered Royal Cypher had changed to that of Queen Victoria, (*See Fig: 25B*.).

Encircling the waist of the cap, a band of two inch deep gold lace having a central blue stripe, with below this band, three bands of gold braid, with the upper band being the deepest of the three. The front peak was of black patent leather, embroidered with three strips of gold braid of differing widths, the widest strip being to the centre of the peak. To the rear of the skull, a black patent leather false peak (folded upright) embroidered with gold braid, this being the last pattern cap to have the false turned-up rear peak. N.B. In the 16th Lancers the central silk stripe to the waist lace was blue (5).

The gilt metal rated plate bore the Royal Arms, regimental devices and title, together with battle honours (where applicable), the plate measuring some five and a half inches in height, and ten inches in width. N.B. It has been stated that in military badges the Royal Helmet and Mantling are omitted (43).

Sometime prior to the introduction of the 1856 pattern plate, the band at the base of the plate mentioned previously was omitted, as may be seen in an excellent black and white illustration of an officers pattern cap of the 12th Lancers that appears on page 69, of 'Head Dresses of The British Army - Cavalry' (6). Also in this illustration it can be seen that the Prince of Wales's feathers (in silvered metal) is positioned immediately above the Royal Arms, this distinction being unique to the 12th amongst the lancer regiments. N.B. It is possible that for the rank and file the Prince of Wales's feathers were omitted on the lance cap plate, although this has yet to be confirmed.

The black cocktail feathers plume as described in regulations, within a gilt metal socket, this being a corded ball having four upright leaves. N.B. By this period the drop and rise of the plume had been reduced considerably (6).

The lion's head bosses, chinchain and cap-lines as previously described, no information being available regarding the head lining.

The Regimental Pattern Cap of the 9th Lancers (*See Fig: 29.*).
The special pattern cap for officers of the 9th Lancers is noted in the Dress Regulations of 1846 thus '*The 9th Lancers have permission to wear a cap of the regimental pattern with gilt metal ornaments*', the regulations of 1855 giving a similar brief description. Hardly an informative description of this regiments cap, particularly as the cap of the 9th differed quite considerably from the cap of the other lancer regiments. Therefore a more detailed description of this cap is given below, with the important regimental variations being given in bold text.

The overall dimensions were as for the other lancer regiments, with the top of the cap being of black patent leather having gilt metal ornaments covering the four corners, with a gilt metal ring attached to the right hand ornament as illustrated in *Fig: 29A*. The upper section (sides) were covered with blue ribbed cloth, with the angles being covered with strips of gilt metal.

To the upper front of the ribbed cloth section, a gilt metal gimp boss (rosette), being not dissimilar in appearance to a coiled rope, having some eight 'rings', the size of each of the rings reducing in size as they approached the centre of the boss (*See Fig: 29.*). N.B. Unlike the post 1856 pattern gilt metal boss, on this, the earlier pattern there was not a regimental pattern button to its centre.

The skull was also of black patent leather, with around the waist, a two inch wide gilt metal band having the appearance of being a

Figure 27: 'An officer in the uniform of the 16th Lancers.' A dismounted officer wearing the uniform of the 16th Lancers, though to be Lieutenant General Beckwith C.B. Note the fine feather plume to the cap, the bullion tassels of the cap lines, and the Mameluke pattern sword. Lt. General Beckwith commissioned Cornet 1813: 16th Light Dragoons (L/D). Lieutenant 1815: 16th L/D. c.1817 to 14th L/D. Captain 1822. Major 1828. Lt. Colonel 1833. Colonel 1846. Major General 1854. Lt. General 1861. General 1869. Made a Knight of Hanover 1831. Died 23rd Feb. 1871. Copyright D.P.& G.

semi-circular rope, each of the two sections being bound together by a double rope at the centre (6). The front peak of black patent leather bound with gilt metal.

The gilt metal rayed plate bore the Royal Arms comprised of two crowned oval shields, below which in silver was A.R. reversed, with the title scroll in gilt metal[12] as illustrated in *Fig: 29B*.

Gilt metal lion's head bosses as for the other lancer regiments, with the chinchain being of regimental pattern beaded/corded chain mounted on black patent leather and lined with black velvet. N.B. The hook attached to the lion's head boss on the left side (facing the cap) was also of special pattern as illustrated in *Fig: 29*.

The Senior N.C.O.' Pattern Cap
This was the pattern of cap, but minus its plume and holder, and covered by the black foul weather cover, that was worn men of the

Figure 28: '9th (The Queen's Royal) Light Dragoons (Lancers).' Mounted officers and other ranks c.1842 by Michael Angelo Hayes. Reproduced by kind permission of the Parker Gallery.

Figure 29: 9th Lancers. A fine example of the pre 1856 officers pattern lance cap, minus plume. Note the large gilt metal plume boss, and the ring to the top left hand corner of the top of the cap. Courtesy of Charles Griffin.

Figure 29A: 9th Lancers. Rear view of the officers pattern cap illustrating the gilt metal pattern band to the waist of the cap. Courtesy of Charles Griffin.

Figure 29B: Close-up view of a cap of a similar pattern cap, in which may be seen the reversed 'A.R' cypher on the lance cap plate, and the regimental pattern chinchain. Courtesy of Christopher Bryant. Photo: R. Biondi.

17th Lancers holding rank below that of commissioned officer whilst on active service in the Crimea. The 17th Lancers together with the 8th Hussars, 11th Hussars, 4th Light Dragoons, and 13th Light Dragoons formed the Light Brigade, who rode into history when they made their famous charge against the Russian guns on the 25th October 1854.

The cap for senior non commissioned officers such as a Troop Sergeant or Sergeant, though less ornate, was similar in overall appearance to the officers pattern cap, the major differences being as follows. N.B. The following description would not necessarily be relevant to the 9th Lancers, whose Senior N.C.O's would most probably have worn a special regimental pattern cap. The top of the cap was covered with black patent leather, the four angles (corners) being adorned with gold braid, and having gilt metal ornaments to the top of each corner, there being a hook for the chinchain attached to the left hand corner ornament[13] (when facing the cap).

The plume boss was of gold bullion cord, being wound around the body of the boss approximately five/six times, with a cotton/woollen centre mounted with a small regimental pattern button (19).

Around the waist of the cap was a band of gold lace having a central stripe, but being without the additional three bands of gold braid present on the officers pattern cap. The front peak was of black patent leather being adorned with a single band of braid to its edge, with the rear folded peak being of black patent leather.

The lance cap plate was a one piece die-struck plate, possibly gilded.[14]

Brass, leather backed chinchain, the head lining of leather and waxed cotton.

The Other Ranks Pattern Cap

For those soldiers below the rank of N.C.O. the cap was of similar shape to that described above, but was much less ornate, the major differences being as follows. The plume boss was of wool (red upon yellow in the 16th), the four angles were adorned with yellow cord braid the corners having brass/gilding metal ornaments, with there being a hook for the chinchain attached to the left hand ornament (when facing the cap). Around the waist of the cap was a band of yellow cotton braid having a central stripe of regimental colour (red in the 16th). The front peak was of unadorned black patent leather, with the lance cap plate of gilding metal/brass, being die-struck and of one piece. See chapter ten for an example of the other ranks pattern plate of the 16th Lancers having eight battle honours and retaining the numeral '16'.

Figure 30: '17th (Light) Dragoons (Lancers).' Dismounted Private c.1854 by M. & N. Hanhart after Wm. Sharpe from *'British Expeditionary Army of the East'*, published 1854. Reproduced by kind permission of the Parker Gallery.

NOTES

1. This excellent painting is on permanent display at the National Army Museum, Chelsea, London.

2. There is a black and white photograph said to be of an officers lance cap of the 19th Lancers, and a coloured line drawing of a differing pattern officers cap of this regiment in Issue 47 of *Regiment Magazine*, which illustrates the facing colour of yellow.

3. The excellent photograph of an officers pattern lance cap of the 23rd Lancers c.1816-1817, illustrated in Fig: 20. originally appeared in 'Head Dresses of the British Army - Cavalry' (6).

4. An account of the bullion boss/rosette for the cap of the 17th Lancers was made by Herbert in 1827, it being described as 'well raised of cork, hollowed for feather socket, silver embroidered double GR, shaded black with rough and smooth border on white'. The head-dress which illustrates this period appears to be in a transitional stage to the next pattern cap (6).

5. The order that was needed by Messrs Herbert Military Tailors for the officers caps of the 23rd Lancers is still preserved, and is reproduced below as written:

> '21 ins. crimson & silver new pattern lace, 3 inches
> 22 ins. crimson & silver new pattern lace, 2 inches
> 1 2/3 yards silver 5/8 in. French braid
> 1 2/3 yards silver 1/8 in French braid
> 1/2 yard silver engine Royal cord
> 1 1/3 yards silver round engine cord
> A silver No.2.1/2 twisted bullion rose with silver embroidered GR in centre on crimson cloth'.

N.B. Messrs Herbert made such lace, braid and cords for Messrs Hawkes who made the basic lance cap (5).

6. A note in Messrs Herbert files quotes the following for the Dress cap of the 16th Lancers:

'21 ins. silver 4.1/4 ins wave with scarlet stripe on one edge, deep scallop with Russia braid on same side
1.1/2 yard silver
5/8 in. basket braid
1.1/2 yard silver
3/16 in basket braid
1/2 yard basket cord for peak
1.2/3 yard basket cord for the top Boss
2.7/8 x 1.1/2 – silver embroidered double GR with border on scarlet
2 silver Russia braid loops with small basket olives – richest gold basket cord cap line all bullion tassels' (5).

7. In December 1823 Messrs Herbert recorded the following details for the fittings on the 17th Lancers officers pattern cap:

'18 sloped off to 17 inches gold and silver mixed
3 inch oak brocade
18 inches gold and silver mixed blue vellum and orris
1 yard 22 inches silver
3/4 inch braid
1 yard 15 inches silver
3/16 inch braid
14 inches Royal cord
1 yard 22 inches gold basket cord for the top Boss – well raised of cork hollowed for feather socket, silver embroidered double GR shaded black with rough and smooth purl border on white' (5).

8. On an existing example cap with a 'GR' boss, the plate comprised a gilt metal rayed back plate upon which was a silver '12' mount instead of the actual Sphinx. The Royal Arms and Prince of Wales's feathers were also in silver, but the separately mounted honours scrolls of 'Waterloo' and 'Peninsula' were in gilt metal, with the word 'Egypt' being part of the die-struck back plate (5).

9. On the 11th December 1823 it was stated (WO 3/242) regarding the 17th Lancers that 'In future supplies of caps, the regimental badge to be stamped in one with the cap plate, instead of being soldered on in a separate piece, as in the case of the sealed cap-plate of 17th Lancers'. This refers to the plate being worn by the other ranks, and did not apply to lance cap plates worn by the officers, who had gilt mounts and a silver back plate (5).

10. In the search for contemporary evidence relating to the height of the cap, four differing editions of the dress regulations were consulted, they stating as follows:

1822: 11 inches.
1831: 9 inches.
1846: 8.3/4 inches - 9.1/2 inches.
1857: 7.1/2 inches - 8.1/2 inches. (5).

11. As the measurements indicate, this pattern of cap 'shows a departure from the cap previously worn, which was straight across and not deeper at the back' (6).

12. The plate of the 9th Lancers was said to have born the Royal Arms of Queen Adelaide, which comprised 'two shields; the dexter containing the arms of Great Britain and Ireland, quartering Hanover on an escutcheon of pretence, the whole surrounded by the Garter; the sinister, the fifteen quarterings of Mecklenberg -Sterlitz, surrounded by a Chaplet of Rue-Leaves, a special mark of the House of Saxony. The Supporters and Crown are those of England. The Regimental device below the above is the double cypher A.R.'(40).

13. In a photograph of a sergeant's pattern cap (19), there is no evidence of a hook having been attached to the right hand corner ornament.

14. In Issue 20 of *Regiment Magazine*, there is an excellent colour illustration of a lance cap of the 17th Lancers, being of officers quality, complete with a bullion rosette bearing 'WR above IV' cypher, and having a black feather plume. The plate however is not the officers pattern that normally comprised a gilt rayed back plate upon which was mounted the silvered overlay of Royal Arms, skull and crossed bones etc, but in its place there being a brass coloured die-struck one piece plate. Could this cap possibly once have belonged to the Regimental Sergeant Major?

Chapter Seven

The 1856 Officers Pattern Lance Cap

The sealed pattern date for this particular lance cap is given as the 11th July 1856, in *'The Dress Regulations for Officers of The Army 1900'* published by The War Office (43). N.B. The sealed pattern indicates that the particular pattern of uniform etc has been deposited at the War Office for reference and guidance, in order that officers are able to ensure that articles according to the sealed pattern are being supplied to them.

Notwithstanding the above, the following description of this pattern of lance cap is based on the first official description of the lance cap, as described on pages 95 and 96 of *'Regulations for the Dress of General, Staff, and Regimental Officers of The Army 1857'* issued by the Adjutant-General's Office, Horse Guards, the relevant paragraphs being reproduced below as originally published.

Dress Regulations 1857

NINTH LANCERS. (*See Fig: 33.*)
'Cap-skull and top covered with black patent leather, the upper part only covered with blue cloth; dimensions of the cap same as other Lancers regiments; gilt metal ornaments at four corners of top attached to gilt metal strips covering the angles; on left side a gilt metal rosette with regimental screw and button in centre, and at back of rosette a socket for plume stem. A gilt metal one inch band round waist, at back a ring and hook for line and chain. A gilt plate with double A.R. cypher and gilt arms to match, with badges according to regimental pattern as deposited. Black patent leather peak with gilt metal quarter inch binding, gilt corded chain five-eighths of an inch, attached to lion's heads at side of cap'. N.B. The gilt metal rosette referred to above is illustrated in *Fig: 33A.*

'Line and Plume-Socket-as in other Lancer regiments'.

'Plume-black and white cocktail feathers, size as in other Lancer regiments'.

TWELFTH, SIXTEENTH, AND SEVENTEENTH LANCERS. (*See Fig: 36.*)
Cap-skull covered with black patent leather, the upper part and top with cloth same colour as facing; height in front six and half inches, side seven inches, back eight and a half inches, top, seven and a quarter inches square. Gold gimp and orris cord across the top and down the angles; on left side a gold bullion rosette with embroidered V.R. on blue velvet for 12th and 17th Lancers and scarlet for 16th Lancers, at the back of which a socket for plume stem. A band of gold one inch lace round waist, with two bands of gold braid below, the upper half inch wide the lower quarter inch wide, a space of one-eighth of an inch being left between the lace and the two braids; a similar double band of braid round the bottom of the skull; the half inch braid at the bottom and the quarter of an inch above it with a space of an eighth of an inch between. A gilt plate with silver arms and badge, according to regimental pattern as deposited. Black patent leather peak embroidered with three rows of gold purl, in all one inch and a quarter wide. Plain gilt burnished five-eighths of an inch chain attached to lion's heads at side of cap. Gilt rings and hook at back of waist for line and chain'.

'Line-Gold gimp and orris cord with slide and olive ends passing through ring at back and encircling the cap singly and worn round the neck'.

'Plume-cocktail feathers, twelve inches long and standing four and a half inches above top of the cap. Colour for-12th Lancers, scarlet, 16th " scarlet and white, 17th " white (*See Fig: 37.*)

Gilt plume socket corded ball with four upright rays'.

N.B. Whilst the official regulations state 'Plume-cocktail feathers', photographic evidence appears to show that the hair plume was also worn prior to 1874, possibly whilst the officer was in 'undress' uniform.

There were very few changes to the description of the cap and plume for several years, although by 1874, the following particulars appeared under the heading 'Lancers' Full Dress, on page 33 of the dress regulations for that year, in which details relating to the 'youngest' of the lancer regiments, the 5th Lancers appeared, the remaining changes being mainly to the text, and of a finite nature. Never the less, the 1874 description is reproduced below with the amendments/changes being identified by being given in bold text. N.B. For the purpose of cross-referencing, the lance cap dimensions quoted in the Dress Regulations for both 1857 and 1846 have been given below in words (as printed), rather than in numerals as used in the later official text of 1874.

Dress Regulations 1874

'Cap [except for 9th Lancers]-Lancer pattern; six and a half inches high in front, seven inches at the sides, and eight and a half inches at the back; seven inches square at the top. Skull covered with black patent leather, the upper part and top with cloth of the same colour as the facings. Gold gimp and orris cord across the top and down the angles. On the left side, in front, a gold bullion rosette, with the Royal Cypher, embroidered on blue velvet in the 12th and 17th Lancers, on green in the 5th, on scarlet in the 16th; at the back of the rosette, a spring socket for the plume stem. A band of inch lace round the waist, with two bands of gold braid below, the upper half-inch wide gold braid; the lower quarter-inch; and a similar double band of braid round the bottom of the cap, the half-inch braid being the lower; the lace and the several bands of braid to be eighth inch apart. A gilt plate in front, with silver badge of regimental pattern. Black patent leather peak, embroidered with three stripes of gold purl. Plain burnished chain, five eighth inches wide, attached to gilt lion's heads at the sides. Gilt rings and hook at the back of the waist, for the cap-line and chain'. N.B. If the above dimensions are accurate, then the top has been reduced in size from seven and a quarter inches square, to seven inches square.

'Cap Line-Gold gimp and orris cord, with slide and olive ends, encircling the cap once, passing round the body and looped on the left breast'.

'Plume-Horse-hair, of the colours stated below, twelve inches long, and rising four and a half inches above the top of the cap; plume socket, a gilt corded ball, with four upright leaves'.

(Text resumes on page 76)

Figure 31: 'An Officer of the 5th Lancers.' A fine study of an officer of the regiment, thought to be Captain Vandeleur c.1865. Records show that there were two officers serving in this regiment c.1865-70 with the surname of Vandeleur, these being Captain Boyle Vandeleur, and Captain David Roche Vandeleur. Regrettably it was not possible to identify which of these two officers is depicted in this photograph. Note the crown and star devices to the collar of the tunic indicating the rank of Captain. N.B. These combined devices were also worn by an officer holding the rank of Lieutenant Colonel, the difference between the two ranks concerned being indicated by the extra lace for the senior of these two ranks (26). Copyright D.P.& G.

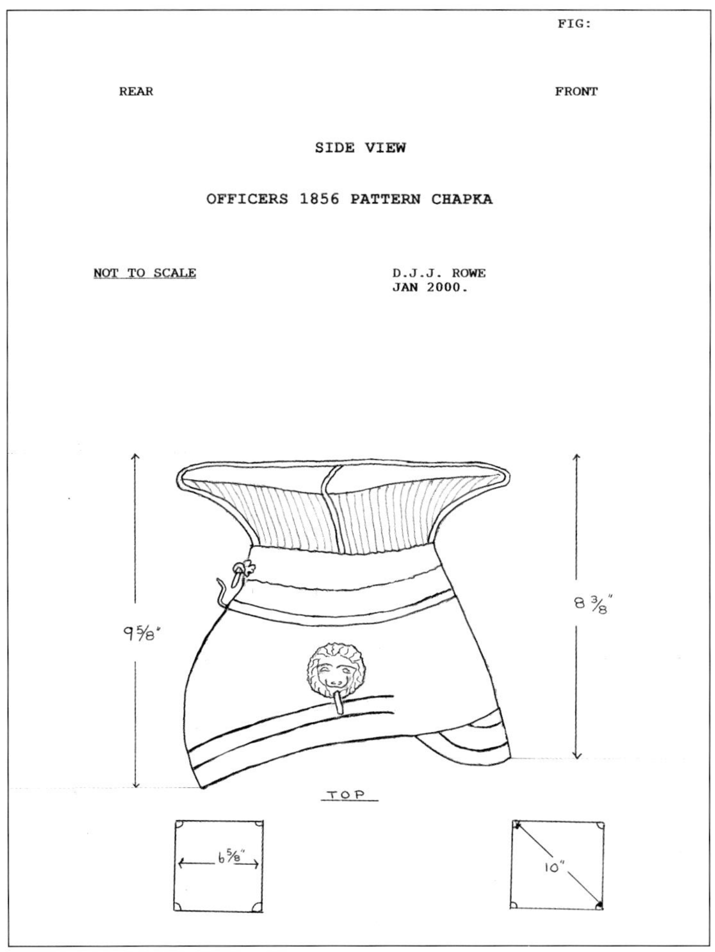

Figure 32: Sketch of the officers 1856 pattern lance cap giving dimensions of the top, the height at the front, and the height at the rear. David J.J. Rowe.

Figure 33: 9th Lancers. A fine officers Victorian pattern cap complete with feather plume, the plate having twelve battle honours. Compare this example with the earlier pattern illustrated in *Fig: 29*. Courtesy of Meng-Chi Tsen. Photo: R. Biondi.

OPPOSITE - *Figure 33A:* 9th Lancers. The cap with the plume removed to reveal the gilt metal plume boss. Note the metal strips covering the angles, and the gilt metal waistband. Courtesy of Meng-Chi Tsen. Photo: R. Biondi.

SOBRAON
CHILLIANWALLAH
DELHI
CHARASIAH
ROYAL LANCERS
PUNJAUB

Figure 33B: 9th Lancers. The extremely rare officers pattern cap having the white cloth sides thought to have been made for a Bandmaster. Note that the plume is of horsehair and not swan feathers. Courtesy of Christopher Bryant. Photo: R. Biondi.

Figure 34: 12th Lancers (Prince of Wales's Royal). A Victorian officers, early 1856 pattern cap, having battle honours to '*Central India*'. Note the 'V.R.' Royal Cypher to the centre of the bullion rosette. Courtesy of Meng-Chi Tsen. Photo: R. Biondi.

Figure 34A: 12th Lancers. Close-up view of cap, in which may be seen the fine detail to the plate, bearing six battle honours. Note the metal framework visible through the cloth at the top (centre), and right side of cap. Courtesy of Meng-Chi Tsen. Photo: R. Biondi.

Figure 34B: 12th Lancers. A similar pattern officers cap. Compare the bullion rosette and the plume socket on this cap with the pattern illustrated in *Fig: 34A*. Courtesy of Charles Griffin.

'For 5th Lancers *Green.*
'For 9th Lancers *Black and white.*
'For 12th Lancers *Scarlet.*
'For 16th Lancers *Red and white.*
For 17th Lancers *White.*

N.B. It is of interest that the plume is no longer described as being cocktail feathers as in the Dress Regulation of 1857.

Cap of the 9th Lancers

The cap for the 9th Lancers was basically as described in the 1857 regulations, there being little, or no changes of any significance.

It is judicious to say that the above descriptions are reasonably informative, they being 'sufficient for the needs of the day'. However for collectors of lance caps, military artists, military modellers, and students of military head-dress, these official descriptions are somewhat lacking in finite detail when describing some of the fittings etc, and therefore offered below is an alternative description on this pattern of cap, based on the official wording in the dress regulations. The alternative narrative has been divided into sections (as listed in chapter five) for ease of reference, with the additional details included by the author's, being given in bold italic text.

Officers Lance Cap [except 9th Lancers]. *See Fig: 36.* for an example of the 16th Lancers cap.

Based on the premise that the dimensions of the cap as given in the Dress Regulations of 1846, and those listed for 1874 are reasonably accurate, then the overall size of the 1856 pattern cap was considerably smaller overall, being two and a quarter inches shorter in front, one inch shorter at the rear, with the top being reduced by two and a half inches square.

The Skull and Top

The skull was covered with black patent leather, the upper part (sides) and top with cloth, known to have sometimes been referred to as 'melton cloth'. The four cloth covered sides of the cap were strengthened, by having thin strips of cane inserted into the 'pockets' that were sewn into the material, thereby creating its ribbed appearance. This material was of the same colour as the facings, these being scarlet in the 5th, blue in the 9th, scarlet in the 12th, blue in the 16th, and white in the 17th. Gold gimp and orris cord ran across the top of the cap extending down the angles (from north to south, and east to west). N.B. In an auction house catalogue, it is not unusual to find the top and sides of an officers pattern cap of the 16th Lancers described as being of black cloth. See appendix three, 'Appreciation of Lance Cap Prices', June 1983 - Sotheby's, May 1984 - Wallis and Wallis, and February 1996 - Bosleys, for three examples. In respect of the blue cloth sides to the cap of the 9th Lancers, there is photographic evidence that at one period in time a cap was manufactured having white cloth sides[1] as illustrated in *Fig: 33B*. The plate fitted to this cap was the pattern having eight battle honours, suggesting that it was manufactured prior to 1900,

Figure 35: An Officer of the 16th Lancers.' A study of an unknown officer of the regiment c.1860. Note the red/scarlet and white plume to the cap, and the crown device to the collar of the tunic. Copyright D.P.& G.

and although not confirmed, it is thought likely that this particular cap was a 'one off' example made especially for the Bandmaster of the regiment.

To the upper left front of the ribbed cloth section, a gold bullion rosette, with the Victorian Royal Cypher being of embroidered gold bullion/wire on velvet as illustrated in *Fig: 34A.*, the regimental colours for the velvet being as follows:

5th Lancers on green velvet.
9th Lancers have gilt metal gimp boss.
12th Lancers on blue velvet.
16th Lancers on scarlet velvet.
17th Lancers on blue velvet.

At the back of the rosette, a flat 'oblong' gilt/brass socket for the stem of the plume as illustrated in *Fig: 17F.*, this stem being secured within the socket by a small 'wing' bolt, or knurled knob bolt, accessible from within the upper skull section of the cap.

The actual skull of the cap (the part that enclosed the wearer's head) was also of black patent leather, having a band of gold inch wide lace round the waist of the pattern shown under the section 'Designs for Lace' of the Dress Regulations 1900, with positioned immediately below, two bands of gold braid, the upper being half-inch wide; the lower being a quarter-inch in width. A similar double band of gold braid round the bottom of the cap, the half-inch band being the lower; the lace and several bands of braid to be an eight of an inch apart. Black patent leather peak, embroidered with three stripes of gold purl of differing widths, the widest stripe being to the centre of the peak, with the inside of the peak being lined with green skiver.

The Lance Cap Plate

In view of the reduced size of the new pattern cap, it was to be expected that the gilt metal plate would also be scaled down accordingly, and this is confirmed by the measurements of the 1856 pattern plate, they being five inches in height, by nine and one quarter inches in width, when measured across the base of the plate.[2] Upon the gilt metal rayed plate was a gilt/silvered overlay, which usually included the Royal Arms[3], current battle honours and regimental devices etc, fuller details of which have been given previously in chapter five. For details relating to each regiments plate, please refer to chapter ten, where will be found illustrations of many of the differing pattern of plate adopted by each of the lancer regiments, together with the relevant text. N.B. The officers pattern

Figure 36: 16th Lancers. An example of an officers Victorian pattern lance cap, which is sadly lacking it's plume. N.B. The plume rosette has fewer rows of bullion and is shallower than normal, also there is no 'lip' to the plume socket entrance. Possibly this is a makers variation, or a replacement fitment. Courtesy of Meng-Chi Tsen. Photo: R. Biondi.

Figure 36A: 16th Lancers. Close-up view of the cap illustrating the fine silvered overlay to the lance cap plate which bears thirteen battle honours. Courtesy of Meng-Chi Tsen. Photo: R. Biondi.

rayed 'back plate' was usually made of copper as this metal was easier to gild (44).

The Chinchain and Ear Bosses
Plain gilt metal burnished chain, three-quarter inch wide, mounted on black patent leather (later being lined with black velvet), attached to gilt metal lion's head bosses at the sides. The lion's head boss to the left side of the cap (when facing the cap) having a closed ring positioned on the lion's chin, to which is attached the secured end of the chinchain, with to the right side, a similar lion's head boss having a gilt metal hook secured to its chin, onto which is secured the 'loose' end of the chinchain.

The Rear of the Waist
At the rear waist of the cap, a gilt metal ring and hook on a gilt metal four petalled leaf, onto which was attached the cap-lines and the loose end of the chinchain as an when required.

The Head Lining
The head lining of tan leather, with the upper section of crimson silk. N.B. Quite often the supplier/tailors 'label' may be found upon the silk lining covering the inner 'crown' of the cap, this usually being in the form of a gold embossed stamp bearing the companies name, address, and trade mark, as may be seen in the photograph of the inside of the East Riding of Yorkshire officers pattern cap, which is illustrated in chapter thirteen.

The Plume
The horsehair plume was a described above, with the cocktail feathers plume possibly being worn at levees etc.

The Cap-lines
The gold gimp and orris cord cap-lines were passed through the gilt metal ring at the rear of the waist, the lines encircling the cap once, and then looped around the wearers body to loop up upon the left breast. N.B. *See Fig: 17H.* for an illustration of the rear view of the 5th Lancers pattern cap, in which the gilt metal ring may clearly be seen.

Officers Lance Cap - 9th Lancers only (*See Fig: 33.*)
The dimensions for the cap are as given in the aforementioned dress regulations, with the top of the skull being covered in black patent leather, with gilt metal leaf pattern ornaments covering the four corners. The upper part of the skull (sides) covered in blue ribbed cloth, with gilt metal strips covering the four angles. To the left upper front, a gilt metal gimp boss, being not dissimilar in appearance to a coiled rope, having some six rings[4], each ring reducing in size towards the centre of the boss, which bore a Victorian regimental pattern button (*See Fig: 33A.*). To the upper rear of the boss a gilt/brass socket as previously described.

The actual skull was covered with black patent leather, however it was without the gold lace waistband with the double band of gold braid below. In its place there was a gilt metal band, one inch wide encircling the waist, (as illustrated in *Fig: 33A.*) possessing the appearance of being formed of semi-circular rope bound together by a double band. The peak was of black patent leather having a binding of gilt metal a quarter inch wide, the inside of the peak being lined with green skiver. N.B. This pattern of cap was also without the usual double band of gold braid around the bottom of the cap.

Figure 36B: 16th Lancers. Side view of an officers pattern cap in which can clearly be seen the regimental pattern lace to the waist of the cap. Courtesy of Charles Griffin.

The Lance Cap Plate
The various patterns of this regiments lance cap plate are listed in chapter ten.

Ear Bosses and Chinchain
Gilt metal lion's head bosses as described for the remaining lancer regiments, the gilt metal beaded link chinchain mounted on black patent leather, later being lined with black velvet. N.B. This regiments special pattern chinchain has also been described as being a gilt metal 'cord' chinchain.

The Plume - All regiments
The horse-hair plume as previously described, within a gilt metal plume socket (holder), having four upright leave above a corded ball, beneath which was a metal stem (prong) that was inserted into the gilt/brass socket located at the upper rear of the bullion rosette, or the gilt metal gimp boss in the case of the 9th Lancers cap.

Dress Regulations 1883

The above regulations advised of the following change of plume colour. '*For 16th Lancers - Black.* N.B. It is thought unlikely that the change of plume actually occurred until 1886 (12).

Dress Regulations 1900[5]

This publication noted several important changes, they appearing on pages 25, 82, 83 and 84 of this book, and being listed below in the order that they appeared in the regulations concerned. N.B. The actual wording used in the regulations is shown as being within the inverted commas, the relevant amendments and changes being noted in bold text, with the author's additions being the text placed within the brackets:

Gold Bullion Rosette: 21st Lancers. '*The Imperial cypher on French grey*' (velvet) as illustrated in *Fig: 38A*.

Chinchain: All regiments (except 9th Lancers):'*Plain burnished chain three quarter inch wide, mounted on black patent leather lined with velvet*' (black).

9th Lancers only: '*Gilt or gilding metal chain three quarter inch wide mounted on black patent leather, lined with velvet*' (black). N.B. There is no mentioned of the chain having beaded/corded links.

Plumes:

'*Drooping swan feathers, length fourteen inches in front, and seven inches behind from the bend of the feathers, of the following colours:-*

For 5th Lancers	*Green.*
For 9th Lancers	*Black and white. (See Fig: 33.).*
For 12th Lancers	*Scarlet. (See Fig: 34B.)*
For 16th Lancers	*Black.*
For 17th Lancers	*White. (See Fig: 37.)*
For 21st Lancers	*White. (See Fig: 38.)*

Plume Socket:

Gilt plume socket with five leaves.

The sealed date for the feather plume is given as being the 29th March 1875. N.B. To the 'crown' of the plume was a gilt metal ring. Two theories have been put forward as to the purpose served by this ring, one being that when storing the plume within its storage tin, a stick with a hook was inserted through the top of the tin to exit at it's base, the hook then being attached to the ring and the stick pulled upwards to draw the plume into the tin. The other theory is that the ring was used to suspend the plume when damp/wet, thereby allowing the feathers to dry naturally.

Lance Cap Plates

Badges-Cavalry, on Full Dress Head-dress:

'5th (Royal Irish) Lancers. On a gilt or gilding metal plate, universal pattern, in silver, the Royal Arms; below, the harp between sprays of shamrock. Across the bottom of the plate "Fifth Royal Irish Lancers". Above "Fifth", two scrolls inscribed "Blenheim", "Oudenarde". Above "Lancers", two scrolls inscribed "Ramillies", "Malplaquet".'

'9th (Queen's Royal) Lancers. In gilt or gilding metal, the universal plate with the Royal Arms, on either side on sprays of laurel scrolls inscribed with the honours of the regiment. On a scroll below, "Royal Lancers". In silver, on the centre of the plate, "A.R.", reversed and intertwined.'

'12th (Prince of Wales's Royal) Lancers. In silver, the Royal Arms with the Prince of Wales's Plume above and the sphinx over Egypt below; the scroll inscribed "Dieu Et Mon Droit" resting on two sprays of rose, thistle, and shamrock intertwined. Below, on three gilt or gilding metal scrolls, the battle honours as on the colours; the outer ends of the scrolls finish in sprays of laurel.'

'16th (Queen's) Lancers. The universal plate in gilt or gilding metal. On the plate, in silver, the Royal Arms. On the lower part of the plate, scrolls inscribed with the honours of the regiment. In the centre of the plate at the bottom a scroll inscribed "Sixteenth Lancers".'

'17th (Duke of Cambridge's Own) Lancers. In silver, the Royal Arms with the death's head and scroll inscribed "Or Glory", and the letters "D.C.O." below. On the right a branch of laurel, and on the left a branch of oak; on the sprays are six scrolls inscribed with the battles as on the colours. A scroll at the bottom of the plate inscribed "17th Lancers".'

'21st Lancers. In silver, on crossed lances, the Royal Arms with a scroll below, inscribed "Khartoum". Below the scroll the Imperial Cypher. On the right a spray of laurel with a scroll below, inscribed "21st (Empress of", and on the left, palm leaves with a scroll below, inscribed "India's) Lancers".'

N.B. With regard to the above descriptions, no mention is made of the crossed lances that are present behind the Royal Arms on the plates of the 9th, 16th, and 21st Lancers.

H.M. Reserve Regiment of Lancers

During the Boer War, garrisons became depleted of regular servicemen when the first line troops were sent abroad on active service. To remedy this situation it was decided to form Reserve Regiments of cavalry[6] and infantry, therefore from April 1900 Reserve Regiments were raised, formed of ex-soldiers who rejoined the Colours for a period home service. A term of service of one year was considered sufficient, and Reserve Regiments now appeared in the Army Lists (up to May 1901). Cap badges were produced for each of these regiment c.1900 (47), the lancer pattern badge being comprised of crossed lances having a Victorian pattern crown between the two pennons, below which were the letters 'RR', surmounting a single scroll inscribed 'Lancers'. N.B. The upper part of the pennons was of gilt with the lower part in silvered metal.

It has been said, that helmet plates were also produced for the Dragoon Guards, Dragoons, and Lancers, although whether these plates were ever actually worn on the full dress head-dress has been the topic of considerable discussion over a period of many years.

(Text resumes on page 88)

Figure 37: 17th Lancers. A good late Victorian example of an officers lance cap, complete with swan feathers plume. Courtesy of Meng-Chi Tsen. Photo: R. Biondi.

Figure 37A: 17th Lancers. Close-up view of cap with plume removed. Note the regimental motto of the skull and crossed bones, and the initials 'D''C''O' on the lance cap plate. N.B. The death's head badge, commonly known as the motto, apparently dates from 1759, being devised by Colonel John Hale, and is unique in the British Army (34). Courtesy of Meng-Chi Tsen. Photo: R. Biondi.

Figure 37B: 16th Lancers. Another example of the officers pattern cap, having the plate bearing thirteen honours, being complete with its red over white feathers plume. It is reliably thought that the plate bearing thirteen battle honours dates from c.1880, and according to the official dress regulations (108), the red over white plume was worn from c.1874 to c.1883 when the colour changed to black (109). Therefore it is likely that this particular cap dates from c.1880-1883, although it is possible the black plume was not actually adopted until 1886 (12). Courtesy of John Reed of Hambleton.

Figure 37C: 16th Lancers. The cap with the feather plume removed. The dimensions of this particular lance cap were measured by the owner, and are as follows: Nine inches high in front, nine and a half inches at the back, seven and a half inches across the top. N.B. Compare these dimensions with those given for the cap in the 1874 Dress Regulation, reproduced earlier in this chapter. Courtesy of John Reed of Hambleton.

Figure 37D: 16th Lancers. Side view of the cap. Of particular interest is the hook to the rear 'North' corner of the cap top, this being a fitment not present on many later examples of this pattern cap. Courtesy of John Reed of Hambleton.

Figure 38: 21st (Empress of India's) Lancers. A superb example of a Victorian officers lance cap, complete with feather plume. Note the superb condition of the ribbed cloth sides. Courtesy of Christopher Bryant. Photo: R. Biondi.

Figure 38A: 21st Lancers. Close-up view with the plume removed. Note the *'VRI'* beneath the honour *'Khartoum'* to the lower centre of the lance cap plate. Courtesy of Christopher Bryant. Photo: R. Biondi.

This subject was raised in a letter that appeared in the Journal of The Crown Imperial Society in 1983, in which reference was made to Army Order No.78 of 1900 which detailed clothing to be provided to the reserve regiments. The author of the aforementioned article stated that "*a study of the individual items show that 'full dress' was not included in the issue*' and goes on to say that "*the only headgear referred to is the field cap or glengarry*". The writer continued by referring to Item No.2 of Army Order 79 which gave details of the officers full dress uniforms, and stated that "*provision of full dress is not necessary, but officers may provide themselves with the full dress of their respective regiments*",[7] and goes on to describe the badge to be worn on the full dress head-dress.

Full dress and undress uniforms were apparently planned, the lancer full dress to have red facings, the lace of Royal pattern with scalloped edge, the buttons of Royal Arms pattern, with the lance cap having a red plume.

The Officers Pattern Lance Cap Plate

Hugh King in his book on British Military Cap Badges (46), describes the plate thus 'Officers lance cap. In gilt-metal the universal plate. On the plate in silver the Royal Arms upon crossed lances. Below the Royal Arms the letters RR. Above, a scroll inscribed Lancers. On either side a spray of laurels'. See endnote seven, 'Her Majesty's Reserve Regiment of Lancers', the section entitled 'On the Lancer cap'. N.B. The authors have never seen, nor have knowledge of any collector who possesses, or has seen an example of the officers plate as described above.

SHE: I don't wonder that officers are such fine fellows.
HE: Why?
SHE: Why, they are all made to order, aren't they?

Figure 39: 'THE OFFICER AND HIS LADY' THE 16TH LANCERS.' David Rowe collection. Previously published in the Regiment Journal 12th September 1896.

NOTES

1. This is not the first known reference to a cap of the 9th Lancers having white sides, the author's having seen two contemporary paintings depicting a member of this regiment of the period c.1830/1840 whose lance cap is shown as having white coloured cloth sides. N.B. Although not confirmed, it is thought that the figure concerned was a trumpeter of the regiment.

2. Measurement of the lance cap plate was achieved by using a fabric tape measure, which permitted the curvature of the plate to be included with the dimensions. The width of the plate was measured across the bottom edge of the plate, from extreme left edge to extreme right edge, the height being measured from the centre of the bottom edge upwards to the top of the uppermost centre rayed tip. N.B. The above measurements were recorded by Geoffrey Frost, using example of both officers and other ranks plates in his collection.

3. On plate number one of the Dress Regulation 1900, it states beneath an illustration of the Royal Arms that '*In Military Badges the Royal Helmet and Mantling are omitted*'. Our research however has identified that this appears not to have been the case during the early years of Queen Victoria's reign. N.B. It is of particular interest, that both the helmet, and the mantling were present on the Royal Arms displayed on the first version plate of the 21st Lancers, and on the plate of City of London Yeomanry.

4. It appears that upon the introduction of the 1856 pattern cap, the gilt metal boss of the 9th Lancers was decreased in size, as the number of 'rings' appear to have been reduced.

5. Dress Regulations for the Officers of the Army (including Militia) 1900. Approved by her Majesty Queen Victoria, by command of the Commander-in-Chief, War Office 9th July 1900, and published by Her Majesty's Stationery Office. Reprinted by Arms and Armour Press in 1969 with the introduction by W.Y. Carman F.S.A. F.R.Hist.S., National Army Museum.

6. In the cavalry section there were Reserve Regiments of Dragoon Guards and Dragoons, Hussars, and Lancers they being raised under Army Order No's 77,78, 79 (April), and 129 (June) of 1900, which gave details of enlistment, terms of service, and dress etc. (48).

7. The Special Army Order issued by The War Office on 29th May 1900 refers to the Reserve Regiments, and details the uniform to be worn by officers, an extract of the section relating to the Reserve Regiments of Lancers being reproduced below:

'*B.-Reserve Regiments of Cavalry.*

1. Dress of Officers. The dress of officers of Her Majesty's Reserve Regiment of Cavalry will be of the following patterns. The provision of full dress is not necessary, but officers may provide themselves with it should they so desire'.

61002
Cavalry
190

Her Majesty's Reserve Regiment of Lancers Full dress and undress - as for Lancers, with facings, & c., of the following descriptions:'

Facings-red. Plume-red Lace-Royal pattern, scalloped edge. Buttons- Royal Arms pattern. Trouser stripes-yellow cloth. Shoulder-belt, full dress-gold lace, 2 inches wide, lined with red morocco leather. Buckle, tip, and slide as for 9th Lancers. No breast ornament. Shoulder-belt, undress-white leather, 2 inches wide, buckle, tip, and slide, as for full dress. Pouch-scarlet leather. Silver engraved flap with "V.R." and Crown in gilt metal. Sabretache ornament - "V.R." and Crown.

Mess dress-Jacket, Lancer pattern. Scarlet cloth waistcoat, closed at the neck. Gilt studs. Fastened with hooks and eyes. No lace.

2. Badges. Her Majesty's Reserve Regiment of Lancers.
On the Lancer cap-In gilt metal, the universal plate, on the plate, in silver, the Royal Arms upon crossed lances, below the Royal Arms the letters R.R. above a scroll inscribed "Lancers"; on either side a spray of laurel.
On the field cap, collar, and shoulder chain-in gilt metal, a pair of crossed lances, on the lances a Crown above the letters R.R.' (50).

Chapter Eight

The 1856 Other Ranks Pattern Lance Cap

As dress regulations were not published for the rank and file, finite details relating to their uniform are far less readily available, and this therefore reduces the amount of substantiated information that may be used when describing this pattern of cap. Despite the above, below is presented a description of the cap worn by the rank and file, based on actual example's seen by the authors, and on examining many contemporary photographs of soldiers wearing their lance cap.

The cap was generally similar in appearance to the cap worn by the officers, but was less ornate, and of a lesser quality, with yellow cord replacing the gold gimp and orris cord, and yellow braid replacing the gold braid that adorned the officers pattern cap. Additionally, the dimensions of the cap differed slightly, details of which are given below, and in *Fig: 41*.

The dimensions of the cap were as follows. Height at the front: eight and seven eighths of an inch, height at the back: nine inches, across the top of the cap (side to side): six and five eighths of an inch, with across the top (corner to corner) measuring: nine and three quarter inches. N.B. It should be clearly understood that the measurements quoted above and obtained on our behalf by Geoff Frost, are given as a general guide only, as it is likely that manufacturers variations exist, and that a cap produced for a soldier having a large skull might be 'taller' overall, and vice versa.

The Skull and Top

The top of the cap was covered with black patent leather[1] with gilding metal ornaments covering the four corners. The upper part of the skull (sides) was covered with ribbed cloth, the facing colour of each regiment being as follows:

5th Lancers Scarlet cloth.
9th Lancers Blue cloth.
12th Lancers Scarlet cloth (*See Fig: 43.*)
16th Lancers Blue cloth (*See Fig: 45.*)
17th Lancers White cloth (*See Fig: 47.*)
21st Lancers French grey cloth.

N.B. With regard to the cap of the 16th Lancer, it is not unknown for the cloth sides of the cap to be described as being in black cloth in catalogues pertaining to militaria auctions, and in the catalogues/sales lists of specialist militaria dealers, possibly due to the very dark blue colour of the material used to cover the upper sides of the cap.

The upper ribbed cloth panels and the leather top, were supported on the inside of the cap by a metal framework made of thin metal 'rods' as illustrated in *Fig: 47C.*, the four corners (angles) of the cloth being covered with yellow cord braid, which terminated under the corner ornaments, and did not extend over the top of the cap as on the officers pattern cap. Senior N.C.O's such a sergeants had gold cord braid in place of the yellow braid. N.B. The 9th Lancers pattern cap did not have yellow braid, in its place there being gilding metal strips covering the angles.

To the upper left front of the ribbed cloth section, a worsted (woollen) boss, having a socket at its rear into which was deposited the stem of the plume. To the centre of the boss a small sized regimental pattern button[2] on a short tube, the actual colour of the cotton/woollen boss varying, dependent upon the regiment concerned, the colours being as follows.

5th Lancers Red upon yellow.
9th Lancers A brass/gilding metal gimp boss.
12th Lancers Blue upon yellow (*See Fig: 43C.*)
16th Lancers Red upon yellow (*See Fig: 45.*)
17th Lancers Blue upon yellow (*See Fig: 47B.*)
21st Lancers French grey upon yellow (6).

N.B. It is of interest that in the 5th Lancers, the centre of the worsted boss was red upon yellow for the rank and file, whilst the velvet backing to the Royal Cypher on the officers bullion rosette was green in colour.

To the inside front of the cap immediately behind the position occupied by the worsted boss, was a thin metal 'plate' having a central hole, through which passed a brass threaded wing nut, which when turned to the right tightened down upon the stem of the plume, thereby securing the plume to the cap.

The actual skull of the cap was covered with black patent leather, with around the waist of the cap a band of yellow cotton braid approximately one inch broad, this band having a central coloured stripe as detailed below. N.B. 'The central stripe originally seems to have followed the colour of the coatee, but by the time the 21st Lancers were raised the reason was overlooked' (6).

5th Lancers A red central stripe.
9th Lancers A brass/gilding metal band in place of the cloth band (of similar design to that of the officers).
12th Lancers A blue central stripe[3] (*See Fig: 43B.*)
16th Lancers A red stripe (*See Fig: 45A.*)
17th Lancers A blue stripe (*See Fig: 47.*)
21st Lancers The yellow band was without a central stripe (6).

The peak was of black patent leather, being without either the three strips of gold purl embroidery or the gilt metal binding present of the officers pattern caps. N.B. On the other ranks pattern cap, the inside of the peak was unlined.[4]

(Text resumes on page 98)

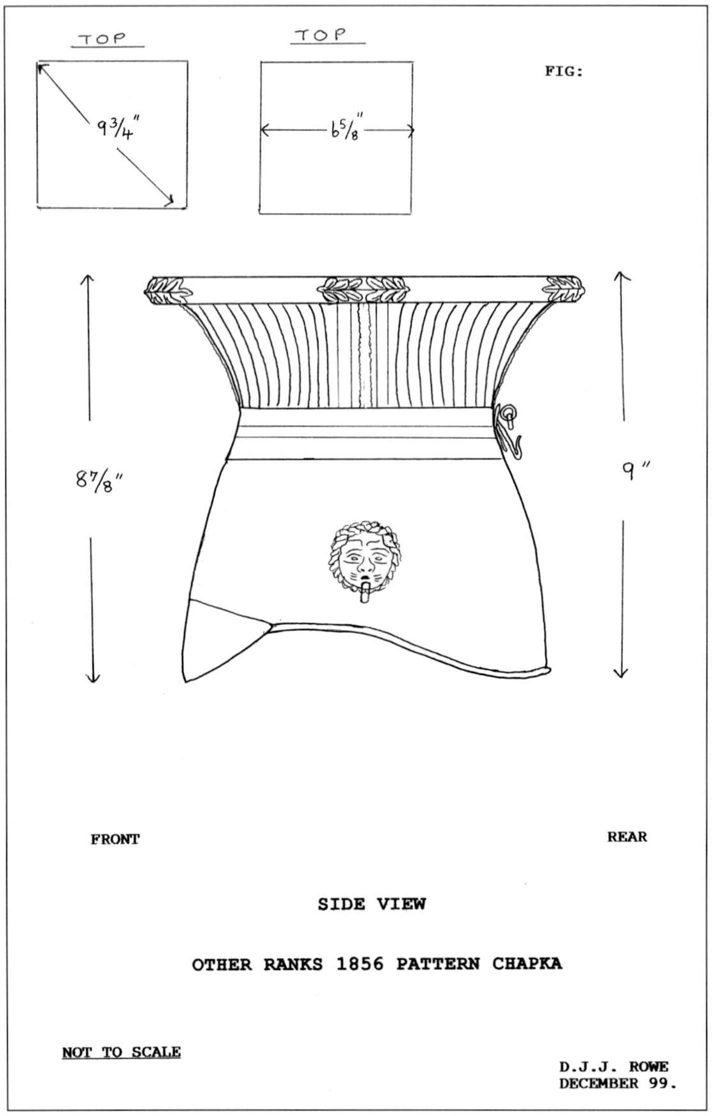

Figure 41: Sketch of the other ranks 1856 pattern lance cap giving dimensions of the top, the height at the front, and the height at the rear. David Rowe. RIGHT - *Figure 42:* 'A VICTIM OF CIRCUMSTANCES' 9TH LANCERS

Figure 40: 'THE SOLDIERS SWEETHEART' 5TH (ROYAL IRISH) LANCERS. David Rowe collection. Previously published in the Regiment Journal 1897.

A VICTIM OF CIRCUMSTANCES.

ANOTHER English veteran has lately been unearthed, this time in the person of William Edwards, who lives near Southampton.

This fine old warrior, if all accounts be true, has participated in no less than ninety different engagements, including the capture and relief of Lucknow, and is now reduced, in his old age, to turning a mangle in order to provide the bare necessaries of life for himself and a sick wife.

William Edwards was in the 9th Lancers, and spent seventeen of his twenty-five years' service in India, which was the scene of all his battles.

It is a noteworthy fact that out of the ninety engagements with which he is credited eighty-four took place in the incredibly short space of a year and a-half—viz., June, '57, to January, '59.

As a reward for his services Edwards receives a pension of 11d. per diem, which he augments in the way described above.

This appears to be a case which calls for some special treatment, and it is to be hoped that the publicity accorded it will be the means of ensuring the veteran either an increase of pension or a sufficiency to comfort his declining years. His age now is eighty-five.

Figure 43: 12th Lancers. A good example of the other ranks pattern cap complete with plume, of the post 1902 period. Note the yellow cap-lines. Courtesy of Geoff Frost.

Figure 43A: 12th Lancers. Close-up view of the post 1902 lance cap plate. Note the battle honours which include '*South Africa 1899-1902*', and '*Relief of Kimberley*'. Courtesy of Geoff Frost.

OPPOSITE - *Figure 43B:* 12th Lancers. Side view of the cap, illustrating the ear boss, and the hook with ring to the rear of the cap. Courtesy of Geoff Frost.

Figure 43C: 12th Lancers. Close-up view of the worsted plume boss, with regimental pattern Victorian button to the centre. Courtesy of Geoff Frost.

Figure 44: '16th (The Queen's) Lancers.' 'A trooper in marching order' c.1891 after John Charlton, published as a supplement to 'The Graphic' in 1891. By courtesy of the Parker Gallery.

Figure 45: 16th Lancers. An excellent example of an other ranks pattern cap complete with plume of the post 1902 period. Courtesy of Schiffer Publishing. Photo: R. Biondi. INSET - *Figure 45B:* 16th Lancers. A fine example of the other ranks pattern plume complete with holder. Note. The brass ring surrounding the hair of the plume is an unofficial fitting. Courtesy of Hugh King. Photo: R. Biondi.

Figure 45A: 16th Lancers. Close-up view of the cap illustrating the post 1902 pattern lance cap plate with honours to '*South Africa 1900-02*' Courtesy of Schiffer Publishing. Photo: R. Biondi.

Figure 46: 'Light Brigade Heroes.' An early post 1856 photograph of a sergeant and three privates of the 17th Lancers proudly wearing the Crimean campaign medal. Note that at this period the top of the cap was of black patent leather, and that the plume also was black. Copyright D.P.& G.

The Lance Cap Plate

For the rank and file, the plate was of brass/gilding metal, being a one piece die-struck item, measuring approximately five inches in height, by nine and one eighth inches in width across the base (as measured by Geoff Frost). The plate generally displayed the regiments battle honours, the Royal Arms, and the regimental title, all as displayed on the officers pattern plate, though usually being less well defined than on the former pattern plate. The lance cap plate was attached to the cap by means of two short threaded studs, which were passed through corresponding holes in the skull of the cap, where brass washers and hooped nuts (thumbscrews) were attached to the studs to secure the plate in place. N.B. Details of each regiments lance cap plate are given in chapter ten.

The Chinchain and Ear Bosses

The plain brass chinchain was backed with leather and measured some five eighths of an inch in width, by sixteen inches in length, and usually had four unbacked links at the 'loose' end of the chinchain, making a total overall length of seventeen and a half inches. The chain was attached to the cap by being secured to a closed ring, positioned upon the chin of the left hand lion's head boss, with the loose end of the chain being hung upon the hook secured to the chin of the right hand lion's head boss.

The Rear of the Waist

At the rear waist of the cap, a brass/gilding metal ring and hook, on a four petalled leaf of similar metal, onto which was attached the cap-lines and the loose end of the chinchain as an when required. *(See Fig: 43B.)*

Figure 47: 17th Lancers. A superb condition example of the other ranks pre 1902 pattern cap, complete with hair plume and a set of cap-lines. Note the unique white patent leather top. Courtesy of Christopher Bryant. Photo: R. Biondi.

The Head Lining

For the rank and file there was not the 'luxury' of a soft leather and silk head lining, in its place there normally being a black leather and oilskin/waxed cotton head lining/sweatband of the type illustrated in *Fig: 47C.*, or alternatively a lining of black calico. N.B. It is not unusual to find the suppliers paper label and/or the War Department issue stamp within the cap, e.g. W.D. 1903 as illustrated in *Fig: 47D.*

The Plume (*See Fig: 45B.*)

The plume was of horsehair, being bound to wood in three places using cord, and having a brass 'slide' to its base, which had an oblong slot cut into its face close to the bottom of the slide. The plume was contained within a brass socket (holder) similar in general appearance to the officers pattern socket, but having a plain ball (uncorded) with a pronounced cut-out recess to the lower rear of the ball, as illustrated in *Fig: 48.* As for the officers cap, the colour of the plumes differed dependent upon the regiment concerned, they being as follows.

5th Lancers Green plume.
9th Lancers Black over white plume.
12th Lancers Scarlet plume. (*See Fig: 43.*)
16th Lancers Black plume. (*See Fig: 45B.*)
17th Lancers White plume. (*See Fig: 47.*)
21st Lancers White plume.

Figure 47A: 17th Lancers. Close-up view of the cap, in which can just be seen the regimental pattern button to the centre of the woollen boss. Note the initials 'D''O''C' close to the centre of the plate. Courtesy of Christopher Bryant. Photo: R. Biondi.

Figure 47B: 17th Lancers. Offset view of similar pre 1902 other ranks pattern cap, in which can clearly be seen the shape of the other ranks pattern plume socket. Note the leather backing to the chinchain is absent, enabling the shape of the links to be seen. Copyright W.Y. Carman.

Figure 47C: 17th Lancers. View of the inside of the cap illustrating the other ranks pattern lining, and the metal support rods for the top of the cap. Copyright W.Y. Carman.

Figure 47D: 17th Lancers. View of the interior of another, other ranks pattern cap in which can be seen remains of the makers paper label, and the 'W.D. 1903' issue stamp. Courtesy of Hugh King. Photo: R. Biondi.

In the 9th Lancers the horsehair was stitched in place to form a permanent black, white, black plume, and was then crimped. N.B. There are three excellent photographic illustrations showing other ranks of the 9th Lancers wearing their lance caps complete with crimped plumes, in *Regiment Magazine*, issue 47.

The crimping of the plume was achieved by placing the dampened plume within a pair of wooden crimping sticks, the inner surfaces of which were undulated, having a saw-tooth surface. When the plume was dry, it was removed from the crimping sticks and would have had a most noticeable 'wavy' appearance (38).

The practice of crimping the plume does not appear to have been adopted by all the lancer regiments, it being known that both the 5th Lancers and the 17th Lancers did not adopt this practice, whilst the 9th, 16th and 21st Lancers are all known to have crimped their plumes. *See Fig: 49.* for an illustration of a soldier of the 21st Lancers in which the crimped plume may be seen. N.B. At one period the plumes worn by the rank and file of both the 1st and 5th Dragoon Guards appear to have been crimped.

The Cap-lines (*See Fig: 43.*)

The cap lines were similar in general appearance to those of the officers, and were worn in the same manner. However, they were of a lesser quality being of yellow worsted cord, they being stated as being some two hundred and forty six inches in length (39).

Figure 48: The other ranks pattern plume holder. Compare this example with the officers pattern illustrated in *Fig: 17U*. Courtesy of Geoff Frost.

The Warrant Officers/Senior N.C.O.'s Pattern Cap

As mentioned previously in chapter four, the War Office publication of 1907 entitled '*Clothing and Necessities*', advised that three differing grades of lance cap existed for men below the rank of commissioned officer, these being divided into the following classes. (1) Warrant Officers and Staff Sergeants, (2) Sergeants, and (3) Lower ranks.

Whilst is quite evident how the cap for the 'lower ranks' varied from the sergeant's pattern cap, quite what the actual difference between the Warrant Officers pattern of cap and that of the Sergeant is a mystery, for whilst the author's have seen many actual examples of lance caps formerly worn by soldiers holding the rank of Warrant Officer/Non Commissioned Officer, there has been nothing noticeable to differentiate one pattern of cap from the other. That said, in the official 1911 publication '*Priced Vocabulary of Clothing and Necessaries*', it is clear that at that period there was a marked difference between the Warrant Officers/Staff-Sergeants cap and that of the sergeants, details of which are given in appendix two. It is however known, that at one time, Warrant Officers holding the position of either Regimental Sergeant Major, or Bandmaster in certain lancer regiments wore a plume of swan feathers in

RIGHT - *Figure 49:* 'A SENTRY OF THE 21ST LANCERS.' A contemporary commercial postcard of a sentry on guard at Hampton Court Palace c.1905. Note the crimping to the plume. Card dated 1906. David Rowe collection.

BELOW - *Figure 50:* 'THE GUARD OF THE 21ST LANCERS c.1906.' A contemporary commercial postcard, the photograph taken at either Aldershot or Hounslow Barracks, card dated 1906. Note that once again crimped plumes are being worn. David Rowe collection.

Figure 51: 21st Lancers. A fine study of a Victorian other ranks pattern cap complete with plume. Just visible is the regimental pattern button to the centre of the worsted plume boss. N.B. This cap bears the regiments second pattern lance cap plate. Copyright W.Y. Carman.

their caps, and perhaps this was the difference between these two pattern of caps, although this has not been confirmed.

The known major differences between a 'troopers' cap and that of a Warrant Officers/N.C.O.'s pattern are worthy of being recorded, and are therefore listed below. N.B. These variations would probably not apply in the 9th Lancers, where their special pattern of cap would have been worn.

(a) The four angles (corners) of the ribbed cloth section were covered with gold braid as opposed to yellow cord, and it is possible that the metal ornamental corner pieces were gilded.

(b) The plume boss was of gold gimp and orris cord[5], as illustrated in *Fig: 52.*, being wound around the 'body of the boss' some eight times, with to the centre of the boss a worsted centre in the regimental facing colour, mounted with a small metal regimental pattern button. N.B. Although not confirmed, it is likely that the centre button was of gilt metal.

(c) Encircling the waist of the cap, a one inch band of gold lace in place of the yellow cotton braid on the troopers cap. N.B. It is known that in the 12th, and 17th Lancers the gold lace had a central blue lace stripe. N.B. *See Fig: 52.* for an example of the 17th Lancers cap.

(d) The standard pattern, one piece die-struck plate was of gilded metal.

(e) The cap lines were of gold cord as opposed to the yellow worsted cord for the troopers cap (39).

(f) As mentioned earlier, it appears to have been the accepted practice for Warrant Officers holding the post of R.S.M. or Bandmaster to wear officers pattern swan feathers plumes in their caps.

H.M. Reserve Regiment of Lancers

As stated in the previous chapter, Reserve Regiments of Dragoon Guards, Dragoons, Hussars, and Lancers were raised during the period c.1900 to 1902. Army Order No's 77, 78[6], 79 (April), and 129 (June) of 1900, gave details of enlistment, terms of service, and dress etc.[7] (48), with the cap badge also a previously described, but being of brass and white metal.

An Other Ranks Pattern Plate (*See Fig: 53.*)

Examples of what is incorrectly claimed to be the other ranks pattern plate of the Reserve Regiment of Lancers have over the years frequently been offered for sale in militaria auctions. However the shape of this particular plate did not 'lend' itself to being fitted to the full dress lance cap, and of the various ideas put forward regarding the wearing of this plate, the authoritative opinion that these plates were worn on the foreign service helmet (as detailed below) does seem to be the most credible, although it is likely that the debate regarding the wearing of these plates on any form of headdress will probably continue for many years to come.[8]

The pattern of plate concerned[9] was made of brass/gilding metal, and comprised of a twelve-pointed star[10], to the centre of which was the garter inscribed with the garter motto of "Honi. Soit. Qui. Mal. Y. Pense". The centre of the garter was voided, having a Victorian crown upon crossed lances, backed by black leather, the pennons and butts of the lances extending beyond the outer oval of the garter. N.B. To the reverse of this pattern of plate were two brass loops.

The original design for this plate was on thin card, with written in ink the reference 'PC/CAV/123 2584/1879 For foreign pattern cork helmet Universal for Regts of Lancers'. The actual 'badges' had a fixing at the back of screws and nuts, which could easily go through the white covered helmet worn on service abroad. This pattern of helmet which was described in G.O. 27 of 1877, was to be worn during the hot season by Staff and Departmental officers at all foreign stations etc (116).

The order for introducing the new white covered helmet included the words for 'All men of our Army' and so the date of 1879 must be when a plate was produced to be worn on the helmet of the lancers. Whether it was used or not has not been proven in photographs etc, but designs were made for both the 12th, and the 17th Lancers.

Figure 52: 'A Sergeant of the 17th Lancers.' A fine study of a sergeant of the regiment c.1890, in which he proudly displays his medals. Note. Just visible is the gold gimp and orris cord plume boss, and the gold lace to the waist of the cap. Also of interest is the skull and crossed bones arm badge worn upon his sergeants chevrons. Copyright D.P.& G.

NOTES

1. At some period in time, the black patent leather top of the other ranks cap of the 17th Lancers was changed to white patent leather, possibly upon the introduction of the plate bearing honours to '*South Africa 1879*'. N.B. Examples of the other ranks cap of the 17th Lancers having the black leather top are extremely rare.

2. With regard to the regimental button positioned to the centre of the plume boss, it is not unusual for a cap to have a Victorian pattern button to the boss, but bear a post 1902 King's crown pattern cap plate.

3. 'The 12th Lancers had a blue central stripe as early as 1843' (6).

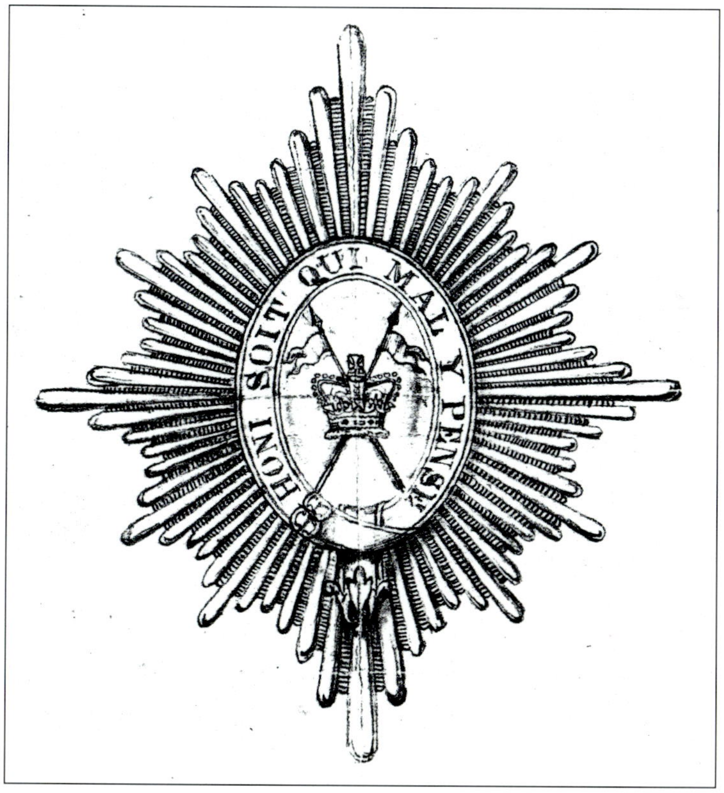

Figure 53: A detailed sketch of the plate for the foreign service pattern, cork helmet, frequently wrongly referred to in Auction House saleroom catalogues as being for the Reserve Regiment of Lancers. Copyright W.Y. Carman.

Figure 53A: An example of the actual plate often inaccurately referred to as being for the Reserve Regiment of Lancers. Courtesy of Hugh King. Photo: R. Biondi.

4. The peak of the cap should be proportionate to the skull of the cap. This point is well worth checking, as it is not unknown for the peak to have been reduced in depth by the edge of the peak having been trimmed, either officially (possibly to aid wearers visibility), or due to the edge of the peak having been damaged.

5. This gold cord was similar in appearance to the gold cord that extended across the top and down the angles on the officers pattern cap of the 5th, 12th, 16th, 17th, and 21st Lancers.

6. The Special Army Order 29th May 1900, states '3. Clothing of Men'. '*The scale of clothing will be notified in paragraph 8 of Army Order 78 of 1900 for mounted men, with the addition of gloves for regiments not receiving gloves with the free kit of necessaries*'. '*The general description of clothing will be the same as that for officers referred to in preceding paragraphs*'.

'The instructions regarding clothing contained in the Order quoted above, will, so far as they are applicable, govern the supply to Her Majesty's Reserve Regiments of Cavalry'.

'*Field cap, collar, and shoulder chain badges will be of the same design as approved for officers*' (50).

7. 'The reserve regiments were formed from retired soldiers who signed on for a twelve month period. They were not required to serve abroad, their only function being to garrison the cavalry stations in this country to enable these garrisons (regular regiments) to be sent abroad. In the original Army Orders of the period, instructions to the doctors examining these men on enrollment made these points quite clear, pointing out that since they were not required for active service abroad, they need not be too particular with regards to their general fitness.' (49).

8. Walter Lambert of the Crown Imperial Society, who has made a special study of this subject states that he is of 'the opinion that the star type helmet plates bearing the *VR* cypher or that of *Edward VII* have nothing to do with the Boer War Reserve Regiments. These regiments had a very short life, being replaced by Provisional Cavalry Regiments, as a study of the Army Lists covering the period shows. I think it follows from this they would not have had two helmet plates bearing the *VR* or *ER VII* cyphers, there would just not have been enough time' 'This should be borne in mind when covering that other fiction put about regarding the alleged Reserve Regiment of Lancers lance cap plate.' (49).

9. A plate described as being of the Reserve Regiment of Lancers that sold at a Sussex Auction Saleroom, was set forth as being 'a gilt HP of HM Reserve Regiment of Lancers, probably for senior N.C.O.'s'.

10. Both the star and the garter on the Foreign Service plate of 1879 were similar, if not identical to the pattern worn on the other ranks full dress helmet of both the dragoon guards and dragoons.

Chapter Nine

The Bandsman's Lance Cap

In the past it had been the practice to clothe regimental trumpeters in 'reversed' clothing, that is to say if the jacket of the regiment was blue and had red facings, then the trumpeters would wear a red jacket with blue facings, however as this easily distinguished them and made them an easy target for the enemy, it was decided to clothe trumpeters the same as the privates of the regiment.

Thereafter to distinguish a musician they wore red plumes to their head-dress, and when regimental bands became popular, with the expenses of their uniforms being borne by regimental funds, white garments were chosen. This is illustrated in paintings of Lt Colonel T. Wildman and Captain P.B. Williams who are accompanied by trumpeters wearing white topped caps having large red plumes, and white jackets, and although these paintings are not dated they are of the pre 1830 period. N.B. In November 1834 a general order stated that cavalry trumpeters were to be dressed in red, thus forbidding the white garments including the white topped cap, however the red plume continued to be worn by bandsmen and trumpeters (5).

The practice of trumpeters and musicians wearing a plume of a different colour to the that worn by the other members of the regiment continued in the heavy cavalry regiments[1], examples of which are given below. In Addition to this head-dress distinction, it was not unknown for the kettle-drummer to have worn a plume that contrasted in colour from the plumes of the other musicians in the band, as was the case in the 1st (Royal) Dragoons c.1895 who wore a black over white plume, whilst his band colleagues wore white plumes. N.B. Kettle-drummers and trumpeters were members of the regiment, and not of the band.

Regimental Plume Colours c.1900

Regiment	Band Members	The Regiment
1st Dragoon Guards	White[2]	Red.
2nd Dragoon Guards	White	Black.
3rd Dragoon Guards	White[3]	Black over red.
4th Dragoon Guards	Black & white	White.
5th Dragoon Guards	Red	Red over white.
6th Dragoon Guards	Red	White.
7th Dragoon Guards	Black	Black over white.
1st Dragoons	White	Black.
2nd Dragoons	Red[4]	White.
6th Dragoons	Red	White. (6).

In light of the above, it might have been expected that the band members of each of the six regular lancer regiments would also have adopted distinguishable coloured plumes. This however was not to be, for it is known that the plume of the musicians and trumpeters was of the same colour as that of the other members of the regiment concerned. This uniformity may clearly be seen in the photographic illustration of the kettle-drummer of the 9th Lancers c.1912 that appears in *Regiment Magazine*, issue Forty-Seven (14), and the copy of a coloured painting by Doug Hagger of the kettle-drummer of the 16th Lancers c.1888 that also appeared in this magazine. This uniformity of plume colour may also be seen in the copy of a contemporary commercial postcard depicting the dismounted band of the 21st Lancers of the period c.1907/08 illustrated in *Fig: 56.*, and a similar photographic illustration of the kettle-drummer of the same regiment c.1905 as illustrated in *Fig: 54.* Notwithstanding the above, it is recorded that in the notes of R. Ebsworth, that c.1850 the trumpeter of the 9th (The Queen's Royal) Light Dragoons (Lancers) wore a scarlet coloured lance cap[5] complete with a plume of the same colour (45), and even earlier, it appears that a cap having a white top had for a short period been worn by trumpeters of the 9th. Additionally although not textually recorded, it is observed in illustrations and pictures of the post 1823 period, that the trumpeters of the 17th Lancers are on occasions depicted as having red and yellow lace, and large red hair plume to their cap (5).

The Post 1918 Period

Sometime prior to the outbreak of hostilities in 1914, the wearing of full dress uniform was discontinued and never officially restored. That said, with this war eventually over and a return to peace, there

Figure 54: Drum horse of the 21st Lancers 1905. A contemporary commercial postcard, the photograph probably taken at Hounslow. Card dated 21st December 1905. Note the white plume to the kettle-drummers cap. Author's collection.

were occasions when this order of dress was once again to be seen, being worn by members of a regiment performing in a musical ride, engaged in a recruitment drive, or performing as members of a regimental band, the musicians of which are known to have worn full dress uniform through the 1920s, and up until sometime before the outbreak of World War II.

The Post 1945 Period

With the return once more to peace, it might have been hoped that the band members might have been permitted to return to the full dress uniform of the pre war era, this however was not to be. The musicians of the respective bands were apparently restricted to wearing 'Blues' (No.1 Dress) complete with peaked caps, it being recorded that the band of the 17th/21st Lancers were still wearing this order of dress in 1970 (51), albeit that full dress was to occasionally be seen being worn by soldiers detailed for marker duty etc, on ceremonial occasions (52).

The 1980s

By the early 1980s (53), the bands of the three regular lancer regiments had once more taken to wearing the full dress uniform complete with lance caps and plumes, albeit that the caps were no longer made of patent leather and cloth, but of fibre glass.[6] The lance cap plate borne on these 'new style' lance caps were those of the former

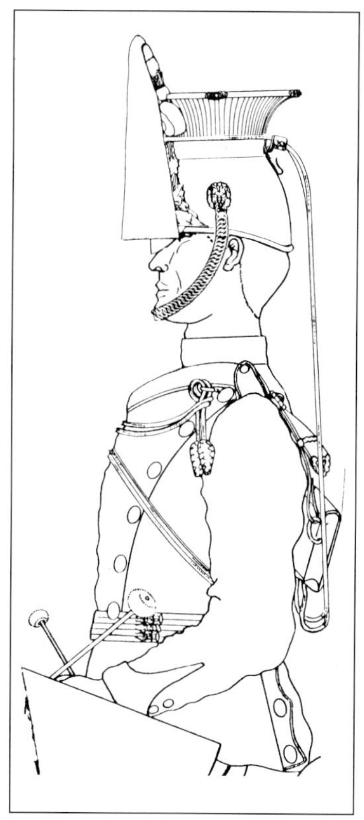

Figure 55: An excellent line drawing of the kettle-drummer of a lancer regiment in full dress uniform. Artist unknown. Author's collection.

Figure 56: The Band of the 21st Lancers leaving church after a regimental church parade. A contemporary commercial postcard, the photograph most probably taken at Aldershot Garrison c.1907/08. N.B. Photographs of this period show that the above weekly event was extremely popular with the residents of a garrison town. Card undated. Author's collection.

combined 9th and 12th Lancers, and the united 16th and 5th Lancers, although for the 17th/21st Lancers for some unknown reason, their caps bore a new pattern of plate as illustrated in *Fig: 57.*

The 1990s

The theme of the Royal Tournament, which up until 1999 was held annually at the Earls Court Exhibition Centre, varied each year, the main subject of the 1991 show being the cavalry. Performing at this important military spectacle were the massed bands of all the cavalry regiments in existence at that time, many of which have subsequently been amalgamated.

This was a glorious event, with all the musicians present wearing their full dress uniforms, there being a mixture of head-dress comprised of the following. The white metal helmets of the Household Cavalry, the brass helmets of the 1st The Queen's Dragoon Guards, the 4th/7th Royal Dragoon Guards, and the 5th Royal Inniskilling Dragoon Guards, the bearskins of The Royal Scots Dragoon Guards, the busbies of The Queen's Own Hussars, The Queen's Royal Irish Hussars, The Royal Hussars (PWO), the 13th/18th Royal Hussars (QMO), the 14th/20th King's Hussars, and the 15th/19th The King's Royal Hussars, the lance caps of the 9th/12th Royal Lancers (Prince of Wales's), the 16th/5th The Queen's Royal Lancers, and the 17th/21st Lancers, and last, but by no means least, the berets of The Royal Tank Regiment (54).

Whilst the performing musicians of the three lancers bands wore their fibre glass lance caps, two of the Bandmaster's present wore original caps. W.O.I. (Bandmaster) G.J. Bright[7] of the 9th/12th Royal Lancers (Prince of Wales's) wore an officers pattern lance cap of the former 12th (Prince of Wales's Royal) Lancers, complete with silvered and gilt plate, and scarlet swan feathers plume, the remainder of his uniform being similar to the officers pattern (55). W.O.I (Bandmaster) G.O. Jones[8] of the 16th/5th The Queen's Royal Lancers also wore an officers pattern cap, this being an example of the former 16th (Queen's) Lancers, complete with Victorian pattern lance cap plate, and black swan feathers plume (58), the remainder of his uniform also being similar to the officers pattern (55).

The cap worn by the Bandmaster of the band of the 17th/21st Lancers, W.O.I. K.J. Harrod[9] was the Warrant Officers pattern lance cap, being similar to the cap worn by the other members of the band, being made of fibre glass and having the one piece lance cap plate, but having gold braid covering the major part of the leather peak, and being worn with a white feather plume in place of the hair plume (21), the remainder of his uniform being of similar quality to that of the other Bandmasters.

Some twelve months after the amalgamation of the 16th/5th Lancers and the 17th/21st Lancers on the 25th June 1993, the bands of the two former regiments combined to form the band of The

Figure 57: Bandsmans lance cap plate of the 17th/21st Lancers. die-stamped plate, the rayed plate being in gold anodised finish, with the 'motto' (skull and crossbones), and the title scroll being in silver anodised finish. N.B. These plates were apparently produced for the band, and 'ceremonial party' only (123). Courtesy of Hugh King Photo: R. Biondi.

Queen's Royal Lancers, under the leadership of Bandmaster[10] W.O.1. G.O. Jones mentioned earlier. The uniform worn by the band members at that time was that of both the two former regiments concerned until c.1995, when they merged with the band of the 9th/12th Royal Lancers (Prince of Wales's) to form the Lancers Band.[11]

The newly formed band was stationed at Bovington, Dorset, the musicians wearing the full dress uniforms of the three former regiments (9th/12th, 16th/5th and 17th/21st Lancers), until for a period of time they reverted to wearing 'blues'(No.1 Dress). They later adopted a full dress uniform, similar to that worn by the band of the 9th/12th, although it appears that lance caps were not worn. N.B. In 1999, the Lancers Band was posted to Munster, Germany for a five/six year tour of duty (57).

The Year 2000 and Onwards

Approximately six years later in 1999, our friend Hugh King informed us that he had loaned lance cap plates of the former 17th Lancers, and the 21st Lancers to Messrs Firmin and Sons[12], and that John Gaylor had loaned this same company an other ranks pattern lance cap. We were further advised that the reason for these items being loaned, was that Firmin's had been awarded the Ministry of Defence contract to supply the lance caps for the '*Lancers Band*'.

Nothing more was heard regarding the above, until early March the following year when David Rowe contacted Louis Chalmers of The Plumery to discuss the various patterns of plumes produced by his business. During this conversation Mr Chalmers mentioned that they were making thirty-four lance caps for the Lancers Band, with one number cap being retained by the Ministry of Defence as a sealed pattern. Coming across such positive information was a real revelation, even more so when Louis kindly invited the author to visit his premises to view the component parts being used in the construction of this cap. N.B. Further relevant information regarding The Plumery, and its extensive range of plumes may be found at the end of this chapter.

Two months later, David Rowe accompanied by his friend Geoff Frost, who very kindly volunteered to photograph the component parts of the cap on our behalf, visited The Plumery, at their premises in Chiswick, West London, where they were made most welcome by Louis Chalmers. In a taped interview, Louis explained at great length the various methods used in the manufacture of a lance cap, all of which are hand made, and the following description is based on an edited transcript of this taped interview, reproduced below by kind permission of Mr Chalmers. Regrettably, at the time of our visit, there was not a completed example of the new lance cap available for Geoff to photograph. N.B. The metal fittings, such as the lance cap plate, the top corner ornaments, the lion's head bosses, the hook and ring to the rear waist of the cap, and the chinchain, are all being supplied by Messrs Firmin and Sons, of Birmingham.[12]

Figure 58: The Royal Yeomanry. A fine study of the Bandmaster of the regiment c.1985 by the respected military photographer Brian Daly. Of special interest is the officers pattern shoulder belt, the 1908 pattern sword, and the gold braid to the peak of the cap. The uniform is closely based on that of the former City of London Yeomanry (The Rough Riders). Note. The body of the lance cap appears to be made of fibre glass.

Sealed Pattern

As the Ministry of Defence always work on a sealed pattern basis, they would normally send a sealed pattern example of the item to be produced to the manufacturer concerned to enable a sample to be made. However, no sealed pattern of an other ranks pattern lance cap appeared to exist, and for some reason the possibility of seeking the assistance of the regimental museum was overlooked. At a meeting held with the M.O.D., the only example put forward by their representative upon which to base a sample cap was the fibre glass cap with the black skull and white top, worn by the musicians of the band of the 17th/21st Lancers.

The Plumery were requested to produce a sample cap based on dress regulations, and this was accordingly carried out. However, at an arranged meeting, and upon seeing the sample cap provided, the Ministry's representative remarked that 'it does not look like one of these' drawing a comparison with the overall shape, and the waist on the 17th/21st Lancers fibre glass cap.

The team from The Plumery were constantly disappointed with the inherent weakness of the unintelligible ideas that were presented to them when discussing the revival of the bandsman lance cap. In spite of the above, the shape of the waist and other modifications identified were duly taken account of, and were carried out on the next sample cap made. This cap was duly accepted, albeit that The Plumery team felt very strongly that the newly designed cap had suffered in its overall appearance, due to the final say in its design resting with people who had no knowledge of the history of this form of head-dress. Authors note. It is hardly surprising that the first sample cap produced did not look like the fibre glass cap, as the only lance cap described in dress regulations is the officers pattern, which differs considerably in appearance and shape from the other ranks cap.

The Lance Cap of the Lancers Band

The Top and Upper Section

The top of the cap is of *black leather*, the scarlet cloth (web) sides being backed with buckram, and having machine made 'pockets' into which are inserted thin strips of cane, originally being of real cane, but later substituted for plastic cane to give extra strength. The insertion of these 'cane' strips gives the scarlet cloth sides a 'ribbed' appearance (*See Fig: 59A.*), the sides of the caps strength being in the combination of the web/buckram, cane inserts, and the stitching. Additionally, wire supports are used on the inside of the cap, being positioned at the four corners (angles), which are embellished on the outside by the use of square yellow cord/braid which is secured by adhesive, and sewn into place, the four top corners being decorated with gilding metal corner pieces. *See Fig: 59B.* for an illustration of the square yellow braid/cord. It is not surprising that the upper part of the cap, comprising the square leather top and ribbed cloth sides is the hardest part of the cap to make, with the leather top being sewn to the top of the scarlet cloth sides, it taking some four hours to complete this task. N.B. Scarlet was the facing

The authors express their sincere thanks to Louis Chalmers ofThe Plumery for kindly permitting the following photographs (taken by Geoff Frost) relating to the bandsmans lance cap of the Lancers Band, to be taken at his premises.

Figure 59: An assemblage of many of the component parts that are used in the manufacture of the other ranks lance cap. Photo: Geoff Frost.

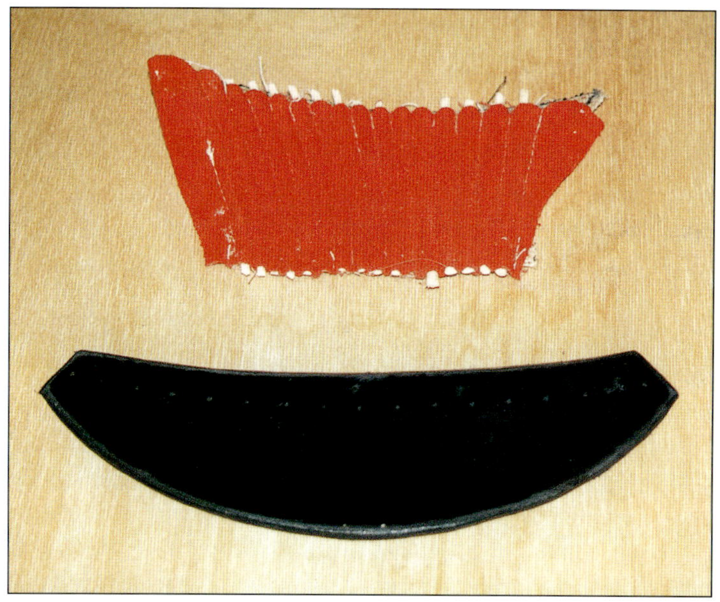

Figure 59A: The scarlet ribbed cloth section (sides), with the 'cane' inserts just visible at the top and bottom of the ribbed pockets, below which is the black leather front peak. Photo: Geoff Frost.

Figure 59B: An unused 'bundle' of the square yellow braid that is used to decorate the four angles (corners) of the scarlet cloth section of the cap. Photo: Geoff Frost.

colour of the former 5th Royal Irish Lancers, it being the colour used for the cloth sides of their lance caps prior to their amalgamation in 1922.

To the upper left of the cloth sides of the cap is mounted a plume boss made of wood, covered with red upon yellow wool and having a regimental pattern button to its centre, behind which is located the brass socket to accommodate the stem of the plume. N.B. The red and yellow boss is the colour used on the caps of both the former 5th, and 16th Lancers.

The Skull and Peak

The skull is of black leather lined with shellac felt, which is steamed into shape (*See Fig: 59D.*). The leather is immersed in water to soften it, then stretched over a wooden head block to form the shape of the skull, an example of which is illustrated in *Fig: 60.*, whereupon the leather is sewn together by a leather specialist. To take account of varying head sizes, four different size head blocks are used, plus one additional block that opens and closes to accommodate other different cap sizes, such as might be required for a female member of the band.

Once sewn and dry, a coat of black coach paint is applied to the leather skull, which when fully dry, is sanded down and then sprayed. N.B. Problems were experienced with the original patent leather used for the skulls, as these days the leather is no longer oil based, but plastic based, which resulted in the plastic element causing the patent leather to return to its original shape when stretched. This problem however has now been addressed.

The scarlet cloth side section of the cap is attached to the leather skull by these two component parts being sewn together with linen thread, the stitching and join being hidden from view by a band of yellow braid[13] which is sewn, and held in place by adhesive. This braid has a central red stripe and encircles the waist of the cap, red being the colour of stripe used on the waistband of the cap of both the former 5th Royal Irish Lancers and the 16th Queen's Lancers. The leather peak (*See Fig: 59A.*) is sewn to the lower front edge of the skull, the join being hidden from view by the lance cap plate.

Figure 59C: Front view of the shaped leather skull. Note the shellac felt to the interior of the skull. Photo: Geoff Frost.

Figure 59D: Side view of the skull illustrating the familiar shape of the skull. Photo: Geoff Frost.

Figure 59E: A roll of the yellow braid that encircles the waist of the cap. Note the red stripe to the centre of the braid, as used on the former 5th Lancers cap. Photo: Geoff Frost.

The Lance Cap Plate (*See Fig: 61.*)

The brass plate is very closely based on the pattern used by the former 21st Lancers (Empress of India's), being the example bearing the Royal Arms, and not the version having a circlet surmounted by a crown. To the lower centre of the plate is a scroll bearing the title '*Lancers Band*', upon which is the motto of the former 17th Lancers (Duke of Cambridge's Own) being a skull and crossed bones. N.B. It is of interest that the title on the scroll of the plate includes the word 'band', for if lance caps are to be worn by other members of the regiment engaged on ceremonial duties etc, then this pattern of plate would be inappropriate, this point having been pointed out to the representative of the M.O.D. by the respective management of both Firmin and Sons and The Plumery.

RIGHT - *Figure 60:* Front view of the wooden head block, upon which the leather of the skull is stretched and shaped. Note the makers name carved into the bottom edge of the block. Photo: Geoff Frost.

FAR RIGHT - *Figure 60A:* Offset view of a head block. Photo: Geoff Frost.

Figure 61: The bandsmans pattern lance cap plate. Compare the Royal Arms on this plate, with the arms on the plate of the 21st Lancers cap illustrated in *Fig: 50.* Photo: Geoff Frost.

The Chinchain and Ear Bosses
The brass chinchain is backed with black leather, being complete with standard pattern lion's head bosses.

The Head Lining

The head lining is comprised of a black leather sweatband backed with foam, having an upper section of black cotton, purchased at Shepherds Bush street market, complete with a drawstring. N.B. On the Victorian pattern caps the upper part of the lining was frequently of waxed cotton.

The Plume (*See Fig: 62.*)
The plume is of black Mongolian horsehair (humanely gathered), which measures sixteen inches overall, rising six inches, and dropping ten inches. The horsehair is woven onto a string, which is then wrapped around a square shaped metal stem, this particular task taking approximately one hour. The brass plume holder is of the standard other ranks pattern, just above which is positioned a brass ring, with a little way above the ring there being a piece of thread around the hair of the plume. The attaching of a piece of thread to the plume appears to have been unofficially introduced many years ago by the troopers to stop the plume 'going all over the place', and is continued on the present day plumes at the request of the Ministry of Defence. N.B. The black plume as mentioned above was the colour of plume of the former 16th The Queen's Lancers.

Officers pattern caps are also to be made, and these will have plumes made not of swan feathers as stated in the Dress Regulations of 1934, but of black cockerel feathers[14], this variety of feather having previously been used quite frequently for officers plumes.

Figure 62: The black horse hair plume for the bandsmans lance cap. Note. Just visible is the thread around the hair, used to 'stop the hair going all over the place'. Photo: Geoff Frost.

Figure 62A: The horse hair plume with the plume holder removed. Note the square shaped plume stem. Photo: Geoff Frost.

The Plumery
The Plumery originated in 1991 as a result of a workers buy-out of the small military plume department of Appleton Brothers, of Thames Works, Church Street, Chiswick, London, this company having been making plumes for nearly two hundred years. N.B. The workers buy-out was assisted both financially and logistically by Messrs Hobson & Sons, Military Tailors.

The Managing Director of the then, newly formed business trading as The Plumery, is Mr Louis Chalmers, who joined Appleton Brothers at the age on nineteen and 'served his time' under the watchful, but friendly eye of the late Elizabeth (Nellie) Smith. Nellie, who joined Appleton's in 1918, lived in London's famous Drury Lane, and frequently recounted tales of her experiences during the London Blitz. She continued making plumes right up until 1988, being awarded the British Empire Medal. Nellie is fondly remembered by Louis as being 'how your grandmother should be'.

Under Mr Chalmers leadership, The Plumery tendered for, and were successful in being awarded the sole contract for the supply of plumes to the Ministry of Defence, whose Defence Clothing and Textiles Agency oversees the purchase of military uniforms.

There are in excess of sixty different plumes being worn by the regiments and corps of the British Army, which includes the plumes worn by the famous regiments of the Brigade of Guards and the Household Cavalry Regiment, the plumes of the latter being made from best quality Mongolian horsehair, humanely gathered by being trimmed from the tails of live horses, which grow back for the following season's crop. They also make the beards (throat plumes) for the officers chargers of the Blues and Royals, the drum horses of both regiments, and for the trumpeters mounts of the Life Guards. N.B. In The Blues and Royals regiment, the officers helmet plumes are once again made of yak hair.

The Plumery also make the plumes for the King's Troop, Royal Horse Artillery, famed for their spectacular appearances at the now defunct Royal Tournament, as well as making plumes for both hussar and lancers officer head-dress. The lancer officers plumes measure some fourteen inches in front, and seven inches behind, from the bend of the feathers.

The supply of plumes is by no means confined to the many regiments of the British Army, the Botswana Defence Force, the Dutch Stitching Cavalerie Ere-Escorte, Lord Strathcona's Horse (Canada), and the Second Legion Augusta are but a few of the plume maker's recent customers. Plumes have also been produced for the makers of the famous 'Sharpe' television series, with the motion picture 'Gladiators' and the futuristic film epic 'Star Wars' being amongst numerous other film and theatre productions for which their services have been required.

In concluding the above, it is perhaps reasonable to say, that those of us who have a specific interest in military full dress, would wish to 'doff their caps' to Louis Chalmers and the staff at The Plumery, for without their stalwart efforts the head-dress of the present day British Army would most probably be bereft of their plumes, and collectors of busbies, helmets, and lance caps etc, would be hard put to obtain replacements for those items of head-dress missing their plume.

With regard to the products produced by The Plumery, and employing the old saying 'a picture is worth a thousand words', below are illustrated a small selection of the extensive range of plumes produced by The Plumery, that it is thought may be of interest to the reader.

Figure 63: Feathers as used in making an officers plume. One cannot but help wonder, just how many officers lance cap plumes could be made from this quantity of feathers. Photo: Geoff Frost.

Figure 63A: A selection of other ranks pattern plumes, including Coldstream Guards, The Life Guards, Welsh Guards, and Royal horse Artillery. Photo: Geoff Frost.

Figure 63B: Other ranks plume of the Kings Troop, Royal Horse Artillery (left), and Welsh Guards (right). Photo: Geoff Frost.

Figure 63C: Other ranks plume of The Royal Highland Fusiliers (left), and The Black Watch (right). Photo: Geoff Frost.

Figure 63D: Plume of the Polish Lancers Re-enactment Society. Photo: David Rowe.

NOTES

1. In the Life Guards, the trumpeters continue the tradition of wearing scarlet plumes in their helmets.

2. At this moment in time, the members of the band of the 1st The Queen's Dragoon Guards comprising the former 1st (King's) Dragoon Guards and 2nd Dragoon Guards (the Queen's Bays) wear white plumes in their helmets. N.B. The Bandmaster however wears a scarlet plume in his helmet.

3. The helmet plume of the band members of the 3rd Dragoon Guards changed from white to yellow c.1902.

4. In the present day band of the Royal Scots Dragoon Guards formed by the merger of the (3rd Carabiniers (Prince of Wales's Dragoon Guards) and The Royal Scots Greys (2nd Dragoons), the musicians wear scarlet hackles in their bearskins.

5. At this period in time, the regimental plume colour for the 9th was black, as was the colour of the sides of the cap (45).

6. The one-piece fibre glass caps had fluted sides to the upper (side) section, with leather being stretched over top of the cap and glued into place (44).

7. W.O.I. G.J. Bright, ARCM, LTCL, ALCM, Bandmaster of the 9th/12th Royal Lancers (Prince of Wales's), 1991. (54).

8. W.O.I. G.O. Jones, ARCM, Bandmaster of the 16th/5th The Queen's Royal Lancers, 1991 (54).

9. W.O.I. K.J. Harrod, BBCM, Bandmaster of the 17th/21st Lancers, 1991 (54).

10. Upon the formation of the newly titled '*Lancers Band*', the band came under the leadership of the Director of Music, this appointment being held by a commissioned officer (57).

11. In an article on The Queen's Royal Lancers in Regiment Magazine, it is recorded that 'the final parade of the regimental band of The Queen's Royal Lancers took place on 11th July 1994 at Osnabruck' (16).

12. Firmin & Son of Birmingham, originally established in London more than three hundred years ago, manufacture the helmets and cuirasses of the Household Cavalry Regiment, as well as supplying specialty items to the Queen's Bodyguard for Scotland, the Royal Company of Archers, and cap badges to the regiments of the British Army.

13. The yellow cord and braid for the waist of the cap is supplied by Messrs Wydean Weaving (44).

14. Cockerel feathers are used, as approximately only eight inches of feather can gainfully be put to use from the wing of a swan (44).

Chapter Ten

Guide to Patterns of Lance Cap Plate

It was often the practice, that following the award of new battle honours to a lancer regiment, that a new pattern lance cap plate was produced on which was displayed the additional honours awarded. This, together with the change of lance cap plate occasioned by the accession to the throne of Queen Victoria, and later King Edward VII resulted in each of the lancer regiments having had several differing patterns of lance plate during the period that the lance cap was worn. Additionally it is known that for some of the regiments, the position of the various battle honours on the plate were changed. It is also not unknown for the date of the battle for which the honour was awarded, to be added after the honour concerned, e.g. Kandahar becoming Kandahar 1880 (9th Lancers), the consequence of these additions and amendments resulting in several differing pattern plates being manufactured.

The following regimental guide of the many differing types of lance cap plate produced, is compiled of the various patterns of plate known to the authors. Whilst this guide may be judged to be comprehensive, it should not be considered as definitive, as confirmed information relating to the 1816 pattern plate is to say the least extremely scarce, and it is possible that a plate shown as Type: A., may not in fact be the very first pattern for the regiment concerned. Additionally, following the list of lance cap plates relating to each of the regiments is the date each battle honour was awarded. N.B. The date given for each battle honour is the date the honour was granted which may not always be the same date as the actual battle or campaign concerned, as honours were frequently awarded retrospectively.

Whilst as already stated, this guide is considered to be reasonably comprehensive, it is acknowledged that it is possible that within a private collection there may exist a rare pattern of plate which has as yet, remained unrecorded.

The following abbreviations have been used in the aforementioned 'Regimental Guide' to describe different patterns of crown that surmounted the Royal Arms on the lance cap plate. N.B. When describing the position of the various battle honours, the honours left and right relate to the reader directly facing the lance cap.

HAV: The full Hanoverian coat-of-arms complete with Royal Helmet and Mantling.

KC: The post 1902 'King's pattern crown surmounting the Royal Arms on the plate.

QA: The Royal Arms of Queen Adelaide.

QVC: The post 1837 pattern of Royal Arms.

RA: The Royal Arms of Mecklenberg-Sterlitz.

N.B.*: Indicates that this particular pattern of plates is illustrated within this chapter.

Once again the authors express their sincere thanks to Hugh King, President of the Aldershot Militaria Society, for kindly permitting the lance cap plates in his collection to be photographed and used as illustrations for this book. N.B. *Fig: 79* owned by G. Frost, and *Fig: 94* owned by W.Y. Carman.

Figure 64: A view of the standard pattern of officers rayed 'backplate', in which may be seen the holes for the 'pins' of the overlay, with the outer holes being used when the plate is secured to the skull of the cap.

5TH (ROYAL IRISH) LANCERS

		TITLE SCROLL	HONOURS LEFT	HONOURS CENTRE	HONOURS RIGHT
A	QVC[1]	Fifth Royal Irish	None	None	None
B*	QVC	Fifth Royal Irish Lancers	None	None	None
C*	QVC	Fifth Royal Irish Lancers	Blenheim Oudenarde	None	Ramillies, Malplaquet
D*	QVC[2]	Fifth Royal Irish Lancers	Suakin, Blenheim, Oudenarde	None	1885 Ramillies, Malplaquet
E	KC[2]	Fifth Royal Irish Lancers	Suakin, Blenheim, Oudenarde	None	1885 Ramillies Malplaquet
F*	KC	Fifth Royal Irish Lancers	Blenheim, Oudenarde, 'Defence of Ladysmith'	Suakin 1885	Ramillies, Malplaquet, 'South Africa 1899-1902'

1882: The battle honours 'Blenheim', 'Ramillies', 'Oudenarde', and 'Malplaquet' that had been awarded to the former 5th Royal Irish Dragoons to be carried by the 5th Lancers.
1885: Battle honour for 'Suakin' awarded.
1902: Battle honours for the 'Defence of Ladysmith' and 'South Africa 1899-1902' awarded.

Figure 65: A fine example of a Victorian officers, second pattern plate, having the word 'Lancers' within the title scroll.

Figure 66: Other ranks, second pattern plate. Compare this example with the officers pattern illustrated in *Fig: 65.*

Figure 67: Other ranks pattern plate now bearing the battle honours *'Blenheim', 'Oudenarde', 'Ramillies'* and *'Malplaquet'.*

Figure 68: A superb condition example of the officers post 1902 pattern plate, having the additional battle honour *'Suakin 1885'.*

Figure 69: Other ranks post 1902 pattern plate, having the additional battle honours of *'Defence of Ladysmith'*, and *'South Africa 1889-1902'*.

9TH (QUEEN'S ROYAL) LANCERS

		TITLE SCROLL	HONOURS LEFT	HONOURS CENTRE	HONOURS RIGHT
A	HAN	None	None	Peninsula	None
B	RA & QA	Royal Lancers A.R.[3] reversed	None	None[4]	None
C	QVC RA & QA	Royal Lancers A.R. reversed	Punniar, Sobraon, Peninsula	None	Chillianwallah, Goojerat, Punjaub
D*	QVC RA & QA	Royal Lancers A.R. reversed	Punniar, Sobraon, Peninsula[5], Delhi	None	Chillianwallah, Goojerat, Punjaub, Lucknow
E*	QVC RA & QA	Royal Lancers A.R. reversed	Punniar, Sobraon, Delhi, Peninsula[5]	None	Chillianwallah, Goojerat, Lucknow, Punjaub
F	QVC RA & QA	Royal Lancers A.R. reversed	Peninsula, Sobraon, Chillianwallah, Delhi, Charasiah, Kandahar	None	Punniar, Punjaub, Goojerat, Lucknow, Kabul, Afghanistan
G*	QVC RA & QA	Royal Lancers A.R. reversed	Peninsula, Sobraon, Chillianwallah, Delhi, Charasiah, Kandahar 1880	None	Punniar, Punjaub, Goojerat, Lucknow, Kabul 1879, 'Afghanistan 1878-80'
H	KC[6] RA & QA	Royal Lancers A.R. reversed	Peninsula, Sobraon, Chillianwallah, Delhi, Charasiah, Kandahar 1880	None	Punniar, Punjaub, Goojerat, Lucknow, Kabul 1879, 'Afghanistan 1878-80'
I*	KC RA & QA	Royal Lancers A.R. reversed	Peninsula, Sobraon, Chillianwallah, Delhi, Charasiah, Kandahar	None	Punniar, Punjaub, Goojerat, Lucknow, Kabul, Afghanistan
J*	KC RA & QA	Royal Lancers A.R. reversed	Sobraon, Peninsula, Charasiah, Chillianwallah, Delhi, Kandahar 1880, 'Relief of Kimberley'	Modder River (left) Paardeberg (right)	Punniar, Punjaub, Lucknow, Goojerat, Kabul 1879, 'Afghanistan 1878-80', 'South Africa 1899-1902'
K	KC RA & QA	Royal Lancers A.R. reversed	Peninsula, Sobraon, Chilliamwallah, Delhi, Charasiah, Kandahar 1880, 'Relief of Kimberley'	Modder River (left) Paardeberg (right),	Punniar, Punjaub, Goojerat, Lucknow, Kabul 1879, 'Afghanistan 1878-80', 'South Africa 1899-1902',

1815: By 1815 the battle honour 'Peninsula' had been awarded.
1844: Battle honours for 'Punniar', 'Sobraon', 'Chillianwallah', 'Goojerat', and 'Punjaub' awarded.
1857: Battle honour for 'Delhi' awarded.
1858: Battle honour for 'Lucknow' awarded.

1879: Battle honour for 'Kabul 1879' awarded.
1880: Battle honours for 'Afghanistan 1878-80', 'Charasiah', and 'Kandahar 1880' awarded.
1899: Battle honour for 'Modder River' awarded.
1900: Battle honours for 'Relief of Kimberley', and 'Paardeberg' awarded.
1902: Battle honour 'South Africa 1899-1902' awarded.

Figure 70: A fine example of a Victorian officers pattern plate, having eight battle honours.

Figure 71: The other ranks pattern plate. Compare this example with the officers pattern illustrated in *Fig: 70.*

Figure 72: Officers Victorian pattern plate, having the battle honours *'Delhi'* and *'Lucknow'* positioned differently. Compare this plate with the officers pattern illustrated in *Fig: 70*.

Figure 73: Other ranks pattern plate, having the additional battle honours of 'Charasiah', 'Kandahar 1880', 'Kabul 1879', and Afghanistan 1878-80'.

Figure 74: Officers post 1902 pattern plate on which the date is not given after the battle honour.

Figure 75: A fine example of the Officers post 1902 pattern plate, having the additional battle honours of *Relief of Kimberley', 'Modder River', 'Paardeberg',* and *'South Africa 1899-1902'.*

Figure 76: An other ranks pattern plate of the post 1902 period. Compare with the officers pattern as illustrated in *Fig: 75.*

12TH (PRINCE OF WALES'S ROYAL) LANCERS

		TITLE SCROLL	HONOURS LEFT	HONOURS CENTRE	HONOURS RIGHT
A	HAN[7]	None	Waterloo	12 Egypt	Peninsula
B[*]	HAN[8]	None	Waterloo	Sphinx Egypt	Peninsula
C[*]	QVC	None	Peninsula	Sphinx, Egypt, Sevastopol	Waterloo
D	QVC	None	Central, Peninsula	Sphinx, Egypt, Sevastopol	India, Waterloo
E[*]	QVC	None	'South Africa 1851.2.3.', Peninsula	Sphinx, Egypt, Sevastopol	Central India, Waterloo
F[*]	KC[9]	None	'South Africa 1851.2.3', Peninsula, 'South Africa 1899-1902'	Sphinx, Egypt, Sevastopol, Paardeberg	Central India Waterloo, 'Relief of Kimberley'

1816: By this time the battle honours 'Sphinx' for Egypt, 'Peninsula', and 'Waterloo' had already been awarded.
1853: Battle honour for 'South Africa 1851-2-3' awarded.
1855: Battle honour for 'Sevastopol' awarded.
1858: Battle honour for 'Central India' awarded.
1900: Battle honours for 'Relief of Kimberley', and 'Paardeberg' awarded.
1902: Battle honour 'South Africa 1899-1902' awarded.

Figure 77: A really fine example of a post 1837 pattern plate. Note the early pattern Royal Arms on which the Royal Helmet and Mantling are shown.

Figure 78: Rear view of the above plate. Of interest is the method of affixing the five piece overlay to the plate, by use of nuts and studs. N.B. the overlay was comprised of (1) the P.O.W. feathers and coronet, (2) the Royal Arms, (3) the sphinx over '*Egypt*', (4) the scroll bearing '*Waterloo*', and (5) the scroll bearing '*Peninsula*'.

Figure 79: A fine and rare example of the N.C.O.'s post 1837 pattern plate. Of particular interest is the silver Prince of Wales's feathers which is attached to the die-stuck brass plate by means of four thin metal pins attached to the rear of the 'feathers' being pushed through corresponding holes in the rayed plate, and then bent flat. Geoff Frost collection. Photo: G. Frost.

Figure 80: Other ranks Victorian pattern plate, having the additional battle honour '*Sevastopol*'.

Figure 81: Officers Victorian pattern plate having the additional battle honours '*South Africa 1851.2.3*' and '*Central India*'.

Figure 82: The Other ranks pattern of the plate illustrated in *Fig: 81*.

Figure 83: Other ranks pattern plate, a makers variation on the pattern illustrated in *Fig: 82*.

Figure 84: A further variation on this pattern of plate. Compare the shape of the P.O.W.'s feathers and coronet, and the detail to the sphinx on *Figs: 82.* and *83*.

Figure 85: View of the reverse of the plate illustrated in Fig: 84. Note the steel washers, and brass 'hooped' nuts used to secure the plate to the skull of the cap.

Figure 86: A fine officers post 1902 pattern plate, having the additional battle honours '*South Africa 1899-1902*', '*Paardeberg*', and '*Relief of Kimberley*'.

Figure 87: An other ranks post 1902 pattern plate. Compare this plate with officers pattern illustrated in *Fig: 86.*

16TH (QUEEN'S) LANCERS

		TITLE SCROLL	HONOURS LEFT	HONOURS AND DEVICES CENTRE	HONOURS RIGHT
A	HAN[10]	None	Peninsula	Queens	Waterloo
B	HAN[11]	None	Peninsula	Bhurtpore, Queens 16	Waterloo
C*		None	Peninsula, Bhurtpore, Maharajpore	Queens, Ghuznee, Aliwal 16	Waterloo, Afghanistan, Sobraon
D	QVC	None	Fuentes, D'Onor, Vittoria, Aliwal, Afghanistan[12], Bhurtpore	Nive, Peninsula, Waterloo	Talavera[12], Salamanca, Sobraon, Maharajpore, Ghuznee
E*	QVC	Sixteenth Lancers	Talavera, Fuentes, D'Onor, Afghanistan, Nive, Waterloo, Salamanca	Maharajpore	Vittoria, Bhurtpore, Sobraon, Ghuznee, Peninsula, Aliwal
F*	KC	Sixteenth Lancers	Talavera, Fuentes, D'Onor, Afghanistan, Nive, Waterloo, Salamanca, 'South Africa 1900-02'	Maharajpore, Paardeberg	Vittoria, Bhurtpore, Sobraon, Ghuznee, Peninsula, Aliwal, 'Relief of Kimberley'
G*	KC	Sixteenth Lancers	Beaumont, Talavera, Fuentes, D'Onor, Afghanistan, Nive, Waterloo, Salamanca, 'South Africa 1900-02'	Maharajpore, Paardeberg	Willems, Vittoria, Bhurtpore, Sobraon, Ghuznee, Peninsula, Aliwal, 'Relief of Kimberley'

1815: By this time the battle honours for 'Peninsula' and 'Waterloo' had been awarded. 1826: Battle honour for 'Bhurtpore' awarded.
1840: Battle honours for 'Afghanistan' and 'Ghuznee' awarded.
1844: Battle for 'Maharajpore' awarded.
c.1848: Battle honours for 'Aliwal' and 'Sobraon' awarded, with late recognition of honours 'Talavera' (May 1809), 'Salamanca' (July 1812), 'Vittoria' (June 1813), 'Nive' (Dec 1813), and 'Fuentes D'Onor' (April 1818). N.B. According to Major Parkyn's book 'Shoulder-belt-Plates' the honours for Talavara, Salamanca, Vittoria, Nive, and Fuentes D'Onor are quoted as being granted on the 16th April 1818, although these honours do not appear on the lance cap plate at that period, nor do they appear for many more years to come.
1900: Battle honours for 'Relief of Kimberley', and 'Paardeberg' awarded.
1902: Battle honour 'South Africa 1900-02' awarded.
1910: The battle honours for 'Beaumont', and 'Willems', both dating from 1794 were awarded retrospectively c.1910.

Figure 88: An extremely rare pre 1856 pattern other ranks plate. Of interest is the helmet and mantling to the Royal Arms, the title '*Queens*' above the arms, and the number '16' to the centre base of the plate.

Figure 89: Reverse of the above plate, is which can be seen the square securing nuts.

Figure 90: A fine example of an Victorian officers pattern plate having thirteen battle honours.

Figure 91: The other ranks pattern plate having thirteen battle honours. Compare this plate with the officers version illustrated in *Fig: 90*.

Figure 92: A post 1902 other ranks plate with the additional battle honours '*South Africa 1900-02*', '*Paardeberg*', and '*Relief of Kimberley*'.

Figure 93: A truly superb example of a post 1902 officers pattern plate having eighteen battle honours, the additional honours being '*Beaumont*' and '*Willems*'.

17TH (DUKE OF CAMBRIDGE'S OWN) LANCERS

		TITLE SCROLL	HONOURS LEFT	HONOURS CENTRE	HONOURS RIGHT
A	HAN	Skull upon crossed bones and motto	None	None	None
B*	HAN	Skull above crossed bones and motto	None	None	None
C	HAN	Skull upon crossed bones and motto	None	None	None
D*	QVC	Skull upon crossed bones and motto, Seventeenth Lancers	Alma, Inkerman	None[13]	Balaclava, Sevastopol
E*	QVC	Skull upon crossed bones and motto D.O.C., Seventeenth Lancers	Alma, Inkerman, Central India	None	Balaclava, Sevastopol, 'South Africa 1879'
F*	KC	Skull upon crossed bones and motto D.O.C., Seventeenth Lancers	Alma, Inkerman, Central India	'South Africa 1900-02'	Balaclava, Sevastopol, 'South Africa 1879'

1856: The battle honours for 'Alma', 'Inkerman', 'Balaclava' and 'Sevastopol' awarded.
1858: The battle honour for 'Central India' awarded.
1879: The battle honour for 'South Africa' awarded.
1902: The battle honour 'South Africa 1900-02' awarded.

Figure 94: A Hanoverian pattern plate having the skull facing front and above the crossed bones - pre 1837. Courtesy of W.Y. Carman.

Figure 95: A Victorian other ranks pattern plate with four battle honours to '*Sevastopol*'.

Figure 96: A superb example of a Victorian officers plate, having six battle honours, the additional honours being '*Central India*' and '*South Africa 1879*'.

Figure 97: The other ranks pattern plate, having six battle honours to '*South Africa 1879*'.

Figure 98: A fine example of the post 1902 officers pattern plate, having seven battle honours, the additional battle honour being '*South Africa 1900-02*'.

Figure 99: The other ranks pattern plate, having seven battle honours. Compare this plate with the officers version as illustrated in *Fig: 98.*

19TH LANCERS

	TITLE SCROLL	HONOURS LEFT	HONOURS CENTRE	HONOURS RIGHT
HAV	None, An 'Elephant' below the honour 'Seringapatam'	Assaye[14]	Seringapatam	Niagara

This regiment was awarded the battle honours 'Seringapatam' (1799), 'Assaye' (1807), and 'Niagara', (1815).

21ST (EMPRESS OF INDIA'S) LANCERS

		TITLE SCROLL	HONOURS LEFT	HONOURS CENTRE	HONOURS RIGHT
A*	QVC	21st Lancers	None	None	None
B*	IMP[15]	Twenty First Lancers (circlet), VRI (centre of circlet), Empress of India's[16] (scroll)	None	Khartoum	None
C*	QVC	21st Empress of (left scroll), India's Lancers (right scroll), VRI	None	Khartoum	None
D*	KC	21st Empress of (left scroll), India's Lancers (right scroll), VRI	None	Khartoum	None

1898: The honour for 'Khartoum' was awarded.

Figure 100: A superb example of the first pattern officers plate. Note, both the helmet and the mantling are displayed upon the Royal Arms.

Figure 101: The other ranks first pattern plate. Compare the detail on this plate with that of the officers pattern illustrated in *Fig: 100.*

Figure 102: The officers pattern of plate having the 'Imperial' pattern crown. Note that on this plate, the Royal Arms has been omitted, that the title '*Empress of India's*' replaces '*21st Lancers*' on the lower scroll, that the battle honour '*Khartoum*' has been included, as have the initials '*VRI*' to the centre of the circlet.

Figure 103: An other ranks pattern plate bearing the Victorian crown, with the Royal Arms now again being displayed, with the regimental title now being on a two-part scroll, and the initials 'VRI' being positioned below the battle honour.

Figure 104: A truly fine example of the post 1902 officers pattern plate. Compare this Kings' pattern plate with the other ranks Victorian pattern illustrated in *Fig: 103*.

23RD LANCERS

	TITLE SCROLL	HONOURS LEFT	HONOURS CENTRE	HONOURS RIGHT
HAN	None	Peninsula, Waterloo	None, The Sphinx	Talavera, Egypt

1801: The 'Sphinx' for Egypt awarded.
1809: The battle honour for 'Talavera' awarded.
1815: The battle honours for 'Peninsula', and 'Waterloo' awarded.

Figure 105: 9th Lancers. A sketch of an early pattern plate by Messrs Hawkes Military Tailors, that was not adopted for use. Note the Royal Helmet and Mantling to the Royal Arms. Courtesy of the National Army Museum.

Figure 106: 9th Lancers. A sketch of an early pattern other ranks plate thought to be post 1830, by A.R. Cattley. Author's collection.

Figure 107: 12th Lancers. A sketch of a plate of the Post Crimean War period by Messrs Hawkes & Co, that was not adopted for use. Author's Collection.

Figure 108: 16th Lancers. A sketch of an early pattern plate on which the numeral '16' is omitted, by A.R. Cattley. Author's collection.

Figure 109: 17th Lancers. A drawing of an early pattern plate having the skull facing to the left (when facing the plate). Author's collection.

BEDFORDSHIRE IMPERIAL YEOMANRY

	TITLE SCROLL	HONOURS LEFT	HONOURS CENTRE	HONOURS RIGHT
KC None	None	None	None	

1ST CITY OF LONDON IMPERIAL YEOMANRY

	TITLE SCROLL	HONOURS LEFT	HONOURS CENTRE	HONOURS RIGHT
KC *	Rough Riders (upper centre scroll), of London (lower left scroll), Imperial (lower right scroll), Yeomanry (upper right scroll)	South Africa	None	1900-1902

EAST RIDING OF YORKSHIRE IMPERIAL YEOMANRY

	TITLE SCROLL	HONOURS LEFT	HONOURS CENTRE	HONOURS RIGHT
KC	East Riding of (left scroll), orkshire (centre scroll), Imperial Yeomanry (right scroll)	None	None	None

Figure 110: A superb example of the officers pattern plate of The City of London Imperial Yeomanry. Note the fine detail to the '*Arms of The City of London*' to the centre of the wreath of oak leaves.

Figure 111: An example of the other ranks die-struck plate of The City of London Imperial Yeomanry. Compare the quality of this plate, with that of the officers pattern illustrated in *Fig: 110*.

LANARKSHIRE YEOMANRY

	TITLE SCROLL	HONOURS ACROSS BASE OF PLATE
KC	Lanarkshire (left of strap), Yeomanry (right of strap)	South Africa 1900-02

LINCOLNSHIRE IMPERIAL YEOMANRY

	TITLE SCROLL	HONOURS LEFT	HONOURS CENTRE	HONOURS RIGHT
KC	Lincolnshire (left scroll), Imperial (centre scroll), Yeomanry (right scroll)	None	None	None

SOUTH BUCKS YEOMANRY LANCERS

	TITLE SCROLL	HONOURS LEFT	HONOURS CENTRE	HONOURS RIGHT
QVC *	None, 'South Bucks Yeomanry Lancers'	None	None	None

Figure 112: An extremely rare other ranks pattern plate of the South Bucks Yeomanry Lancers. Of interest are the 'Union Flowers' comprising the rose, shamrock, and thistle, above the scroll bearing 'Yeomanry'.

NOTES

1. 5th Lancers: Photographic evidence would appear to indicate that this, the first pattern plate for this regiment, was still being worn c.1880.

2. 5th Lancers: Plates type: D. and E. have identical battle honours, the only variation between these two pattern of plates being the change from Victorian to King's pattern crown.

3. 9th Lancers: The reversed A. R. cypher relates to the regiment being granted the title '*9th Queen's Royal Lancers*' in honour of Queen Adelaide in July 1830 (6). Queen Adelaide was married to King William IV who ruled Great Britain from 1830 to 1837. N.B. On an example of an officers cap bearing this pattern plate, that is on display at the National Army Museum, London, the plate was comprised of three separate pieces, these being (1) the gilt metal rayed back plate, (2) the gilt Royal Arms, spray of leaves, and title scroll, and (3) the silvered A.R. reversed.

4. 9th Lancers: It is of interest that whilst the battle honour '*Peninsula*' was displayed on the earlier pattern plate (type: A.), it appears to have been omitted from the later pattern plate (type: B.).

5. 9th Lancers: On plates D. and E., the battle honours '*Delhi*' and '*Peninsula*' are in reverse positions, as are the honours '*Lucknow*' and '*Punjaub*'. N.B. *See Figs: 70.* and *72.* for an example of each of these pattern of plates.

6. 9th Lancers: Plates G. and H. have identical battle honours, the only variation between these two pattern of plates being the change from Victorian to King's pattern crown.

7. 12th Lancers: On this pattern of plate the honour 'Egypt' is die-stamped on the rayed backing plate and positioned on the band at the base of the plate. *See Fig: 22.* for an illustration of this plate affixed to an officers pattern lance cap.

8 12th Lancers: On the officers pattern plate Type: B., the P.O.W.'s feathers, the Royal Arms, the scroll bearing '*Waterloo*', the scroll bearing '*Peninsula*', and the sphinx were all separate overlay pieces secured to the backing plate by threaded studs affixed to the back of each 'piece' and fastened with nuts. This plate was made up of a total of six individual pieces. N.B. *See Figs: 77.* and *78.* for an illustration of the front and reverse of this pattern of plate.

9. 12th Lancers: On the officers pattern plate Type: F., seen by the authors, the silvered Royal Arms were die -stamped, however the eight gilded battle honours were cast as a one-piece overlay, making a three-piece plate.

10. 16th Lancers: The description of this pattern of plate is based on a sketch of the plate concerned (42).

11. 16th Lancers: This pattern of plate is thought to have been worn during the period 1830-37 (98).

12. 16th Lancers: Although not confirmed, it is possible that the honours '*Afghanistan*' and '*Talavera*' are actually revered.

13. 17th Lancers: Various sources have made reference to there having been a lance cap plate bearing the honours '*Alma*', '*Inkerman*', '*Balaclava*', and '*Sevastopol*' with the additional honour of '*Central India*', thus making five battle honours. However, the authors have been unable to verify the existence of such a plate.

14. There is an illustration of an officers pattern cap, said to be of the 19th Lancers, bearing a plate without battle honours in *Regiment Magazine*, issue 47.

15. 21st Lancers: It is of interest that the pattern of plate listed as Type: B. as illustrated in *Fig: 102.*, appears to display an 'Imperial' pattern crown, but omits the Royal Arms. Hugh King, in his excellent book on British Army cap badges lists this example as being the second pattern of plate for this regiment, and this invites the following question. Why was the Royal Arms, as displayed on the first pattern plate omitted from the second pattern, when on the third and last pattern plate the Royal Arms are present. In fact there exist examples bearing both the Victorian Type: C. (*See Fig: 103.*) and the King's crown Type: D. (*See Fig: 104.*) Is it possible that the pattern of plates having the 'Imperial' pattern crown were produced unofficially, and that the War Office ordered that this regiments plate should bear the Royal Arms, thereby creating the plates listed as Types: C. & D., although this has not been confirmed.

It is likely that we may never know the answer to this question, should however a reader of this book have a explanation, then the authors would be pleased to hear of same. N.B. Whilst the authors have seen examples of officers pattern plates of Type: B., they have never seen an other ranks pattern plate.

16. The origin of the title 'Empress of India' is most interesting. Apparently, when in 1858 Queen Victoria's eldest daughter (Vicky) married the man who was to become the future Emperor of Germany (H.I.M. Kaiser William II), her mother was not best pleased at the prospect of her daughter outranking her, upon Vicky becoming Empress of Germany.

Several years later on the 1st May 1876 a solution was proposed by the eminent politician Benjamin Disraeli, and subsequently a Royal Titles Bill was submitted and approved by parliament, creating Queen Victoria 'Empress of India'.

Chapter Eleven

The Undress Cap and the Foul-Weather Cap

The Undress Cap

The initial pattern of undress cap to be worn by the Lancer officers was really an ornamental cloth head-dress which varied in style according to regimental ideas, with the first 'official' description to be found recorded in the Dress Regulations for April 1822, page 56. as reproduced below. N.B. As these regulation are based on the dress of the senior regiment in the group, they agree with what is expected for the 9th Lancers, they being the senior lancer regiment,

Dress Regulations 1822

Undress

'Cap-crimson cloth, trencher top nine and a half inches square, front angle in a direct line with centre of peak; fluted sides three and a half inches deep, gold and crimson cord round corners, running transversely over crown; gold bullion rosette with embroidered G.R. on crimson velvet in the centre; scull three and a half inches deep, encircled with gold and crimson lace in the centre two inches wide, and a narrow gold quarter of an inch braid top and bottom; plain black peak in front; a small screw socket for plume.'

'Plume-red and white horse-hair.'

When comparing the above particulars with the official description of the dress cap as described in chapter six, it would appear that the main differences between the dress and undress caps were, when considering the latter cap, as follows. The square trencher top is reduced by half an inch overall, albeit that the fluted sides were the same. The skull is described as being three and a half inches deep, although the material used is not described. The lace to the waist is reduced by one inch in width down to two inches, there being additional quarter inch braid top and bottom, with the front peak being unadorned. Omitted from the description was the large lance cap plate, and the rear peak, whose absence presumably made for a lighter and more comfortable cap.

Contemporary illustrations of the undress cap are rare, however there is one in 'The Military Costumes of Europe' published by Goddard and Booth, where the plate concerned is dated May 29th 1822. The illustration is named '12th (Prince of Wales's) Royal Regiment of Lancers' and although contemporary, may not be entirely accurate. The cap illustrated has the red top with gold or yellow lace around the edges and the peak, but no lance cap plate. A small red and white plume is worn as described in the aforementioned regulations.

There is also a coloured plate dated 1822 illustrating an officer of the 17th Lancers in 'stable dress'. The officer is depicted wearing a small cap with a trencher top edged with silver lace, from the centre of which is hung the strands of a silver tassel. N.B. Although not mentioned in the Dress Regulations of 1822, the officer appears to be wearing silver chinscales attached to his cap.

Amongst the uniform items that formerly belonged to Caesar Bacon of the 23rd Lancers that are preserved in the Isle of Man, there is a fine undress cap. This item of head-dress however does not follow the description given in the official printed regulations, for it is in fact a peaked cap. The cap has the crimson trencher top with silver lace and embroidery, the top of which is sunk down to rest on a surround of silver lace (of wave and vellum, like that on the sabretache). Lace criss-crosses the top of the cap in true lancer quartering and around the four sides, the peak having neither braid nor lace, but having instead impressed designs (116).

These fancy pattern undress caps did not remain in use for very long, and the regulations of 1826 note that this style of undress cap was replaced by one of simple oiled silk. The Dress Regulations of 1831 also describe the same pattern of undress cap, the relevant extract of which is reproduced below. N.B. This oiled silk cap was in fact a foul-weather cap, although not so named at this period of time.

Dress Regulations 1831 and 1846

Undress

'Cap-oiled silk, shape and dimensions as Dress Cap; gilt chain, lined with black velvet'.

N.B. It is interesting to compare the reasonably descriptive account of the undress cap as given in the 1822-26 regulations, with the brevity of the particulars given for the 'same' cap in the Dress Regulation of 1831 as the old cloth type gave place to the foul-weather pattern.

The Foul-Weather-Cap

Considering the considerable expenses incurred by an officer when purchasing his full dress cap, it is hardly surprising that not to long after its introduction, it was decided to protect the dress cap against the elements. To this end, an 'oilskin' cover was introduced which buttoned over all parts of the cap, there being no provision however for the plume. The full dress cap when worn with this oilskin cover was a heavy affair, being uncomfortable to wear, especially in action, and therefore by the 1830's a special pattern of foul-weather cap was introduced to replace the wearing of the combination of dress cap and oilskin cover during periods of inclement weather.

The new pattern of undress[1] cap was similar in its dimensions to the dress cap, and was worn complete with cap-lines, but not with the plume. The cap had a 'thin body covered with black oilskin' (6), being unadorned by either braid or lace, albeit, as a matter of necessity the lion's head bosses, chinchain, and the ring and hook on the four-petalled hook to the rear waist of the cap were retained. The 'seams of the body were raised on the quarters' and a 'false boss' was positioned up on the left hand side of the cap in the position occupied by the gold bullion rosette on the dress cap. There were some four number false buttons running along the side seam of the cap, the lower button being positioned just above the lion's head boss, with the other buttons being evenly spaced and extending upwards to the top of the cap (19). N.B. On the Post 1856 pattern cap, the number of false buttons appears to have been reduced to three in number.

With regard to this rare pattern of cap, the author's were fortunate in possessing a copy of the description for the undress cap of the 16th Lancers c.1850 (Hanbury-Williams kit), made by B.T.A. Griffiths, an account of which is reproduced below verbatim:

> '16th Lancers. undress czapka. Hanbury-Williams Kit, c.1850. The whole covered with thin black oilskin (or oiled silk?). The buttons at sides are dummies, the opening being stitched down & without buttonholes. Buttons of bone-blackened. A gilt hook under right-hand corner & a similar one on top at back. Gilt Lion's head bosses & remains of a gilt curb-chain.'
>
> 'Lined with crimson silk, below that a yellowish brown leather band (might have been white originally?) peak lined green.'
>
> 'Both drawings to scale of 1/2 inch to the inch, not allowing for perspective of course.'
>
> 'Line of stitching down front, back, & both sides' B.T.A. Griffiths.

It would appear that the above narrative by B.T.A. Griffiths was in fact his abridged description of this cap for there exists an illus-

DEATH OR GLORY BOY.

Figure 113: 'Death Or Glory Boy.' An officer of the 17th Lancers in undress?. David Rowe collection. Previously published in the Regiment Journal 1987.

Figure 114: A sketch depicting an officers pattern undress cap of the 16th Lancers c.1820 from Johnson's (Dublin) pattern book, together with brief description of same. Copyright W.Y. Carman.

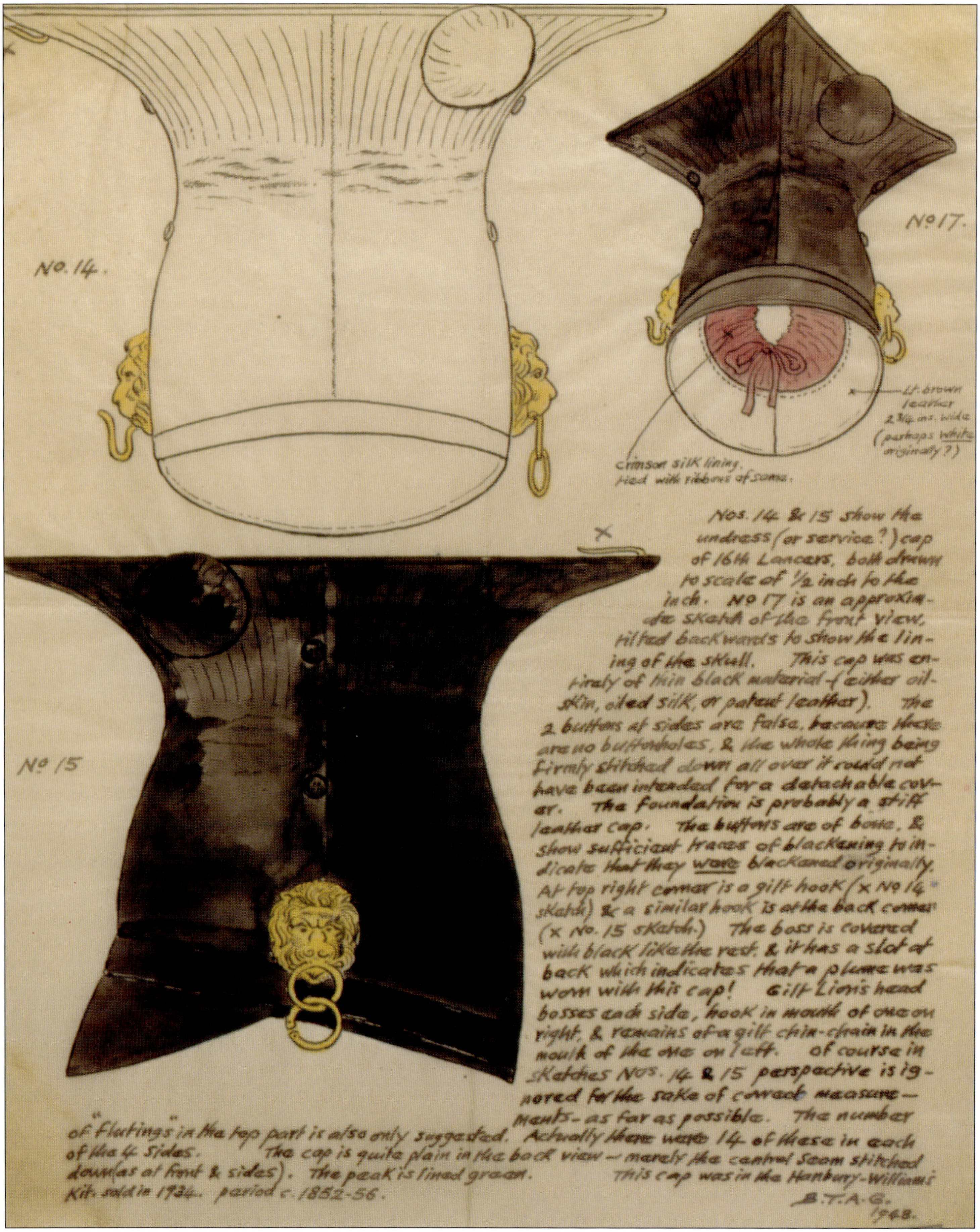

Figure 115: Three sketches of the undress cap of the 16th Lancers of the period c.1852-56, together with a detailed description of this pattern of cap by B.T.A. Griffith. Copyright W.Y. Carman.

trated and more comprehensive account dated 1948, a copy of which is reproduced in *Fig: 115*.

With the introduction of the 1856 pattern full dress lance cap, the dimensions of the undress cap were reduced accordingly, so as to more closely resemble the later pattern dress cap. With the cap being unadorned by a lance cap plate or plume, there was little to differentiate the cap of one regiment from that of another. It is however known that the 9th Lancers retained their regimental pattern corded chinchain, and at some time during Queen Victoria's lengthy reign, the 17th Lancers adopted gilt metal skull bosses in place of the usual lion's head bosses on their undress caps as illustrated in *Fig: 116A*. N.B. The interior of this pattern of cap was as similar to that of the full dress version, having a leather and silk lining.

Figure 116: An officers pattern undress (foul-weather) lance cap of the 17th Lancers. Note the 'false' plume boss. Courtesy of Meng-Chi Tsen. Photo: R. Biondi.

Figure 116A: Side view of the cap, illustrating the unique regimental pattern skull pattern ear bosses, and the hook and ring upon the four-petalled leaf to the rear to the cap. Courtesy of Meng-Chi Tsen. Photo: R. Biondi.

The Other Ranks Pattern

For the rank and file, there was not to be the expense of providing a second cap, in its place being issued a black oilskin cover which fitted over the dress cap, worn complete with cap-lines, but minus of course the plume. This was the pattern of foul-weather 'cap' worn by members of the 17th Lancers when they made their famous charge into 'The Valley of Death' as part of the Light Brigade during the Crimean campaign.

The foul-weather cover continued to be worn long after the Crimean campaign, being listed in the official publication 'Priced Vocabulary of Clothing and Necessaries' of 1911 as catalogue number 277 and described as Covers-cap, lance, oilskin, and priced at £0 1s 0.1/2d per item. *See Figs: 117.* and *118.* for an illustration of this cover being worn.

The White Cap Cover

In a most informative article relating to British Lancer Regiments (*Military Modelling Magazine*, March 1986), that formed part of a series of articles entitled 'The Cut of the Cloth' by Don and Bryan Fosten, the authors, when describing the uniforms worn by the lancer regiments of the 19th Century, make reference to the 'white calico quilted cover[2] with a curtain to protect the neck, worn' in hot climates. This cover, complete with buttons, enclosed the dress cap in a similar manner to that of the oilskin cover, and is known to have

Figure 117: '9th (Queen's Royal) Lancers.' An extremely rare photograph of a corporal and two privates, who are all wearing the foul-weather cover over their full dress lance caps. Note how the cap lines are 'looped' around the outside waist of the cover/cap. Copyright D.P.& G.

been worn in action by the 16th Lancers whilst serving in India.[3] N.B. The 16th (Queen's) Lancers served in India from 1823 to 1846 (4).

NOTES

1. The Dress Regulations of 1846 merely describe the Undress Cap as '*Cap*-oiled silk, shape and dimensions as *Dress* Cap; gilt chain, lined with black velvet'.

2. It is recorded that a white calico cover was worn to cover the shako worn by members of light dragoon regiments whilst on service in countries having hot climates. Additionally, it is known that a white quilted cover complete with neck curtain, was worn to cover the 1847 heavy cavalry helmet worn by the 1st (King's) Dragoon Guards whilst serving abroad.

3. There is an excellent illustration in Philip Warner's book on the British Cavalry (62) of the 16th Lancers in action at Bharatpur, India, c. 1825 in which the lancers are wearing the white calico cap cover.

Figure 118: '16th (Queen's) Lancers.' A most unusual and interesting photograph of a group of 16th Lancers 'strolling along the road' c.1914. Of particular interest is the foul-weather cap worn over the full dress cap by several of the soldiers. Also of interest is the full dress lance cap being worn without the cover, the service dress cap worn by many of the troopers, the mixture of riding boots and puttees being worn, the variety of weapons and equipment carried, and the almost 'at the slope' sword held by the soldier to the centre of the group. Copyright D.P.& G.

OPPOSITE
Figure 119: A member of the 9th Lancers in 'marching order' c.1890, said to be the Regimental Sergeant Major. Whilst the light background does little to improve the quality of the image, it is just possible to see that the foul-weather cap is being worn. Copyright D.P. & G.

Chapter Twelve

1902 and Onwards

A Change of Royal Cypher

Following the accession to the throne by King Edward VII in 1902, and the subsequent inauguration of King George V in 1911, the Royal Cypher to the centre of the gold bullion rosette changed to first to ER VII, and later to GRV.[1] Additionally, sometime into the reign of King Edward VII, a new pattern of silvered overlay for the lance cap plate was produced bearing a King's pattern crown as illustrated in *Figs: 123.* and *127.*, with the battle honours awarded for the war in South Africa being added to the plates of the 5th, 9th, 12th, 16th,and 17th Lancers.

For the rank and file, the change of monarch resulted in the button to the centre of the cotton/woollen plume boss being gradually changed from a Victorian pattern button to one bearing a King's pattern crown, with the die-struck lance cap plate being amended accordingly over a period of time.

The Officers Full Dress Uniform into Storage

With the outbreak of the First World War the wearing of full dress was discontinued, however as the officers purchased their lance cap and uniform, these items were put into storage, usually in a black japanned metal storage chest. Sadly, for many of these officers, this would be the last occasion that they would ever see their full dress uniform, for what was thought to be the 'War to end all Wars' was to claim the lives of many lancer officers, including Lieutenant J. Eden[2] (12th Lancers), and the Victoria Cross heroes, Captain F.O. Grenfell V.C.[3] (9th Lancers), and Captain (Later Brigadier) P.A. Kenna V.C. (21st Lancers).

Came the end of The Great War, and the resumption of peacetime soldiering for the returning heroes. Regrettably, they did not as a general rule return to wearing the splendid colourful uniforms of the pre war period, for the wearing of the full dress uniform was never to be officially restored. There were however occasions when an officer wore this order of dress, such as when attending an award ceremony, an investiture, at a levee, or at an officers wedding etc.

The Other Ranks Full Dress Uniform

Khaki service dress had been worn for quite a while prior to 1914, however with the outbreak of the war in Europe and the British Army being 'warned for active service', the wearing of full dress for the rank and file was officially discontinued, with the lance caps, tunics, and other items of 'ceremonial uniform' (sword and scabbard excepted) being returned to the regimental clothing stores.

With the return of peace, it might have been hoped that upon the gradual return of the various regiments from abroad, that some form of full dress uniform would once again be taken into wear by the rank and file, this however was not to be, for as with the officers, the wearing of this order of dress would not be officially sanctioned. Notwithstanding the above, there were occasions when some members of a regiment were permitted to wear the full dress uniform of their regiment, these rare opportunities including such official events as when attending a military tattoo, performing in a musical ride, at the presentation of a new regimental standard, when providing a guard of honour, such as at an officers wedding, whilst taking part in a recruitment drive, whilst performing at the Royal Tournament, and last, but by no means least, by military musicians when performing as members of a regimental band.

The Amalgamations of 1922

The month of April for the year 1922 heralded a new 'financial' year for the accountants, bankers, investors, and stockbrokers, with the prospect of great new ventures to come. It was not however to be a good year for many famous and proud regiments of the British Army, for it was in April of this year that the decrease in the size of the army was made known, these reductions to the standing army being frequently referred to as being due to 'The Geddes axe'.[4]

Under Army Order 133 of April 1922 the regiments to be amalgamated were named, the effect upon the cavalry being that, two regiments of Household Cavalry, five regiments of Dragoon Guards, one regiment of Dragoons, six regiments of Hussars, and four regiments of Lancers lost their age old regimental titles. The lancer regiments affected by these mergers were the 5th[5], 16th, 17th, and 21st Lancers, these regiments becoming the *16th/5th Lancers,* and the *17th/21st Lancers*, with all 'secondary' titles being dropped, e.g. Royal Irish, The Queen's, Duke of Cambridge's Own, and Empress of India's.

Figure 120: A contemporary commercial postcard depicting the 5th Lancers changing guard, post 1904. N.B. The original photograph was almost certainly taken outside the guardroom of the former Beaumont Cavalry Barracks, Aldershot. David Rowe collection.

Mechanization 1928

The first two British cavalry regiments to lose their horses and to become mechanized were the 11th Hussars and the 12th Lancers, who in April 1928 (15) converted to a cavalry armoured car regiment.

Dress Regulations 1934[6]

Once again there were few changes relating to the lance cap, those that there were appeared on pages 62, 63, 66, and 67 of the above publication, the amendments and changes being reproduced below, with the significant changes being in bold text.

The Rosette

'A gold bullion rosette, with the Royal Cypher embroidered on blue velvet in the 12th and 17th/21st Lancers; on scarlet in the 16th/5th; at the back of the rosettes, a ventilated spring socket for the plume stem'.

Rings and Hook

'Rings and hooks on a metal leaf at the back of the waist, for the cap-line and chain'.

The Plume

'Plume.-Drooping swan feathers, 14 inches long in front and 7 inches behind from the bend of the feathers, of the following colours:

9th Lancers	*Black and white.*
12th Lancers	*Scarlet.*
16th/5th Lancers	*Black.*
17th/21st Lancers	*White.'*

Badges

Badges: On Full Dress Head-dress.

9th Queen's Royal Lancers. As per Dress Regulations 1900:

12th Royal Lancers (Prince of Wales's). **'***On a gilt or gilding metal plate in silver, the Royal Arms, with the Prince of Wales's Plume above, and the Sphinx over Egypt below. Below, on gilt or gilding metal scrolls, the honours; the outer ends of the scrolls finish in sprays of laurel'*. N.B. The scroll inscribed "*Dieu Et Mon Droit*" has been omitted on the above description.

16th/5th Lancers. '*The universal plate in gilt or gilding metal. On the plate in silver, the Royal Arms and scroll "Sixteenth-Fifth Lancers". No battle honours.'*

17th/21st Lancers. *'On a gilt or gilding metal plate, in silver, the Royal Arms with the death's head and scroll inscribed "Or Glory".*

(Text resumes on page 162)

Figure 121: 'An Officer of the 5th (Royal Irish) Lancers.' A fine study of Lieutenant (Q.M.) G. Burridge of the 5th Lancers in dismounted review order pre 1915 proudly displaying his three medals. Commissioned – Q.M. & Hon. Lieutenant: 27th Nov. 1909. Q.M. & Hon. Captain: 3rd June 1915. Q.M. & Hon. Major: 3rd June 1919 (16). Note how the cap lines are worn around the collar of his tunic. Copyright D.P.& G.

Figure 122: 'An Officer of the 9th (Queen's Royal) Lancers.' A superb illustration of a dismounted Captain of the regiment in dismounted review order c.1904 by Rodney Player. Kindly reproduced by kind permission of the artist, and the Parker Gallery.

Figure 123: 9th Lancers. An excellent example of the post 1902 officers pattern cap with the plume removed, the plate bearing sixteen battle honours, as also illustrated in *Fig: 75*. Courtesy of Charles Griffin.

Figure 124: 9th Lancers. Offset view of the officers pattern cap with the feather plume now in situ. Courtesy of Charles Griffin.

Figure 125: '9th Lancers at Church Parade.' Officers and other ranks of the regiment in dismounted review order, returning from church parade at Aldershot Garrison c.1904. Copyright D.P.& G.

Figure 126: 12th Lancers. A superb condition post 1902 officers cap complete with scarlet feather plume. N.B. The plate on this cap bears nine battle honours and is further illustrated in *Fig: 86*. Courtesy of Christopher Bryant.

No battle honours'. N.B. The initials "D.C.O." (Duke of Cambridge's Own) are no longer listed for this regiments lance cap plate.

Regarding the above three plates, the authors have no knowledge of any collector, museum, or militaria specialist that has ever seen or heard of the existence of the these pattern of plates, and are of the opinion that even if manufactured, they were never taken into wear.

Mechanization 1936/1938/1940

The second regiment of lancers to lose their horses, were the 9th Lancers, this sad event occurring in the spring of 1936, with some two years later, the last mounted parade of the 17th/21st Lancers taking place at Meerut, India on the 4th January 1938 (115). For the 16th/5th Lancers the last horsed ceremonial parade for the regiment is said to have taken place whilst the regiment was stationed at Risalpur, India, (now in Pakistan) in 1940 (8). N.B. Other sources give the date of mechanization as 1929 for the 12th Lancers, with the last ceremonial parade of the 16th/5th Lancers being given as the 1st January 1939 (121).

Amalgamation of the 9th and 12th Lancers

On the 11th September 1960 (52) the two remaining lancer regiments previously unaffected by the mergers of April 1922, they being the 9th The Queen's Royal Lancers, and the 12th Royal Lancers (Prince of Wales's) were amalgamated to form the *9th/12th Royal Lancers.*

Amalgamation/Merger of the 16th/5th and 17th/21st Lancers

On the 4th July 1991, the then Defence Secretary, Tom King M.P. announced a dramatic change to the structure of the existing British Armed Forces (55). These changes included the proposed mergers of many famous regiments of the British Army, including that of the 16th/5th The Queen's Royal Lancers and the 17th/21st Lancers. The proposed amalgamations brought fourth many headaches, such as which of the regimental distinctions would be retained from each of these two regiments, with the 16th/5th wishing to retain their crimped lance pennons, and the 17th/21st their death's head cap badge and motto "Or Glory", both of which in the event, were adopted by the new regiment.

The amalgamation parade of these two fine regiments took place on the 25th June 1993 at Tidworth, when Her Majesty the Queen presented the newly formed regiment, *The Queen's Royal Lancers* with their new guidon (16). N.B. For readers wishing to further their knowledge of the newly formed regiment, Issue Twenty of *Regiment Magazine* is devoted to this regiment, and contains many fine illustrations of the four former parent regiments, the 5th, 16th, 17th, and 21st Lancers, in addition to several illustrations of The Queen's Royal Lancers.

The Queen's Royal Lancers Regimental Museum

The museum of the newly formed regiment was opened in 1995 by His Grace, the Duke of Rutland, and is located at Belvoir Castle, Lincolnshire, being some six miles from the A1 at Grantham, and 12 miles from Melton Mowbray. From the end of March to the 30th October, the museum is open to the public from 11am to 5pm on Tuesday, Wednesday, Thursday and Saturday, and is open on Sundays, Good Friday, and Bank Holidays from 11am to 6pm during the same period (56). The Curator of the Museum is Captain M. Holtby (0115-957-3295).

Included within the museums collection of fine and rare military antiques that are on display, is the famous Balaclava Bugle[7], carried by Trumpeter William 'Billy' Brittain of the 17th Lancers in the Charge of The Light Brigade on the 25th October 1854 during the Crimean campaign. This proud regimental treasure was presented to the former 17th/21st Lancers by the late actor, Lawrence Harvey who starred alongside John Wayne in the epic film 'The Alamo'.

The museum also contains arms, military decorations, paintings, personal artifacts, silver, and most importantly for readers of this book, uniforms of the 5th, 16th, 17th, 21st, 16th/5th, 17th/21st, and The Queen's Royal Lancers. There is also a small museum gift shop offering a fine range of gift wares and souvenirs, and a licensed restaurant (16).

Figure 127: 16th Lancers. A fine example of the post 1902 pattern cap with black feather plume which partially obscures the battle honours on the lance cap plate. *See Fig: 93.* for an example of this pattern of plate. Courtesy of Christopher Bryant.

Figure 128: 'A sentry of the 16th Lancers.' A sentry of the 16th Lancers in dismounted review order c.1903. His tunic bears collar badges, and he has two long service and good conduct chevrons to his left sleeve. Note that both his lance cap plume, and lance pennon are crimped. Copyright D.P.& G.

Figure 129: 'An Officer of the 17th Lancers.' Lieutenant Lord George Crespigny Brabazon Vivian Bt D.S.O.T.D.A.D.C. D.L. J.P. (1878-1940) c.1903 of the 17th Lancers. Served as a Major in the 1st Royal Devon Yeomanry, Brevet Colonel, the 4/5 Battalion D.C.L.I. Awarded the Chevalier Legion of Honour, Officer Order de Leopold, French Croix de Guerre, Belgian Croix de Guerre (33). A fine study of an officer wearing the post 1902 mounted review order of dress. Reproduced by kind permission of the Queen's Royal Lancers Museum.

NOTES

1. Sometime after 1902, for the officers of the 9th Lancers, the regimental pattern button to the centre of the gilt metal gimp boss on the lance cap would have changed from the Victorian crown pattern, to one having a King's crown.

2. The younger brother of Lieutenant John Eden, of "B" Squadron, 12th Lancers, was Anthony Eden M.C., who many years later was to become Sir Anthony Eden, three times appointed Foreign Secretary, and later in April 1955 became Prime Minister of Great Britain (63), eventually being elevated to the peerage as Lord Avon.

3. Captain Francis Octavius Grenfell V.C., 9th Lancers, was awarded the first Victoria Cross of the First World War for gallantry in action whilst at Andregnies, Belgium, on the 24th August 1914 (64).

4. Sir Auckland Campbell Geddes (first Baron Geddes) G.C.M.G. C.B. K.C.B. P.C. (1879-1954). Sir Auckland Geddes sat on a War Office Committee whose task was to considerably reduce the national expenditure of the United Kingdom.

5. The 16th The Queen's Lancers were senior in order of precedence to the 5th Royal Irish Lancers, by reason of the this regiment having unbroken service dating back to 1759, unlike the 5th Lancers who were re-raised in 1858. As a result of the above, the title of the then newly formed regiment, became the 16th/5th Lancers, and not the 5th/16th Lancers as might have been expected.

6. Dress Regulations for the Army 1934, by command of the Army Council, The War Office 30th June 1934, were approved by his Majesty King George the Fifth. They were originally published by His Majesty's Stationery Office in 1934, and some thirty-five years later reprinted by Arms & Armour Press in 1969.

7. The bugle carried in the Charge of the Light Brigade by Trumpeter William Brittain of the 17th Lancers, and known as the Balaclava Bugle sold in auction at Sotheby's on the 20th April 1964 for the then princely sum of £1,600 (20). A differing cavalry musical instrument, having a distinct connection with the former 17th/21st Lancers, is the trumpet carried by Sergeant Trumpeter Frederick Knight of the 21st Lancers during the regiments famous charge at Omdurman on the 2nd September 1898. This instrument sold at Christies Auction House some ten or more years ago, realising £4,200 and being purchased by an unknown collector.

Chapter Thirteen

The Yeomanry Cavalry Regiments and Volunteer Troops

Introduction to the Yeomanry

Whilst it was not properly organised until 1794, the yeomanry can trace its history back to 1761. Command was on a county basis, with the regiments at that time consisting of the officers (county gentlemen) and other ranks (farm workers), all of which provided their own horses.

In 1885 the War Office drew up a 'Yeomanry Table of Precedence' for the first time, which ranked the regiments in order of seniority. Further changes took place with the introduction of the Defence Act of 1888, which amended the terms of service for the yeomanry so that all ranks were liable for service anywhere in Great Britain, with yet another change occurring in 1893 when all yeomanry regiments were ordered to reorganise on a squadron basis (65).

Prior to 1901, the number of yeomanry regiments on the official establishment was thirty-eight, with a further two regiments being classed as Volunteer Light Horse. The uniforms of these volunteer regiments closely followed those of the regular regiments of cavalry, albeit in many cases they were far more elaborate. Eleven yeomanry regiments dressed as Dragoons, twenty-five as Hussars, one as Lancers (Lanarkshire Yeomanry), and one as Mounted Rifles, with the two regiments of Volunteer Light Horse being dressed similar to Dragoons (65). Whilst as stated, the uniforms of the volunteer regiments followed those of the regulars, the colour of their tunics varied considerably, especially so from c.1902, ranging from the striking French grey of the Rough Riders, the maroon of the East Riding Yeomanry, the scarlet of the Montgomeryshire Yeomanry, to the more sombre colours of dark blue for the Oxfordshire Hussars, khaki of the Sussex Yeomanry, and the Lincoln green of the Lincolnshire Yeomanry.

In 1899, with the outbreak of the Boer War, it was quickly realised that there was a requirement for additional mounted troops to be sent to the seat of war. The yeomanry cavalry regiments were not slow if responding to the call for more men, and many regiments provided drafts of men to form Companies of Imperial Yeomanry.

Under the Militia and Auxiliary Forces Act of 1901, together with Army Order 109, the name of the Yeomanry Cavalry was changed to Imperial Yeomanry. The years 1900-1902 also saw the raising of several new volunteer regiments, not the least amongst them being the Bedfordshire, 1st County of London, Lincolnshire, Surrey, and Sussex, regiments of Imperial Yeomanry.

With the introduction of the Territorial Force in 1908, which encompassed the volunteer artillery, the cavalry, and infantry etc, those yeomanry regiments who had changed their title to include the word 'Imperial' should in theory have changed again, and indeed a great many regiments did so. However, in spite of this change to their title, a limited number of regiments retained the word 'Imperial' on their head-dress plates, the City of London (Rough Riders), East Riding Yeomanry, and Lincolnshire Yeomanry having been known to have kept their lance cap plate bearing the word 'Imperial' on their lance caps, through to, and some cases through the reign of King George V.

It is of interest that within the volunteer regiments it appears to have been usual for the post of Adjutant was held by an officer seconded from a regular army regiment, and this was the case in the yeomanry, where the permanent staff posts such as the Regimental Sergeant Major and the Squadron Sergeant Majors were also regular serving soldiers on temporary secondment.[1]

What is most interesting about these temporary postings, is the uniform worn by the soldiers holding these appointments, as contemporary photographs tend to show the permanent staff, i.e. the R.S.M. and S.S.M.'s wearing the uniform of the yeomanry regiment to which they were seconded, whilst the regular officer serving with the same yeomanry regiment wears the full dress uniform of his parent regiment. A possible explanation for this variation in uniform, is that the full dress yeomanry uniforms worn by the R.S.M. and S.S.M's would have been an official issue, whilst the officer (Adjutant), would have been expected to meet the cost of the additional expense incurred by providing the full dress yeomanry uniform from his own pocket.

This slight mixture of uniforms, occasionally resulted in a group photograph being taken of the officers of a yeomanry regiment wearing their particular full dress uniform, which perhaps might be in the style of either a dragoon or hussar, whilst included amongst this group of officers would be the regiments adjutant, who, being for example a lancer officer, would be wearing the lancer pattern full dress uniform. Such photographs are rare, they do however occasionally 'turn up', and are of great interest to students of cavalry uniforms.

Included within this chapter, is a description of the full dress uniform worn by the officers of those yeomanry regiments who adopted the lancer style uniform. It should be understood, that the information available to the authors relating to these uniforms was somewhat limited, and may regrettably therefore be less than totally complete.

Also within this chapter has been included a 'thumbnail' history relating to the formation of each regiment, accompanied by changes of regimental title where applicable, that occurred up until the outbreak of the First World War, the address of each regiments station as at 1914 (47), together with information on the uniform worn by members of the detachments taking part in the coronation procession in 1911. N.B. All fifty-six yeomanry regiments, including two Special Reserve Regiments, took part in this coronation parade, they being formed into either the 1st Battalion, or the 2nd Battalion, the exception being the London regiments who made up The London Mounted Brigade (66).

With regard to the above, when writing on the subject of army regiments, either regular army or volunteer, it is the accepted practice to list the regiments concerned in order of seniority. However, of the seven yeomanry listed in the Army List of 1914 that were designated as being lancers, only five regiments adopted the lance cap for full dress wear, therefore the aforementioned accepted method has not been adhered to, and instead the regiments concerned have been listed alphabetically, which it is hoped will not cause offence to the readers of this book. Coincidentally, this method of listing those regiments, places the two yeomanry regiments that did not take into wear the full dress lance cap, at the end of this listing.

The regiments included in this chapter are The Bedfordshire Imperial Yeomanry, The City of London Yeomanry (Rough Riders), The East Riding Yeomanry, The Lanarkshire Yeomanry, The Lincolnshire Yeomanry, The Surrey Imperial Yeomanry, and The Sussex Imperial Yeomanry.

In addition to the above seven regiments, has been included the limited information available to the authors relating to The Duke of Cornwall's Yeomanry Cavalry, the West Essex Yeomanry, and four little known Troops of yeomanry, they being the Adlington Troop, the Long Melford Troop, the Radbourne Troop, and the Taplow Troop, each of which adopted a lancer style uniform, complete with lance cap, before either being absorbed into a newly formed regiment, or being disbanded entirely. N.B. Whilst it is known that not all of the volunteer corps that styled themselves as lancers actually adopted the lance cap, never the less, in our wish to be comprehensive we have included these units within the following text.

Yeomanry Bands

As with their brothers-in-arms, the regular cavalry, many yeomanry regiments had a band, either mounted or dismounted, and some of the more ambitious and perhaps affluent regiments that had a mounted band, emulated the 'regulars' by having a kettle-drummer resplendent upon his drum horse. It is a sad fact, that accurate details relating to yeomanry bands is very scarce, and therefore the only information presented on this subject, has been taken from an authoritative source such as R.G. Harris's excellent booklet on yeomanry drum banners and mounted bands (67).

The Yeomanry Regiments

Bedfordshire Imperial Yeomanry

Whilst authority to raise a Troop of volunteer cavalry within the County of Bedfordshire was granted in 1794, it was not until 1797 that the first troop was raised. By the following year there were four troops in existence, these volunteer Troops serving for many years before being united to form a regiment in 1803. However, as appears to have been occurring across the country at that period, disbandment of the individual Troops took place at intervals, and by 1810 the *Bedfordshire Yeomanry Cavalry* as they had become known, ceased to exist (68).

The year 1817 saw two new Troops of yeomanry being formed in the county, and by 1820 there were six established Troops. In 1827, once again disbandment reared its 'ugly head', with all the Troops being disbanded. 1860 saw the raising of a Troop at Bedford, with another being formed at Sharnbrook, being titled the *1st Huntingdonshire Mounted Rifles (The Duke of Manchester's Light Horse).*

On the outbreak of the war in South Africa in 1899, it soon became apparent that there was a requirement for additional mounted troops, with the result that several companies of volunteer cavalry were raised and sent to the war. As the war progressed the need for further troops resulted in the raising of more companies, amongst them being the 28th (Bedfordshire) Company Imperial Yeomanry, also being informally known as '*Compton's Horse*' after Lord Alwyne Compton who raised the Company. Members of this battalion provided the foundation for the raising of a new regiment in 1901 to be known as the Bedfordshire Imperial Yeomanry (68), the word '*Imperial*' being dropped from the regiments title sometime after 1908.

The regiment's detachment attending the military parade and coronation procession in 1911, formed part of the 1st Battalion of the yeomanry contingent, being commanded by Major the Hon S.C. Peel[2], who wore a uniform quite different from the full dress uniform described below. Major Peel's uniform[3] consisted of the blue cloth peaked cap with white piping, having a white band around the waist, with an embroidered cap badge. A blue serge tunic with white piping, having a stand up collar with white gorget patches with collar badges, and steel shoulder chains. Overalls of blue cloth, having double cloth white stripes, worn with wellington boots and

Figure 130: A fine study of an officer of the Bedfordshire Yeomanry in full dress uniform by W.Y. Carman.

OPPOSITE - *Figure 131:* Bedfordshire Yeomanry. A fine example of this pattern of cap complete with swan feathers plume. Note the wooden stand bearing a regimental pattern cap badge used to display this cap. Courtesy of Geoff Frost.

ABOVE - *Figure 131A:* Bedfordshire Yeomanry. The cap with the plume removed, in which can be seen the plain patent leather peak, bound with gilt metal. Courtesy of Geoff Frost.

spurs. The full dress gold lace shoulder belt with pouch was worn, and he carried what appears to be the 1896 cavalry officers sword with steel scabbard (66).

The regiment's station in 1914 was at Ashburnham Road, Bedford (47).

The Band

No information was available to the authors regarding this regiment's band, other that it is recorded that a dismounted band existed post 1902 (67).

The Officers Full Dress Uniform[4] (*See Fig: 130.*)

The Head-Dress (*See Fig: 131.*)

It was observed by the authors that when studying officers pattern helmets of heavy cavalry regiments, that there were slight differences in the dimensions quoted in the Dress Regulations 1900, and the measurements taken of actual helmets in the authors collection.

In view of the above, it was decided to obtain the measurements of an actual example of an officers pattern lance cap, and for this purpose we enlisted the assistance of Geoffrey Frost of the Aldershot Militaria Society, who kindly undertook to take the necessary measurements of an officers chapka of the Bedfordshire Yeomanry that was amongst his collection of military head-dress and militaria.

Figure 131B: Bedfordshire Yeomanry. Close-up view of the lance cap plate illustrating the number of component parts that make up the plate. Courtesy of Geoff Frost.

The dimensions of the cap as measured by Geoff, are as shown in *Fig: 32.*, they being as follows. Height in front: eight and three eighths of an inch, height at back: nine and five eighths of an inch, across the top of the cap (side to side): six and five eighths of an inch, with across the top (corner to corner): measuring ten inches.

The Skull, Sides and Top

The top of the skull was covered in black patent leather, with gilt metal leaf pattern ornaments covering the four corners. The upper part of the skull (sides) in ribbed blue cloth (sometimes referred to as melton cloth), with gilt metal strips covering the four angles.

To the upper left front of the ribbed cloth section, a gilt metal gimp boss, resembling a cord, being wound some six times with a regimental pattern plain gilt metal (half ball) button to its centre (*See Fig: 131D.*). To the upper rear of the boss, a flat 'oblong' shaped socket into which was inserted the curved prong of the plume (69).

The actual skull, (the part that enclosed the wearers head) was covered with black patent leather, with a gilt metal band one inch wide around the waist, having the appearance of being formed of semi-circular rope, bound together by a double rope to the centre, as illustrated in *Fig: 131C*. Due to the presence of the aforementioned band, the skull of this regiments chapka was without the gold lace waist band with the double band of gold braid below, and the double gold braid around the base of the cap, as on the officers caps of the other lancers regiments. The peak was of black patent leather, but differed in that it had a binding of quarter inch wide gilt metal, in place of the more usual three stripes of gold purl. N.B. The peak binding was similar to that on the officers cap of the 9th Lancers, as illustrated in *Fig: 33.*

The Lance Cap Plate (*See Fig: 131B.*)

The gilt metal plate consisted of the standard pattern gilt metal rayed plate, upon which was mounted a wreath of laurel leaves to the left and oak leaves to the right (when facing the cap) surmounted by a King's crown, with to the centre of the wreath the Arms of Bedford, comprised as follows: 'Argent, an eagle displayed with wings inverted looking towards the sinister, ducally crowned and surmounted upon its breast by a castle of three degrees' (70), all in silvered metal. The assembled lance cap plate consists of five separate pieces, these being (1) the gilt rayed back plate, (2) the white metal (wm) 'King's' crown, (3) the wm wreath of laurel and oak leaves, (4) the wm eagle displayed, and (5) the wm castle superimposed upon the breast of the eagle (69).

The Ear Bosses, Chinchain and Hook

A gilt metal lion head boss to the right side of the cap (when facing the chapka) having a closed ring positioned on the lion's chin, to which was secured a three quarter inch wide gilt chinchain mounted on black leather. The actual linked chinchain measured eighteen inches in length, with the leather backing measuring sixteen inches (69). Although not illustrated in the lance cap shown in *Fig: 131C.*, it is not unknown for this regiments cap to have been fitted with the pattern of chinchain having links often referred to as being 'beaded'. There is an excellent photograph of the cap formerly worn by Lt Colonel Shuttleworth, within the archives at the National Army Museum (accession number 46297) in which the beaded link chinchain may be seen as being fitted to this cap. N.B. Considering the similarity of the Bedfordshire Yeomanry pattern of cap, and the officers cap of the 9th Lancers, which was fitted with the beaded link chinchain, it does not seem out of place that the Bedfordshire Yeomanry cap might also be fitted with this distinctive pattern of chinchain.

To the left side of the cap, a similar gilt metal lion head boss having a gilt metal hook secured to its chin, onto which is secured the loose end of the chinchain. To the rear of the waist of the skull, a gilt metal ring and hook secured to a gilt metal four petalled leaf, onto which was attached the cap-lines and the loose end of the chinchain, as and when required.

The Head Lining, Plume, and Cap-Lines

The sweatband of light fawn leather, with the upper section of dark red silk.

The plume of black over white swan feathers, or alternatively of horsehair in the same colours within a gilt metal socket, consisting of a corded ball beneath five upright leaves (69). (*See Fig: 131E.*).

The cap-lines were of gold gimp and orris as previously described in the aforementioned dress regulations, and encircled the cap once, passed around the body of the wearer, and looped up on the left breast.

The Tunic, Overalls and Accoutrements

The following information relating to the officers full dress uniform is based on a black and white photographic illustration of Lord Alwyne Compton[5] that appears in P.J.R. Mileham's most informative book on the yeomanry regiments (68).

The tunic of blue cloth, the piping to the plastron, to the back seams, and skirt edge in the facing colour of white. The collar and cuffs also in white, being adorned with gold lace. The tunic was somewhat unusual, in that the plastron was of the fold-back pattern, having the appearance of being 'butterfly shaped', the edges being piped in white. It appears that this effect was achieved by the left side of the plastron being unbuttoned down to the top two gilt metal regimental pattern buttons, and then turned back upon itself and held in place by the top two gilt buttons on the opposite side of the tunic (68). N.B. The practice of wearing the plastron 'butterfly style' is known to have been in use by officers of several of the regular lancer regiments c.1860 (16).

The waist girdle was of gold lace, having two white stripes (71), with the sword slings being of gold lace on black morocco leather (66). The overalls of blue cloth, having a double white stripe to the outer seams, worn with black wellington boots and spurs.

The shoulder belt was of gold lace, complete with a white leather flask cord attached by small loops running down the centre of the belt (71), being backed with black morocco leather. Regrettably no information was available to the authors regarding the pat-

Figure 131C: Bedfordshire Yeomanry. Side view of the cap, in which can clearly be seen the gilt metal band that encircles the waist of the cap. Courtesy of Geoff Frost.

Figure 131D: Bedfordshire Yeomanry. Close-up view of the gilt metal corded boss, in which can be seen the regimental pattern plain ball half-button, and the slot for the plume stem. Courtesy of Geoff Frost.

Figure 131E: Bedfordshire Yeomanry. Close-up view of the plume socket fitted to the feather plume. Courtesy of Geoff Frost.

tern of pouch worn with the belt. White wrist gloves, and the 1822 officers light cavalry pattern sword with sword knot, and a steel scabbard completed the uniform (66). N.B. There is a fine colour illustration on an officer of the regiment in full dress uniform, based on the painting by E.A. Campbell, in R.G. Harris's book 'Fifty Years of Yeomanry Uniforms'.

The Other Ranks Uniform

The full dress uniform as worn by the rank and file whilst attending the processions and military parades at the Coronation of 1911 was comprised as follows. A blue cloth cap having a white band and piping, with the quarter seams being similarly piped, and worn without a cap badge. N.B. There is no known record of the other ranks of this regiment ever wearing the full dress lance cap.

The tunic of blue serge having a stand collar upon which was a white gorget patch bearing the regimental collar badge (the Eagle and Castle badge of the Bedford Corporation), with additional white piping around the base of the collar. The tunic was further piped white down the back and hind seams, with the edging to the pointed cuff (which had two buttons) also being piped in white. To the front of the tunic, two breast pockets with buttons, the centre fastening having half-ball buttons of Royal Artillery pattern. Shoulder chains without pads were worn, with a leather shoulder bandolier completing the upper wear. The nether wear consisted of blue cloth overalls having double white stripes, worn with black boots (66).

1st City of London Imperial Yeomanry (Rough Riders)

This regiment can claim descent from the volunteer corps formed in 1798, and known as *The Loyal Islington Troop*. In 1802 this corps was disbanded, only to be re-raised in 1803, becoming known as the Loyal London Volunteer Cavalry and suffering disbanded in 1814 (68). N.B. With regard to the '*Islington*' referred to above, Islington is one on the London Boroughs that borders with the City of London.

In December 1899 the 'Rough Riders' and The Sharpshooters (3rd County of London Yeomanry Hussars) were raised for service in South Africa, the former being numbered the 20th Battalion Imperial Yeomanry, they taking their name from Colonel Theodore Roosevelt's volunteer cavalry formed during the Spanish-American war in Cuba (68), the battalion landing at the Cape towards the end of 1900 (73).

In 1901[6] members of the battalion returning from active service in South Africa formed the 1st County of London Imperial Yeomanry (Rough Riders) with the new corps being allowed the battle honour 'South Africa 1900-02'. At the request of the then Lord Mayor of London, the Arms of the City of London was granted to the regiment (71), and upon the Lord Mayor petitioning the War Office, the regiments title was changed to the 1st City of London Yeomanry (Rough Riders) (73), its first Commanding Officer being Colonel, Viscount Maitland.[7] N.B. One of the regiments earliest and staunchest friends was Lord Baden-Powell, the 'Hero of Mafeking' and founder of the Boy Scout Movement (73).

In 1908 the 'Imperial' was dropped from the regiments title, albeit that the full dress lance cap plate retained the title 'The City of London Imperial Yeomanry' right up until the abolition of full dress.

At the 1911 Coronation the regiment's detachment formed part of The London Mounted Brigade, being commanded by Major T.A. Polson[8], there also being present at the coronation and military parade, a party on horseback wearing mounted review order. The of-

Figure 132: 'Sir John French and an officer of the Rough Riders.' The Inspector-General of the Forces, Sir John French (later Field Marshall the Earl of Ypres K.P. G.C.B. O.M. G.C.V.O. K.C.M.G.) (4) at Smithfield, City of London c.1911. To the right of the photograph is an unknown officer of the City of London Yeomanry in dismounted review order. Copyright D.P.& G.

ficer commanding the mounted detachment is recorded as having worn the mounted review order uniform as described below, complete with lance cap. The other ranks however, are reported as wearing French grey forage caps in place of the full dress lance cap. N.B. 2nd Lieutenant E.W. Goldsworthy is thought to have been the officer commanding the mounted party (66).

The year 1919 saw another change to the regiments title, this time to 'The City of London Yeomanry Lancers (The Rough Riders)' (71).

The regiment's station in 1914 was at 39 Finsbury Square, London, E.C. (47).

The Band

It is recorded that at one period the regiment had a mounted band, and that the band took part in the Lord Mayor of London's procession of 1903, and again in 1909 (67). Indeed taking part in this famous London event continues to the present day, with the musicians of the dismounted band of the Royal Yeomanry parading in full dress uniform similar to that of the former Rough Riders, complete with lance cap with cherry coloured plume. N.B. This dismounted band may also be seen at the Cavalry Old Comrades Parade, held annually on a Sunday morning early in May, in London's Hyde Park, close to Knightsbridge Barracks.

The Officers Full Dress Uniform (*See Fig: 132.*)

The Head-Dress

The Slouch Hat and Peaked Cap

Prior to the introduction of the lance cap, a slouch hat of Colonial pattern was worn. The hat thought to have been French grey in colour, had a purple coloured pugri around its waist, and was worn with an upright black cock's feather plume with a regimental pattern badge on the on the left turned up side of the brim. This pattern of head-dress was replaced circa 1906 by a French grey peaked cap with a purple welt and a purple band around its waist (71), worn with a regimental pattern cap badge. The peaked cap was replaced as the full dress head-dress by the chapka, upon the introduction of the lancer style uniform.

The Lance Cap (*See Fig: 133.*)

The Skull, Sides and Top

For the lance cap, the overall dimensions are approximately as described in the Dress Regulations of 1900 for officers of regular lancer regiments. The upper part of the skull was in French grey ribbed cloth, with the top of the cap in the same colour cloth, having gold gimp and orris cord extending across the top and down the angles, from north to south, and east to west.

To the upper left front of the ribbed cloth section, a gold bullion rosette bearing the GRV Royal Cypher embroidered in gold bullion/wire on a French grey velvet ground, as illustrated in *Fig: 133A*. To the upper rear of the rosette a flat 'oblong' brass/gilt socket, into which was inserted the 'stem' of the plume.

The actual skull was covered with black patent leather, having a band of one inch wide gold lace around the waist, being similar in appearance, if not identical to the pattern shown in 'Designs for Lace' *Fig: No.35*, plate No.75 of the aforementioned dress regulations. Positioned immediately below the gold lace waist band, a band of half inch wide gold braid, above a similar band of one quarter of an inch wide gold braid. Around the base of the cap a band of one quarter inch wide braid, above a similar band of half inch wide gold braid. The peak was also of black patent leather, being embroidered with three differing width stripes of gold purl, the widest stripe being to the centre. (*See Fig: 133A.*).

The Lance Cap Plate (*See Fig: 110.*)

A gilt metal rayed plate of standard size and shape, upon which was a silvered overlay comprised of a wreath of oak leaves surmounted by a King's crown, beneath which was a scroll inscribed '*Rough Riders*'. Upon the wreath of oak leaves, four scrolls inscribed as follows. Upper left scroll '*South Africa*', lower left scroll '*The City of London*', upper right scroll '*1900-1902*', and lower right scroll '*Imperial Yeomanry*' To the centre of the wreath, the 'Arms of The City of London' comprised as follows:- (A shield), 'Argent a cross gules, in the first quarter (upper left quarter) of the shield, a sword in pale, point upwards, of the last. Crest-A dragon's sinister wing argent, charged with cross gules, above the helmet of a Peer with mantling. Supporters-On either side of the shield, a dragon with wings elevated, endorsed and charged on the wing with a cross gules. Beneath the supporters and shield, a tripartite scroll bearing the motto "*Domine Dirige Nos*"' (Lord direct us) (70). N.B. The silvered overlay comprising the crown, title scroll, wreaths, battle honour scrolls, and Arms of the City of London, was a one-piece overlay.

The Ear Rosettes, Chinchain and Hook

A gilt metal lion head boss to the right side of the cap having a closed ring positioned on the lion's chin, to which is secured the three quarter inch wide gilt metal chinchain, mounted on either black leather, or on black patent leather, backed with black velvet. To the left side of the cap, a similar gilt metal lion head boss having a gilt metal hook secured to its chin, onto which is secured the loose end of the chinchain. To the rear of the waist of the skull, a gilt metal ring and hook secured to a gilt metal four petalled leaf, onto which was attached the cap lines and the loose end of the chinchain, as and when required.

The Head Lining, Plume, and Cap-Lines

The head lining of tan leather, with the upper section of crimson/red silk, as may be seen illustrated in *Fig: 133B*.

The full dress plume was of light blue swan's feathers, set in a gilt metal plume socket, and it is highly likely that a light blue hair plume was used for undress (74).

Figure 133: The City of London Imperial Yeomanry, officers pattern lance cap complete with plume. Of interest is the distinctive colour of the feather plume, and the fine condition of this cap. Courtesy of Christopher Bryant Photo: R. Biondi.

Figure 133A: The City of London Yeomanry. Close-up view of the cap with the plume removed, in which can be seen the intricate detail of the silvered overlay on the lance cap plate. Note the Arms of the City of London to the centre of the plate. Courtesy of Christopher Bryant. Photo: R. Biondi.

The cap-lines were of gold gimp and orris and encircled the waist of the cap once, passing round the body of the wearer, and being looped up on the left breast.

The Tunic, Overalls and Accoutrements

The regular pattern lancer style tunic in French grey cloth, with the plastron and piping all in the regimental facing colour of purple, with regimental pattern gilt buttons. The cuffs and collar were also in the facing colour, being adorned with gold lace, although collar badges were not worn. Shoulder cords of gold wire completed the tunic (66).

The waist girdle of French grey material with a double purple stripe. The sword slings of gold lace, backed with leather, and having a purple strip to the centre of the lace (66). The overalls/pantaloons were of French grey cloth with a double purple stripe down each outer seam.

A shoulder belt of gold lace, backed with morocco leather, having a central purple silk stripe. The breast ornaments, buckle, tip, and slide, and the prickers and chains were all in silvered metal (66). The full dress pouch[9] was of blue leather, the flap being silvered and originally bearing the Royal Cypher of ER VII, the cypher later changing to GRV (75).

White leather gauntlets, black knee boots with spurs (for mounted duties), or wellington boots with spurs (for dismounted duties), and either the 1822 officers light cavalry sword (71), or the 1896 pattern cavalry officers sword with sword knot (66), and steel scabbard completed the uniform. N.B. There is a coloured illustration of a subaltern officer of the regiment in full dress uniform, based on the painting by E.A Campbell, in Ron Harris's book on yeomanry uniforms (71).

The Other Ranks

The full dress uniform of the rank and file[10] generally followed that of the officers, and was worn with either a peaked cap having a French grey top, complete with purple headband, and cap badge, or the full dress lance cap[11] which was similar to the pattern worn by the other ranks of the regular lancer regiments. The cloth upper section of the cap was in French grey material, with a band of yellow cotton braid around the waist. The purple plume was supported by a blue and yellow woollen plume boss, having a plain gilt/gilding metal button to the centre, with the lance cap plate being one piece die-struck item. (*See Fig: 111.*)

The tunic was of French blue material, sometimes referred to as being cornflower blue, having purple facings, with collar badges and steel shoulder chains being worn. Yellow braid/cord was substituted for the gold braid/cord/lace used on the officers pattern tunic.

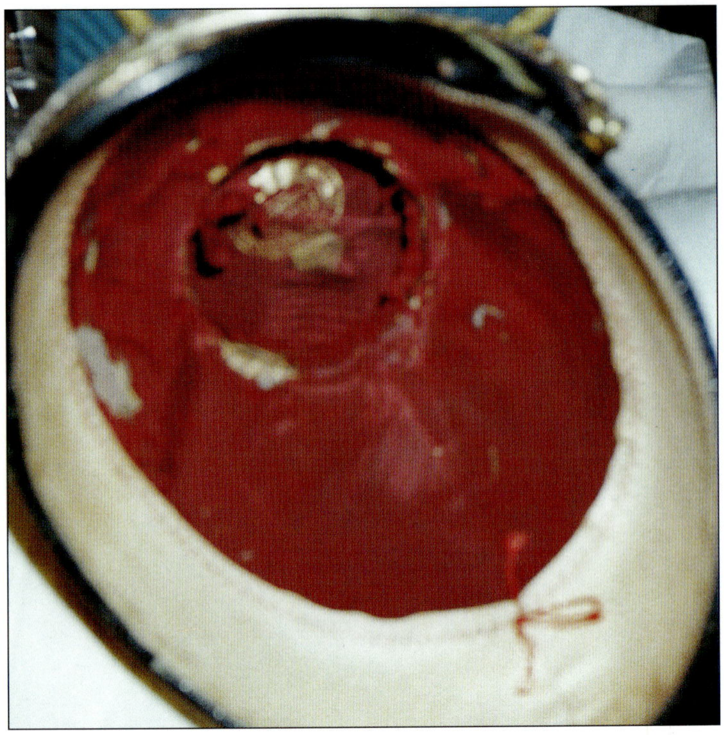

Figure 133B: The City of London Yeomanry. Inside view of the cap illustrating the leather and silk lining. N.B. Just visible is the gold embossed makers stamp. Copyright W.Y. Carman.

East Riding of Yorkshire Yeomanry

Following a request by H.M. Government that within the limits of the County of East Riding a regiment of yeomanry cavalry be raised, public meetings were held at Beverley, Hull and Driffield in April 1902 to 'drum up support for the new regiment' (76).

These discussions were obviously fruitful, for there was soon sufficient volunteers to form the new regiment, and in 'September, the Regimental Headquarters was set up in Railway Street, Beverley'. The regiment was 'officially accepted by the Government on the 15th May 1903', being titled the *East Riding of Yorkshire Imperial Yeomanry*, the regiment being known locally as 'Wenlock's Horse' after its Colonel, Lord Wenlock.[12] Major (later Lt Colonel) John Bourchier Stracey-Clitherow C.B.E., T.D., D.L., was appointed as second-in-command, with Lord Herries becoming Honorary Colonel (77). N.B. *See Fig: 134.* for a contemporary illustration of Lt Colonel Stracey-Clitherow.

The newly raised regiment was comprised of four squadrons, the recruiting area for each of the squadrons being as follows. A Squadron from the City of Hull. B Squadron from Holderness, with its headquarters at Beverley. C Squadron from the York area, with an headquarters at Escrick. D squadron which included a maxim gun section, with headquarters at Bridlington (77).

Following the introduction of the Territorial Act of 1908, which brought into being the term 'Territorial Army' the word '*Imperial*' became obsolete and was dropped from the regiments title, although as with the 1st City of London Yeomanry, the word '*Imperial*' continued to be borne on the title scroll of the plate on the officers lance cap into the reign of King George the Fifth.

Figure 134: Lt. Colonel J.B. Stracey-Clitherow C.B.E., T.D. (1853-1931). He was appointed as second-in-command to Lord Wenlock in 1903, and commanded the East Riding Yeomanry from 1907 to 1912. Courtesy of Queen Own Yorkshire Yeomanry.

Figure 135: 'A group of the East Riding Yeomanry.' An unknown squadron of the regiment c.1914. The officer in the centre of the group is thought to be Lieutenant Colonel Langdale, with on his left Captain W.R. Tylden-Wright the Adjutant of the regiment, wearing the uniform of the 3rd Hussars, this being his parent regiment (76). Copyright D.P.& G.

The 1911 Coronation detachment formed part of the 2nd Battalion of the yeomanry contingent, being commanded by Lieutenant J. Walker[13] who wore the full dress uniform, complete with lance cap. The other ranks in the detachment also wore the lancer style uniform, their head-dress however was a maroon staff pattern peaked cap with welts, lancer piping, and regimental pattern cap badge (66).

The regiments station in 1914 was at Railway Street, Beverley, East Riding (47).

The Band

It is recorded that the regiment's official band was formed in 1907, the strength of the band being increased by seventeen members of the brass band of Thomas Wilson, Sons and Co. The musicians appear to have 'been dressed like the men, with lancer tunics and staff pattern forage caps, but with heavy epaulettes of twisted cord, possible red'. N.B. In May 1940 the bands instruments were lost 'somewhere in France', however they were retrieved by a Frenchman who hid them from the occupying troops throughout the occupation of France, he returning the instruments to the regiment during the liberation of his country in 1944 (77).

The Officers Full Dress Uniform (*See Fig: 136F.*)

The following details relating to the full dress uniform of this regiment, designed in 1906, are based on information contained in the most detailed article entitled 'The East Riding Yeomanry (Wenlock's Horse) 1902-47 by Major Roy Wilson that appeared in *Military Modelling Magazine* in April 1983, the same authors book entitled 'Yeomanry of the East Riding', and written correspondence from Roy Wilson to the authors.

The Lance Cap (*See Fig: 136.*)

The Skull, Sides and Top

Once again the dimensions approximate to those given in the Dress Regulations of 1900 for officers of regular lancer regiments. The upper part of the skull, was in light grey ribbed cloth with gilt metal strips covering the four angles, the top of the cap being covered with black patent leather, with gilt metal leaf pattern ornaments covering the four corners. N.B. The upper cloth section has also been described as being in French grey (66).

To the upper left front of the ribbed cloth section, a unique pattern silvered metal rose of Yorkshire as illustrated in *Fig: 136A.*, secured to the ribbed cloth section of the cap by means of two small 'looped' nuts (79), with to the upper rear of the rose, a flat oblong socket into which was inserted the 'stem' of the plume. N.B. Within the skull, positioned behind the Yorkshire rose, a metal 'wing bolt' to secure the plume stem in place (79).

The actual skull was covered with black patent leather. having a gilt metal band of acanthus design, being approximately half an inch wide around the waist of the cap (*See Fig: 136B.*). The unadorned peak was also of black patent leather, having a gilt metal binding, three sixteenth's of an inch wide (76).

The Lance Cap Plate (*See Fig: 136C.*)

The gilt metal plate of standard shape and size, carried the Royal Cypher of ER VII[14] surmounted by a King's pattern crown. Below the cypher and crown, the 'running fox', below which was a tripartite scroll bearing '*East Riding of*' (left), '*Yorkshire*' (centre), and '*Imperial Yeomanry*' (right). Immediately above the left scroll was a spray of laurel leaves, with a spray of palm leaves immediately

Figure 136: East Riding of Yorkshire Yeomanry. An Edwardian example of the officers lance cap complete with feather plume. Note the extremely fine condition of this rare lance cap. Courtesy of Christopher Bryant. Photo: R. Biondi.

above the right scroll, with a small '*Yorkshire*' rose beneath the centre scroll (65). The crown, cypher, fox, scroll, and rose were all in silvered metal, and it is confirmed that this pattern of plate was comprised of six separate pieces, they being (1) the gilt plate, (2) the crown, (3) the Royal Cypher, (4) the running fox, (5) the Yorkshire rose, and (6) the wreath/title scroll. N.B. The five silvered overlay pieces were attached to the gilt rayed backing plate with copper wire (79), in a similar method as described earlier in chapter five, for the officers pattern plate of the 5th Lancers.

The Ear Rosettes, Chinchain and Hook

A gilt metal lion head boss to the right side of the cap, having a closed ring positioned on the lion's chin to which is secured the three quarter inch wide gilt metal chinchain, mounted on black patent leather, and backed with black velvet. To the left side of the cap, a similar gilt metal lion head boss having a gilt metal hook secured to its chin, onto which is secured the loose end of the chain. To the rear of the waist of the skull, a gilt metal ring and hook secured to a gilt metal four petalled leaf, onto which was attached the cap-lines and the loose end of the chinchain, as and when required.

The Head Lining, Plume, and Cap-Lines

The head lining of tan leather, with the upper section of crimson silk (79). (*See Fig: 136D.*).

The plume was of French grey (although more blue in actual colour) over white swan feathers, measuring fourteen inches in the front, and seven inches behind (from the bend of the feathers), hav-

Figure 136A: East Riding ofYorkshire Yeomanry. Close-up view of the regiments unique silvered Yorkshire rose pattern plume boss. Courtesy of Major R. Wilson.

Figure 136B: East Riding of Yorkshire Yeomanry. Close-up view of the gilt-metal, leaf pattern band that encircled the waist of the cap. Courtesy of Major R. Wilson.

Figure 136C: East Riding of Yorkshire Yeomanry. Front view of the cap with the plume removed. Of particular interest is the fine gilt and silvered lance cap plate. Courtesy of Christopher Bryant Photo: R. Biondi.

Figure 136D: East Riding of Yorkshire Yeomanry. Inside view of the cap, in which may be seen the suppliers gold embossed 'stamp' of H. Poole & Co. Note. Just visible to the lower left of the illustration is the 'wing bolt', which when turned to the right, tightened down upon the plume stem. Courtesy of Major R. Wilson.

Figure 136E: East Riding of Yorkshire Yeomanry. Close-up view of the gilt metal ring located at the centre of the 'crown' of the feather plume. Courtesy of Major R. Wilson.

ing a gilt metal ring to the centre 'crown' of the plume, as illustrated in *Fig: 136E.*). The plume was set within a gilt metal plume socket, comprised of a corded ball beneath five upright leaves (79).

The cap-lines were of gold gimp and orris as previously described in the aforementioned dress regulations, and encircled the waist of the cap once, and were then passed around the body of the wearer and looped up on the left breast.

The Tunic, Overalls and Accoutrements[15]

The most impressive tunic was of maroon cloth, the plastron, piping to the outer seam of the sleeves, the rear seams, and the shoulder straps all being in the regimental facing colour of light blue, complete with gilt regimental pattern buttons 'bearing a scroll inscribed 'East Riding of Yorkshire', and within the scroll a crown and fox, and below the letters IY' (76). Gilt metal running fox collar badges were also worn, with the collar and cuffs being in the facing colour and adorned with gold lace. N.B. There exists an officers pattern full dress tunic having gold twisted shoulder cords, this tunic being reserved for levee dress (76).

The girdle was of gold lace having two crimson silk stripes, with the sword slings also of gold lace (not having a silk stripe), being backed with red morocco leather.

The overalls were of dark blue cloth having a light blue stripe down each outer seam, worn with black wellington boots and steel spurs (76).

The shoulder belt of gold lace (lace design No 53 of Dress Regulation 1900) being without a central stripe[16], backed with leather, with the buckle, tip, and slide in gilt metal.[17] The pouch of black patent leather, the flap of the pouch bearing a gilt crown, with beneath, a gilt metal running fox on a silver coloured scroll bearing "*Forrard*". White buckskin/doeskin wrist gloves were worn, and the 1896 cavalry officers pattern sword with gold sword knot, and steel scabbard completed the uniform. N.B. The word "Forrard" is taken from the hunting term 'Hark forrard' (76).

The Other Ranks Full Dress (*See Fig: 135.*)

The rank and file wore a 'maroon staff pattern forage cap, with light blue piping around the edge of the cap and on the quarter welts', and a pale blue cap band', worn with the regimental cap badge.[18] Maroon cloth, lancer style tunic, 'the collar, cuffs, and shoulder strap were light blue, and there was light blue piping down the front of the tunic, round the skirts, down the rear seams and on the pocket flaps'. 'Collar badges were only worn by senior N.C.O.'s (these had the scroll added below (the fox) at the same time as the cap badge was changed' (76). Yellow cap-lines, the girdle of light blue with maroon stripes, overalls of dark blue cloth with a single blue cloth stripe, worn with black wellington boots. N.B. There is no record of the other ranks of this regiment wearing the full dress lance cap.

Lanarkshire Yeomanry

Prior to 1819 there were no yeomanry in the County of Lanarkshire, however in that year three Troops were raised in the Upper Ward (82) with a single further Troop being raised at Airdrie on the 2nd November 1819 by Walter Frederick Campbell M.P. of Islay. The winter of 1819 was one with problems in northern England, in Glasgow and other towns in the west of Scotland, with riots an general insurrection being threatened, this situation soon being settled by the yeomanry. The Airdrie Troop was added to the

Figure 136F: A fine study of an officer of the East Riding of Yorkshire Imperial Yeomanry c.1908. Based on photographs, and items of head-dress and uniform in the York Castle Collection by courtesy of Dr. P. Newman, and the Yeomanry Collection in the Art Gallery, Beverley, by courtesy of East Yorkshire Borough of Beverley Council. Reproduced by kind permission of the artist W.R. Younghusband.

Lanarkshire Yeomanry in 1826, their uniform being described as 'blue, full skirted, facings yellow' with 'some sort of helmet'. For administrative purposes the four Troops were termed the *Upper Ward of Lanarkshire and Airdrie Yeomanry Cavalry* (80).

It is said that the regiment were selected to perform official duties, upon the occasion of the royal visit to the City of Glasgow in August 1849 by Her Majesty Queen Victoria, accompanied by her sons and daughter, the Lanarkshire Yeomanry guarding the route taken by the royal party (81). In 1852 the regiment was re-named the *Lanarkshire Regiment of Yeomanry Cavalry*, and by 1868 three additional Troops had been added. Six of the Troops were armed with carbines and swords, however, in the case of the Airdrie Troop, lances were carried, this being the first recorded indication of their lancer role. It appears that the lances were considered a source of danger, both to themselves and their friends, rather than a terror to their foes, and so were withdrawn about 1870 (80). N.B. It is said that the regiment served without a break in service, being frequently called upon the assist the Civil Powers, and in fact the regiment was on permanent duty for six weeks 1856 (68).

The uniform of this period is described as being blue double-breasted tunic, with red collar and cuffs, as well as red lapels, with girdles of yellow and red indicating a lancer style of dress. However the head-dress of this period was a shako, and remained so until 1884 when it was withdrawn, being replaced by a infantry style blue cloth helmet (80). N.B. A pre 1880 pattern dark blue tunic having a large scarlet lapels (in lancer fashion), a red collar with rank badges, and pointed cuffs, is preserved.

In 1888, the then Prince of Wales (later H.M. King Edward VII) opened the Glasgow Exhibition, when the Lanarkshire Yeomanry took part in the proceedings, where they apparently 'made a fine appearance' (81). There was however still no evidence of the regiment wearing lance caps.

During the Boer War the regiment provided both officers and men for the 17th Company of the 6th Battalion Imperial Yeomanry, with the Ayreshire Company (68). In 1901 following the end of this conflict, an Act of Parliament re-organised the yeomanry who were now to be 'Imperial Yeomanry' after the South Africa war veterans, with the word 'Imperial' to be included within the their regimental titles. However upon the formation of the Territorial Force in 1908, the volunteer cavalry regiments who had earlier incorporated the word 'Imperial' within their regimental title experienced yet another title change, when this word was deleted from their respective titles. It is not hard to imagine the 'great joy' this change of title must have meant to the manufacturers of regimental buttons and cap badge etc. N.B. It was sometime after this period, that the Lanarkshire Yeomanry adopted their badge of a two-headed eagle surmounted by a crown.

The Coronation detachment of 1911 was part of the 1st Battalion of the yeomanry contingent, being commanded by Captain W.M. Tower (formerly of the 3rd Hussars), who wore regulation pattern khaki service dress of peaked cap with badge, service dress tunic with a stand up collar, having collar badges comprised of a black eagle with gilt claws, beneath a gilt crown. A Sam Browne belt, khaki pantaloons and riding boots, leather wrist gloves, with sword and scabbard (pattern unknown) completed this uniform. The rank and file of the detachment also wore khaki service dress with peaked caps, and would probably have worn leather bandoliers (66). N.B. The respected author Ron Harris, in his excellent booklet on the yeomanry force at the 1911 Coronation, makes the important observation that 'It is difficult to know why this Scottish regiment should have chosen to send its detachment to London in khaki. Certainly full dress does not seem to have been worn after the South African War, but by 1911 all ranks had blue patrols which would have been quite adequate' (66).

The regiments station in 1914 was at Lanark (47).

The Band

It is recorded that the regiment had a band complete with drum-horse circa 1887, and in 1899 the band performed outside the Clydesdale Hotel at the Lanark Racecourse, regrettably however, no information was available relating to the uniform worn by members of the band on the aforementioned occasion. The mounted band eventually became a dismounted band in circa 1901/02. N.B. Some forty years on and the regimental band was still performing for in July 1938, a set of new silver kettle-drums were presented to the regiment by the then Colonel, Sir John T. Usher (67).

The Officers Full Dress Uniform

As mentioned above, in 1884, the shako that was being worn at that period gave place to an infantry style helmet, as described below, this type of dress being worn up to the Boer War, when the practical drab coloured service dress was worn by all.

The Head-Dress[19]

The Blue Cloth Helmet

The following is an abridged description of the above mentioned item of head-dress, as worn by corps and infantry officers, it being known as the 'Universal Home Pattern' helmet. The skull of cork covered blue cloth, the front peak being bound with gilt metal, the rear peak with patent leather. To the crown of the skull, a gilt spike mounted upon a gilt cross-piece base, with each of the terminations of the base having a small rose, with to the rear of the helmet, a convex gilt metal bar down the centre of the back. Gilt metal rose pattern ear bosses (rosettes) with a gilt metal chinchain mounted on black patent leather and backed with black velvet. Tan leather and scarlet silk head lining, with a regimental pattern helmet plate to the front of the helmet (43). N.B. On an officers helmet illustrated in Issue Five of *Regiment Magazine*, the small rose fitted to each of the terminations of the cross-piece base was said to be in silver.

Notwithstanding the above, on an officers blue cloth helmet of this regiment that sold at a Sussex Auction House, the helmet concerned differed from the regulation infantry officers pattern helmet, by having a gilt metal laurel wreath band[20] above the front peak, running from ear socket to ear socket, being fitted with an acanthus base supporting the spike, with the leather backed chinchain having beaded links, being secured to the skull with lion's head bosses (83).

The helmet plate fitted to this regiments blue cloth helmet was comprised of a gilt metal hobnailed eight-pointed rayed star, not dissimilar in appearance to the pattern of star fitted to the 1871 pattern yeomanry officers helmet. Upon the star, a gilt metal strap inscribed 'Lanarkshire Yeomanry', to the centre of which was a silvered double-headed eagle grasping a bell in its right claw, surmounted by a crown on a gilt metal ground, (this device being from the Seal of the Royal Burgh of Lanark) (46).

The Lance Cap[21] (*See Fig: 137.*).
On an officers pattern cap that some short time ago appeared in the saleroom of a London Auction House, the lance cap plate carried a single battle honour, that being for the South Africa 1900-02 campaign, (the plate being as described below). This might suggest that this plate was produced prior to the outbreak of the First World War, however there is no evidence of such a pattern of plate existing prior to 1914. In fact it was not until c.1961 that this pattern of plate was mentioned, it being recorded that there was an actual specimen in the Regimental Room, Brook Street some six years later in 1967 (118). The actual cap as mentioned above, appears to have been very different from the other ranks pattern cap as mentioned below under the heading 'The Other Ranks Uniform', being firmly based on the special pattern cap of the 9th Queen's Royal Lancers, as described in chapter seven. N.B. The year 1947 saw the issue of Army Order No.44 of 1947 which stated that the Lanarkshire Yeomanry was now part of the Royal Armoured Corps and was to be affiliated to the 9th Queen's Royal Lancers (118).

Figure 137: The Lanarkshire Yeomanry. Officers pattern lance cap complete with feather plume. Courtesy of Blunderbuss Antiques.

Figure 137A: The Lanarkshire Yeomanry. Side view of the cap. Courtesy of Blunderbuss Antiques. Photo: W.Y. Carman.

Figure 137B: The Lanarkshire Yeomanry. Close up view of the gilt metal plume boss. Note. Just visible on the left, below the waistband is part of the silvered thistle wreath overlay to the lance cap plate. Courtesy of Blunderbuss Antiques. Photo: W.Y. Carman.

The Skull, Sides and Top

The dimensions of the cap are as previously described in chapter seven for officers of regular lancer regiments, with the top of the skull being covered in black patent leather and having gilt metal leaf pattern ornaments covering the four corners. The upper part of the skull in ribbed black cloth, with gilt metal strips covering the four angles.

To the upper left front of the ribbed cloth section, a gilt metal gimp boss, resembling a cord being wound some six times, with to the centre of the boss a regimental pattern gilt metal scallop edged button bearing an eagle with two heads as illustrated in *Fig: 137B*. To the upper rear of the boss a flat 'oblong' socket, into which was inserted the 'stem' of the plume. On the inside of the cap, immediately behind the gilt metal boss, was a small brass knurled knob, which when turned, secured the plume stem within the oblong socket.

The actual skull was covered with black patent leather, with a gilt metal band one inch wide around the waist, having the appearance of being formed of semi-circular rope, being bound together by a double rope to the centre. The skull of this regiments chapka did not have the gold lace waist band with the double band of gold braid below, nor the double gold braid around the base of the cap, as on the officers caps of the Lincolnshire Yeomanry, and The Rough Riders, this specific pattern of band being illustrated in *Fig: 137A*. The peak was of black patent leather, having a binding of quarter inch wide gilt metal in place of the more usual three stripes of gold purl.

The Lance Cap Plate

The standard shaped gilt metal rayed plate, bore a silvered thistle wreath encircling an oval shaped strap bearing the title *'Lanarkshire Yeomanry'*, the strap surmounted by a King's pattern crown. Within the strap in silvered metal, the Arms of Lanark comprised as follows:- 'Argent, an eagle with two heads displayed sable, beaked and membered gules, a bell azure pendent from the dexter leg by a string of the last'. Beneath the thistle wreath, a gilt metal single scroll inscribed with the battle honour *'South Africa 1900-02'*. The lance cap plate was comprised of four separate pieces, these being (1) the gilt metal rayed plate, (2) the silvered crown/thistle wreath/ strap & ground, (3) the gilt 'double-headed eagle', and (4) the gilt metal battle honour scroll. N.B. The actual, Arms of Lanark also includes the following 'devices' that are omitted from the 'badge' on the lance cap plate. 'In chief, two lion's counter-passant of the third, and in base, as many salmon naiant from the centre' (70).

With regard to the gilt metal 'double-headed' eagle, and title scroll as mentioned above, there is known to exist an example of an officer pattern cap bearing a plate having both the 'double-headed' eagle and the title scroll 'South Africa 1900- 02' in silvered metal[22], as opposed to being in the gilt metal as mentioned above. The existence of two differing examples of the same pattern of plate for this regiment, is to say the least somewhat strange and rather disconcerting. It is not however within the authors remit to speculate upon the authenticity of particular items of head-dress, and therefore no opinion is offered at this time.

The Ear Rosettes, Chinchain and Hook

A gilt metal lion head boss to the right side of the cap having a closed ring positioned on the lion's chin, to which is secured the three quarter inch wide gilt corded metal chinchain (similar to the hussar pattern), mounted on black leather. To the left side of the cap, a similar gilt metal lion head boss having a gilt metal hook secured to its chin, onto which was secured the loose end of the chinchain. To the rear of the waist of the skull, a gilt metal ring and hook secured to a gilt metal four petalled leaf, onto which was attached the cap-lines and the loose end of the chinchain, as and when required.

The Head Lining, Plume, and Cap-Lines

The head lining of tan leather, with the upper section of scarlet silk (84).

The plume of black cock's feathers (85), or alternatively of black horsehair, in a gilt metal lancer pattern socket.

The cap-lines were of gold gimp and orris, and encircled the waist of the cap once, passing round the body of the wearer, then being looped up on the left breast.

The Tunic, Overalls and Accoutrements

The Khaki Uniform

Following the Boer War, and upon becoming Imperial Yeomanry, the regiment was ordered to wear a basic uniform of drab coloured tunic having red collars, worn with 'IY' upon the shoulder straps. The nether wear comprised drab breeches, with brown leather leggings and boots, with the head-dress being a similar coloured slouch hat having one side turned up, upon which was worn the regiments badge. N.B. Officers were permitted to wear the old levee dress if desired.

The Full Dress Uniform

In 1905 many Imperial yeoman sought more attractive uniforms, and it was decided that they were to be permitted to wear a blue tunic with scarlet facings, with gold lace for the officers. In 1908 following the introduction of the previously mentioned Territorial Force, a new uniform was introduced and eventually the head-dress was to be the lance cap. N.B. A special parade of the Territorial Army held in 1909 saw many yeomanry regiments parading in their new full dress uniform (82).

The blue tunic had the upper part of the plastron[23] and the piping in the regimental facing colour of scarlet, the collar and cuffs being in like colour and adorned with gold lace. Regimental pattern gilt buttons, and gilt bullion shoulder cords of regular lancer officers pattern completed the tunic (86) N.B. It appears that the officers did not wear collar badges on the full dress tunic.

Figure 138: The Lanarkshire Yeomanry. A fine study of the unique, other ranks pattern cap, based on that of the 12th Lancers, complete with plume. Note the most unusual plate fitted to the front of the cap. Courtesy of the Scottish War Museum, The Castle, Edinburgh.

Figure 138A: The Lanarkshire Yeomanry. Side view of the other ranks pattern cap. Courtesy of the Scottish War Museum, The Castle, Edinburgh.

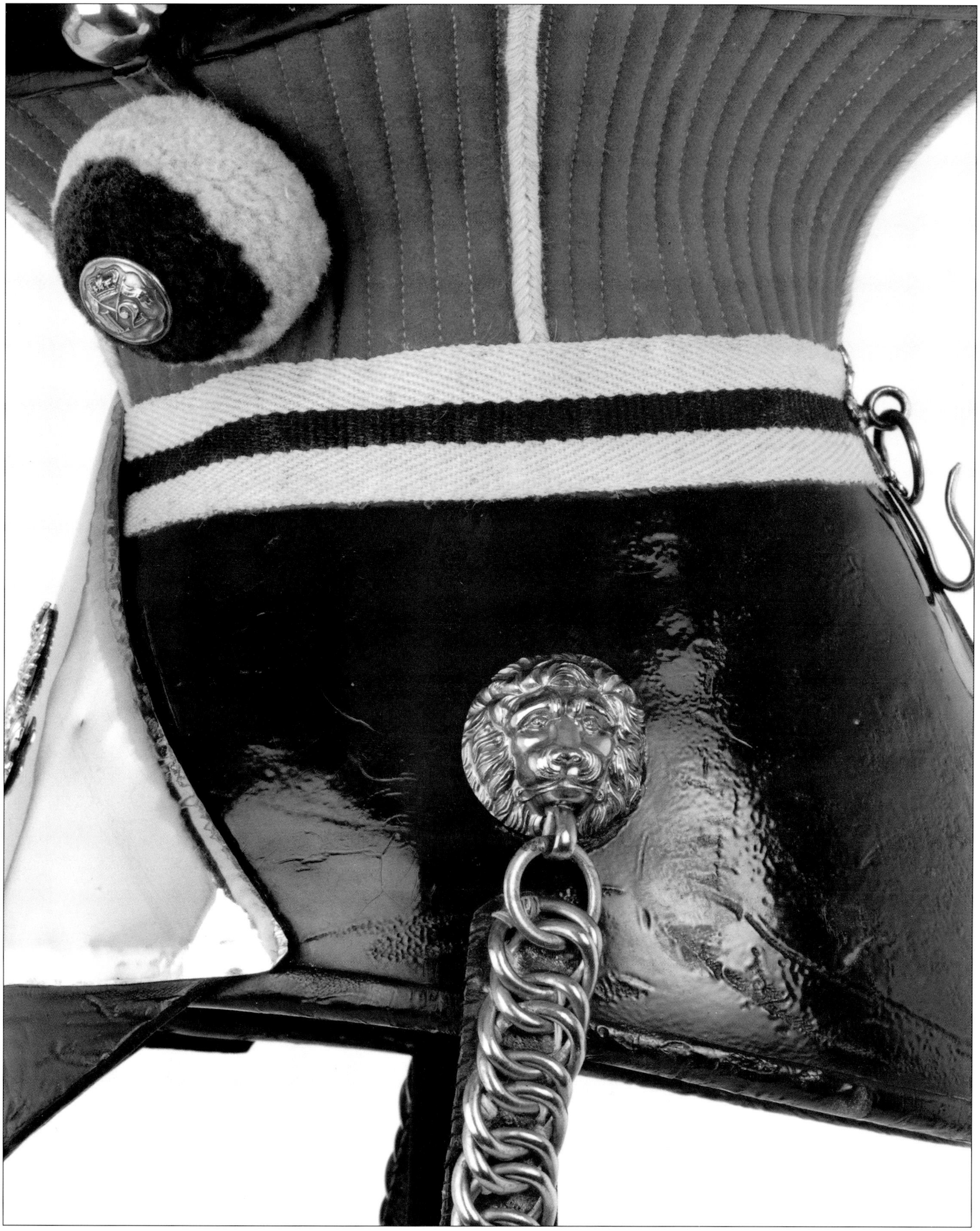

Figure 138B: The Lanarkshire Yeomanry. Close up view of the side of the cap, in which may clearly be seen the 'Victorian' pattern button of the 12th Lancers to the centre of the plume boss. Courtesy of the Scottish War Museum, The Castle, Edinburgh.

The waist girdle was of gold lace with two scarlet stripes (85), and it is reasonable to conclude that the sword slings would also have been of gold lace.

The overalls were of dark blue cloth with a double stripe down each outer seam of either gold lace or yellow cloth, worn with black wellington boot and spurs.

The shoulder belt was of gold lace having a central silk stripe, backed with leather, complete with silvered breast ornament[24] with prickers and chains (85). White wrist gloves were worn, with the 1912 pattern sword with gold sword knot, and steel scabbard completing the uniform (85). It is regretted that no information was available regarding the pattern of shoulder belt pouch worn. N.B. It is thought that the above pattern of full dress uniform, complete with lance cap, is similar, if not identical, to that worn by the officer attending the Glasgow Exhibition of 1938.

The Other Ranks Uniform

Lance Caps

It appears that there had been a desire for the rank and file to wear a lance cap, but there is no evidence of there ever having been an official issue of this form of head-dress.

In 1934 information was sought by the regiment from Messrs Stephen Simpson who made lace and cords for such a cap, and details were sent to a Captain Sanderson. It appears that it was at this period that other ranks pattern lance caps were purchased from the 12th Lancers, they being provided with a special pattern plate, there apparently being a surviving example of this pattern of cap, which retains a 12th Lancers regimental pattern button to the centre of the plume boss. It would seem that the 12th Lancers pattern cap was chosen because the red ribbed cloth sides to the upper part of their cap matched the facing colour of the Lanarkshire Yeomanry. N.B. It has been said that the other ranks pattern lance cap appeared at the Glasgow Exhibition held in 1938.

The Lance Cap (*See Fig: 138.*).

The following description of the lance cap, is based on the pattern of cap thought to have been worn by the trooper, who wore the full dress uniform when representing his regiment at the Glasgow Exhibition of 1938, as mentioned above.[25]

The Skull and Top

The top of the cap was covered with black patent leather, with gilding metal ornaments covering the four corners. The upper part of the skull (sides) was covered with ribbed cloth, the facing colour being of scarlet. The four corners (angles) of the cloth section were covered with yellow cord braid, which terminated under the corner ornaments, but did not extend over the top of the cap. N.B. It is of interest the cloth sides to this particular cap were of scarlet, whilst that of the officers pattern cap were of black cloth as described above. Surely, such a disparity in colour must be unique, even for a yeomanry regiment.

To the upper left front of the ribbed cloth section, a blue upon yellow worsted boss, having a socket at its rear into which was deposited the stem of the plume. To the centre of the boss a small sized 12th Lancers regimental pattern button on a short tube. N.B. The small button, as illustrated in *Fig: 138B.* appears to bear the Victorian crown.

The actual skull of the cap was covered with black patent leather, with around the waist of the cap a band of yellow cotton braid approximately one inch broad, this band having a central blue stripe. To the rear waist of the cap, a brass/gilding metal ring and hook, on a four petalled leaf of similar metal, as illustrated in Fig: 138B. The peak was of black patent leather, being without the gilt metal binding present of the officers pattern cap.

The Lance Cap Plate (*See Fig: 138.*).

The lance cap plate was totally unique, consisting of a plain (not rayed) triangular shaped brass plate, without a border, and having the appearance of being home made. To the centre of the plate was what appears to be a regimental pattern 'eagle with two heads above a title scroll' pattern cap badge.

The Chinchain and Ear Bosses

The plain brass chinchain was backed with leather, being attached to the cap by being secured to a closed ring, positioned upon the chin of the left hand lion's head boss, with the loose end of the chain being hung upon the hook secured to the chin of the right hand lion's head boss.

The Head Lining

Although not confirmed, it is thought that the lining was comprised of a black leather and oilskin/waxed cotton head lining/sweatband, or alternatively of black calico.

The Plume (*See Fig: 138.*)

The plume was of black horsehair, within a brass socket (holder) similar in general appearance to the officers pattern socket, but having a plain ball (uncorded).

The Tunic and Overalls[26]

Blue tunic with full scarlet plastron, scarlet collar and cuffs, yellow piping. Yellow waist girdle with double scarlet stripes, blue pantaloons having a double yellow stripe, worn with black knee boots and spurs (85).

Lincolnshire Imperial Yeomanry

The County of Lincolnshire's first troops of volunteer cavalry were raised in 1794, they serving until 1828.[27] The *Lincoln Light Horse* comprised four Troops, and at one period a further ten Troops of cavalry existed. Re-raised in 1831, the *North Lincolnshire Regiment of Yeomanry Cavalry* served for some fifteen years, until it was disbanded in 1846 (68).

The regiment with which this chapter is concerned, received the royal approval of His Majesty King Edward VII on the 18th May 1901[28], the Earl of Yarborough being appointed to command the newly formed regiment (71).

Although raised during the Boer War, the regiment was too late for any action. Never the less, 'regular training persisted with annual camps rotating between Belton, Riseholme and Grimsthorpe Parks, each being the seat of a senior officer'. 'N.B. The Army Lists of the day were virtually a 'Who's Who' of the county gentry' (88).

As with other yeomanry regiments, sometime after 1901 the regiments title changed to include the word 'Imperial', however the amended title of Lincolnshire Imperial Yeomanry was in use for only a few years, for with the formation of the Territorial Force in 1908 the regiments title was simplified to the Lincolnshire Yeomanry, albeit that the word 'Imperial' was still present on the title scroll on the officers lance cap plate.

The regiments detachment that attended the Coronation of King George V in 1911 formed part of the 1st Battalion on the yeomanry contingent, being commanded by Captain R. Sleight[29] who wore the regiments full dress uniform, complete with lance cap (66). The rank and file of the detachment wore dark green forage caps with a white band and lancer piping, complete with white metal cap badges. A green frock coat with built-in belt, collar badges and shoulder chains was worn, the overalls being of like colour having double white stripes down each outer seam. A brown leather bandolier and tan wrist gloves were also worn (87). N.B. Metal initials of 'LIY' could be worn on the shoulder straps, the title later being changed to T/Y/Lincoln upon the formation of the Territorial Force (88).

The regiment continued to serve until 1920, when its disbandment was announced under Army Order 512 of November 1920 (87).

The regiments station in 1914 was at Old Barracks, Lincoln, Lincolnshire (47).

The Band

It is recorded that the regiment maintained a dismounted band during the post 1902 period (67), and based on a photograph of a member of the band that appeared in the county magazine, the uniform appeared to be very similar, if not identical to that worn by other members of the regiment (88).

The Regiments Uniform

When formed, the common dress for the Imperial Yeomanry was drab coloured, with a slouch hat, although it was not long before the Lincolnshire Yeomanry added green to their uniform. It was to be expected that 'Lincoln green' which was made in Lincoln should be their distinguishing facing colour, to be used on the collar and piping of the tunic. This appeared in the Army List (1905 etc) as 'Uniform drab - facings - Dark Green' (72), with their badge inspired by the Arms of the City of Lincoln, this consisting of a fleur-de-lis (lys) upon the Cross of St. George within laurel leaves (88).

Figure 139: The Lincolnshire Yeomanry. A fine study of a dismounted officer in Review Order, and a sergeant in Parade or Walking Out Dress, as worn by members of the regiments contingent on parade at the Coronation of Their Majesties King George V and Queen Mary on the 22nd June 1911. N.B. This painting previously appeared in the May 1980 edition of Military Modelling Magazine. Reproduced by kind permission of the artist R.J. Marrion.

By 1905, permission had been granted for the officers mess dress uniform, the green jacket having a white collar and silver lace, and by 1907, a tunic of lancer style having white facings as described below was being worn, as was a peaked cap having a white band with lancer style piping (72).

The Officers Full Dress Uniform *(See Fig: 139.)*

The Lance Cap[30] *(See Fig: 140.)*

The following information relating to the lance cap is based on an example that at one time was within the collection of artifacts housed at the Castle, Lincoln, supplemented with additional details based on a lance cap formerly owned by Eric Dickinson of Nottingham, the latter cap having been made by Messrs Hobson and Sons, Military Tailors. N.B. It is though that only four or five of these lance caps were ever made, they being worn by the senior officers of the regiment (89).

The Skull, Sides and Top

The dimensions of the cap are as described in the Dress Regulations of 1900 for officers of regular lancer regiments, with the upper part of the skull in white ribbed cloth, with the top of the cap also in white cloth having silver gimp and orris cord extending across the top and down the angles, from north to south, and east to west as illustrated in *Fig: 140A*.

To the upper left front of the ribbed cloth section, a silver bullion rosette bearing the Royal Cypher of ER VII.[31] as illustrated in *Fig: 140.*, embroidered in silver bullion/wire on a green velvet ground.[32] To the upper rear of the rosette a flat 'oblong' brass/gilt socket into which was inserted the 'stem' of the plume, which was secured within the socket by means of the knurled 'knob' located within the inside of the cap as illustrated in *Fig: 140F*.

The skull was covered with black patent leather, with a band of one inch wide silver lace having a green central stripe around the waist (71), with positioned immediately below the waist band, a further band of half inch wide silver braid above a similar band of one quarter of an inch wide silver braid, as illustrated in *Fig: 140B*. Around the base of the cap, a band of one quarter inch wide braid, above a similar band of half inch wide silver braid. The peak was also of black patent leather, being embroidered with three differing width stripes of silver the widest stripe being to the centre. (*See Fig: 140.*).

Figure 140: Lincolnshire Yeomanry. A fine example of the officers cap with the feather plume removed. Note the silvered overlay to the plate, comprised of the wreath, crown, shield, and title scroll, and the bluish tinge to the velvet backing to the ER VII Royal Cypher on the plume rosette. Courtesy of Eric Dickinson.

The Lance Cap Plate (*See Fig: 140.*)

A silvered metal rayed plate of standard shape and size (89), upon which was the silvered overlay comprised of the following. A wreath of laurel leaves surmounted by a King's pattern crown, to the centre of which was the Arms of the City of Lincoln comprised as follows: 'Argent, a cross gules upon a shield, charged with a fleur-de-lis to the centre of the cross' (70). Below the wreath a five-part scroll bearing the title '*Lincolnshire Imperial Yeomanry*' as follows. Part 1: '*Lincolnshire*', Part 2: Blank, Part 3: '*Imperial*', Part 4: Blank, Part 5: '*Yeomanry*'. The assembled lance cap plate consisted of three separate pieces, these being the (1) the silvered rayed back plate, (2) the crown, wreath and shield, and (3) the title scroll (120). (See also *Fig: 141.*).

The Ear Rosettes, Chinchain and Hook

The lion head bosses were quite unique being silver in colour, the boss to the right side of the cap having a closed ring positioned on the lion's chin, to which was secured the three quarter inch wide silvered metal chinchain, mounted on black patent leather, and

Figure 140A: Lincolnshire Yeomanry. The officer lance cap, together with cross belt with prickers and chains and the silver flapped pouch bearing the ER VII Royal Cypher. N.B. The flap to the pouch, and all the belt fittings are hallmarked 1905. Courtesy of Eric Dickinson.

Figure 140B: Lincolnshire Yeomanry. The officers lance cap complete with feather plume. Courtesy of R.J. Smith.

Figure 140C: Lincolnshire Yeomanry. Offset front view of the cap in which can be seen the 'GRV' Royal Cypher in silver embroidery. Note. The plume holder appears to be in gilt metal. Courtesy of David McAlpine. Photo: W.Y. Carman.

Figure 140D: Lincolnshire Yeomanry. Offset rear view of cap illustrating the silver gimp and orris cord to the angles of the sides of the cap, the silver lace to the waist of the cap, and the silvered lion's head boss. Courtesy of David McAlpine. Photo: W.Y. Carman.

Figure 140E: Lincolnshire Yeomanry. Rear view of the cap showing the silvered hook and ring to rear of the waist of cap. Courtesy of David McAlpine. Photo: W.Y. Carman.

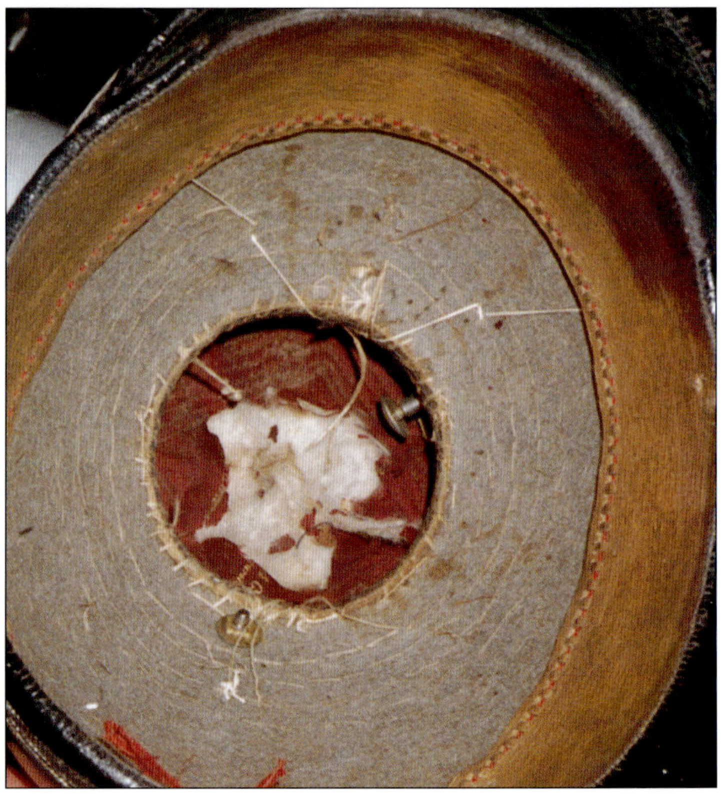

Figure 140F: Lincolnshire Yeomanry. Inside view of the cap. Note the knurled 'knob' (upper right) used to tighten down onto the plume stem to secure the plume in place. N.B. The upper silk lining is absent on this cap. Courtesy of David McAlpine. Photo: W.Y. Carman.

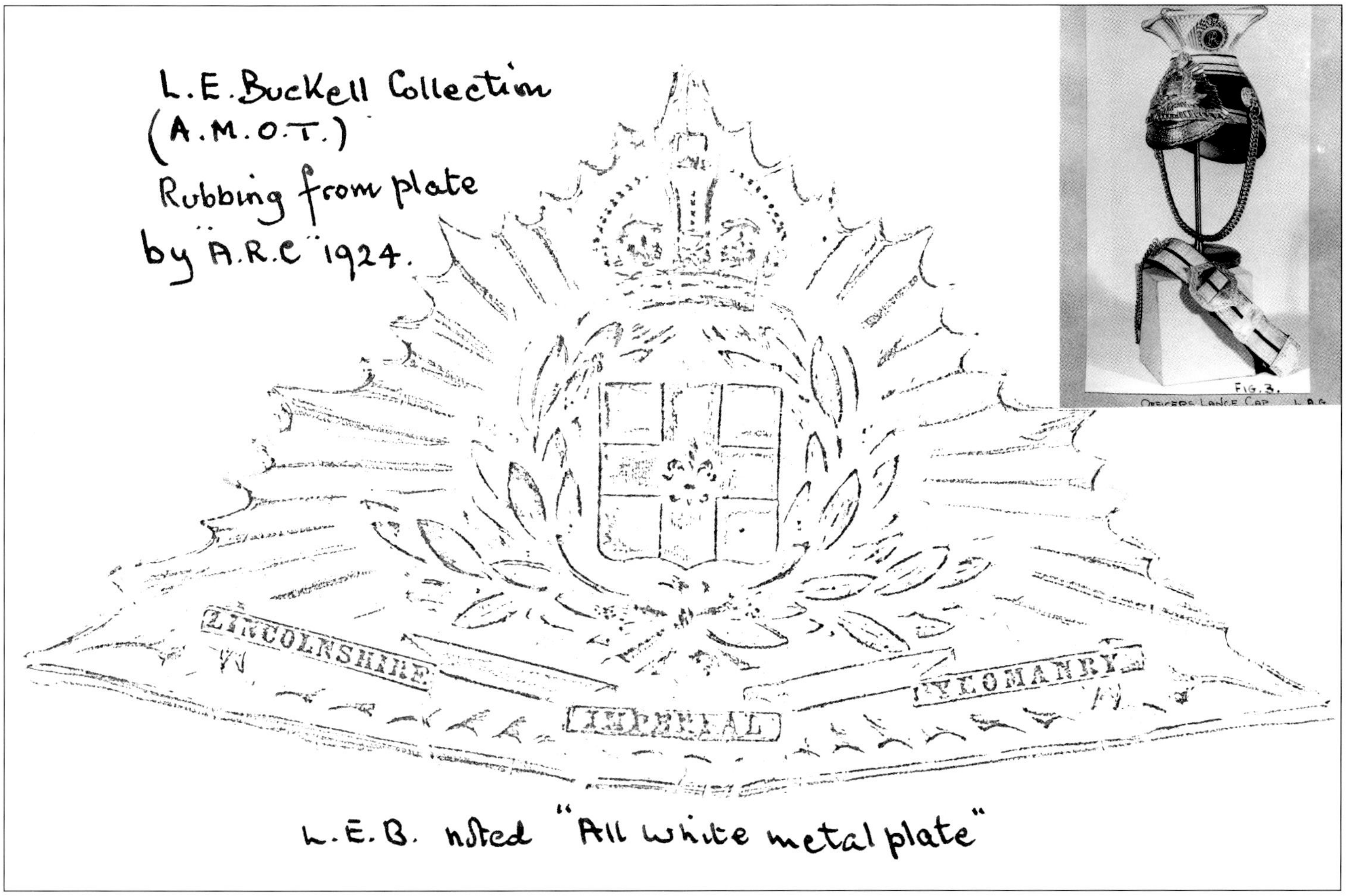

Figure 141: Lincolnshire Yeomanry. A rubbing of the officers lance cap plate of the Lincolnshire Imperial Yeomanry c.1924. L.E. Buckell. Courtesy of Army Museums Ogilby Trust.

backed with either black or blue velvet. To the left side of the cap, a similar silvered metal lion head boss having a silvered metal hook secured to its chin, onto which was secured the loose end of the chinchain. To the rear of the waist of the skull, a silvered metal ring and hook secured to a silvered metal four petalled leaf, just visible in *Fig: 140E*. Onto this ring was attached the cap-lines, with the loose end of the chinchain being attached to the hook, as and when required.

The Head Lining, Plume, and Cap-Lines

The head lining of tan leather, with the upper section of scarlet silk (120).

The plume of greenish black cock's feathers mounted in a silvered metal plume holder having four upright leaves above a corded ball. N.B. On an example of this pattern of cap exhibited in the Yeomanry section of the Museum of Lincolnshire Life, the plume holder is of gilt metal.

The cap-lines were of silver gimp and orris, and were as previously described in the aforementioned dress regulations for officers of regular lancer regiments.

The Tunic, Overalls and Accoutrements (*See Fig: 139.*)

The following details relating to the officers uniform are principally based on information dedicated to this regiments full dress uniform, and presented in a most informative article (87) by the respected author and military artist R.J.(Bob) Smith, the article being illustrated by the equally respected military artist R.J.(Bob) Marrion.

The lancer style tunic of deep Lincoln green[33], the plastron in the facing colour of white, with the edge of the tunic, back seams etc having white piping. Silver coloured lancer style shoulder cords, with silver coloured regimental pattern buttons, the collar and cuffs also being in the facing colour of white, being adorned with silver lace having a green stripe (87). N.B. R.G. Harris states that the white plastron was edged with green piping (71).

The waist girdle was of silver lace, with two green stripes, the sword slings being of silver 'check' pattern lace, having a green stripe, backed with green morocco leather (87).

The overalls of deep Lincoln green cloth, having a double white stripe down each outer seam, worn with black wellington boots and steel spurs.

The shoulder belt was silver 'French check' patterned lace[34], having a central green silk stripe, originally backed with black leather, but later changed to green morocco leather (90). The breast ornament, buckle, tip, and slide, and prickers and chains were all in silver coloured metal. The pouch was originally of black leather (later green leather), having a silvered coloured flap bearing the Royal Cypher of ER VII (89) as illustrated in *Fig: 140A.*, the cypher changing sometime after 1911 to GRV. White wrist gloves, and the 1822 light cavalry officers pattern sword, with silver sword knot, and steel scabbard completed the uniform (71). N.B. An interesting point relating to the shoulder belt pouch worn by yeomanry officers, is that unlike the silver flap on the pouch formerly worn by regular lancer officers, the flap on many of the pouches that were worn by officers of the various yeomanry regiments, will often be found not to be of hallmarked silver.

The Other Ranks Uniform *(See Figs: 139 and 142.)*
The uniform worn by the rank and file members attending the 1911 Coronation is stated as being the 'walking out dress', and comprised a dark green staff pattern forage cap having a white band with Lancer piping round the crown and quarter seams, complete with regimental pattern cap badge.

A dark green frock coat with stand collar (with collar badges) having two breast patch pockets (without pleats) with silver coloured buttons, a built in belt of green cloth with a silver coloured buckle to the front, with shoulder chains completing the upper wear. Overalls of dark green cloth with two white stripes were worn, with tan wrist gloves, and wellington boots completing the uniform (66). N.B. It is though that leather bandoliers were also worn by the other ranks attending this ceremonial occasion.

Surrey Imperial Yeomanry

Within the County of Surrey, various independent troops were raised from 1794 onwards, they being formed into a regiment in 1797, and being disbanded some thirty years later in December 1827. Four years later in January 1831, the *Southwark Troop,* was re-raised, eventually becoming a full regiment being titled the *Surrey Regiment of Yeomanry Cavalry*, only to suffer disbandment in 1848 (68).

The raising of the *Surrey Imperial Yeomanry* was authorised on the 30th April 1901, and under Army Order No.160 of 1902 it was granted the title of the *Surrey (the Princess of Wales's Lancers) Imperial Yeomanry* (91).

When the volunteers were declared to be a Territorial Force in 1908, the word 'Imperial' was discontinued, and the regiments title became the *Surrey (Princess of Wales's Lancers) Yeomanry*. Some two years later in 1910, the title was once again changed when Princess Mary became Queen, this time to the *Surrey Yeomanry (Queen Mary's Regiment)*, with a new badge being taken into wear.

At the Coronation procession of King George V in 1911, the regiments commanding officer Lt Colonel the Hon H. Cubitt TD, rode in the procession in his capacity as Marshalling Officer, with the coronation detachment forming part of the 1st Battalion of the yeomanry regiments contingent, being commanded by Captain R.W. Barclay. The latter officer wore the lancer style uniform, with sil-

Figure 142: 'A detachment of the Lincolnshire Yeomanry.' A rare photograph of an officer, thought to be Captain R. Sleight in full dress uniform, leading a detachment of the regiment c.1910/11. Note the leather bandoliers worn by the rank and file. Copyright D.P.& G.

ver cap-lines around the body and looped up on the left breast, complete with the staff pattern peaked cap, all as described below. However his shoulder belt differed, it being of silver lace backed with leather, the lace having a central scarlet stripe, being complete with silvered breast ornament, buckle, tip, and slide, and prickers and chains (66).

The rank and file wore a similar style of uniform, however, their caps were without the scarlet band around its waist, their cap-lines being of yellow cord. N.B. The shoulder belt was not worn by the rank and file members of the contingent. (66). In 1914, the regiments station was at King's Avenue, Clapham Park, S.W. (47).

The Band

It is recorded that there exists a painting c.1830 showing the drum horse of the regiment, with a pair of kettle-drums on the ground (67). However, the authors found no record of there being a band for the post 1902 period.

The Regiments Uniform

As Imperial Yeomanry the compulsory uniform was official 'drab' for tunic, breeches and slouch hat, but by 1902 colour was added in the way of red facings, and a red lancer style plastron as described below. The desire for more colourful dress of blue with scarlet facings came in 1908, but only for mess dress and undress.

The Officers Full Dress Uniform

The Head-Dress

Although a lancer style uniform was worn, the officers did not take into wear the lance cap, in its place being worn a camel coloured slouch hat[35], having a pagri (turban) with a red edge, wound around the waist of the hat, with a regimental pattern silver coloured badge[36] worn on the upturned brim of the hat (left side), with a green cock's feather plume completing the head-dress. Alternatively a staff pattern peaked cap of drab camel colour with lancer piping, having a scarlet band around the waist, complete with a regimental pattern cap badge was worn. (92). N.B. In the text accompanying a photograph of a dismounted officer that appeared in Issue Five of *Regiment Magazine*, the cock's feather plume is described as being black, possibly because the darkness of the green gave the feathers the appearance of being black in colour.

The Tunic, Overalls and Accoutrements

The tunic was of a deep shade of camel (not unlike khaki), with the plastron of scarlet cloth, with the piping to the outer seam of the sleeves, and rear skirt seams in like colour, as was the collar and cuffs, silver coloured regimental pattern buttons, and silver wire shoulder cords being worn. The collar was also adorned with silver lace, having silver coloured collar badges, being a smaller version of the cap badge. Silver cord cap-lines were worn encircling the body, with the top end (having the olives) being looped up on the left breast, the lower end of the cap-lines being looped up onto the 6th plastron button (counting down from the top) on the right hand side of the tunic. The waist girdle was of silver lace material having two crimson stripes (92).

For dismounted duty, overalls of the same colour as the tunic, having double red stripes down the outer seams were worn with wellington boots and spurs, or alternatively for mounted duties breeches replaced the overalls, being worn with tan coloured knee boots and spurs.

A shoulder belt of tan coloured leather[37], the breast ornament, buckle, tip, and slide, chain and prickers all being silver in colour. The pouch was also of tan leather, and had the regimental badge of a spearhead emerging from a coronet, in silvered metal upon the flap. Wrist gloves of brown leather[38], and the 1822 light cavalry pattern sword, or possibly the later, 1912 officers pattern sword with brown leather sword knot, together with a steel scabbard, completed the uniform (92). No confirmed information relating to either the sword belt, or the sword slings was available to the authors, although it is reasonable to assume that they would each have been of brown leather to complement the shoulder belt.

Sussex Imperial Yeomanry

Four Troops of volunteer cavalry were raised within the County of Sussex as early as 1794, under the title of the *Sussex Troops of Gentlemen and Yeomanry*, however by 1802 most of the volunteer corps in the County were disbanded, only to be revived upon war breaking out in 1803. Some two years later, there were no less than ten Troops within the County, but once again, as in most other counties, disbandment frequently occurred and by 1817 only the Lewes Troop, and the Midhurst Troop still existed. The year 1831 saw the *Arundel and Bramber Yeomanry Cavalry* being raised, they eventually being disbanded in 1848 (93).

In 1871, the '*1st Sussex Light Horse Volunteers*' was raised, their headquarters being located at Brighton. This volunteer cavalry corp was in existence for only some four years, they being disbanded in 1875 (93). Notwithstanding the above, during the 1880s the County of Sussex was not completely without volunteer cavalry, as a Brighton Troop was serving with the Middlesex Hussars at this period. In 1900, the 69th Company Imperial Yeomanry was formed within the county, their members being sent to take part in the conflict in South Africa (68).

On the 4th June 1901, His Majesty King Edward VII gave his approval for a regiment of yeomanry to be formed within the County, the name of this regiment to be the '*Regiment of Sussex Imperial Yeomanry*', they being officially accepted on the 11th June 1901 (93).

As with other Imperial Yeomanry regiments, the 'Imperial' in their title was discontinued some time after the formation of the Territorial Force in 1908.

At the procession and military parade held on the occasion of the Coronation of King George V in 1911, the Sussex Yeomanry detachment formed part of the 1st Battalion of the yeomanry contingent, being commanded by Captain R.V. Gwynne, who wore the officers pattern full dress uniform of the period, worn with a peaked cap as described below, whilst the other ranks of the detachment wore parade dress with caps, complete with a leather bandolier. N.B. It is recorded that Captain Gwynne's cap had a white cover, and that the peak was adorned with gold braid (66).

In 1914 the station for the regiments was, The Drill Hall, Church Street, Brighton, Sussex (47).

The Band

Thanks to the excellent booklet on this regiment, produced by the Robert Ogilby Trust (93), information has been recorded of the uniform worn by the regiment's band. In this booklet there is a photograph of fifteen members of the dismounted band circa 1912 that shows the musicians wearing the blue peaked forage cap, having yellow piping in the seams of the crown, with a yellow band around the caps waist, and a brass cap badge.[39] The bandsmen are seen to be wearing the blue serge parade frock coat, having brass collar badges, complete with chains to the shoulders. Their overalls are also of blue serge with a single yellow stripe down each outer seam. Black boots are worn, and although not visible in the photograph, it is assumed that spurs were also worn.

The Bandmaster to the centre of the aforementioned photograph wears a forage cap of similar, if not identical pattern to that of the bandsmen. However, in place of the parade frock, he wears an old pattern cavalry frock coat, being similar in appearance to the frock coat illustrated in Dress Regulations for The Army 1900 (plate number 19.). The Bandmaster also wears leather wrist gloves, colour unknown.

The Officers Full Dress Uniform

The Head-Dress

As with the Surrey Imperial Yeomanry, the lance cap was never adopted for wear by the officers of this regiment, in its place being worn a light drab, greenish shade slouch hat.[40] This hat had a narrow brown leather band around the base, with a gilt regimental badge[41] being worn on the turned-up brim, the hat being complete with a small bright blue emu feather plume. Another form of head-dress worn at this period was the blue staff pattern peaked cap, having a yellow band around the waist, and worn with a regimental pattern cap badge. Gold cord cap-lines were worn encircling the body, the upper end being looped up on the left breast (93), the lower end being attached as previously described for the Surrey Yeomanry.

The Tunic, Overalls and Accoutrements

The tunic of khaki cloth, and of lancer cut[42], having the plastron, the piping down the front and round the skirts, to the back seams and three pointed flaps, all in the regimental facing colour of blue (as shown in the Army List 1905), complete with dead gilt buttons bearing the Royal Arms. Regimental pattern gilt collar badges, the collar and cuffs also in blue, being edged with blue mohair braid. Blue plaited shoulder cords completed the tunic.

The waist girdle was of blue material with two yellow stripes, with the overalls being of khaki material and having a double blue stripe to each outer seam. Black wellington boots were worn with silver coloured spurs. The shoulder belt was of tan leather, with the breast-ornament, buckle, slide, and tip, and the pickers and chains all in gilt metal, complete with a tan leather pouch. Brown leather wrist gloves, and the 1912 officers pattern sword with sword knot, together with a steel scabbard completed the uniform (93).

The Duke of Cornwall's Yeomanry Cavalry

Very little is recorded about this Cornish volunteer cavalry regiment, the origins of which date back to 1794. In that year plans were made to form a *Falmouth Troop* of cavalry, and by 1797 Troops had in fact been formed at Falmouth and elsewhere in the county. These Troops of cavalry were reorganised in 1803, when two Troops were named *The Loyal Meneage*. In 1814, it was proposed that six Troops of Cornish cavalry should form a regiment, and by 1817 they became recognised, the regiment being unofficially called the *1st Cornwall Yeomanry Cavalry* (59).

In 1835, the regiment was unofficially called *The Duke of Cornwall's Yeomanry*, its title being made official in 1836, the regiment then being commanded by Major Commandant George S. Borlase. However there existence under their new title was short lived, for on the 3rd March 1838, His Majesty's Government ordered that many yeomanry units, including The Duke of Cornwall's Yeomanry to disband.

The Full Dress Uniform

No information was available to the authors regarding the full dress uniform of this regiment, other than that the pouch badge was of white metal, and comprised an eight-pointed star, to the centre of which was the Prince of Wales's plume within a strap bearing the regiments title (59).

The Lance Cap

Information was however forthcoming on the lance cap, the details given below being based upon an example, thought to be the sole remaining specimen in existence, that sold at an auction house sale-room in England, early last year (2000). N.B. This cap had a very wide top, high sides, and a narrow waist, all of which gave it an almost continental appearance.

The Skull, Sides and Top

The square shaped top was of black patent leather, the upper part of the skull (sides) of scarlet ribbed cloth. Silver coloured cord covered the four angles, there being a small silvered lion's head complete with hook, upon the front angle, onto which could be attached the ribbon joining the two chin scales. N.B. There was no plume boss/rosette present on this unique example.

The actual skull of the cap was covered with black patent leather, having the waist decorated with a band of bullion lines, thought to have been silver coloured. The peak was of black, unadorned patent leather.

The Lance Cap Plate
To the front of the cap, a plate of Sheffield silver plate, upon copper, having sharp-cut ends. To the lower centre of the plate, the 'Prince of Wales's' feathers and coronet, above which, and partially enclosing the P.O.W.' feathers was a single scroll bearing the title '*Duke of Cornwall's Yeomanry*'.

The Ear Bosses, Chinchain, Head Lining, and Plume
To each side of the skull, a silvered lion's head boss supporting a set of Sheffield silver plate chin scales, backed with velvet, and joined at the centre by a ribbon. The skull was lined with quilted silk, the cap being accompanied by a scarlet and white horse hair plume. N.B. It is thought that this pattern of lance cap was worn only for the short period between the years 1836 to 1838 (59).

West Essex Yeomanry
In December 1830, George Palmer Jnr of Nazeing Park, near to Waltham Abbey raised a Troop of yeomanry numbering between eighty to ninety all ranks.[43]

The Troop was called into action as early as the night of the 1st April 1831, when a riotous mob set fire to some hay stacks close to the gunpowder mills, the fire being eventually extinguished by the men of the West Essex Yeomanry, assisted by Ordnance officers, for which they received the thanks not only of the Master-General of the Board of Ordnance, but also the directors of the Sun Fire Office who had insured the hay stacks.

Following the taking place of other incendiary incidents, a second and third Troop was soon raised, with George Palmer Jnr being appointed Major Commandant. Other events involving the regiment were however more peaceful, with the West Essex Yeomanry forming a guard of honour and escort to His Royal Highness Prince Albert, from Lea Bridge and back, upon the occasion of his visit to the Infant Orphan Asylum at Wanstead on the 27th June 1841.[44] (60).

Further royal escort duties[45] took place two years later on the 27th June 1843, when the corps carried out similar duties for Prince Leopold of Saxe Coburg (later King of the Belgians), and again to H.R.H. Price Albert in 1844 on a return visit to the Infant Orphan Asylum. On the occasion of the visit to Cambridge University by Queen Victoria and Prince Albert on the 5th July 1847, the corps, 'at a few hours notice' mounted guard at both Tottenham Station as illustrated in *Fig: 143.*, and at Bishop's Stortford Railway Station.[46]

EXTERIOR OF THE RAILWAY PAVILION AT TOTTENHAM AND ESSEX YEOMANRY GUARD OF HONOUR FOR QUEEN VICTORIA

The above illustration appeared in the "Illustrated London News" of 10th July 1847, and shows the West Essex Yeomanry guard of honour provided at Tottenham Station for the commencement of Queen Victoria's train journey to Cambridge on 5th July 1847 for the installation of Prince Albert as Chancellor of the University. The Essex Yeomanry also furnished a guard of honour at Bishops Stortford Station where the royal train stopped to take in water.

Figure 143: West Essex Yeomanry, a contemporary illustration of the regiment providing an escort to H.M. Queen Victoria at Tottenham Station in 1847. Courtesy the Illustrated London News.

In October 1867 the corps provided a guard of honour and escort for the Duke of Wellington upon the occasion of his review of the South Herts Yeomanry held at Hatfield Park, when the Duke, when referring to the West Essex, 'expressed himself highly pleased with your smart and soldier like appearance and efficiency in the field'. All did not continue to go well for the corps however, they being reduced to eighty men, and at the Chelmsford Review of 1876 they could only muster forty-six men, and so on the 4th March 1877 the West Essex Yeomanry Cavalry was disbanded (60).

The Band

There seems to have been a mounted band[47] comprised of eight musicians and a kettle-drummer, the bandsmen wearing the same uniform as the privates of the regiment, but being distinguished by having their shakos covered in scarlet cloth, and having a scarlet plume. The kettle-drummer was a negro who had been in the Coldstream Guards, his uniform was of Moroccan style, his head-dress being a high white turban criss-crossed with gold lace, with from the top a high upright white feather. He also wore a blue zouave jacket with gold lace, a crimson waistcoat, and voluminous trousers of like colour (60).

The Regiments Uniform

The Head-Dress

The Albert pattern shako appears to have been worn c.1845, the officers pattern shako having silver lace around the top, and a gilt metal Maltese cross plate to the front. The shako was worn with a large cock-tail or swans feather plume of white, having a small red base, although the plume of the rank and file appears to have been plain white. N.B. Whilst the regiment generally appear to have worn the shako, according to accounts that appeared in the *Illustrated London News* in 1843 and 1847, lance caps were worn by members of the regiments lancer troop (60), although regrettably no actual details of the cap were available.

The form of head-dress worn during the early 1860s is not know, but it must have followed the regular fashion, for in 1861 when the corps was doing permanent duty, the Lieutenant Colonel remarked that the regiment might have been 'mistaken for very fine Frenchmen, as they dressed so much like the National Guard', which seems to indicate that they were wearing the tapering leaning forward shako based on the French pattern (60).

By 1870, the busby had been taken into wear, it having a scarlet bag decorated with silver lace, complete with white over scarlet plume (61), this being the form of head-dress worn by the corps until its disbandment in 1877.

The Jacket

No information was available on the first uniform worn by this corps, it has however been suggested that their jackets would have been red. The earliest piece of evidence, dated 10th March 1832 (if correct) is that Messrs Hawkes, the military tailors were making an officers jacket, being blue in colour, with the lancer shaped plastron and the collar and cuffs all in the facing colour of scarlet.

In a contemporary print by Messrs Fores (Publishers) dated 1845, an officer is depicted wearing the above style of jacket, having silver buttons, epaulettes, and lace, and although this style of uniform could have been worn up to the Crimean War. The yeomanry tended to follow the changes adopted by the regular cavalry, and so the tunic came into wear, this having the same regimental distinctions. N.B. Messrs Fores who had premises at 41 Piccadilly, London, produced eight yeomanry prints c.1844 to 1847.

The hussar style of uniform had been adopted c.1870, comprising a tunic having silver lace, worn with pantaloons and black knee length boots with spurs. A shoulder belt having silver lace, prickers and chains, with a silver and scarlet pouch was also worn, together with a sabretache having silver lace, with the 1822 light cavalry officers pattern sword being carried (61).

The Troop(s) of Yeomanry

Buckinghamshire Yeomanry - The Taplow Troop

In May 1794, the first yeomanry cavalry in the County of Buckinghamshire was formed, being known as the *Bucks Armed Yeomanry.* In 1802, following the Peace of Amiens, the Troops within the county were formed into three regiments, they being the *1st or Southern Regiment*, the *2nd or Mid Bucks Yeomanry Cavalry*, and the *3rd or Northern Regiment* (68).

In 1827, the 1st or Southern Regiment, and the 3rd or Northern Regiment were disbanded, the 2nd Regiment of Bucks Yeomanry Cavalry however remained in service, this despite they receiving no allowances or pay. This regiment was frequently known as the *Second or Hussar Regiment of Buckinghamshire Yeomanry* (94).

On the 6th September 1830 riots occurred locally and the 2nd Mid Bucks Yeomanry had to be present. A few months later, on the 27th December 1830 the *Marlow Troop* was raised by Captain Viscount Kirkwall (later to become the Earl of Orkney), the title of the Troop soon changing to Taplow, albeit that they were known locally as the South Bucks Yeomanry Cavalry.

The first training of the Taplow Troop took place in 1831 at Beaconsfield, and more than once they were engaged in local troubles. This must have been a testing time for the Troop, particularly as for a time the Troop had only a Lieutenant in command. In March 1838 when the regiment was ordered to disband, the Taplow Troop offered to serve without pay, and did so until 1842 when they were again placed on pay lists. When the Mid Bucks Yeomanry were no longer titled the 2nd, the Taplow Troop then became the 2nd Bucks Yeomanry, however, they were not known officially as the Taplow Troop, although 'Taplow' was on their head-dress.

The Taplow Troop retained a separate identity long after their parent regiment had ceased to exist, and as *The South Bucks (Taplow) Yeomanry Lancers* served under the Earl of Orkney in the south of the county during the 1850s and 1860s. By 1863 the Troop was under the command of a Captain Commandant, they at this time having adopted the lance cap as their form of head-dress. N.B. The Troop were known as lancers, even though they were equipped with carbines (95).

When in 1871 the War Minister ordered all yeomanry regiments to have at least four troops, the Taplow Troop had to be disbanded (94), although many of the men continued to serve as yeomen by forming 'B' (Reading) Troop of *The Royal Berkshire Yeomanry Cavalry* (97). N.B. At no time did the Taplow Troop have anything to do with the Bucks Hussars, they being a strong regiment who wore hussar dress. It is possible that there has been some confusion in the past, because the Hussars were once numbered the 2nd (95).

The Regiments Uniform

It would appear that when raised, the Troop were given a helmet converted from the regular heavy cavalry pattern, but having a rayed 'lancer' style plate in front. N.B. This plate also served as a pattern when the lance cap was taken into wear in 1856.

Scarlet coatees with dark blue facings and a double row of buttons down the front are known to have been worn, the buttons on this garment having a crown over 'TYC' for Taplow Yeomanry Cavalry. By 1845 the lancer coatee with wide blue lapels was being worn. N.B. Scarlet was the colour of the new tunic worn in 1856.

Officers Full Dress Uniform:

The Lance Cap

The Skull, Sides and Top

The dimensions of the cap were as for a regular lancer officers cap of the period concerned. The upper part of the skull and the top of the cap in crimson/red cloth, with gold gimp and orris cord extending across the top and down the angles, from north to south, and east to west.[48] To the left upper front, a gold bullion rosette, with the Royal Cypher embroidered in gold bullion/wire on a blue velvet ground (75). To the upper rear of the rosette, a flat 'oblong' brass/gilt socket into which was inserted the prong/stem of the plume.

The actual skull was covered with black patent leather. having a band of gold lace with a central blue silk stripe around the waist. The peak also of black patent leather, being bound with gilt metal (75).

The Lance Cap Plate

The gilt metal rayed plate bore the Royal Arms of Queen Victoria above a scroll bearing the title 'South Bucks Yeomanry *Lancers*'. *See Fig: 112.* for an illustration of the other ranks pattern of lance cap plate. N.B. It is likely, that on the officers pattern plate that the title scroll was in silvered metal, although this has not been confirmed.

Figure 144: A copy of a fine study of a member of the Taplow Lancers by the artist Bill Younghusband. Courtesy of Bill Younghusband.

The Ear Bosses and Chinchain

A gilt metal lion head boss to the right side of the cap (when facing the cap) having a closed ring positioned on the lion's chin to which is secured the gilt metal chinchain, mounted on leather. To the left side of the cap, a similar gilt metal lion head boss having a gilt metal hook secured to its chin, onto which is secured the loose end of the chinchain. Although not confirmed, it is probable that to the rear of the waist of the skull was a gilt metal ring and hook secured to a gilt metal four petalled leaf, onto which to secure the cap-lines and the loose end of the chinchain, as and when required.

The Plume and Cap-Lines

No information was available to the authors regarding the head lining fitted to this regiments lance cap, although it is reasonable to assume it would have been the same as for other officers lance caps of this period.

The plume of white swan feathers within a gilt metal socket having five upright leaves.

The cap-lines were of gold gimp and orris as previously described in the extract from the relevant dress regulations.

The Tunic, Overalls and Accoutrements

The tunic was scarlet cloth, with the 'butterfly' plastron (as described for the Bedfordshire Yeomanry), and the seams being in the facing colour of blue (pale blue). The collar and cuffs were also in the facing colour of blue, and adorned with gold lace. Regrettably the authors have no knowledge as to the colour/type of shoulder cords/straps on the officers pattern tunic of this regiment.

The waist girdle was of gold lace with two blue stripes, with the sword slings also being of gold lace, and having a central crimson/red silk stripe, being backed with leather. Breeches of blue cloth having to each outer seam a double red stripe, with a light colour to the centre of the stripe, being worn with black knee boots and spurs (75).

A shoulder belt of gold lace having a central crimson/red silk stripe, being backed with crimson/red leather, the breast -ornament, buckle, slide, and tip, and the prickers and chains all in silvered metal. The pouch of crimson/red leather having either a silver, or silver plated flap bearing the 'V.R.' Royal Cypher in gilt metal. White leather gauntlets, and the 1822 officers light cavalry pattern sword with gold cord sword knot, together with a steel scabbard, completed the uniform (75).

Figure 145: South Bucks Yeomanry Lancers (Taplow Lancers). The other ranks pattern lance cap complete with plume. Source unrecorded.

The Other Ranks Pattern Cap (*See Fig: 145.*)

Of similar appearance overall to the officers pattern cap, the gold gimp and orris cord being replaced with yellow cord which extended across the top and down the angles. To the left upper front a plume boss of blue upon yellow worsted, there being a 'gilt' regimental pattern button to its centre.

The skull of black patent leather having around the waist a band of yellow cotton braid with a central blue stripe, the plate being of die-struck brass bearing the title '*South Bucks Yeomanry Lancers*' on a tri-part scroll as illustrated in *Fig: 112*. The ear bosses were of brass/gilding metal, the brass chinchain being leather backed, the white horsehair plume in a brass socket. N.B. No information was available to the authors regarding the head lining on this particular pattern of cap, although it is reasonable to assume that it would have been similar to that fitted to the caps worn by the rank and file of the regular lancer regiments of the period.

Cheshire Yeomanry - Adlington Troop

The Adlington Troop of Lancer was raised by Richard Townley Crosse, the son of Richard Legh of Adlington, and consisted of some twenty-four to thirty members, the Troop being attached to the Macclesfield Squadron of the Cheshire Yeomanry in January 1820.

In March, the Cheshire Legion (formed in 1806) under the command of Sir Fleming Leicester was denominated the '*King's Cheshire Volunteer Legion*', and as they were 'conceived to be Royal', they were entitled to wear the royal facing colour of blue on their uniforms. It was remarked that when in February 1820 they were on parade in Macclesfield, that the 'looked well in their new facings'. On the 10th June of that year, the cavalry of the Legion assembled at Liverpool for a six day drill period, and the Adlington Lancers attended a review by Major General Sir John Byng, when the Troop was praised for their expertise in the use of the lance, and the docility of their horses.

In 1824, when there were civilian risings in Cheshire, the Adlington Troop were called out to aid the Macclesfield Squadron of the Cheshire Yeomanry in restoring peace, this being soon achieved. In 1826, the infantry contingent of the Legion was disbanded, and the London Gazette announced that the new name was to be '*The King's Regiment of Cheshire Yeomanry Cavalry*'. Some twelve years later in 1838, the reorganisation of the regiment was fixed at ten Troops, each of sixty men, and the Adlington Troop had to be disbanded (59).

Full Dress Uniform

Very little is known relating to the dress of this Troop, other than that their uniform was similar to other troops within the Cheshire Yeomanry, except that the men wore the lance cap having a red top, with 'white' fittings', worn with a red and white plume. The skirt of their blue jacket was made smaller, having a red collar and cuffs, and a broad red plastron, the officers jacket being decorated with silver lace (98). All items of uniform were made under the direction of the regimental Adjutant, Captain Joseph Barra[49] late of the 16th (The Queen's) Light Dragoons (Lancers). Their belts, pistols, and sabres were supplied by the Board of Ordnance, however the lances used by the troop were to be provided at the members own expense. As with other regiments of lancers, the pennon atop the lance was red over white, this being the colours of the Cross of Saint George, the English flag.

Derbyshire Yeomanry - The Radbourne Troop

Following the reorganisation of the volunteer cavalry in 1803, the Radbourne Troop was added to the *Derbyshire Yeomanry Cavalry* under the command of Sir Henry Harpur in July 1803. The five other Troops that made up the regiment at this period were, the Ashbourne, Calke, Chesterfield, Derby, and Locko Troops. The yeomanry engaged in a peacekeeping role in 1811, when the Radbourne Troop, together with two other Troops were called out to aid the civil powers during the Luddite Riots that occurred in the county (99).

A letter was sent to the Lord Lieutenants of the Counties of England in December 1827, to the effect that, no further allowances would be made to any Yeomanry Force that had not been called out in aid of the civil power within the last ten years. As a result of this decision, the *Derbyshire Yeomanry Cavalry* ceased to exist as a regiment, with only the Radbourne Troop continuing to serve, the officers offering to serve without pay in 1828 (59), they 'soldiering on' free of public expense until they were placed in pay in December 1830. However in 1831 following reform riots in Derby, *The Derby and Chaddesden Hussars* was formed on the 15th December 1831, with the *Repton and Gresley Troop* being raised on the 9th April 1832. The latter Troop was disbanded on the 3rd March 1838, only to be raised again on the 20th March 1843 (99).

In 1863, it was agreed that The Derby and Chaddesden Hussars, the Repton and Gresley Troop, and the Radbourne Troop, should be formed into a single regiment, to be known as the *Derbyshire Regiment of Yeomanry Cavalry*, authorization for the formation of this new regiment being approved on the 31st March 1864.

Full Dress Uniform

The following limited information pertaining to the uniform worn by the members of the Radbourne Troop is based on a fine black and white illustration by Richard Scollins, of a trooper of the regiment c.1832. This illustration accompanied an article on '*The Volunteer Cavalry of Derbyshire*' by M.D. Brittain, together with a very brief description of the uniform concerned, that appeared in the journal of the Crown Imperial Society (99).

The Lance Cap

According to the above mentioned illustration, an early pattern lance cap appears to have been worn, being complete with lance plate, chinscales, a horsehair plume (colour unknown), and a set of caplines with flounders. N.B. December 1830 is the only known official reference to the wearing of lance caps (59).

The Jacket, Overalls, and Accoutrements

A light dragoon pattern jacket of scarlet cloth, having a full plastron (possibly green, as this was the facing colour), complete with brass shoulder scales, the jacket being similar in appearance to the lancer tunic of the period.

The waist girdle was of yellow material having a double scarlet stripe, with the overalls being of dark grey cloth having a double scarlet stripe to the outer seams (98). The 1829 pattern light cavalry troopers sword complete with sword knot, and steel scabbard completed the uniform.

Suffolk Yeomanry - The Long Melford Troop

The official date for the Suffolk Yeomanry being accepted is given as 4th May 1794. During this period, nine units were raised, however by 1828 the last of these Troops had been disbanded. Recorded information relating to the above little known Troop of volunteer cavalry is extremely scarce, however it is recorded that c.1868 the Long Melford Troop joined with the Bury St. Edmund's Troop (formed in 1831) to become known as the "West Suffolk Yeomanry". N.B. The Long Melford Troop had been dressed as lancers from c.1847, and according to 'The Royal Militia and Yeomanry Cavalry List' arranged and compiled by Arthur Sleigh Esq (published in April 1850), the Troop was commanded by Captain Commandant N.C. Barnardiston, the strength of the Troop being five Officers, three Sergeants, three Corporals, one Trumpeter, and sixty-one Privates (65).

Full Dress Uniform

The Officers Lance Cap *(See Fig: 146.)*

The Skull, Sides and Top

The skull of black patent leather, the upper part (sides) of ribbed scarlet cloth, the top in cloth of the same colour, with gold cord extending up the four angles and across the top of the cap. To the top left hand corner of the cap was located a gilt metal hook onto which could be attached the chinchain, with joined to the gold cord

Figure 146: Long Melford Troop. A fine example of the officers pattern cap minus plume. Note the method by which the loose end of the chinchain is attached to the hook attached to the top left corner of the cap. Copyright W.Y. Carman.

Figure 146A: Long Melford Troop. Offset view of the cap in which may be seen the bullion rosette bearing the 'VR' Royal Cypher, and the pattern of lace to the waist of the cap. Copyright W.Y. Carman.

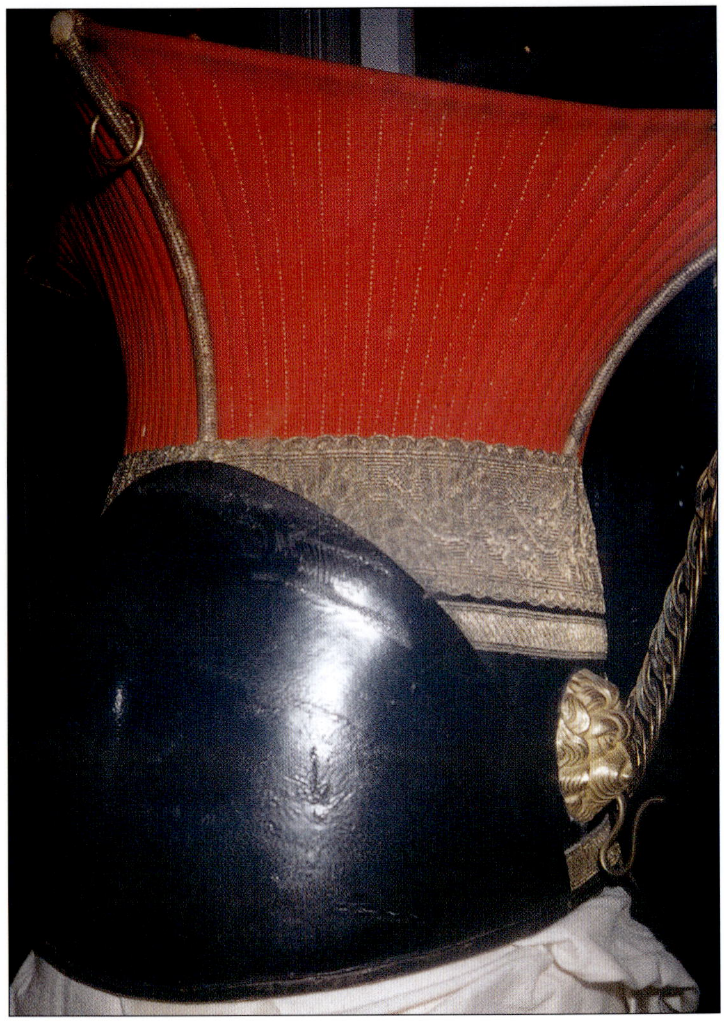

Figure 146B: Long Melford Troop. Rear view of the cap illustrating the plain black patent leather 'false' peak. Note the ring attached to the cord of the rear angle, and the hook to the top of the cap (right side of photograph). Copyright W.Y. Carman.

adorning the rear angle there being a gilt metal ring as illustrated in *Fig: 146B*. To the upper left of the ribbed cloth section, a gold cord rosette having the 'V.R' Royal Cypher to the centre on a blue ground as illustrated in *Fig: 146A*.

Around the waist of the cap, a band of gold lace, though to have been some two inches in depth, the peak of black patent leather, the outer edge of which was decorated with gold braid as illustrated in *Figs: 146* and *146A*., with to the rear of the cap a large constantly turned-up patent leather peak. N.B. Unlike on the pre 1856 pattern lance cap of regular lancers officers, the rear peak on this cap was unadorned by gold braid as illustrated in *Fig: 146B*.

The Lance Cap Plate

To the front of the cap, a large rayed die-stamped plate bearing the Royal Arms, above a tripartite scroll inscribed '*Dieu Et Mon Droit*' as illustrated in *Figs: 146*. and *146A*.

The Ear Bosses, Chinchain and Plume

The lion's head bosses were of the standard pattern in gilt metal, as was the chinchain as illustrated in *Fig: 146A*., which sadly lacks its backing. It is regretted that no information was available to the authors regarding the lining to this pattern of cap. The plume however would have been of white swan feathers for officers, and white horsehair for the rank and file.

The Officers, Jacket, Overalls, and Accoutrements

The very nominal information relating to the uniform worn by the members of this little known Troop is based on a black and white illustration of a print by Messrs Fores (Publishers) depicting an officer and private of this Troop, mounted and in full dress uniform c.1847, that appeared in *Regiment Magazine* Issue Five, together with the brief text that accompanied this picture.

The jacket of dark green cloth, having a full plastron, complete with bullion epaulettes, to the centre of which was a silver crown and "S.Y", the jacket being similar in appearance to the lancer tunic of the period (100).

The waist girdle was of gold material having a double stripe, thought to have been scarlet in colour, the overalls being of dark green cloth having a double stripe to the outer seams. A white patent leather shoulder belt complete with prickers and chains was worn. White leather gauntlets, black leather boots with steel spurs, together with the light cavalry pattern sword with scabbard completed the uniform. N.B. No information was available to the authors regarding the pattern of shoulder belt pouch worn.

NOTES

1. In 1903 the 3rd County of London Yeomanry (Sharpshooters) had amongst their permanent staff, R.S.M. Lesley (13th Hussars), S.S.M. Eatwell (3rd Dragoon Guards), S.S.M Morris (15th Hussars), and S.S.M. Taylor (17th Lancers) (101), and in 1907, the Adjutant to the North Somerset Yeomanry (who dressed as dragoons) was Captain O.W. Brinton (21st Lancers) (102).

2. The Hon Sidney Cornwallis Peel was commissioned Major on the 27th May 1903, coincidentally The Hon W.R.W. Peel was also commissioned in the rank of Major on that same date (103). In 1901, a book entitled 'Trooper 8008 IY' by the Hon S. Peel was published, being an account of his service in the 40th (Oxfordshire) Company Imperial Yeomanry.

3. Major Peel, wearing the uniform described in chapter thirteen, is included in a group photograph of twenty -nine officers who were part of the Yeomanry force at the 1911 Coronation, this photograph being reproduced in the excellent booklet published by The Army Museum Ogilby Trust, entitled 'The Yeomanry Force at the 1911 Coronation'.

4. The actual date the lancer uniform was first adopted by the officers of the regiment is unclear. However, it is known that an oil painting of Colonel F. Shuttleworth by the artist W.W. Oules R.A. was exhibited at the Royal Academy, London in 1904, in which Colonel Shuttleworth is depicted as being in lancer style uniform, complete with lance cap and feather plume. N.B. F. Shuttleworth (late of the 7th Hussars) was commissioned Lt Colonel of the regiment on the 19th September 1901 (103), and Honorary Colonel 10th Feb. 1906 (104).

5. Lord Alwyne F. Compton DSO saw service with the 10th (Prince of Wales's Own Royal) Hussars, and was the brother of the 10th Marquess of Northampton (68). Major: 25th September 1901 (103) Lt Colonel: 27th May 1905 (104).

6. The date given by the authoritative writer R.G. Harris, for the forming of the Rough Riders is 18th July 1901 (67).

7. Colonel The Viscount Maitland was responsible for introducing the regiment's most distinctive lancer style uniform, originally styled as being in Austrian blue, later to be known as French grey (67).

8. Major T.A. Polson later became Colonel Sir T.A. Polson KBE CMG TD.

9. It is known that a brown leather officers pattern pouch, bearing on its flap a bimetal badge, similar to the regiments cap badge also existed.

10. Photographs of the uniform worn by the regiment appeared in an issue of *The Navy and Army Illustrated*, published on the 28th February 1903 (67).

11. It is recorded that a former member of the regiment recalled how the rank and file could purchase the (optional) lance cap for £1 0s 0d (66).

12. Colonel, Lord Wenlock (3rd Baron) PC GCSI KCB VD was the regiments first commanding officer, his second-in- command being Major J Bouchier Stracey-Clitherow CBE TD DL (76).

13. Lieutenant J. Walker went on to become Lt Colonel James Walker CBE DSO TD DL JP (66).

14. Following the accession to the throne by King George V in 1911, the Royal Cypher on the lance cap plate changed from ER VII to GRV, the title scroll however remained unchanged (77).

15. *Fig: 134.*, and *Fig: 136F.* both previously appeared in an article by Major Roy Wilson, published in *Military Modelling Magazine*, February 1986.

16. Major Roy Wilson in his most interesting and informative article on this regiment that appeared in *Military Modelling Magazine*, records that a later version of the officers shoulder belt had a quarter inch wide central crimson stripe.

17. Within this regiment, the officers shoulder belt was not fitted with the breast ornament, nor the prickers and chains.

18. It is recorded that the cap badge was designed by Lord Wenlock and Major Stracey-Clitherow. 'It was the latter who had the inspiration behind the design, having seen a fox on a panel from an old stagecoach, the device struck him as a suitable one for the regiment' (76).

19. There is a most interesting copy of a painting in a bin book (85) at the National Army Museum, by Godfrey H. Brennan depicting a mounted officer of this regiment. The officer wears the lancer style tunic with what appears to be the 1871 pattern heavy cavalry helmet complete with flowing plume. N.B. It is likely that this item of head-dress is 'artist's licence'.

20. A photograph in a National Army Museum bin book (85) illustrates an example of the blue cloth pattern helmet of this regiment, however unlike the example sold at Messrs Wallis & Wallis, this particular helmet was fitted with a narrow patterned band around its waist, and the base to the spike surmounting the helmet was of the standard infantry officers pattern. Additionally, on a helmet illustrated in Issue Five of *Regiment Magazine*, the gilt band encircling the waist of the helmet was described as being 'a gilt chain band', having a small rose to the centre of the band, and furthermore the ear bosses had the appearance of being of rose pattern, but being totally dissimilar in size and appearance to the regulation infantry pattern 'rose fastenings'.

21. The actual date that the lance cap was taken into wear by the officers of the regiment is uncertain, although it is unlikely to have been before 1910, as there is no mention of the cap in the regimental history published in 1910. It is believed that the Scottish United Services Museum have information relating to a new pattern of undefined badge being authorised in 1909, which was in use c.1910/11. N.B. The Scottish United Services Museum was re-named the Scottish War Museum sometime late in the year 2000.

22. The officers lance cap concerned, was seen by the authors at the premises of an established militaria shop in London, in February 2000. Upon examining this cap, it was observed that the workmanship and patina to the silver of both the 'double-headed' eagle and the title scroll 'South Africa 1900-02' appeared to be of the same standard and in a similar condition to that of the crown, strap and ground, and the thistle wreath.

23. It would appear that in this regiment, the officers plastron was worn 'butterfly style' as described for the uniform of the Bedfordshire Imperial Yeomanry.

24. In a bin book (85) at the National Army Museum, there is a photograph of a painting of Major, Sir Norman Macdonald Lockhart of Lee and Carnworth c.1870 in full dress uniform. In this photograph it can be seen that his shoulder belt has a breast ornament, the chains of which are attached to a St. Andrew's Cross. (N.A.M. accession number 7412-10-4).

25. There is an example of the other ranks lance cap in the Scottish War Museum. N.B. The general view of those who have seen this cap appears to be that it is a 'terrible concoction', this cap having being 'made up' for a special occasion, and worn by a trooper in 'full dress uniform'.

26. For the rank and file of the regiment, evidence of the full dress uniform being worn is even more scarce than for the officers. It is however known that at The Glasgow Exhibition held in the City of Glasgow in 1938, that an officer and a member of the other ranks represented the regiment, both soldiers wearing full dress uniform, complete with lance caps.

27. A rare copper Georgian oval shaped shoulder belt plate bearing the inscription '*The Loyal Lincolnshire Yeomanry*', thought to have been worn c.1800, was offered for sale at Wallis and Wallis, Sussex in 1970.

28. Army Order 155 of 1901 announced the formation of the new regiment, which was placed 44th in order of regimental precedence (71).

29. Captain Rowland Sleight saw service with the Imperial Yeomanry in both Rhodesia and South Africa, being awarded the Queen's South Africa Medal with six clasps. He is amongst a group of yeomanry officers photographed at the 1911 Coronation, this most detailed photograph being reproduced in the Ogilby Trust booklet No.10. (66).

30. In R.G. Harris's most informative book on the yeomanry regiments (71), he records that in February 1902, Messrs Hamburger Roger & Co, of Covent Garden, London, produced a trial pattern full dress uniform for the Commanding Officer of the Lincolnshire Imperial Yeomanry, based on the uniform of the 17th Lancers, complete with lance cap and white plume. He also records that 'There is no evidence that the other officers of the regiment purchased dress uniforms until several years later, by which time there were various modifications' to the uniform.

31. Sometime after 1911, the Royal Cypher to the centre of the bullion rosette for the plume would have changed from ER VII to GRV as illustrated in *Fig: 140C.*

32. On the cap illustrated in *Fig: 140.*, the colour of the velvet backing to the Royal Cypher appears to be almost blue in colour. Eric Dickinson, the Hon Secretary of The Military Historical Society, who formerly owned this particular cap, and is an acknowledge authority on the Lincolnshire Yeomanry, is of the opinion that the bluish tinge on the boss is due to the velvet having weathered with age (89). This could certainly explain this colour anomaly.

33. The Lincolnshire Yeomanry were the only lancer regiment regular, or otherwise to be clothed in Lincoln green.

34. The officers of this regiment wore the leather Sam Browne belt when wearing the substitute full dress comprised of peaked cap, green patrol jacket, and overalls (90).

35. At the Coronation procession of King George V in 1911, Captain Barclay wore a camel coloured staff pattern cap, having a scarlet band and piping of the same colour, and worn with a silver coloured cap badge (66).

36. The regimental pattern cap badge was a spearhead emerging from a coronet, this being the crest of Lord Middleton, the Regimental Colonel (66).

37. At the 1911 Coronation procession, Captain Barclay wore a shoulder belt of silver lace with a scarlet centre stripe, fitted with the normal belt ornaments (66).

38. Captain Barclay wore white wrist gloves on the above mentioned occasion (66).

39. From c.1908, the other ranks cap badge was in brass/gilding metal, and was as described below for the officers (endnote number 41.), but having a scroll bearing 'Sussex Yeomanry' (93).

40. It is recorded that c.1909-1937, some officers of the regiment adopted a white metal 1871 pattern dragoon helmet, having gilt metal fittings, and being surmounted by a yellow over blue horsehair plume. N.B. See '*Head Dress of the British Heavy Cavalry*' by D.J.J. Rowe for full details of this helmet.

41. The officers cap badge (in gilt metal) represented the Arms of the County of Sussex, being six martlets on a crowned shield, with a scroll below bearing 'Sussex Imperial Yeomanry' (93).

42. It is also recorded that on the 3rd April 1909 approval was given for the officers of the regiment to wear a new full dress tunic, this being of Indian Army pattern. The tunic was of dark blue superfine cloth, having across the breast, five loose loops of black plaited chain gimp cord with olivets and Austrian knots at the ends of the cord. The collar is stated as being yellow in colour, edged all round with flat black mohair braid (worn without collar badges), with similar braid round the skirts of the tunic. The cuffs were adorned with an Austrian knot in gold chain gimp, with the shoulder cords being of plaited gold gimp. Blue overalls with a single yellow stripe were also taken into wear (93). Worn with this order of dress was a shoulder belt and pouch, the belt being of oak-leaf pattern lace on blue leather (66). No information was available as to the pattern of pouch worn. N.B. The helmet referred to above (endnote number 40.) was worn with this tunic.

43. It was Lord Melbourne and the Duke of Wellington who suggested such a force, for the protection of the Government Gunpowder Mills situated at Waltham Abbey, and the small arms manufactory at Enfield Lock (60).

44. The West Essex Yeomanry were the 'first Corps of Yeomanry Cavalry in England to be accorded the honour of providing an escort for His Royal Highness Prince Albert, and the first volunteer cavalry unit seen by him' (60).

45. At the request of the Mayor of Colchester, an escort of 'one and twenty' members of the corps was provided for H.R.H. Prince Albert on the 21st April 1856, on his visit to the town to inspect the newly formed 'camp', and to review the garrison etc (60).

46. *The Illustrated London News* of 10th July 1847, depicted (in a wood-cut) the royal coach under a canopy outside the railway station with the Essex Yeomen mounted, and wearing lance caps, and carrying lances with pennons. N.B. Royal escorts/guards were not purely ceremonial, as two attempts had been made on the Queen's life in 1841, and two more in 1850, which demonstrated that policing by the yeomanry was needed in these troublesome times (60).

47. It is recorded that the band of the West Essex Yeomanry Cavalry, played the National Anthem as the royal train arrived in the railway station, on the occasion of Queen Victoria's visit to Cambridge University (60).

48. The description given in the book from which some of the lance cap details were obtained (75) states, 'the corners being ornamented in brass'. However, as gold gimp and orris cord ran across the top of the cap and down the corners, this would negate the requirement for 'brass ornaments'.

49. Captain Joseph Barra served at Waterloo, and was Adjutant of the 16th (The Queen's) Light Dragoons (Lancers) for sixteen years, before taking up a similar post with the Cheshire Yeomanry (98).

Chapter Fourteen

Theatrical and 'Trial' Pattern Lance Caps

Before proceeding onto the subject of purchasing a lance cap, below are some brief details relating to two theatrical pattern caps, three non-standard lance caps, that may loosely be described as being 'trial' pattern caps, an officers cap with a unusual fitting, a cap restored for display purposes only, and a 'trial' pattern plate.

Theatrical Caps

Occasionally, lance caps are offered for sale that do not conform to the known patterns, these may be caps that have been altered for a military tattoo, for theatrical use, or even caps that have been made to resemble a known pattern of cap for use in a film.

Theatrical Pattern Cap - 27th Lancers

In the First National Picture version of 'The Charge of the Light Brigade' of 1936, the film star Errol Flynn played the part of Major Geoffrey Vickers of the 27th Lancers[1], and wore the full dress uniform of this then fictitious regiment. The cap he wore in the film appears to be loosely based on the shape of the pre 1856 officers pattern cap, having a large none standard rayed plate, superimposed upon which was what appears to be a 'mock up', comprised of a 'post 1902 version of the Royal Arms upon crossed lances, as illustrated in *Fig: 149*. Regrettably when the film director Tony Richardson made his famous film of the same name in 1968, actor Mark Burns[2], who played the part of Captain Morris of the 17th Lancers wore a forage cap when in dress uniform, even when taking part in the re-enactment of the famous charge.

Theatrical Pattern Cap - 19th Lancers

This particular cap has the initial appearance of being a variation on the officers pattern cap of the 19th Lancers, being an early pattern cap having yellow cloth sides and top, with gold cord running up the four corners (angles), and transversely over the crown of the cap (*See Fig: 150.*).

To the upper left side of the cloth section, a gold bullion rosette bearing 'GR' to its centre, on a yellow velvet ground as illustrated in *Fig: 150A*. Around the waist of the cap a wide band of lace (*See Fig: 150B.*), the front peak being adorned with gold braid, as was the rear 'false' peak as illustrated in *Fig: 150C*.

The gilt metal lance cap plate bore the Hanoverian Royal Arms including the motto 'Dieu Et Mon Droit', but being devoid of any regimental number, title, or battle honours.

The head lining of leather and silk, the gilt chinscales being attached to the cap by means of most unusual pattern ear bosses having four flats scalloped terminals as illustrated in *Fig: 150B*.

Not unnaturally it has been suggested that this is a cap of the 19th Lancers, and indeed it is reasonable to say that having the yellow cloth sides and top, this cap does superficially resemble the officers pattern cap of the 19th Lancers. However as may be seen in *Figs: 8.* and *8A.*, the top of the cap for the 19th is of patent leather and not of yellow cloth.

The lance cap plate of the 19th Lancers bore three battle honours and various regimental devices, as may be seen in *Fig: 8.*, however, the plate fitted to the 'theatrical' cap bears neither honours nor regimental distinctions of any kind, being comprised solely of the Royal Arms overlay superimposed upon the rayed plate.

The authors can think of no logical reason why a regiment such as the 19th, which it is known displayed battle honours on their lance cap plate should suddenly adopt an alternative pattern cap having a 'naked' plate, and it is their view that the head-dress in question is in fact a cap to which a basic pattern plate has been affixed, possibly for theatrical purposes.

Trial Pattern - Bandmasters Cap

This cap was offered for sale by auction at a renowned Sussex Auction House in May 1969, being described as follows. 'A British Tailor's Pattern Officers Type Lance Cap (possibly Bandmaster) of the 19th Lancers c.1835. Scarlet top, gilt wire lace, lion head bosses, fancy wings to chinchain, the H.P. not orig. quite G.C., no plume. See illustration.' A black and white photographic illustration accompanied the description in the saleroom catalogue. N.B. The abbreviation H.P. refers to the helmet (lance cap) plate.

The general shape of the above cap appeared to be that of the pre 1856 pattern, having the larger sized square cloth top, extending across the top of which and down the angles there being a narrow cord. Although not given in the catalogue description, the colour of the cloth sides and top looked as if they might be scarlet in colour. N.B. There was no bullion plume rosette fitted to this cap.

Around the waist of the cap, there was what appeared to be two equal width bands of lace, below which was a slightly narrower band of lace. The peak of black patent leather, the edge of which was adorned by a single embroidered band of wide braid/lace.

To each side of the cap, a lion's head boss, having a corded pattern hook secured to the chin of the lion's head, the chinchain being of the beaded/corded pattern. N.B. The corded pattern chinchain hook was to be found on the pre 1856 officers pattern cap of the 9th Lancers, as illustrated in *Fig: 29B.*

The lance cap plate was of similar size to the pre 1856 pattern, superimposed upon which was the Royal Arms. N.B. This particular pattern of Royal Arms had a single scroll beneath the lion and unicorn supporters in place of the more usual two part (twin) scroll.

Trial Pattern - 12th Lancers

This particular example was described and illustrated in the same catalogue as the cap above, its description being as follows. 'An interesting trial pattern of an officer's lance cap of the 12th Lancers c.1922. Scarlet top with yellow corded boss bearing "GRV" cypher badge as officer's No. 1 pattern. Lion head gilt bosses with gilt chin chain. GC. inside lining as found. N.B. A black and white illustration accompanied the text of the catalogue.

This cap was of the 1856 pattern, having a cloth top and ribbed sides, but being without the usual adornment of the gold gimp and orris cord extending across the top and down the angles. To the left side of the ribbed cloth upper a yellow corded boss, having to its centre an embroidered GRV cypher.

Around the waist of the cap, a band of inch wide gold lace, but being without the two bands of gold braid that are normally positioned below the inch wide band of lace on the officers pattern cap. Also absent was the double band of gold braid usually positioned round the bottom of the officers pattern cap. The peak however was of standard pattern, having three rows of gold purl.

Gilt lion's head bosses of standard pattern, with a plain burnished gilt metal chinchain.

No lance cap plate was fitted to the cap, in its place there being what appeared to be a post 1903 (47) regimental pattern cap badge, comprised of crossed lances with a King's pattern crown positioned between the left and right pennon, with the roman numerals XII positioned between the butt of each of the lances. To the centre of, and upon the lances, the Prince of Wales's plume and coronet.

Trial Pattern - Yeomanry Officers Cap

The third example appeared as a photograph in a National Army Museum's bin-book (105) accompanied by the following text. 'Submitted for identification by the Military Memorabilia of California, August 1975'. continues 'I would therefore conclude that, if genuine, your lance cap was an experimental model possibly for the Bedfordshire or the Lincolnshire Yeomanry. R.G. Harris mentions in Fifty Years of Yeomanry Uniforms 'That the Commanding Officer of the Lincolnshire Yeomanry had a lance cap with white top made by Hamburger, Rogers and Co, of Covent Garden in 1902, a

Figure 147: 'THE ARMY OF THE FUTURE - THE DEATH OR GLORY BOYS.' David Rowe collection. Previously published in the Regiment Journal 1897.

Figure 148: 'THE 12TH LANCERS OF THE FUTURE?' Courtesy of Lynda Rowe.

Figure 149: The film star Errol Flynn as Major Geoffrey Vickers the 27th Lancers, from the film 'The Charge of The Light Brigade'. Of interest is what appears to be a post 1902 version of the Royal Arms on the lance cap late. Author's collection. Courtesy of First National Pictures.

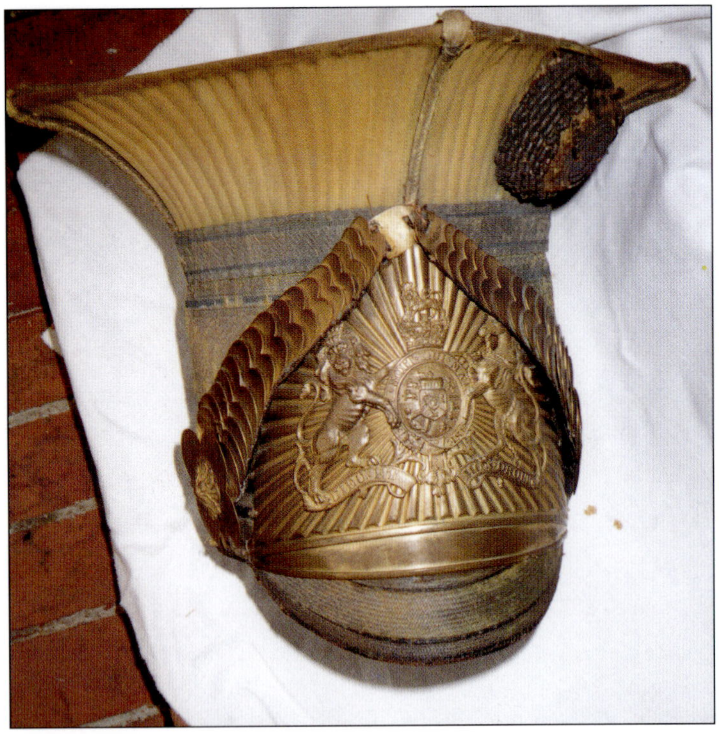

Figure 150: Front view of the 'theatrical' pattern lance cap illustrating the Hanoverian pattern plate void of any battle honours. Copyright W.Y. Carman.

Figure 150A: Close up view of the bullion rosette of the 'theatrical' pattern cap illustrating the 'GR' Royal Cypher. Copyright W.Y. Carman.

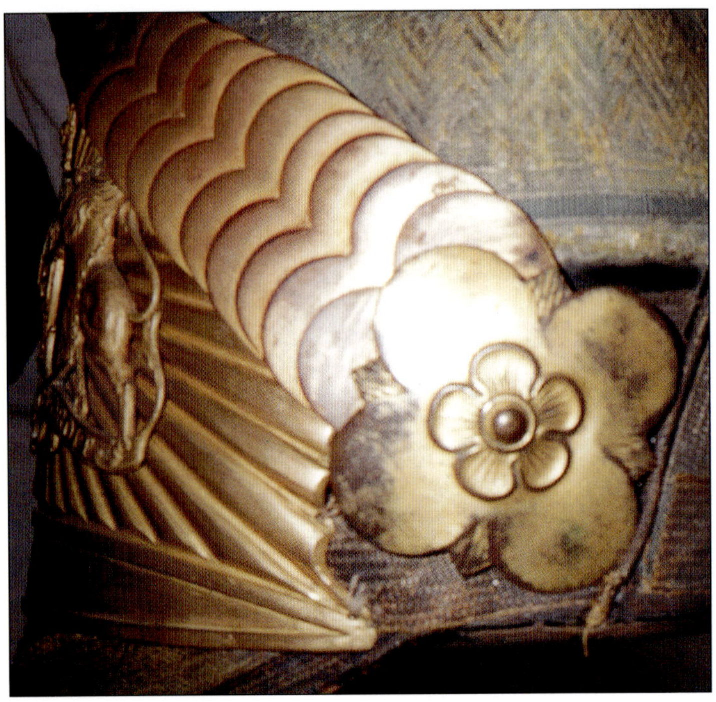

Figure 150B: Close up view of the unusual pattern bosses to the chinscales fitted to the 'theatrical' pattern cap. Copyright W.Y. Carman.

Figure 150C: Rear view of the 'theatrical' pattern cap illustrating the 'false' rear peak. Copyright W.Y. Carman.

considerable time before the regiment introduced lancer dress. The lance cap was based on that of the 17th Lancers, but no details of the plate or the lace are given'. Continues 'Such experiments took place fairly frequently in connection with yeomanry uniforms which, as you will appreciate was subject to much less official scrutiny than was the uniform of regular units'. N.B. Regrettably the author of the above observations and conclusions was not named in the bin-book.

This cap was based upon the 1856 officers pattern cap, having the ribbed sides and the top covered with white cloth, with what appears to be gold gimp and orris cord across the top and down the angles. To the upper left front a bullion rosette, with the Royal Cypher of ER VII embroidered to the centre.

The skull and peak of black patent leather, having braid and lace as described in chapter seven for the caps of officers of regular lancer regiments.

The lance cap plate consisted of the standard pattern gilt metal rayed plate, surmounted by the overlay comprised of, the Royal Cypher of ER VII surmounted by a King's pattern crown within a wreath of laurel. The overlay is thought to have been of three separate pieces, these being (1) the wreath of laurels, (2) the crown, and (3) the Royal Cypher, all parts being in silvered metal.

Standard pattern lion's head bosses, and burnished chinchain completed the head-dress, there being no plume fitted to the cap concerned.

Based on the above description, the authors are of the considered opinion that the cap in question had no connection with the Bedfordshire Yeomanry, as the facing colour, cloth top, bullion boss etc bear no resemblance to the those on the pattern of cap adopted by the officers of this particular regiment. It is however possible that this cap had some connection with the Lincolnshire Yeomanry, although this has not been confirmed.

Figure 150D: Inside view of the 'theatrical' pattern cap. Copyright W.Y. Carman. Photo: David Rowe.

A Cap having a None Standard Fitting *(See Fig: 151.)*

This cap was the standard post 1856 pattern officers cap of the 17th Lancers, however it differed from other known examples it that a skull and crossed bones fitment replaced the standard pattern lion's head bosses. N.B. The author's reserve their right not to express an opinion as to the authenticity of this none standard fitting.

A Cap for Display Purposes *(See Fig: 152.)*

This cap appears to be a post 1856 officers pattern, but having light yellow cloth sides and top, with gold cord extending up the corners and transversely across the crown of the cap. All other fittings appeared to be of standard pattern except for the plate as described below.

The plate comprised a rayed back plate upon which was superimposed a large crown, not unlike the pattern fitted to the helmet plate of the heavy cavalry of the pre 1871 period, with immediately below the crown an intertwined double 'GR' in gilt/brass metal. As

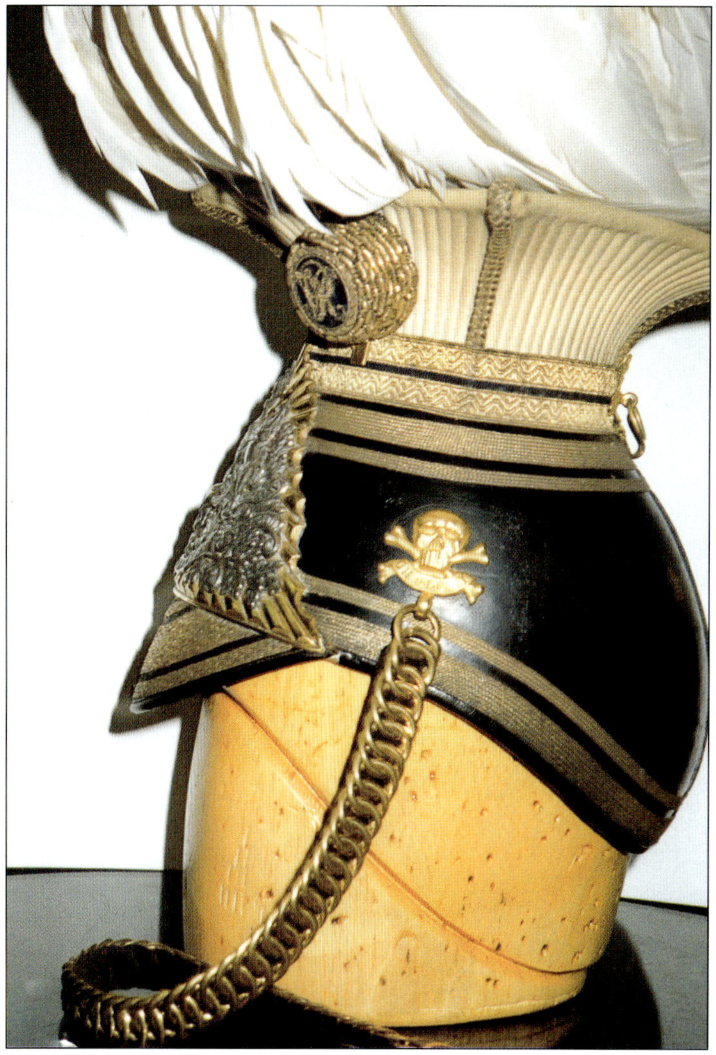

Figure 151: A Victorian officers pattern cap of the 17th Lancers fitted with ear bosses of a spurious nature. Note. The 'stand' supporting this cap is in fact a head block used to stretch and form the skull during the manufacture of a lance cap. Copyright W.Y. Carman.

stated previously this cap was restored for display purposes only. N.B. Although not exactly the same the intertwined 'GR' was not unlike the pattern fitted to the helmet plate of the Household Cavalry helmets of the 1814-16 period.

A Trial Pattern Lance Cap Plate (*See Fig: 153.*)
This 'trial' pattern lance cap plate is amongst the extensive collection of head-dress plates and cap badges owned by the renowned collector Hugh King, its design being as follows.

A standard pattern gilt rayed 'back plate', superimposed upon which was a silvered two-piece overlay comprised of the following. (1) The post 1902 pattern Royal Arms, having the crown surmounted by the Prince of Wales's feathers and cornet, the arms partially surrounded by (2) A wreath of laurel leaves.

Having handled this particular item, and examined both sides of the plate, it was evident that both the silvered overlay, and the gilt metal rayed 'back plate' were genuine. The back plate being of the standard officer pattern holds no specific interest, it being the silvered overlay that invites speculation as to the reason why this plate was produced. Therefore, the component parts of the overlay are listed below for consideration, with a more detailed description of each part being given, together with the author's observations:

(A) The Prince of Wales's feathers, coronet, and motto of '*Ich Dien*' that surmount the crown to the Royal Arms, is, amongst

Figure 152: The restored officers pattern cap used for display purposes only. Note the reversed and intertwined double 'GR' superimposed upon the rayed plate. Courtesy of Alan Fordham.

BELOW - *Figure 153:* Unidentified Victorian officers pattern lance plate. Of interest is the Prince of Wales's plume and coronet surmounting the crown of the Royal Arms. Courtesy of Hugh King Photo: R. Biondi.

regular lancer regiments unique to the lance cap plate of the 12th Lancers.

(B) This particular pattern of Victorian Royal Arms is the version being without the crossed lances behind the arms, that is to be found on the lance cap plate of the 5th, 12th, and 17th Lancers, albeit that in the case of the 5th, and 17th Lancers[3], a lion guardant surmounts the crown of the Royal Arms.

(C) The laurel leaf wreath that partially encloses the Royal Arms is unlike any other pattern of wreath known to have been used on a lance cap plate. This pattern is less profuse than the oak leaf wreath of the Bedfordshire Yeomanry as illustrated in *Fig: 131B.*, or the oak leaf wreath of the 1st City of London Yeomanry illustrated in *Fig: 110.* It is also of an entirely different design to the laurel and palm leaf decoration on the plate of the East Riding of Yorkshire Yeomanry as illustrated in *Fig: 136C.*, of different shape to the thistle wreath on the plate of the Lanarkshire Yeomanry, and is less profuse and of different design to the laurel leaf wreath of the plate of the Lincolnshire Yeomanry illustrated in *Fig: 140.* Taking account of the above, this lance cap plate appears to be an unadopted officers 'universal' trial pattern, the overlay being comprised of the Royal Arms from a regular lancer officers plate, with the wreath being in the style of a yeomanry lance cap plate, which regrettably brings us no nearer to identifying for which regiment/s it was designed. Should any reader have a substantiated theory regarding this item, perhaps they would be kind enough to contact the authors via Schiffer Publishing Limited.

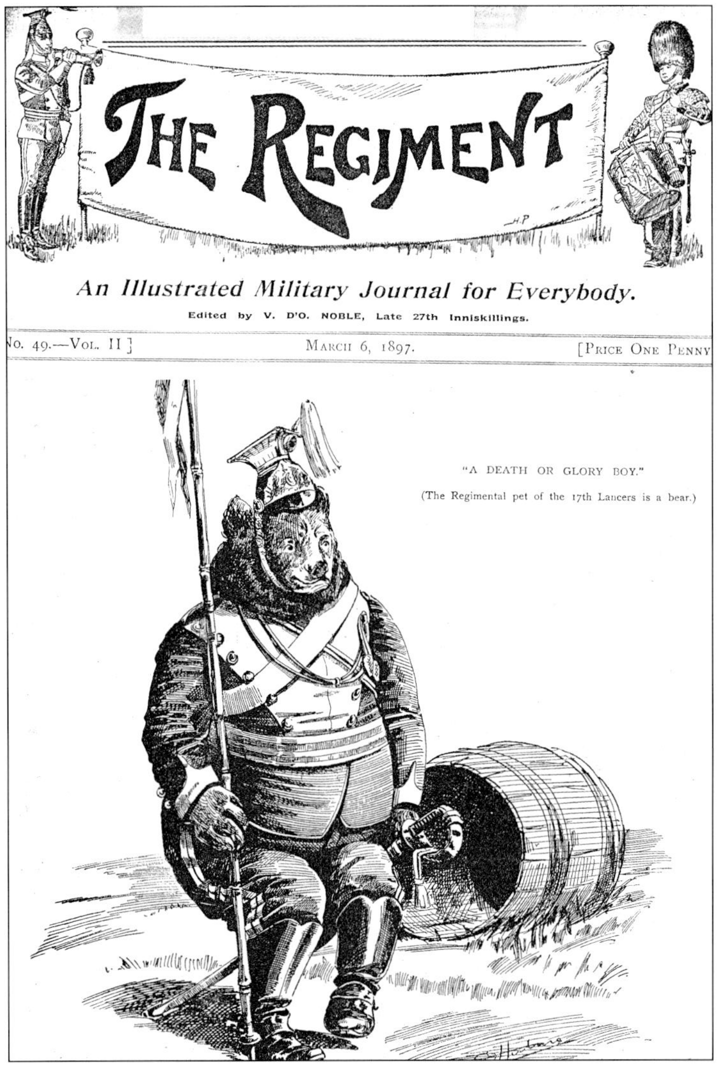

Figure 154: 'A Death Or Glory Boy' A Victorian cartoon depicting the then regimental pet of the 17th Lancers. David Rowe Collection. Originally published in the Regiment Journal 6th March 1897.

NOTES

1. At the time of the charge of the Light Brigade, that occurred on the 25th October 1854, there was no such regiment as the 27th Lancers in the then current Army List. It would be some eighty-six years before the 27th Lancers appeared in the Army List, this occurring when the short-lived war raised regiment having this title was raised in 1940 (47).

2. The actor Marks Burns, who played the part of Captain Morris, actually served in a British cavalry regiment, being at one time a short-service officer in the 15th/19th Hussars (106).

3. On the plate of the 17th Lancers, the 'union flowers' are absent from the scrolls inscribed 'Dieu Et' and 'Mon Droit' that form part of the Royal Arms (*See Fig: 37A.*).

Chapter Fifteen

Purchasing a Lance Cap

Choosing a Theme

Having decided to collect lance caps, and with there being several different regiments and various differing pattern of caps to choose from, just how the collector new to militaria decides what lance cap will start their collection will depend on many differing factors, including perhaps the amount of money available to spend, and the caps being offered for sale at the time concerned. However, once a cap has been chosen upon which to build a collection, it is strongly advise that this theme is adhered to, as it can be extremely costly changing from one to another, and there is always the possibility that difficulties may be experienced when attempting to 'sell off' the original items purchased without a monetary loss being incurred.

The chosen theme may take the form of collecting head-dress of a particular lancer regiment from its formation to the withdrawal of full dress, the lance caps worn by the regiment concerned during a given period of time, officers pattern caps, or caps worn by the rank and file. It could however be concentrated on a particular period in time such as the early or late Victorian era, or the post 1902 to 1914 period.

Seeking Advice

It is not our place to preach to collectors new to this field of militaria, nor to established militaria collectors who might be considering the purchase of a full dress lance cap to complement a cavalry tunic with overalls/pantaloons that are already in their collection. We do however offer the following words of advice, which it is sincerely hoped will be of some assistance in this respect.

As with the purchase of any expensive article/item, if the intending purchaser has little or no knowledge regarding the subject concerned, they should attempt to recruit the assistance of an established collector or a friend, who hopefully will be able to offer constructive advise. If such a person is not already known to the prospective buyer, a good way to meet people with a similar interest is by joining a militaria collectors society, always provided that such an organisation exists within your city/town. If however this avenue is not available, it may be well worth finding out if there is a Model Soldier Collection Society in your locality, as collectors of model soldiers often also collect items of militaria to complement their model soldier collection.

Alternatively, a look at the classified advertisement section of a militaria magazine such as *Classic Arms & Militaria, Military Illustrated, Military Modelling*, or *Regiment Magazine* may well provide the names of some reputable militaria dealers who may be approached for advice. N.B. It is worth remembering that a dealers who sells a variety of militaria, and whose stock may range from cap badges to complete uniforms may not necessarily be knowledgeable on all aspects of this hobby, and therefore may only be able to offer a considered opinion on a particular item.

With the current and foreseeable shortage of genuine, good condition, undamaged lance caps available for purchase by collectors from either arms fairs, auction house salerooms or specialist militaria dealers, coupled with the ever increasing cost of same, a prospective buyer need to feel confident that the item under consideration is 'all belonging', and that it has not been 'restored' and fitted with associated parts sometime in its life. It therefore goes without saying, that any lance cap under consideration should be examined very carefully before parting with any hard earned cash.

Theatrical Head-dress

It is well known that over the years items of head-dress have been adapted for theatrical use, and therefore may have had parts removed or added to alter the caps appearance to suit the wardrobe managers/mistress's requirements, and that some of these items have found there way onto the 'open market'. Additionally items of head-dress sometimes become available for purchase that have been modified to resemble an earlier, rarer, and more collectable pattern. N.B. A good example of a 'theatrical' lance cap is illustrated in *Fig: 149.*, which depicts the actor Errol Flynn wearing the uniform of the then fictitious 27th Lancers, including a lance cap, further details of which have already been given in chapter fourteen.

Military head-dress and items of uniform known/thought to have been worn by actors in films, the theatre, or television should generally be viewed as being of dubious authenticity, for it is known that Directors are inclined to amend facts relating to characters, dates and dress to suit the script concerned. A prime example is the 1968 Tony Richardson film *'The Charge of The Light Brigade'*, in which despite professional advice, all the regiments involved in the charge wore cherry coloured overalls (19). Additionally, this film 'changed history', as Captain Lewis Nolan was depicted as the officer involved in the 'Black Bottle' affair of 1854, when in fact the incident occurred in 1840 and involved Captain John Reynolds of the 11th Hussars. Additionally, both Captain Nolan and Paymaster Henry Duberly were depicted as serving in the 11th Hussars, whilst in fact the former served in the 15th, the latter in the 8th Hussars (20).

Tattoo Head-dress

There are also caps/helmets that have been specially modified or produced for use by re-enactment societies, or for use at official military tattoos, albeit that genuine parts may have been fitted to these items of head-dress, thus making it difficult to authenticate such items. Items of head-dress thought to be possibly either theatrical, from military tattoos, restored or made, up should always be examined most carefully, for as we all know, there are unscrupulous people who will stop at nothing to make a 'fast buck', and such items should normally be avoided by the serious collector.

In relation to the 'restoration' of a lance cap, the following are some 'not quite right' aspects of restoration known to the authors that have been carried out to the officers pattern lance cap.

The Cloth Top and Sides

Extensive moth larvae damage, major splits/tears, or bad staining are probably the three main reasons for the cloth sides and top of an officers pattern cap being replaced. At one time this form of 'restoration' was comparatively unknown, however, early last year (2000) in a militaria auction held at the premises of a respected London auction house, on four out of the five officers pattern lance caps offered for sale, the cloth tops had been replaced. In this particular instance the saleroom catalogue clearly stated this fact, and the auctioneers are to be commended for there attention to detail. There are however other known 'outlets' from which may be purchased such desirable items, whose proprietors might have the 'you pay your money and take your choice' attitude, and who would certainly be less forthright when describing the condition of such a cap.

Regarding restoration to the cloth sides and top of the cap, the authors have been advised by collectors of militaria who have handled such items of head-dress, that on caps that have had the sides/top recovered, the grade of material used appears to be of an inferior quality and the nap has a 'fuzzy' feel when touched. When examining the top of an officer pattern cap, we would recommend that the gold gimp and orris cord that runs across the top and down the angles of the cap is also carefully scrutinized, as it is likely that upon this cord being removed from the original cloth sides/top that the gimp and orris cord would have been damaged, thereby making it impractical to re-use, and needing to be replaced.

The gold lace encircling the waist of an officers pattern cap should also be examined carefully and its condition compared with the level of tarnishing on the braid immediately below the lace and around the bottom of the skull, as the waist lace would also need to be removed if replacing the cloth upper section and top.[1] Careful attention should also be paid to the gold lace encircling the waist of an N.C.O.'s pattern cap, and the worsted band on the other ranks pattern cap, as it is not unknown for a damaged waistband to be replaced by a modern replacement.

The Bullion Plume Rosette

It is also not unknown for the gold bullion rosette to have been replaced, possibly due to either damage to the gold bullion, moth damage to the velvet backing to the Royal Cypher, or both. The known replacement rosettes appear to be of inferior quality, having only five rows of bullion, whereas the genuine fitment had seven/eight rows thereby making it somewhat deeper, and standing further 'proud' from the side of the cap. Additionally, the Royal Cypher is less defined, being of lesser quality, with the plume socket that protrudes from behind the top of the rosette being without a 'lip', and having the appearance of being an other ranks fitting.

The Head Lining

Over the period of many years, which in many cases will be in excess of a hundred, the crimson silk material to the upper part of the lining may have become dry and 'brittle', and in many instances have disintegrated completely, with the leather sweatband drying out and 'rotting' away. The 'lack' of a head lining to a cap will obviously have an effect on its value, and may result in a replacement sweatband and silk lining being fitted to the cap.

This part of the cap should be carefully examined to ascertain if the leather and silk elements of the lining are contemporary with the remainder of the cap. An original lining should normally show signs of service wear (staining and wear) to both the leather sweatband and the silk upper section, which may have minor splits or tears to the material. The silk lining may also retain the gold embossed stamp of the maker/supplier as illustrated in *Fig: 136D*. N.B. If permitted to do so, carefully examine the stitching to the sweatband/lining exercising extreme care, as an age old lining may split or tear if not handled gently.

Should a replacement lining have been fitted, the leather sweatband is likely to be very soft and supple and the silk element will probably be made of a synthetic material, neither of which are likely to show signs of service wear. Evidence of the 'makers' gold embossed stamp referred to above may not necessarily indicate that the lining is the original one for that particular cap. N.B. The authors have seen examples of Dragoon Guards officers helmets where the quilted cloth head lining has been replaced by a modern day replacement lining of synthetic material.

Replacement Fittings

It not unusual to find an item of head-dress that has at some time been fitted with either associated/replacement parts, or reproduction fittings, such as the plume, the corner ornaments, the gilding metal strips covering the angles (9th Lancers only), the head lining, ear bosses, and the chinchain. It is a matter of personal choice as to whether or not to purchase a cap fitted with 'associated' parts, one view on this matter being that if as a whole the lance cap is a collectable piece, then it is worth purchasing the item in the hope that the required genuine items may at some later date be acquired from either a fellow collector or a specialist militaria dealer.

Having taken account of the above, a prospective purchaser would be wise to take account of any replacement items fitted to the cap concerned before agreeing a price and concluding the sale, as an item of head-dress with associated fittings is not as saleable as an untouched item. In view of this fact we offer the following information relating to lance caps, and the component parts which are most likely to have been replaced with associated or replacement fittings, all of which will effect the value of a cap.

The Sides, Skull and Top

Some degree of crazing to the patent leather top of the other ranks pattern cap (also 9th Lancers officers pattern), is to be expected, as is minor crazing to the skull and peak, and should not effect its value to any degree. Excessive crazing, congealing of the leather, or cuts to the patent leather peak, skull, or top, will however have a marked effect on the value of a cap, as will severe moth damage to the cloth sides or top of a cap, or having the top and sides replaced (officers caps) as mentioned earlier. Other ranks pattern caps having an unmarked[2] top should be examined very carefully, for unless an unissued example, it is possible that the patent leather top has been replaced. It is also worthwhile checking the condition of the edge of the peak on an O.R.'s pattern cap for possible evidence that the peak has been reduced in depth (shortened).

Avoid caps with peaks or tops having pieces of linen or paper adhering to the patent leather. This 'problem' appears to have usually occurred when the cap has been left in an area very prone to either heat, sunlight or both. The patent leather becomes warm and congeals, and the linen/paper that has somehow come into contact with the peak, skull or top of the cap, bonds into the patent leather. This may also be found to have happened to the patent leather flaps of undress sabretache's, and regrettably it is almost impossible to separate these materials from the leather.

The Plume Holder

Occasionally on an officers pattern plume, the gilt metal holder will be found to have been replaced with a brass/gilding metal other ranks pattern holder. It is also not unknown for a hussar officers pattern plume socket to have been used to replace a missing holder on a lancer officers plume, or for the holder to be simply absent, all of which will have some effect on the overall value of the plume concerned. N.B. The hussar officers pattern plume holder has only four upright leaves, which are of a different pattern to those on the lancer officers holder. Additionally, the band above the corded ball is slightly deeper on the hussar pattern holder.

The Head Lining

On an officers pattern lance cap, the tan leather sweatband and crimson silk lining will frequently be in a stained condition, however this should not usually affect the value of the cap to a great extent, as many collectors prefer to own a cap showing signs of service wear. A torn, perished, or missing lining, whether on a officers or other ranks[3] pattern cap, will almost certainly have the affect of reducing the caps value.

The Lance Cap Plate

On an officers pattern cap, it is always worthwhile looking closely at the method by which the plate is attached to the skull to see if there is any reason to suggest that the plate has at some time been removed for cleaning or restoration purposes etc. N.B. This is most important, for it is not unknown for a plate to have been 'married' to the skull of a cap lacking its original plate.

Careful examination of the silvered overlay on an officers pattern plate should be carried out, as frequently, slight damage may have been sustained, such as the orb of the crown being absent, the tails of the supporters (lion and unicorn) being bent or missing, or the horn of the unicorn being broken off etc. Missing ray tips to a lance cap plate will detract from its appearance, particularly if the top tip is missing or distorted.

Reproduction Lance Cap Plates

Notwithstanding the above, plates in the above condition are still collectable, unlike 'fake' plates, it being known that reproduction other ranks lance cap plates have been produced for in excess of thirty years. N.B. The author's have seen Victorian examples of both the 16th, and the 17th Lancers plates, and it is not unreasonable to presume that the plates of other regiments have also been produced.

When looking at what is thought to be a reproduction plate, it is not always that easy to tell if the item concerned is genuine or not. One reason why at first glance these plates appear to be genuine, is borne in the suggestion that these 'fake' plates are struck using the original lance cap plate dies, first used over a hundred years ago, although to date this has not been verified. That said, it is when looking down at the edge of a reproduction plate that the difference between a genuine plate and a 'fake' item becomes noticeable, the rays on a genuine plate being angular giving them dimension, whereas the rays on a modern reproduction plate are almost flat. Additionally, the Royal Arms, battle honour scrolls, and title scroll are less 'proud', and have little depth.

An alternative method of reproducing an exact copy of an object such as a lance cap plate, without incurring the rigorous problems and expense involved in making and using a steel die is the Electro Form (Type) method, which dates back to Victorian times (44).

This method involves making a rubber mould of the item to be copied, say for example a lance cap plate, the mould then being dusted with a copper powder, or painted with metallic paint. A tank filled with copper sulphate, sulphuric acid, and de-ionized water is required, into which is immersed a suitable amount of copper. A positive charge of a couple of amps is run through the copper, the positive charge then being transferred to the rubber mould which is left in place for some twenty-fours hours or so. The copper builds a deposit onto the flat surface of the mould, which at the prescribed time may be removed from the tank, the reproduced lance cap plate then being cleaned (44). The major difference between this type of plate and a die -struck item is that the latter plate is usually made of brass, and not copper, and scratching the reverse of the electro form plate will identify that the plate is made of copper. N.B. As dangerous chemicals are used in the above process, it is recommended that the this method of creating a lance cap plate etc is only carried out by a highly trained specialist.

The Plate - To Purchase or Not

Our advice in respect of purchasing a lance cap plate, is try to always buy from an established reputable source, and as soon as possible compare the newly purchased item with a plate known to be the genuine article. It in doubt, leave well enough alone, as other ranks pattern plate are reasonable plentiful and are frequently offered for sale at auction salerooms, or by specialist militaria dealers.

The Lion's Head Bosses and Chinchain

Lion's head bosses should be carefully examined as it is rumoured that 're-struck' pattern ear bosses have been produced using the original dies, although perhaps it is better to have such a boss, than none at all. On an officers pattern cap, the bosses should be checked to ensure that they are not replacement fittings, or from an other ranks lance cap. To establish if the bosses are contemporary with the cap, unscrew one of the bosses, and hold it against the hook and ring mounted upon the four-petalled leaf at the rear waist of the cap, to compare the colour of the gilt metal. N.B. In theory, there should be no reason why a lion's head boss could not be reproduced using the electro form method described above, thereby making it even more important to examine this component part most carefully.

Chinchains are frequently either in a worn condition, missing completely, or have had the backing replaced, nether the less, a worn or re-backed chinchain is better than no chain at all. For regiments having a distinctive pattern chinchain such as the 9th Lancers and Lanarkshire Yeomanry, the chain should be examined to ensure that it is of the corded pattern.

If possible, check the length of the chinchain using a tape measure, as several examples seen by the author's have been shortened by having some of the links removed. The normal length of an officers pattern chinchain should be approximately sixteen to eighteen inches, with the other ranks pattern measuring approximately sixteen to seventeen and a half inches. N.B. The later figure includes the four unbacked links at one end of the chinchain).

The Plume

In the author's opinion, the plume is the crowning glory of any item of military head-dress, and a lance cap without its plume does not quite have the same appeal, and this should be reflected in the asking price for such an example.

Officers swan feather's plumes should be carefully examined, as it is known that good quality modern reproduction feather plumes are being produced. It is reasonable to expect that on a genuine plume, that given its probable age, there should be some fading to the colour of the feathers, although this cannot be taken as 'proof positive' as there are those who will age a plume to give it an authentic look. The prospective purchaser should look to see if the gilt metal ring is in place at the centre crown of the plume, as the modern day reproduction plumes appear to lack this fitting.

Reproduction Officers Pattern Caps

Respected collectors of militaria in both the United Kingdom and the United States of America, have informed the authors that 'reproduction' officers pattern lance caps complete with feather plumes, of the both the 17th and the 21st Lancers, and possibly other regiments are 'doing the rounds', being offered for sale at a price one would normally expect to pay for the genuine article.

These caps are all in 'mint' condition, and whilst at first this might seem to be a dead giveaway as to their authenticity, it cannot be guaranteed, as it is known that there exist genuine officers caps, in unmarked condition, having little or no service wear, which could equally be described as being in fine condition. If the potential purchaser is in doubt, a check of the quality of the cloth top and sides, the bullion rosette, the head lining, and the feather plume might assist in establishing the caps pedigree. Our advice is, if in doubt seek qualified advice, if still in doubt, give it a miss.

Miniature Lance Caps

Finally, before concluding this chapter we include a brief reference to miniature caps, which we felt might be of interest to collectors of militaria who would like to own a lance cap, but for whatever reason are unable to do so.

In respect of the above, it had recently come to the attention of the authors that one-fifth scale miniature lance caps are currently being produced from a 'cottage industry' based in the north of England, these caps being hand made (to order) by craftsmen.

As the production of these miniatures is still somewhat in its infancy, there is only one pattern of lance cap currently available, this being the officers cap of the pre 1830 period as illustrated in *Figs: 155.* to *157.* The body of the cap is made of resin, and hand painted in the appropriate regimental colours, with the fittings such as the plate, ear bosses, plume holder etc all being made of white metal, then gold or silver plated as appropriate. The caps are fitted with a hair plume in its holder, and come complete with a wooden stand.

To date miniature officers pattern caps have been created for the 9th, 12th, 16th, and 17th Lancers, with a foul weather cap also being produced. All of these scale sized caps are produced in a very limited edition, and are available from the sole distributor D.P.& G. of P.O. Box 186, Doncaster, South Yorkshire, England.

OPPOSITE - *Figure 155:* An example of the miniature lance cap of the 16th (Queen's) Lancers complete with hair plume in holder. Copyright D.P.& G.

Figure 155A: Rear view of the 16th Lancer cap showing the 'constantly turned up' rear peak. Copyright D.P.& G.

NOTES

1. On an officers 'Victorian' pattern cap examined by a respected overseas collector, the silk stripe to the centre of the waist band lace was found to be wider than normal. Additionally it was also observed that the plume socket mount was not stitched in place and could easily be removed, and that the hook located to the rear waist of the cap was a new replacement fitting.

2. Other ranks caps of the 17th Lancers having the white patent leather top, should be examined carefully for signs of the leather top have been painted to enhance its appearance.

3. The calico/waxed cotton head lining on an other ranks pattern cap should be carefully be examined for signs of the lining having been replaced.

Figure 156: An example of the miniature lance cap of the 17th (Light) Dràgoons (Lancers). Copyright D.P.& G.

Figure 157: Two examples of the miniature cap, the 17th Lancers (left) and the foul weather cap (right). Copyright D.P.& G.

Chapter Sixteen

Care, Preservation/Restoration of the Lance Cap

Irrespective of whether a particular item of head-dress is to form the basis upon which a collection is to be built, has been acquired to complement a full dress uniform, or is a recent acquisition for an established collection, the proud owner will almost certainly wish the item to look as near as possible to how it would have looked when worn by the soldier concerned many, many years ago. There are differing opinions on whether or not a lance cap in a dirty, but untouched condition should be cleaned, repaired and restored to its former glory. Many collectors prefer to leave the head-dress in the condition it was in when acquired, and one must respect this view. However there are several ways that the appearance of a cap may be improved without actually undertaking any major restoration work, and the following advice is given in the hope that it will be of some assistance to both new and established collectors.

The Plume

It is often the plume, either feather or hair that is in a dirty condition, white plumes frequently having become a dirty yellow in colour. Horsehair plumes in this condition may benefit from being washed with a proprietary brand of shampoo of the type suitable for normal hair, with the plume being immersed in a bowl of lukewarm water and the shampoo being gently massaged into the hairs of the plume. Great care should be taken to ensure that as far as is possible the hairs do not become matted, as once the plume has dried entangled hairs are difficult to brush and may be pulled loose by the hairbrush, thereby thinning the plume. The damp plume should then be rinsed, and gently massaged using a named brand of hair conditioner (also of the type suitable for normal hair), rinsed thoroughly in clean lukewarm water, and hung in a natural position to dry. Once dry the plume may be gently brushed. N.B. It is not recommended that an attempt is made to wash a cock-tail or swan's feather plume.

The Cap

The cleaning of the patent leather skull and fittings is again very much a matter of personal choice, there being some collectors who prefer to see all items in their collection in 'mint condition', whilst other choose to leave the skull and fittings in an untouched state, as this tends to give the head-dress an air of age and authenticity. However, if it is decided that the skull and fittings are to be cleaned, then this task should be carried out with extreme caution and care, and should it be considered necessary to remove the lance plate from the skull (in the case of an other ranks cap only), always unscrew the plate retaining nuts very slowly, and if resistance is met, it is suggested that the attempt is abandoned and that the cap is cleaned with the plate in situ. The removal of the lance cap plate from an officers pattern cap is not recommended unless absolutely necessary, in which case professional assistance should be sought before attempting this task.

The Skull and Top

Leather becomes brittle with age and there is a school of though that recommends that leather should be treated with one of the proprietary brands of leather dressing used by the museum services. In this respect the author's have used lanolin cream for this purpose, the cream being gently rubbed onto the leather part concerned, the leather then being gently polished with a soft clean duster to remove any excess cream. If applying lanolin cream to the patent leather skull of a lance cap, extreme care should be taken to ensure that the cream does not come into contact with the ribbed cloth section, the gold braid/lace on an officers cap, or the cotton braid on the other ranks pattern cap.

The patent leather top, where applicable, may also be treated with lanoline cream, taking extreme care to ensure that the cream does not come into contact with the cloth material below. The ribbed cloth upper sides of the cap may be gently brushed with a small dry brush, such as a tooth brush. However it is not recommended that the cloth sides are in any way dampened to clean them, nor any cleaning agent used, without first seeking professional advice. The skiver lining the inside the front peak however, may benefit from having lanolin cream gently massaged into the skiver, and then wiped over with a soft cloth.

The Braid and Lace

The gold braid and lace on an officers pattern cap is often in a tarnished condition, and may benefit by being cleaned with a mixture of dry bread crumbs and purified cream of tartar (available from a pharmacy), applied in a dry condition, and brushed onto the braid/lace with a soft clean brush, then 'wiped' over with a soft duster. N.B. As always, extreme care should be taken when brushing or wiping the braid/lace.

The Fittings

The gilt fittings, such as the lion's head bosses, the corner finishing pieces to the top of the cap (where applicable), and the rear waist ring and hook may be gently washed with warm soapy water using a soft toothbrush to remove ingrained dirt, then 'wiped over' with a soft dry duster.

The Officers Lance Cap Plate

The Silver plated overlays to the officers pattern lance cap plate may be cleaned by using a long lasting proprietary brand of silver polish, such as 'Goddards Long Term Silver Polish', however care must be taken to ensure that the polish does not come into contact with the gilt metal backing plate, as the very thin layer of gilt on the plate might be damaged or removed completely. It is worth remembering that every cleaning of a gilded/silver plated item represents a minute wearing down of the surface concerned and may result in the removal of a minute layer of the gilding/silver. Notwithstanding the above, if it is considered necessary to give the overlay a 'good clean' using silver polish, once this task has been completed, it is probably best thereafter to merely 'wipe' over the silvered parts with either impregnated wadding, or a silver polishing cloth. N.B. As mentioned earlier, it is not recommended that an attempt to remove the lance cap plate from an officers cap be undertaken, unless absolutely necessary, in which case professional assistance should be sought before undertaking such a task.

The N.C.O.'s and O.R.'s Lance Cap Plate

The lance cap plate on a senior N.C.O.'s cap will most probably be gilded metal, and should therefore be washed with warm soapy water, and no account should metal polish be used as this will almost certainly remove the gilding. The lance cap plate on an other ranks pattern cap may be removed by unscrewing the two brass 'hooped nuts' that secure the plate to the skull of the cap, taking extreme care, as mentioned above. The plate may then be cleaned using a proprietary brand of metal polish, such as 'Brasso' using a small nail brush or toothbrush, the polish then being 'wiped off' using a soft duster and any dried polish removed using a clean dry toothbrush, before re-affixing the plate to the skull of the cap.

The Lining

Officers pattern caps having a combined leather/silk head lining may benefit from having the leather part treated with lanolin cream as previously described, taking extreme care to ensure the cream does not come into contact with the silk section of the lining. It is not recommended that any attempt at cleaning the silk section of these dual linings be undertaken, as the silk is highly likely to be in a fragile condition, and may easily tear.

The Chinchain

Chinchains backed with velvet may benefit from the backing being brushed to improve their appearance, and chains having a leather backing may be treated with lanolin cream as described earlier. The stitching that holds the chain links onto the backing will often be found to have rotted away, with the result that the leather hangs loose from the chain. It is possible to re-stitch the chain to the leather, however this is a most difficult task and may take several hours to complete.

Therefore, unless totally confident about re-stitching a chinchain, it is recommended that the item concerned is taken to a leather specialist to be repaired. If however you are confident enough to attempt this task, please remember not to sew to tightly, or the end result will be a twisted chinchain.

Cap-lines

To reduce the effect of tarnishing on a set of officers pattern gold gimp and orris cord cap-lines, the method described earlier for the braid and lace on the skull of the cap may be used.

Finally with regard to the car and preservation of a lance cap, the importance of protecting the cap and plume from damage by moth larvae cannot be emphasised too strongly, and the possible use a modern moth deterrent should be given serious consideration.

Chapter Seventeen

Storage and Transportation of a Lance Cap

There may well be occasions when a collector may wish to transport a lance cap from their home to another location. This might occur when the collector wishes to take a particular cap to display at a militaria society meeting, to show to a fellow collector, or perhaps to take the item of head-dress to a militaria shop to sell or part exchange.

Irrespective of the actual monetary value of the cap, the last thing a collector would want to occur is for the lance cap to be damaged in transit. In Victorian and Edwardian times an officer would usually transport his cap in a metal carrying tin specifically designed to carry the chapka. We would not however advise the use of this method of transporting a lance cap, should a collector be fortunate enough to possess such a case in their collection, as the item of head-dress concerned will now be in a more fragile condition than when new, and therefore more prone to accidental damage. We do however offer the following advice, which it is felt may be of assistance in reducing the possibility of an item of head-dress being damaged in transit.

The Plume

The plume should be removed prior to packing the actual cap, and if the example concerned is an other ranks horsehair plume, it may be wrapped in a suitable cloth item such as a pillow case or a towel, taking extreme care to ensure that the plumes natural hanging shape is maintained. If however the plume concerned is a feather plume and the collector is fortunate enough to have an officers metal plume case/tin in their collection of the type illustrated in *Figs: 158.* and *159.*, then using such a case/tin is an ideal means of safely transporting a plume.

Should the plume be fitted with a gilt metal ring to its 'crown' as illustrated in *Fig: 136E.*, then the plume may be placed within the case by first pushing a length of wire having a hook at its end down through the top of the plume case and attaching the hook to the ring mentioned. Slowly withdrawing the wire from the plume case by pulling on its 'plain' end will then pull the plume into the case. Extreme care should be used when drawing the plume into tin to ensure that the feathers of the plume are not accidentally pushed downwards as this may well damage the 'stem' of the feather. If the collector does not possess a metal plume tin as mentioned above, a possible alternative may be to use a cardboard tube of the type frequently used to contain certificates, diploma's or posters etc, always providing that the circumference and length of the tube are of a suitable size.

The Chinchain and Lion's Head Bosses

Whilst it is not essential that the chinchain be removed, doing so will ensure that the metal links do not come into contact with the lance cap plate thereby possibly causing damage to same. This is particularly important on an officers pattern cap, for if the chinchain is left in situ, there is always the possibility that during transit the links of the chain may become entangled with the silvered overlay on the plate causing possible damage to the 'proud' parts of the silvered overlay, such as the horn or tail of the unicorn supporter, the tail of the lion supporter, the Prince of Wales's feathers (12th Lancers plate), or the tips of the lances (21st Lancers plate), all of which are very delicate and prone to accidental damage if not handled with extreme care.

If it has been decided to remove the chinchain from the cap then extreme care should be exercised to ensure that the threaded stud at the rear of the lion's head boss does not become cross-threaded, and that the edges of the lion's head mask do not mark the patent leather of the skull when replacing same.

Should in view of the above it be decided that the chinchain is to be removed from the skull of the cap, then it might also be a suitable occasion to pay attention to the backing of the chinchain. For an officers velvet backed chain, gently brushing the velvet lining with a soft brush should remove any fluff etc that might have adhered to the material and assist in restoring its nap. Extreme care should be taken to ensure that the brushing does not cause accidental damage to the cotton securing the chain to its backing. In the case of a leather backed chinchain, the gentle application of lanolin cream will feed the leather and help to prevent it drying out and cracking. N.B. Shortly after the lanolin cream has been applied the leather should be wiped gently with a soft dry cloth to remove any surplus cream and give the leather a smart appearance.

Figure 158: A fine example of a lancer officers plume tin. This example being for a 9th Lancers plume, and having the officers name painted onto the side of the tin. Courtesy of Jon Maguire.

Figure 159: A selection tins for lancer officers plumes. Of interest is the height of the tin of the extreme left of the photograph. Courtesy of Christopher Bryant. Photo: R. Biondi.

Packing the Lance Cap

When transporting a lance cap, an old pillow case to which a 'drawstring' has been attached makes an ideal 'lance cap bag' in which to transport the cap. The 'bagged up' head-dress may then be placed into a suitably sized, strongly constructed cardboard box/carton, the base of which should be lined with either foam rubber or 'bubble pack'. The gap between the walls of the box/carton and the actual chapka may also be lined with a similar protective material, as should the top of the box/carton.

Prior to taking a cap from the collectors home to another location, albeit perhaps for a short period of time, it is advisable to contact the company that insures the contents of your flat/house, to enquire if the company is prepared to issue a temporary cover note in respect of accidental damage to the cap during transit, during the period that the cap is at the temporary location concerned, or possibly even theft of the head dress whilst the item is away from your home. N.B. If the insurance company are prepared to cover the item in respect of the above, then it is likely that a small additional premium will be payable, we would however suggest that any reasonable fee requested will be well worth the investment.

Finally, in respect of theft of an item of head-dress, it is always advisable to photograph all the items in a collection as soon as practical, paying particular attention to photographing any unusual marks on each item that may be of assistance in positively identifying an item of head-dress etc, should one be unfortunate to have a lance cap or entire collection stolen.

Chapter Eighteen

Displaying the Lance Cap

This chapter was originally written for an earlier work entitled 'Head Dress of the British Heavy Cavalry' (38), however as the majority of that text is equally applicable to a lance cap, and there is no sense in 're-inventing the wheel', the chapter concerned has been reproduced here with a few suitable amendments.

Regardless of whether a collector has only one lance cap amongst a collection of uniforms, swords etc, or an entire collection of military head-dress, good condition other ranks chapka's have become extremely costly to buy, and the cost of officers pattern lance cap even more so. It therefore makes sound sense to ensure that the head-dress is cared for and protected from dust, atmospheric pollution, and attack by moth, all of which can have disastrous effects on a feather plume, the cloth upper part of the skull, the velvet backing to a chinchain, and the leather and silk head lining etc.

Display Cabinets

A glass fronted cabinet is ideal for displaying items of head-dress, whilst at the same time helping to protect valuable lance caps from atmospheric impurities. A suitable cabinet will also help protect the swans feather, or horsehair plumes from the effects of tobacco smoke (where applicable), as smoke from a cigarette, cigar, or pipe may discolour a light coloured plume.

In the case of an officers pattern cap, the cabinet will also help to protect the cloth top and upper part of the skull, the quilted cloth head lining, the skiver lining to the inside of the front peak, and the velvet backing to the chinchain from attack by moth, as the larvae of these insects feed on cloth, feathers, fur, and leather etc. One has only to see the cloth top of a lancer officers cap, or a busby bag that has been attacked by moth to see the irreparable damage that occurs if the head-dress is not suitably protected.

Finding a suitable cabinet in which to display a collection of military head-dress may prove to be no easy task, for antique display cases, both genuine and reproduction, whilst being ideally suitable in that they would complement the head-dress are usually extremely expensive to purchase. Also suitable for displaying a collection, are purpose built display cabinets, although these items are also very expensive to purchase, and are probably beyond the financial means of many collectors. Ready made display cabinets may be purchased from large furniture outlets/stores, however the majority of cabinets seen by the authors appear to be intended for displaying glassware and china ornaments etc, and have in our experience been found to be unsuitable for displaying items of head-dress in the face forwards position, due to their lack of depth. Suitable display cases may however sometimes be obtained from one of the suppliers of second hand business equipment and furniture that are to be found in most cities and major towns, where perhaps an open fronted bookcase may be found, to which may be added runners and glass sliding doors, thereby turning the bookcase into a display cabinet.

For the purposes of exhibiting a single item of head-dress, the oval shaped glass domes with fitted wooden bases that were popular in Victorian times to exhibit stuffed animals and birds, of which both antique and reproduction examples may be found in antique shops etc, are, if of the correct dimensions ideal for this purpose. They may not however be suitable for displaying an officers pattern chapka fitted with the swans feather 'dress' plume.

Displaying the Lance Cap

There are several methods of actually displaying an item of head-dress that is contained within a display cabinet, with probably the cheapest and simplest way being to place the lance cap onto a piece of dark coloured material such as velvet. N.B. If using this method to display more than one lance cap, the items of head-dress should be spaced a reasonable distance apart to prevent damage should the cabinet accidental be moved or rocked, which might cause the lance caps within to rock from side to side and come into contact with each other, possibly causing damage.

Supporting the Cap

An alternative method of exhibiting a cap within a display cabinet, is for the head-dress to be supported by a simple wire frame which can easily be made by a collector, or by using one made of plaster. For a more realistic effect, the use of a expanded polystyrene model head of the type used to display wigs may be used, alternatively for those collectors whose pocket can bear the cost, a professionally made studio head as used by window dressers, makes an ideal mode of display.

The Display Stand (*See Fig: 160.*).
A further alternative method of displaying the lance cap is by means of a purpose made wooden stand. A cheap, but effective stand can easily be constructed using a suitable wooden base measuring approximately seven inches x seven inches x three quarter inches, at the centre of which is positioned a piece of wooden dowelling having an approximate diameter of one and a half inches, and being some ten inches in height. N.B. An old wooden broom or mop handle is ideal for this purpose.

The wooden dowelling is first glued into place, and then further secured by a steel screw being passed through the square base of the stand and up into the centre of the wooden dowel. A circular piece of either hardboard or plywood having an approximate diameter of four inches is then affixed to the top of the dowelling by means of a screw. Onto the circular hardboard/plywood base is then placed a suitable sized and shaped piece of foam rubber to form the 'head', which is then covered by piece of strong cloth material, sufficient in size, to not only cover the foam, but to also hang down some five inches below the circular base. The material is then pulled down below the circular base to form a dome shape, where the loose ends of the material are gathered together beneath the base, and held in place by means of string, or by two or three strong elastic bands. The string/elastic bands is/are then covered with PVC insulating tape, and the 'loose' ends of the material trimmed with a sharp knife to 'tidy up' this part of the stand. N.B. It is important that the cloth covered foam 'head' is of sufficient dimensions to ensure that the skull supports the weight of the cap, and that the 'head' of the stand does not support the inside of the top of the cap, which could cause damage to either the cloth material or leather from which the top is made.

The wooden parts of the stand may then be stained and varnished, with the overall appearance of the display stand being enhanced by affixing either a collar badge, or a cap badge (a 're-strike' badge is most suitable for this purpose) of the appropriate regiment, to the centre front of the wooden base.

If a stand of the type described above is to be used, and the cap is complete with a set of cap-lines, then the owner may wish to display the cap with the lines encircling the waist of the cap once, with the remainder of the lines being looped around the base of the stand.

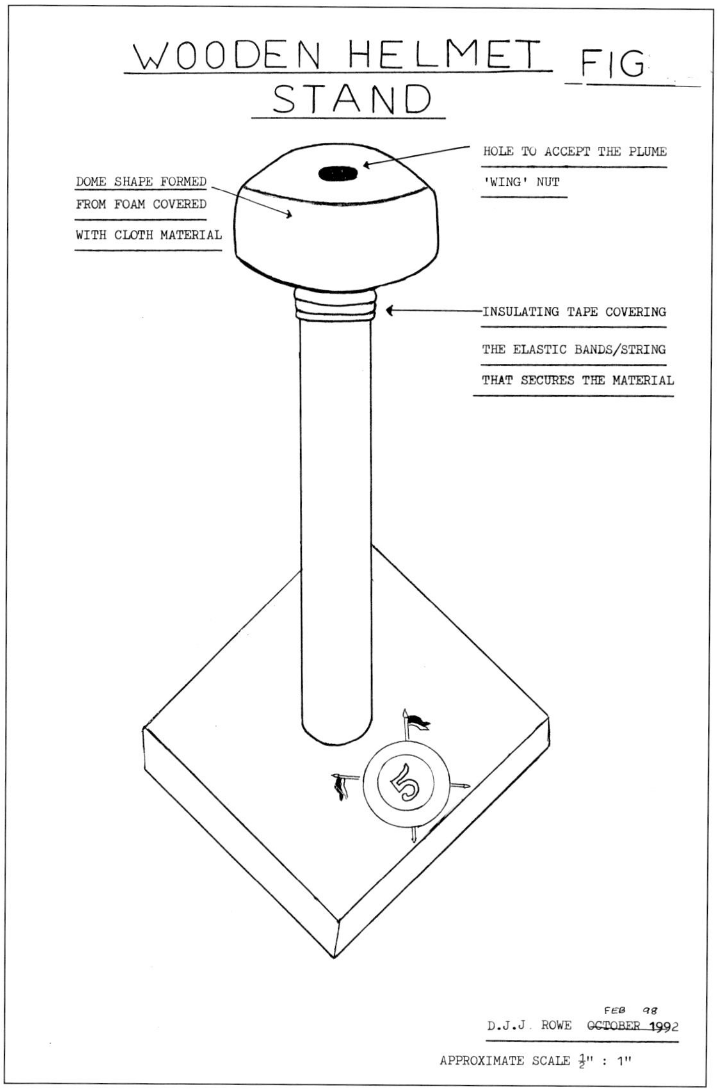

Figure 160: A basic display stand for the lance cap.

Appendices

Appendix I
Sealed Patterns

The following abridged extracts relating to the sealed patterns of officers uniforms have been reproduced from the Dress Regulations of 1900 and 1934 respectively, and are reproduced as originally written.

Dress Regulations 1900. Appendices

1. The Specifications and Instructions in these Appendices are intended to assist the Trade to supply garment or other articles of equipment to Officers strictly according to Regulation Pattern.

2. The Sealed Patterns of Officers Uniform and Equipment are open to inspection at the War Office, where every information on the subject will be afforded to manufacturers and others concerned.

3. Should any manufacturer desire to provide himself with patterns for his own guidance, such patterns will, upon application, be duly examined at the War Office, and, if found correct, passed and certified as being in conformity with Sealed Pattern.

4. All communications should be addressed to the Under Secretary of State, War Office, London, S.W.

Dress Regulations 1934. Section 1, General Instructions

1. Commanding officers are forbidden to introduce or to sanction any deviation from the sealed pattern of dress, clothing, equipment and badges. They will be responsible for the cost of replacing or restoring to the approved pattern any articles worn in their units which may be found not to be in conformity therewith.

2. When obtaining uniform and equipment, officers should make sure, by personal comparison if necessary, that articles according to sealed pattern are being supplied.

3. Sealed pattern of garments, buttons, lace, embroidery, badges of rank, special badges, devices, horse furniture and appointments are deposited at the War Office for reference and guidance. Duplicates of the sealed pattern badges are in possession of officers commanding regiments, battalions and infantry depots.

Appendix II
Cost of Component Parts for the Warrant Officers, Staff-Sergeants, Sergeants and Other Ranks Pattern Lance Cap

The following is an extract from the official publication entitled '*Priced Vocabulary of Clothing And Necessaries (Including Material)*' published on behalf of the War Office by Her Majesty's Stationery Office in 1911. The section of this publication with which this book is concerned is part one, which is composed of the designation and detail of the articles as stored in, and issued from, clothing depots, and their prices without accessories. N.B. Kindly note that the text of this abridged extract has been re-formatted for ease of reference, with the minimal additional text provided by the author's being presented in italics.

It should be noted that only the details relating to the warrant officers and staff sergeants, the sergeants, and the other ranks pattern lance caps have been given below, the information pertaining to the other items of head-dress contained within this publication i.e. the bearskin, bonnet, busby, chaco, and helmet having been omitted as such details do not fall within the terms of reference of this book. N.B. The price quoted against each component part is per item.

Part 1. Bonnets, Busbies, Caps, Chacos & c.

Caps, dress, lance- including body, plate, lines, plume, chain, socket, and oilskin cover. (A)

5th, 12th, 16th, 17th, and 21st *Lancers*.

Cat No.	Designation	Detail	£. s. d.
148	Warrant Officers & Staff-Sergeants	*As described above (A)*	3. 8. 6.
149	Sergeants	*As described above*	1. 7. 3.
150	Rank & file	*As described above*	0.19. 9.

9th *Lancers*

Cat No.	Designation	Detail	£. s. d.
151	Warrant Officers & Staff-Sergeants	*As described above*	3.11. 3.
152	Other ranks	*As described above*	1. 1. 6.

N.B. Of interest is the difference in cost between the Warrant Officers/Staff-Sergeants cap, and that of the Sergeants, which back in 1911 would have been quite a considerable amount.

Components, dress, lance-bodies, without accessories mentioned on page 10.: *As described above in (A).*

5th *Lancers* with scarlet quarters

231	Staff	Plain gold band; silk lined	1.12. 4.
232	Sergeants	Plain gold band	1. 1. 9.
233	Rank & file	Plain yellow worsted band	0.14. 2.

9th *Lancers* with blue quarters

234	Staff	Gilding metal band; silk lined	1.15. 0.
235	Other ranks	Gilding metal band	0.15.11.

12th *Lancers* with scarlet quarters

236	Staff	Gold band with blue centre; silk lined	1.12. 4.
237	Sergeants	Gold band with blue centre	1. 1. 9.
238	Rank & file	Yellow worsted band with blue centre	0.14. 2.

16th *Lancers* with blue quarters

239	Staff	Gold band with crimson centre; silk lined	1.12. 4.
240	Sergeants	Gold band with light crimson centre	1. 1. 9.
241	Rank & file	Yellow worsted band with scarlet centre	0.14. 2.

17th *Lancers* with white quarters

242	Staff	Gold band with blue centre; silk lined	1.12. 4.

243	Sergeants	Gold band with blue centre	1. 1. 9.
244	Rank & file	Yellow worsted band with blue centre	0.14. 2.

21st *Lancers* with French grey quarters

245	Staff	Plain gold band; silk lined	1.12. 4.
246	Sergeants	Plain gold band	1. 1. 9.
247	Rank & file	Plain yellow worsted band	0.14. 2.

Note that the Warrant Officers/Staff-Sergeants cap is listed as being silk lined.

Cockades, Cap, Lance-

5th *Lancers*			£. s. d.
259	Staff	Gold, with Royal Cypher on green velvet centre	0.15.11.
260	Sergeants	Gold cord with scarlet worsted centre	0. 3. 2.
261	Rank & file	Yellow worsted with scarlet centre	0. 0. 6.1/4.

9th *Lancers*

262	All ranks	Gilding metal	0. 0. 8.

12th and 17th *Lancers*

263	Staff	Gold, with Royal Cypher on blue velvet	0.15.11.
264	Sergeants	Gold cord, with blue worsted centre	0. 3. 2.
265	Rank & file	Yellow worsted with blue centre	0. 0. 6.1/4.

16th *Lancers*

266	Staff	Gold, with Royal Cypher on crimson velvet centre	0.15.11.

Sergeants, rank and file: See 5th *Lancers*

21st *Lancers*

267	Staff	Gold, with Queen Victoria's Royal and Imperial Cypher on French grey centre	0.15.11.
268	Sergeants	Gold cord, with French grey centre	0. 3. 2.
269	Rank & file	Yellow worsted, with French grey centre	0. 0. 6.1/4.

N.B. Of particular interest is the reference to the Staff pattern cockade having the Royal Cypher on a velvet centre.

Covers

		£. s. d.
277	Cap, Lance Oilskin	0. 1. 0.1/2.

Lines, Cap, Lance-

313	Staff	Gold cord, with gold acorns and runners	1.11.10.
314	Other ranks	Light yellow worsted cord, acorns and runners	0. 1. 1.

N.B. The price given for the other ranks lines is a guesstimate due to the amount of one shilling only being shown, the pence column being blank on the page concerned due to a printing error.

Plumes

Cap, lance- all ranks			£. s. d.
336	5th Lancers	Green	0. 1. 6.
337	9th Lancers	Black and white	0. 1. 0.
338	12th Lancers	Scarlet	0. 1. 6.
339	16th Lancers	Black	0. 1. 0.
340	17th & 21st	White	0. 1. 0.

Runners

Cap lines, lance-

369	Staff	Gold	0. 0.10.1/2.
370	Other ranks	Worsted	0. 0. 0.3/4.

Buttons, Cockade-

Cap, lance,		all ranks	
593	5th *Lancers*	all ranks	0. 0. 2.1/4.
594	12th *Lancers*	all ranks	0. 0. 2.1/4.
595	16th *Lancers*	all ranks	0. 0. 2.1/4.
596	17th *Lancers*	all ranks	0. 0. 2.1/4.
597	21st *Lancers*	all ranks	0. 0. 2.1/4.

No price was quoted for the cockade button for the 9th Lancers, presumably as the cost of same was included within the higher price charged for their metal cockade.

Chains

603	Lance,	Gilding metal; all ranks; with lion head attachments	0. 0. 9.3/4.

Corners

607 Cap, lance	Gilding metal; all ranks	Not quoted

Hooks

623 Cap, lance	Gilding metal; all ranks	0. 0. 2.1/4.

Lion's Heads

630 Cap, lance	Gilding metal; all ranks	0. 0. 3.1/4.

Plates, Cap lance

641 5th *Lancers*	0. 1. 2.
642 9th *Lancers*	0. 1. 2.
643 12th *Lancers*	0. 1. 2.
644 16th *Lancers*	0. 1. 2.
645 17th *Lancers*	0. 1. 2.
646 21st *Lancers*	0. 1. 2.

Plume - Lancers

679	Gilding metal; grenade large	0. 0. 2.1/2.

N.B. The above assumedly refers to the plume holder.

Thumbscrews

689 Plate, Cap, lance	0. 0. 1.1/4.

The thumbscrews were used to secure the lance cap plate to the skull of the cap.

With regard to the lance cap for the Warrant Officers/Staff-Sergeants as mentioned earlier in chapter four, when taking account of the above reference to this pattern of cap having a gold band with 'coloured' centre; silk lined, and being fitted with a cockade (rosette) of gold bearing the Royal Cypher on a velvet ground it would appear to indicate that c.1911 the lance cap for lancers holding Warrant Officer rank was not unlike the officers pattern cap.

Appendix III
Appreciation of Lance Cap Prices

The price a collector might reasonable expect to pay for a lance cap, whether an other ranks, or an officers pattern has risen consistently in Great Britain over a period of many years. The great interest in these items shown by overseas collectors from such countries as America, Australia, Canada, and New Zealand etc, has meant that some of the better condition, rarer and more desirable chapka's that have been offered for sale in auction house salerooms, and in specialist militaria shops have been purchased by overseas collectors. However, it is pleasing to know that this is not a case of one-way traffic, as items of head-dress are frequently being 'imported' into the United Kingdom from these countries.

Placing a Value on a Lance Cap

Just how one places a value on a particular lance cap will depend on whether the item of head-dress is seen from the vendor's viewpoint, or the purchasers. Many readers will have experienced how the value of a motor vehicle is often calculated on the basis that, it is "in nice condition, in a nice colour, and with low mileage" when seen from the salesman's point of view. However, when a member of the public offers an identical condition car for sale at a used car saleroom, the vehicle is seen with the car salesman's 'wearing a hat of a different colour', and it becomes "a car in only reasonable condition, with the colour being a bad selling point, and the particular model unpopular and hard to sell". N.B. It is of interest that whilst an officers pattern lance cap will normally sell for a higher price that an officers metal helmet of a dragoon guards/dragoon regiment. However, the opposite appears to be the norm when buying or selling an other ranks pattern lance cap, or dragoon guards helmet, the latter type of head-dress nearly always realising a slightly higher price.

Condition of the Lance Cap

The deciding factor that may well influence a collector when considering the purchase a particular item of head-dress, will for many collectors be its overall condition. Lance caps, like all other items of a soldier's uniform were meant to be worn on an almost daily basis, with the full dress uniform being worn not only for escort duty, guard duty, and parades etc, but also often in battle. It is reasonable therefore to expect a certain amount of wear and tear (commonly known as service wear) to have occurred, and this will be evident in the condition of the item of uniform concerned. Just how much the general condition of a particular item of head-dress will influence the prospective purchaser, will obviously be a matter of individual choice, although one can hardly expect a lance cap, or helmet that was worn during the Crimean, or Indian campaigns not to show some signs of service wear etc.

A lance cap that has slight unrepaired damage, such as minor moth to the cloth upper section or a contemporary professional repair, say to the stitching of the chinchain, may to many collector's, be considered a collectable item, whilst a similar cap that has a crude modern day repair may not. Additionally, as mentioned previously, many lance caps have been fitted with replacement items, such as the chinchain, lion's head bosses, plume, plume sockets etc, and this may well influence the potential purchaser's decision whether or not to acquire a particular item of head-dress or not.

It is of regret, that gone forever are the days when visiting a specialist militaria shop, one might reasonably expect to find a lance cap of almost any period, and of any regiment in almost mint condition complete with all its original fittings and plume. In those days (some thirty years ago) busbies lance caps, and helmets were so plentiful that you could almost decide which particular regiment's head-dress you wished to purchase, prior to your visit to the militaria shop.

Auction House Salerooms

For a person wishing to sell a lance cap through the saleroom of a respected auction house, the price the cap is expected to realise is often based on the price originally paid by the vendor, and of course a profit margin, for we all like to make a profit when we sell an item from our collection. In consideration of the above, the price the seller expects the cap to sell for is often far higher than the actual price realised in the sale. Many factors may effect the price realised for an lance cap sold through an auction saleroom, such as the written description given in the auction catalogue, the caps overall condition, its rarity, the current market value of similar condition item, and the number of collectors prepared to bid for the cap.

Moving from the vendor to the buyer, when submitting a bid for a particular item, there are various circumstances that will influence just how much the prospective purchaser is prepared to pay for an item of head-dress. This may include the articles rarity, whether or not the item concerned say a cap/helmet, is required to complement a uniform, and the period of time the collector has been seeking that specific item. Other considerations may include what other sources of supply are open to the collector, such as militaria fairs, or specialist militaria shops, and last, but perhaps most importantly, how much can be afforded, although an impulse buy may on occasion cause the purchaser to disregard the latter.

Finally a word of caution regarding prices realised for items sold in an auction saleroom. It is worth being mindful that the price a particular lance cap/helmet/uniform fetches under the hammer in an auction sale should not be treated as a benchmark for similar items of uniform, as often the price realised may reflect just how much a determined bidder was prepared to pay for the item concerned on that particular day.

Lance caps that frequently sell for a far higher price than is normal will include those that were only worn for a short period of time by a particular regiment, such as the chapka's worn by members of the 19th Lancers and the 23rd Lancers, both these regiments existing as lancers for only a short period of time. Additionally caps formerly owned by an officer who achieved fame, high rank or both, that accord the potential owner the opportunity of researching the service history of the officer concerned, will almost certainly sell for a much higher price than a cap worn by an unnamed officer.

Condition/Grade

The following is a functional system of grading the condition of a lance cap, which will almost certainly be at variance with the grades used by militaria dealers and those given in auction saleroom catalogues. It may, none the less be of assistance to collectors when comparing the condition of items of head-dress offered for sale at various differing sources. For the purposes of grading the condition of a lance cap, an officers 1856 pattern cap of a regular lancer regiment was selected, and therefore for an other ranks pattern cap, brass replaces gilt metal etc.

Excellent Condition

For a lance cap to be graded as being in excellent condition, it should be an example that has hardly ever been worn, being in almost untouched condition, with all fittings, including the plume being original to the cap. Although rare, it is sometimes possible to acquire a cap, that for whatever reason, has in effect, 'being taken down from the military tailors shelf', purchased by the officer, and been worn only once or twice. N.B. As most lance caps are sold minus the cap-lines, this 'accessory/fitting' has not been included within the following descriptions. The plume to be of officers quality, with no sign of the colour/s of the feathers or hair (as appropriate), having faded, being complete with the correct pattern gilt metal socket. The gold bullion on the rosette to be undamaged, with no sign of moth damage to the velvet ground, and the rosette as a whole, being securely affixed in place. N.B. In the case of the special pattern cap of the 9th Lancers, there should be no wear or damage to the gilt metal gimp boss that replaced the bullion rosette normally fitted to an officers pattern lance cap. The patent leather skull should be in an almost unmarked condition, with no sign of crazing to the leather, and with the cloth upper, and top (not 9th Lancers) being free of moth damage. The gold gimp and orris cord should be securely fastened to the top and upper sides of the cap, and all the gold lace to be unmarked and intact. In the case of a 9th Lancers chapka, there should be no damage to the strips of gilt metal covering the angles, nor the leaf pattern ornaments covering the corners of the top of the cap.

The lion's heads bosses should be a matched pair, with the gilt being in 'bright' condition, as should the rear waist hook. The gilt links of the chinchain also to be in 'bright' condition, with the velvet backing being unmarked by either moth or staining, with no evidence of fatigue to the cotton stitching. The leather sweatband and lining silk to be undamaged, with little or no staining, the stitching being intact and in good condition.

The plate to be securely attached to the skull of the cap, with no evidence of the plate ever having been removed from the skull. The tips of the rayed plate should all be present, with the silvered regimental device comprising the Royal Arms, battle honours and title scrolls etc being in undamaged condition. N.B. Particular care should be taken when examining the silvered overlay on the plate, as frequently such items as the tail of either the lion or the unicorn, may be detached or missing completely, likewise the tips of any floral decoration, and the ends of the scrolls should be carefully scrutinised, as they also may be fractured or damaged.

Very Good Condition

The correct pattern plume, the condition being near to that described above, complete with officers pattern gilt metal socket, the bullion rosette with little, or no signs of wear. The patent leather skull might have very minor marks, with there possibly being very minor moth damage to the cloth top or upper side section, the lace to be in good condition. Any such damage however, should not adversely affect the overall appearance of the cap. The gold gimp cord as above. The lion's head bosses and rear hook as above, with perhaps very minor stitching faults to the chinchain backing, the leather sweatband and silk lining might have some signs of service wear. Minor service wear to the plate, with all tips present, with possible rubbing to the high spots of the silver plated overlay, but again with all tips etc being intact.

Good Condition

A correct or associated officer pattern plume, complete with socket, with some wear to the bullion rosette. The skull with some creases or crazing to the patent leather, the cloth upper, or top having a degree of moth damage, with dulling to the gold cord and lace.

Some rubbing to the gilt on the lion's head bosses, and to the rear hook. The chinchain with some stitching faults, with some staining or moth damage to the velvet backing. The sweatband with age and service wear, the silk upper section perhaps showing signs of fatigue to the material, with stitching faults, or possibly showing signs that the silk lining may have been professionally restored.

The gilt and silvered lance cap plate may have signs of rubbing and wear to the high spots, with possibly one or more of the rayed tips slightly distorted, with minor age cracks/wear to the silvered overlay on the plate.

Quite Good Condition

As for good condition, but with the plume either being faded, or missing completely, with the bullion on the rosette being loose, and the velvet possibly mothed. More serious damage to the patent leather of the skull/peak, the upper section and top with serious moth damage, the gold lace dull overall affecting the overall appearance of the cap. None matching lion's head bosses, the chinchain backing hanging loose from the actual chain, or being missing completely, the head lining heavily stained, or with the sweatband, and/or silk upper section missing.

The plate showing signs of having at some time been removed from the skull, and being only loosely re-affixed. The plate may also have some ray tips missing, or/with damage to the silvered overlay, such as the tail of either the lion or unicorn having been broken off. Not a lance cap for the serious collector. It is likely that some readers might not agree with the descriptions/grades given above, however these descriptions and grades are given as a guide only, and should be treated as such.

Appreciation of Prices

The following compilation of lance cap prices is composed of information assembled from auction saleroom catalogues, dealers lists, specialist militaria shops, and interviews with collectors covering the period 1960 to 2001 inclusive and gives an indication of how lance cap prices have risen over the past forty-one years. The descriptions taken from the various auction catalogues, have been reproduced below using the terminology from the relevant catalogue. Notwithstanding the above, these particulars have, where practical, been abbreviated to reduce unnecessary preamble and repetition, and have also been reworded where appropriate. Additionally, where relevant, the authors observations and impression on the condition of a particular item of head-dress have been given in bold text. N.B. With regard to the numerous lance caps and accessories etc, sold through the salerooms of Messrs Bosley, Christie's, Dee & Atkinson, Phillips, Spink's, and Wallis and Wallis, it should be borne in mind that a buyer's premium of approximately 15%, in addition to Value Added Tax at the appropriate rate (where appropriate), should be accrued to the price realised for those items concerned.

Sources Consulted

Blunderbuss Antiques (Central London), Bosley Militaria Auctioneers (Marlow, Buckinghamshire), Christie's Auctioneers (South Kensington, London), Dee & Atkinson (Driffield), Phillips Auctioneers (London), Regimentals Militaria (Islington, London), Spink's Auctioneers (Central London), Tradition (Central London), Geoff White Militaria (Bristol), Wallis and Wallis Auctioneers (Lewes, Sussex), the late David Young, (Paddington, London), The Lyle Official Antiques Review, and various editions of The Lyle Official Arms and Armour Review of the period 1976 to 1983 inclusive (hereafter referred to as the Lyle Arms & Armour Review).

Grade Abbreviations

EXC: Excellent Condition.
VGC: Very Good Condition.
GC: Good Condition.
QGC: Quite Good Condition.
Illus: Indicates that the particular lance cap concerned, was illustrated in the saleroom catalogue from which the written description given below has been taken.

5TH (ROYAL IRISH) LANCERS

1971 February Tradition, London £120.
Officers lance cap with plume, no written text. Authors description: A post 1902 lance cap, KC silvered and gilt plate, Gilt lion's head bosses with chinchain. Green swan's feather plume. Illus. VGC/GC (very minor moth to left upper section).

1980 October Regimentals, Islington £200.
An other ranks Edwardian lance cap, complete with green hair plume and chinchain. GC. *The peak had been trimmed to shorten its length.*

1984 October Wallis & Wallis, Sussex £900.
An Edwardian officers lance cap, no written text. Authors description: Patent leather skull with cloth upper section, gold bullion rosette with 'ER VII' Royal cypher. Silvered and gilt plate with battle honours to '*South Africa 1899-1902*'. Gilt lion's head bosses with chinchain. The gilt and silver good, no sign of moth to cloth top. Plume missing. EXC/VGC.

1996 June Bosleys, Buckinghamshire £3000.
A fine and rare pre 1901 officers lance cap. Black patent leather skull, with scarlet melton cloth upper, with gold gimp cord across the top. Gold bullion rosette, fire gilt cup, with green swan's feather plume. Gilt plate with silver Royal Arms, battle honours and title scroll. Gilt lion's head bosses, velvet backed chinchain. Leather sweatband with crimson silk upper, with suppliers name inside cap. The bullion fresh, (minor wear overall), VGC. With tin for cap with named brass plaque, also plume tin.

1998 October Bosleys, Buckinghamshire £820.
A scarce example of an Edwardian other ranks lance cap.
Regimental lance plate with battle honours to '*South Africa 1899 - 1902*'. Lion's head bosses, leather backed chinchain, Woollen boss

with regimental button to centre support a black horsehair plume in gilt metal cup. Leather and waxed cotton lining with issue date 1902. Good clean condition. VGC.

2000 April Military Antiques, Islington £1800.
A post 1902 officers lance cap with feather plume and chinchain, with service wear. Minor moth to cloth upper, the braid and lace in a dulled condition. *The colour of the feather plume faded, the cap fitted with an incorrect pattern chinchain. Well worthy of restoration and offered at a realistic price.*

9TH (QUEEN'S ROYAL) LANCERS

1969 May Wallis & Wallis, Sussex £250.
A fine and rare officers lance cap c.1832. Black leather skull, top (some damage) and peak. With a fine large gilt and silver lance cap plate. Fancy rings to chinchain and lion's head bosses. A metal boss with black feather plume (mothed). GC (no lining, metal binding of peak cracked). Illus. *No backing to regimental pattern chinchain. An extremely rare pattern cap.*

1973 October Wallis & Wallis, Sussex £550.
A rare early officers pattern Victorian lance cap. Large gilt plate with silvered "A.R." cypher. Gilt metal fittings including large plume rosette, and lion's head bosses. Velvet backed chinchain. GC. The gilt good, the plume missing. (lining, and peak loose, some moth damage to top). With its japanned metal case, named to *Major Octavius Anson*, and a set of cap-lines (worn). Illus. A rare pattern cap, the cap-lines were the 'with flounders pattern'. Major Anson's sword and pouch were also sold in this sale. N.B. *See Fig: 29.* for an illustration of a similar pattern lance cap in fine condition.

1979 Lyle Arms & Armour Review 1980 £300.
A Victorian officers lance cap. Illus. The cap, which was complete with chinchain and black & white feather plume, looked to be in VGC/GC, the gilt bright.

1979 Lyle Arms & Armour Review 1980 £175.
An other ranks lance cap, black hair plume in holder, brass mounts. Illus. The cap looked to be in VGC/GC.

1981 Lyle Arms & Armour Review 1982 £720.
A post 1902 officers lance cap, gilt and silvered badge, gilt mounts with velvet backed beaded link chinchain. Black over white feather plume in gilt holder. With a set of cap-lines. With its tin case, with name of officer painted on tin. Illus. N.B. *See Figs: 123.* and *124.* for two illustrations of a similar cap in excellent condition.

1983 November Blunderbuss Antiques, London £850.
A Victorian Officers lance cap, complete with black and white horsehair plume. Leather and silk lining, twelve battle honours, undress hair plume in gilt holder, gilt to plate bright, stitching to chinchain slightly AF, otherwise in VGC. N.B. *See Fig: 33.* for an illustration of a similar pattern lance cap in fine condition.

1986 April Wallis & Wallis, Sussex £1300.
An Officers lance cap complete with plume, and gold cord cap-lines. *The white hair plume was the incorrect colour for this regiment, otherwise the cap in VGC with no obvious signs of moth to the cloth.*

1990 January Christie's, South Kensington £605.
A troopers lance cap, with black hair plume in brass socket. the K.C. plate with '*South Africa*' honours. Illus. Chinchain stitching looked to be AF, otherwise in GC.

1998 February Bosleys, Buckinghamshire £2000.
A fine scarce example of a pre 1901 officers lance cap. The skull of black patent leather (possibly recovered), the upper part of black melton cloth. A gilt metal simulated gimp boss, mounted with a regimental button. This supports a (replacement) gilt plume cup and black over white swan feather plume. The gilt lance cap plate is mounted with silvered entwined cypher and gilt Royal Arms and battle honours. Gilt metal lion's head bosses, velvet backed chinchain. Leather sweat band with ink name. Gilt extremely fresh, (age wear to plume, the cap body with some restoration). Illus. Eight battle honours to plate. With some service details for the period 1865-1879. The chinchain was not the cord pattern normally fitted to the officers cap of this regiment.

2000 April Spinks, London £1800.
An officers lance cap with fine plate mounted with rich gilt metal devices, QVC, battle honours to '*Afghanistan*' and '*Khandahar*', & '*AR*' reversed (plate re-affixed). Corded chinchain, black & white feather plume. (internal headband replaced, angle pieces and lion's head bosses probably replaced, chinchain shortened, plume socket of other ranks pattern, black feathers slightly faded). Illus. *N.B. Due to the extensive amount of 'restoration' and replacement parts fitted to this cap, it could possibly best be described as a being a 'decorative item only'.*

2000 13 December Bosleys £700.
Troopers uniform: A good post 1901 example. Comprising lance cap, plate with battle honours to *South Africa 1900-02*. Lion's head bosses, leather backed chinchain (leather now af), leather and waxed cotton lining. Black horsehair plume in gilt metal holder, with cap-lines. Some wear to patent leather, otherwise GC. Tunic, overalls, girdle, boots (6 Items). Illus. *N.B. Although plume described as being black, it was in fact the correct colours of black and white. Even allowing for the wear to the patent leather, and the chinchain leather being as found, this would appear to have been very good value at the price for a cap in GC, plus an almost complete uniform.*

2001 February Wallis & Wallis, Sussex £3500.
A Victorian officers cap, black patent leather top, blue cloth sides, gilt ornaments, gilt corded rosette. Gilt and silvered plate bearing twelve battle honours to Afghanistan. Lion's head bosses and velvet backed corded link chinchain, leather lining. Black over white feather plume in its socket. GC. The patent leather closely crazed overall, backing to chinchain as found, the gilt generally good. Illus. N.B. *See Fig: 33.* for an illustration of a similar pattern cap.

2001 March Blunderbuss Antiques £3800
A fine Victorian officers cap, complete with black and white feather plume, leather and silk lining, lion's head bosses and velvet backed chinchain. *No moth. The cap in excellent condition.*

12TH (PRINCE OF WALES'S ROYAL) LANCERS

1972 January Wallis & Wallis, Sussex £32.
A Victorian other ranks chapka. Battle honours to *'Central India'*. Chinchain and lion's head bosses, red hair plume. GC. (some crazing to leather). Illus. *This example looked to be a nice cap, with no obvious signs of moth to the cloth upper section.*

1978 September Wallis & Wallis, Sussex £590.
A good post 1902 officers lance cap. Black patent leather skull with scarlet cloth upper. Silver and gilt plate with honours to 1902, embroidered ER VII, gilt chinchain on leather backing, lion head's bosses. GC (no plume, gilt lace dulled, leather crazed, one minor moth hole). Illus. *In view of the missing plume, dull lace, moth hole etc, this cap was in near GC only.*

1979 Lyle Arms & Armour Review 1980 £190.
A Victorian other ranks lance cap, dated inside 1900. Illus. Cap complete with chinchain, and plume. Looked to be VGC/GC.

1981 Lyle Arms & Armour Review 1982 £950.
A rare officers lance cap c.1856. black leather skull, scarlet cloth sides and top with gilt cord trimmings. Gilt & silvered badge with honours *'Egypt'*, *'Peninsula'*, *'Sevastopol'*, and *'Waterloo'*, but without *'South Africa 1851.2.3'*. Embroidered *'V.R.'* boss, lion's head bosses with velvet backed chinchain. Illus. *The plume missing, otherwise looked to be VGC/GC.*

1983 September Wallis & Wallis, Sussex £1150.
A Victorian officers lance cap. Patent leather skull with scarlet cloth upper. A good, early pattern plate bearing Royal Arms with P.O.W.'s feathers, coronet and motto, sphinx and *'Egypt'* with honours *'Central'* to the left, and *'India'* to the right, with along the bottom *'Peninsula'*, *'Sevastopol'* and *'Waterloo'*. Red feather plume in gilt socket. GC. (No lining, red colours a little faded). This cap had the plate with the battle honour *'Central India'* on two separate scrolls, the later version plates having this honour on a single scroll. *The cap having the lining missing, I would suggest that the condition of this cap was near GC only.*

1984 May Wallis & Wallis, Sussex £800.
A scarce officers lance cap c.1857. Black patent leather skull with scarlet cloth top with gold gimp cord. Plate with battle honours *'Egypt', 'Peninsula', 'Sevastopol'* and *'Waterloo'*. Embroidered boss with *'V.R.'*, velvet backed chinchain with lion's head bosses. GC for age. (chinchain backing and leather sweatband to lining restored). Illus. The plate on this cap was the early 1856 pattern being without the honour *'South Africa 1851.2.3'*.

1990 January Christie's, South Kensington £462.
A troopers Victorian lance cap, with red hair plume in brass socket, and yellow cap-lines (cap now bearing a velvet lined chinchain). The plate with honours inc *'Central India'*. Illus. *Apart from the incorrect pattern chinchain, the cap looked to be VGC/GC.*

1990 June Wallis & Wallis, Sussex £450.
A troopers lance cap, black patent leather skull with scarlet cloth upper. Yellow and blue rosette with Victorian button. Lion's head bosses and beaded chinchain. Near mint condition post 1902 pattern plate, scarlet hair plume in socket. Yellow cord cap lines. GC. (lion's head bosses restored, some patches of congealing to patent leather). *It is not unknown for a Post 1902 cap to have a Victorian button to the centre on the woollen boss. The reference to a 'beaded' chinchain however, suggests that this fitting was possibly a replacement item. N.B. See Fig: 43. for a similar pattern cap.*

1990 October Wallis & Wallis, Sussex £2000.
A Edwardian officers lance cap. No catalogue text available. Author's description as follows: Patent leather skull and peak, with scarlet cloth upper, gold lace with waist, and gold braid to peak. Gold bullion rosette bearing embroidered *'ER VII'* Royal Cypher. Gilt plate bearing silvered KC Royal Arms, P.O.W.'s feathers, and sphinx. Nine gilt metal battle honours including *'South Africa 1899-1902'*. Gilt metal lion's head bosses, with chinchain. Lining not seen. Illus. (plume missing). The gilt bright, the silver tarnished, Very minor moth damage to upper cloth of skull. VGC/GC. N.B. *See Fig: 126.* for an illustration of a similar lance cap.

1992 Dee & Atkinson (Driffield) East Riding £350.
A good Victorian troopers lance cap complete with oilskin head lining, ear bosses with chinchain, scarlet plume, together with a set of cap-lines. An un-touched item in fine, original condition.

1992 Camden Passage Militaria Market £550.
A post 1902 good other ranks pattern cap complete with chinchain and plume. The cap having minor crazing to the skull and peak. A Victorian regimental button to the woollen plume boss, the cloth section free of moth damage. Very minor stitching faults to the chinchain, overall VGC/GC. N.B. *See Fig: 43.* for an illustration of this lance cap.

1993 November Wallis & Wallis, Sussex £470.
A Victorian other ranks lance cap. Patent Leather skull, scarlet cloth

upper, yellow and blue waistband, woollen rosette with button. Plate with honours '*Peninsula', Sevastopol*' and '*Waterloo*'. Correct leather chinchain. Leather and linen lining. Basically GC, an untouched example. (some wear, moth below top, patent leather crazed). Illus. An early 1856 pattern, having only three extra battle honours in addition to the honour '*Egypt*'.

1994 October Bosleys, Buckinghamshire £960.
A fine Troop Sergeants lance cap. Skull of black patent leather, gold lace band around the waist, with a scarlet cloth upper, bullion boss with blue woollen centre & QVC button. Patent leather top, with gold orris cord down the angles. QVC lance cap plate with honours to Central India. Complete with chinchain (backing slightly as found). Various *W.D.* marks, some service wear, otherwise GC to VGC. Illus. *The fact that this is a senior N.C.O.'s cap appears to have been reflected in the price realised.*

1999 August Bosleys, Buckinghamshire £750.
A fine scarce example, black patent leather body. Brass triangular plate with battle honours to *'Sevastopol'*. Lion's head bosses, leather backed brass chinchain. Woollen cord boss with Victorian button, supports a scarlet horsehair plume in gilt metal plume holder. The interior with waxed cotton lining, faint issue stamps. Minor age wear, basically VGC. Illus. An other ranks pattern lance cap.

2000 April Spinks, London £2000.
A good officer cap, with QVC plate bearing battle honours to '*Central India*' in gilt, with P.O.W. feathers, and sphinx in white metal (tip of plate missing). Scarlet feather plume, velvet backed chinchain. (restoration includes the scarlet cloth top, a non regulation plume rosette bearing gold embroidered 'V.R', other ranks pattern plume socket, lining replaced). Illus. *In view of the level of restoration, this was a high price to pay for a purely 'decorative' item.*

2001 March Blunderbuss Antiques £4700.
A fine Victorian officers lance cap with gilt and silvered plate, lion's head bosses and velvet backed chinchain, leather and silk lining, complete with scarlet feather plume. No moth to cloth sides or top, in Exc cond.

16TH (QUEEN'S) LANCERS

N.B. With regard to the officers pattern caps listed below, the cloth material to the top and sides of certain caps are quoted as being either black, or blue in colour.

1975 The Lyle Arms & Armour Review 1976 £370.
An officers lance cap with gilt and silvered cap plate, complete with chinchain. Illus. Plume missing. Thirteen battle honours to plate, and apart from the missing plume this cap looked to be VGC. N.B. *See Fig: 36.* for an illustration of a similar pattern Victorian lance cap.

1980 The Lyle Arms & Armour Review 1981 £190.
A post 1902 troopers lance cap, with black hair plume in holder. Cap dated 1903 inside skull, with lion's head bosses & leather backed chinchain. Illus. Cap looked to be near VGC.

1983 June Sotheby's London £715.
A good officers lance cap c.1905. Black leather skull, black top section, peak with decoration. Lion's head bosses, chinchain with circular links. The plume holder with gold bullion surround with 'ER VII' on red ground. Lance plate with honours to '*Sobraon*'. Black feather plume. Illus. *The lance plate was a rare King's crown pattern having 'thirteen' honours. This cap Looked to be in VGC overall.*

1984 May Wallis & Wallis, Sussex £1000.
A post 1902 officers lance cap with black swan's feather plume in gilt mount. Black patent leather skull and peak, black cloth top with gilt cord crosspieces. Gilt bullion cockade bearing *George V* Royal Cypher, velvet backed chinchain with lion's head bosses. Gilt and silvered lance plate with '*sixteen*' battle honours. VGC. (some wear to cloth lining). Illus. *Both the cap and the plume looked to be in VGC as described in the catalogue.*

1987 April Wallis & Wallis, Sussex £260.
A post 1902 troopers lance cap, complete with black horsehair plume in holder. Leather backed chinchain and lion's head bosses. W.D. stamp inside the cap 1912, complete with a set of yellow cap-lines with acorns and sliders. Illus. *Cap looked to be near VGC.*

1990 January Christie's, South Kensington £462.
A troopers lance cap with K.C. front plate and button, hair plume and brass chinchain. Illus. N.B. *See Figs: 45.*, and *45A.* for two illustrations of a similar cap.

1990 April Wallis & Wallis, Sussex £1200.
A rare pre 1856 troopers pattern lance cap. Black patent leather skull, top and peaks, the sides of blue stiffened cloth, with around the waist a yellow waistband having a red stripe. Yellow and red woollen plume rosette. A large brass lance cap plate bearing the Royal Arms with eight battle honours (*Peninsula to Sobraon*), with *"Queen's"* at the top of the plate and "16" at its base. Lion's head ear bosses. GC for age. (the chinchain, lining, and plume missing, minor crazing and congealing to patent leather, two tears to top, one having been repaired, some repairs to sides). Illus. *Some service wear to woollen plume boss (rosette). A very rare and desirable other ranks pattern lance cap.*

1992 May Wallis & Wallis, Sussex £1400.
A Victorian officers lance cap. Black patent leather skull, blue cloth sides, gilt and silver plated HP with thirteen battle honours (type two). Bosses and chinchain, leather and silk lining, black feather plume. Basically GC (moth to top, patent leather crazed, some service wear). with tin case and nameplate inscribed '*H. De la Poer*

Gough'. Some service details. Illus. See chapter 3, endnote 9, for some service details of this most distinguished officer. N.B. See *Figs: 36., 36A.* and *36B.* for an illustration of a similar, officers pattern cap.

1996 February Bosleys, Buckinghamshire £2800.
A fine & rare officers pre 1901 lance cap. Black patent leather skull, black melton sides and top with gold gimp cord. Gold bullion rosette with Royal Arms. Black swan's feather plume in gilt cup. The gilt lance plate with battle honours and title scroll. Lion's head bosses and velvet backed chinchain. Leather sweat band with paper label and ink name *S. Stanley*, with crimson silk lining retaining suppliers embossed stamp. GC. (wear to gilt & bullion, some blistering to leather). Illus. Some service details. N.B. The Army List for October 1897 lists R.F.A. Sloane Stanley as having been appointed to the rank of Captain on the 27th January 1893.

1997 Dec Spink's London £3200.
A Victorian officers lance cap, the patent leather skull having French braid trim, the top and sides in blue cloth, with rosette having the *VR* Royal cypher. The cap bears a fine Victorian plate, the chinchain being backed with velvet. The cap has a good black swan's feather plume. Illus. The lance cap plate was the pattern with thirteen battle honours, and the cap looked to be in GC overall.

1999 April Bosleys, Buckinghamshire £700.
A good other ranks lance cap post 1901. Standard description, with leather and waxed cotton lining with issue stamp for 1911 to the inside of cap. GC. (some minor wear to patent leather). Illus. Looked to be an example in VGC.

2000 February Regimentals, Islington[1] £885.
An other ranks Victorian cap complete with plume, lion's head bosses and chinchain. With service wear overall in GC. Victorian lance cap plate, KC button to woollen boss, some moth to ribbed cloth.

2000 April Spinks, London £2000.
An attractive officers lance cap with gilt plate now bearing QVC Royal Arms, battle honours to '*Sobraon*', and regimental title etc, all in white metal. Complete with velvet backed chinchain, and black swan feathers plume in an other ranks pattern socket. Restoration includes a non regulation boss with 'V.R.' in gold embroidery on a crimson ground, the blue cloth top, and the headband and lining). Illus. *N.B. The level of restoration to this cap is reflected in the price realised.*

2000 Dec Bosleys, Buckinghamshire £1750.
A scarce example of a post 1902 officers lance cap. Skull of black patent leather, with gold gimp cord across the black melton cloth top and down the four angles. Gilt plate with silvered Royal Arms and battle honours to 'South Africa 1900-02'. Lion's head bosses support the velvet backed chinchain. Lining of quilted cotton with crimson silk edging. A small moth hole to the crown, some age wear, the lining part loose, the plume boss, and the plume and holder absent. Illus. *This cap bore the last pattern lance plate having eighteen battle honours. The lack of the gold bullion plume rosette, the plume and holder are reflected in the price this cap realised.*

17th (DUKE OF CAMBRIDGE'S OWN) LANCERS

1970 October Wallis & Wallis, Sussex £75.
A very fine post 1901 officers lance cap, with white hair plume mounted in cypher boss bearing *ER VII*, complete with chinchain. VGC. (a small, slight moth spot to cloth top, minor marks to skull). With tin storage case. Illus. *The moth spot excepted, this cap looked to be in VGC. Note. This cap fitted with a hair plume.*

1973 October Wallis & Wallis, Sussex £95.
An other ranks lance cap. White leather top to cap, Victorian brass plate, chinchain and mounts (well cleaned). Yellow and blue cockade, white hair plume. Stamped inside cap "W.D. 1903" with original label of *G & W Almond, Army Contractor, London S.E.* GC. Illus.

1978 Lyle Arms & Armour Review 1979 £790.
A Victorian officers schapka, complete with white hair plume and chinchain. Illus. Plate bearing battle honours '*Alma*', '*Balaclava*', '*Inkerman*', and '*Sevastopol*'. Looked to be in GC.

1978 Lyle Arms & Armour Review 1979 £140.
A Victorian other ranks lance cap, complete with chinchain, and plate. Date inside cap 1902. Plume missing. Illus. *N.B. It is not that unusual to find a cap dated 1902, having a Victorian pattern plate.*

1984 May Wallis & Wallis, Sussex £3300.
An early Victorian officers lance cap of the 17th Light Dragoons (Lancers) circa 1840. Illus. No text available. Complete with bullion boss, chinchain, with silvered and gilt plate. Cap looked to be in EX/VGC, plume missing. *This was a record price for a lance cap at that time. N.B. See Figs: 25., 25A. and 25B. for three illustration of a similar pattern lance cap.*

1994 October Bosleys, Buckinghamshire £700.
A good other ranks cap, blue & yellow woollen boss with regimental button, brass QVC lance cap plate with honours to South Africa 1879, chinchain, white plume with socket, and cap-lines. Makers label inside cap, also ink stamp "*3 Years*", and last issue stamp of "*WD/2/1903*", together with paper label "*67/8*". Minor service wear, otherwise VGC. Illus. *A most interesting cap having so many different types of stamp. The date stamp of would appear to indicate that a cap bearing a Victorian plate was still in use in 1903.*

1994 October Bosleys, Buckinghamshire £360.
A 17th/21st Lancers bandsman's fibre glass lance cap. Complete

with blue and yellow woollen boss with KC General Service button. Gilded plate with silver skull and crossed bones & title, brass chinchain, leather sweatband, white nylon plume. VGC. These modern day caps do appear on the 'market' very frequently. However, the price realised appears to reflect the apparent unpopularity of these fibre glass caps amongst collectors. N.B. *See Fig: 57.* for an example of the lance cap plate fitted to this pattern of cap.

1995 November Regimentals, Islington £950.
A very clean Victorian other ranks lance cap, with all its correct fittings, and head lining. Complete with a set of yellow cap-lines. N.B. *See Figs: 47., 47A.* and *47B.* for illustrations of a similar pattern cap.

1996 October Bosleys, Buckinghamshire £6200.
An important and well documented Crimean period Troop Sergeant's lance cap. The rear of the cap with false patent leather folded neck peak, leather and waxed cotton lining, black hair plume. Bullion dulled, minor specks to white cloth, otherwise VGC. Complete with cap lines. Illus. This cap was fitted with a one piece die-struck plate, there being a hook for the chinchain attached to the upper left hand corner ornament. The plume boss was of bullion cord, with the edge of the front peak being embroidered with a single row of braid. The extremely high price realised for this cap reflects the noteworthy rarity of this pattern of lance cap.

1996 December Bosleys, Buckinghamshire £5000.
An extremely fine and scarce 1901-10 example of an officers lance cap. Skull of black patent leather, with the upper portion of white melton cloth, with gold gimp decoration. A gold bullion rosette bearing the Royal Cypher of *ER VII*, supporting a white swan's feather plume. Gilt plate with silvered Death's Head and crossed bones, with battle honours to '*South Africa 1900-02*'. Peak embroidered with gold bullion lines, gilt metal lion's head bosses, with velvet backed chinchain. Leather sweatband to interior with satin lining and makers embossed stamp. The patent leather, gilt and bullion remains fresh, (minor wear to the lining), otherwise in VGC. With original storage tins for both the cap, and the plume. Illus.

1999 August Bosleys, Buckinghamshire £940.
A scarce and fine pre 1901 Troop Sergeant Majors lance cap. Black patent leather skull and peak, white patent leather top. To the waist, gold regimental lace with central blue stripe. Lance plate with honours to '*South Africa 1879*'. Lion's head bosses, leather backed chinchain. Gold bullion and woollen cord boss with regimental pattern button. White horsehair plume in gilt metal plume holder. Leather and cotton lining. Issue stamp of WD 1896 to inside of crown. Minor age wear, basically VGC. Illus. *This cap looked to be an example in VGC, although how the actual rank of the former wearer was identified is open to speculation.*

2000 February Regimentals Catalogue, Islington £1350.
A troopers lance cap complete with plume, lion's head bosses, chinchain etc. 'An untouched' in near excellent condition.

2000 April Spinks, London £750.
A regulation pattern troopers cap complete with its black calico lining bearing traces of Hobson & Sons makers label. Plate with honours to '*Central India*'. chinchain and plume in brass socket. (the cloth upper part now painted white). Illus. *N.B. With regard to the upper cloth section being 'painted' white, it is not unknown for the cloth section to have been 'whitened' using 'white sap' or whitening fluid similar to the type once used on tennis shoes.*

2000 April Spinks, London £2500.
An officers lance cap having gilt plate mounted with KC Royal Arms, deaths head, and honours to '*South Africa 1900-02*', all in white metal. White feather plume, now fitted with Hussar officers gilt holder, complete with boss bearing 'V.R.' in gold embroidery. Velvet backed chinchain. (restoration includes the white cloth top, the lining and headband). Illus. A high price top pay for a restored cap, particularly as the bullion boss appeared to be a replacement fitment having an other ranks pattern plume socket. *N.B. The Hussar officers plume holder differed in that the design of the four upright leaves were dissimilar, and the band above the corded ball was slightly deeper.*

21ST (EMPRESS OF INDIA'S) LANCERS

1970 July Wallis & Wallis, Sussex £100.
A good Victorian officers lance cap. "Khartoum" honour on badge, complete with white feather plume and chinchain. GC. Illus.

1975 March Blunderbuss Antiques, London £110.
A Victorian other ranks lance cap complete with chinchain, plate, plume, and all fittings. GC. The plate was the 2nd pattern. The button to the woollen boss was incorrect, and the lining was worn, otherwise in GC. N.B. *See Fig: 51.* for an illustration of a similar pattern cap.

1981 Lyle Arms & Armour Review 1982 £850.
A Victorian officers lance cap, French blue cloth top and sides with gilt lace, velvet backed chinchain. gilt and silvered lance plate. Illus. The plate was the 2nd pattern with the honour '*Khartoum*'. The plume was missing, otherwise in VGC/GC. N.B. *See Figs: 38.* and 38A. for two illustrations of a similar cap, that is in excellent condition.

1997 Dec Spink's London £5800.
A very fine officers example by *Sandilands & Son.* French grey top, gilt plate bearing KC Royal Arms, regimental devices, and battle honour *Khartoum* in white metal. Complete with chinchain, and white feather plume within a gilt socket. The silk section of the head lining largely absent. Illus. *The damage to the lining excepted, this cap appeared to be in VGC/GC.*

2000 April Spinks, London £2300.
An officers lance cap with fine QVC plate, with white feathers plume in good gilt socket, complete with chinchain. (extensive restoration includes the French grey top, the bullion boss with 'V.R.' in gold embroidery, and the plate and lining re-affixed, and part of the lining absent). Illus. *Although officers caps of this pattern are rare, this was a high price for a cap with this level of restoration. N.B. Note the reference to restoration to the top of the cap.*

2000 October Wallis & Wallis, Sussex £4400.
A Victorian officers lance cap. No written description available to authors. Illus. This cap sold in the Wallis and Wallis Autumn Connoisseur Collectors Auction 2000, and bore the first pattern lance cap plate without the battle honour *Khartoum*. The cap was complete with bullion boss, chinchain, feather plume etc, and appeared to be in VGC/GC.

2001 March Blunderbuss Antiques £5500.
A fine officers lance cap bearing the late pattern 'Kings' crown plate. Gilt lion's head bosses with velvet backed chinchain, leather and silk lining. Complete with white feather plume. No moth to top or sides, in excellent condition.

OFFICERS FOUL WEATHER CAPS

1981 Lyle Arms & Armour Review 1982 £155.
A Victorian officers foul weather lance cap. black patent leather skull and top, with false rosette. Gilt peak binding, lion head bosses and beaded-link leather backed chinchain. Illus. Cap looked to be in VGC/GC. The gilt edge to peak, and beaded/corded link chinchain would suggest that this was a 9th Lancers pattern cap. N.B. The 9th were the only known regular lancer regiment to adopt the beaded/corded pattern of chinchain.

1982 Lyle Arms & Armour Review 1983 £300.
A Victorian officers foul weather cap, black patent leather skull and top, false rosette, gilt metal peak binding, lion's head bosses and beaded leather backed chinchain. Illus. Cap looked to be VGC, and 9th Lancers pattern.

1996 Bosleys, Buckinghamshire £750.
A rare and fine 19th Century example. The cap of black oilskin cloth, with simulated boss also in oilskin, and gilt metal binding to the peak edge. Gilt lion head bosses with gilt cord chinchain backed with velvet. Leather sweatband and crimson lining. Complete with a set of gold bullion cap-lines. Cap is in exceptional condition for age. Illus. N.B. *See Fig: 116.* for an example of the 17th Lancers pattern of foul weather cap.

YEOMANRY LANCE CAPS

BEDFORDSHIRE IMPERIAL YEOMANRY

1989 April Christie's, South Kensington £3300.
A very rare officers chapka with patent leather skull, black cloth sides with gilt metal fittings, with a gilt metal rosette with plain gilt half ball button. The plate with the regimental devices in white metal. Leather headband bearing printed mark of SBR 056, the silk lining missing. Gilt lion's head bosses and gilt burnished chinchain. Black over white hair plume in gilt metal socket. Illus.

1999 April Bosleys, Buckinghamshire £3750.
An extremely fine & scarce post 1902 officers lance cap. The skull and top of black patent leather, the sides of black melton cloth. A gilt metal gimp cord boss with gilt half ball button. Gilt metal plate with silvered wreath surmounted by crown, to the centre a silvered eagle with castle upon its breast. Gilt metal lion's head bosses with gilt metal chinchain. Leather sweat band. Black and white feather plume in gilt plume cup. VGC. Gilt remains extremely fresh, minor age wear, silk lining absent. Illus. An extremely nice example in VGC. *N.B. See Fig: 131. for an illustration of this particular cap.*

1ST CITY OF LONDON YEOMANRY (ROUGH RIDERS)

1984 Wallis & Wallis, Sussex £260.
A scarce troopers lance cap, black patent leather skull with blue cloth upper sides, yellow trim. Yellow and blue woollen rosette with plain button. Brass plate bearing honour '*South Africa 1900-02*'. Lion's head bosses with leather backed chinchain. GC. Illus. Plume missing.

1996 August Bosleys, Buckinghamshire £3900.
A fine and rare officers post 1902 lance cap. Black patent leather skull, the sides and top of pale blue melton cloth, with gold gimp cord. A gold bullion rosette bearing the Royal Cypher of *'George V.'* Gilt metal lance cap plate with silvered '*Arms of the City of London*', battle honour and title scroll. Chinchain and gilt metal lion's head bosses. Label inside cap *'Cater & Co'*. With blue swan's feather plume in gilt plume cup. Edge of cap dried and detached, melton and bullion dulled, but not affecting overall appearance. Illus. GVR cypher would indicate a post 1911 example. N.B. *See Fig: 133.* for an illustration of a similar pattern cap in fine condition.

1997 April Bosleys, Buckinghamshire £600.
A rare Bandsman's lance cap, black leather body, peak and crown with gilt metal fleur bosses to each corner, woollen cord boss with General Service button to centre. Lance plate with battle honour '*South Africa 1900-02*'. Leather backed chinchain with lion's head bosses. With a cherry coloured hair plume in gilt metal plume holder. Leather and waxed cotton lining. Some minor wear, otherwise in GC. Illus. N.B. The musicians of the band of The Royal Yeomanry

currently wear a lance cap based on the Rough Riders pattern lance cap, complete with a cherry coloured plume, when parading in full dress uniform.

EAST RIDING OF YORKSHIRE IMPERIAL YEOMANRY

1994 October Bosleys, Buckinghamshire £8200.
A magnificent officers lance cap. Skull retains original mirror finish to Patent leather, light blue cloth upper with silver Yorkshire rose, gilt metal corner pieces. Gilt acanthus band to waist, gilt lion's head bosses, velvet backed chinchain. Fine gilt plate with silver devices, including *ER VII* Royal Cypher. Light blue over white feather plume set in gilt holder. Red silk lining with gold embossed name of maker. A really superb example. Illus. *The price realised reflects the rarity and condition of this particular cap, however compare this price with that of the Bedfordshire Yeomanry cap mentioned above which was an equally rare example, and in similar condition. N.B. See Fig: 136. for an illustration of a cap in similar condition.*

2001 March Bosleys, Buckinghamshire £1850.
A scarce and fine example. Skull, the upper sides of blue melton cloth, having a silvered Yorkshire Rose plume boss, and gilt metal stripes covering the angles. The gilt metal plate mounted with tripart scroll bearing the regimental title, running fox, and ER VII Royal Cypher. Patent leather peak with gold bullion lines, gilt lion's head bosses with velvet backed chinchain. Leather sweatband with pencil name "C. Wilson". The plume absent, some restoration, silk upper lining to interior absent, some small moth holes to cloth. Illus. The 'peak with gold bullion lines' was in fact the correct pattern unadorned peak having a gilt metal binding. The cap realised a very low price, even allowing for the restoration etc.

LANARKSHIRE YEOMANRY

1972 January Wallis & Wallis, Sussex £18.
An other ranks lance cap plate of the Lanarkshire Yeomanry, being a lance cap of the 12th Lancers modified with a plain brass plate bearing a cap badge of the regiment. N.B. *See Fig: 138.* for an illustration of an actual cap fitted with this pattern of lance cap plate.

1994 December Bosleys, Buckinghamshire £3500.
A fine Officers post 1908 lance cap. Black patent leather skull, the upper sides in black cloth with gilt metal to the corners. The top in black patent leather with gilt ornaments to each corner. Gilt metal rosette with regimental pattern button. A band of gilt metal round the waist. Gilt and silvered lance cap plate, leather corded gilt chinchain with gilt lion's head bosses. Black and white horsehair plume in its gilt metal cup. VGC. With a reference to cap being adopted upon the introduction of the Territorial Force in 1908. Illus. *No reference in catalogue description to the lining to the cap, the 1908 date given in the catalogue for the adoption of the cap is open to comment.*

2001 March Blunderbuss Antiques £4300.
A fine officer lance cap complete with feather plume in gilt holder, silvered and gilt plate, gilt lion's head bosses with gilt chinchain, leather and silk lining. Skull and top minor marks, ribbed cloth untouched by moth, gilt on plate bright, silver nicely toned, lining unmarked. The plume a modern replacement, the chinchain not the correct corded pattern. N.B. *See Fig: 137.* for an illustration of this particular lance cap.

LINCOLNSHIRE IMPERIAL YEOMANRY

1995 April Bosleys, Buckinghamshire £7400.
A rare and fine officers chapka. Black patent leather skull, white buff leather top, bullion boss with cypher of ER VII, fine silvered rayed plate with Arms of Lincoln. Burnished silver chinchain with blue velvet backing, silver ear bosses. Green swan feathers plume in silvered holder. Original lining with tailor's stamp of *Hamburger Rogers and Co etc. Once again, a high price when compared with the price realised for the Bedfordshire Yeomanry cap sold in April 1999. See Fig: 140. for an illustration of this particular lance cap.*

TAPLOW LANCERS: BUCKINGHAMSHIRE

1996 January Wallis & Wallis, Sussex £550.
A Victorian troopers lance cap of the South Bucks Lancers (Yeomanry). Black patent leather skull and peak, with crimson cloth sides, and braided cross lines. Waistband of yellow with two blue stripes, yellow and blue rosette with gilt regimental button. Brass plate, lion's head bosses with velvet backed chinchain. White hair plume in brass socket, leather lining. *Basically GC (some service wear, peak shortened, chinchain and peak binding restored). Despite the restoration to the chinchain, peak, and the velvet backed chinchain, this lance cap realised a low price considering its extreme rarity.*

OFFICERS AND OTHER RANKS CAP PLATES

5th (Royal Irish) Lancers

1998 December Bosleys, Buckinghamshire £100.
A good post 1905 other ranks brass example. Honours to '*South Africa 1899-1902*'. Two studs to reverse. VGC. Illus. N.B. *See Fig: 69.* for an illustration of a similar pattern plate.

1999 October Bosleys, Buckinghamshire £150.
A good brass example without battle honours. Two screw studs to reverse. (brass worn through in one or two places, highlights polished). N.B. *See Fig: 66.* for an illustration of a similar pattern plate.

1999 October Bosleys, Buckinghamshire £85.
A good Victorian other ranks example, with honours '*Blenheim*' '*Malplaquet*', '*Oudenarde*', and '*Ramillies*'. Two screw studs to reverse. VGC. N.B. *See Fig: 67.* for an illustration of a similar pattern plate.

9th (Queen's Royal) Lancers

1970 July Wallis & Wallis, Sussex £13.
A late Victorian officers silver and gilt lance cap plate. VGC.

1980 March Regimentals, Islington £45.
A good brass other ranks pattern Victorian lance cap plate. VGC. The pattern of plate with twelve battle honours. N.B. *See Fig: 73.* for an illustration of a similar pattern plate.

1996 October Bosleys, Buckinghamshire £420.
A very fine officers example circa 1856-79. Gilt plated mounted with gilt Royal Arms, with below in silver the cypher of *Queen Adelaide*, reversed and intertwined. Gilt scroll below bearing "*Royal Lancers*". Scrolls to left and right bearing *six battle honours*. (minor wear to gilt, tiny split to bottom rim) not affecting its fine appearance. VGC.

1998 June Bosleys, Buckinghamshire £65.
A fine post 1905 (unissued) other ranks lance cap plate with battle honours to '*South Africa 1899-1902*'. With two screw studs to back. VGC.

1998 June Bosleys, Buckinghamshire £62.
A good pre 1901 other ranks example with twelve battle honours up to '*Afghanistan 1878-80*'. two screw studs to back of plate. VGC. (pin hole in all three extreme points, not affecting appearance of plate).

12th (Prince of Wales's Royal) Lancers

1970 July Wallis & Wallis £15.
A post 1901 officers silver and gilt lance cap plate. VGC, as new. Compare price realised with that of the earlier pattern sold some two years later, as described below.

1972 September Wallis & Wallis, Sussex £38.
A very fine early officers Victorian cap late c.1845. Gilt ray with '*Waterloo*' (left) and '*Peninsula*' (right) scrolls. Silver British Crest below P.O.W.'s plumes, with silver '*Egypt*'. VGC. Illus. *A very rare and collectable plate. N.B. See Fig: 77. for an illustration of a similar pattern plate.*

1984 October Wallis & Wallis, Sussex £125.
A Victorian officers gilt and silvered plate, with five battle honours, including '*Central India*'. GC. (fixing wires replaced, top ray tip missing). Illus. Although text stated five honours, '*Egypt*' was also on plate, making six honours. N.B. *See Fig: 81.* for an illustration of a similar pattern plate.

1996 December Bosleys, Buckinghamshire £560.
A fine late 19th Century example. A gilt metal, triangular shaped rayed plate bearing a silver Royal Arms, P.O.W.'s feathers, with the Sphinx resting on a tablet bearing '*Egypt*'. Battle honours '*Central India*' '*Peninsula*', '*Sevastopol*' '*South Africa 1851.2.3.*' and '*Waterloo*'. Silver nicely toned, gilt worn, otherwise VGC. (one or two securing wires absent). Illus. *This was an officers pattern plate.*

1999 October Bosleys, Buckinghamshire £110.
A Victorian other ranks post 1860 example, bearing five battle honours to '*Central India*'. Two screw studs to reverse. VGC. N.B. *See Fig: 82.* for an illustration of a similar pattern plate.

16th (Queen's) Lancers

1970 July Wallis & Wallis, Sussex £14.
A late Victorian officers silver and gilt lance cap plate. GC.

1982 April Geoff White, Bristol £195.
A fine officers gilt and silvered lance cap plate QVC. VGC. Illus. *Thirteen battle honours*, extreme top tip of plate as found.

1997 February Bosleys, Buckinghamshire £520.
A fine gilt and silvered officers lance cap plate. *thirteen battle honours.* GC. N.B. *See Fig: 90.* for an illustration of a similar pattern plate.

1997 April Bosleys, Buckinghamshire £150.
A rare 1828-1837 lance cap plate. Gilt triangular rayed plate mounted with silvered Hanoverian Royal Arms, with below the arms a scroll bearing '*Queens*'. Above the arms a scroll bearing '*Bhurtpore*', with to the left side a scroll bearing '*Peninsula*' and to the right a similar scroll bearing '*Waterloo*'. Some wear to gilt, the silver toned, three splits to the rayed backing plate. It is rare to find this early pattern plate, in any condition.

1998 December Bosleys, Buckinghamshire £55.
A good pre 1901 other ranks plate with battle honours up to '*Aliwal*'. the screw studs are old replacements, otherwise GC. Illus. N.B. *See Fig: 91.* for an illustration of a similar pattern plate.

1999 June Bosleys, Buckinghamshire £82.
A Senior N.C.O.'s scarce gilded other ranks lance cap plate, with honours to '*Aliwal*'. With two screw studs to reverse, some wear to the gilt, old lacquer overall. GC. Illus.

17th (Duke of Cambridge's Own) Lancers

1970 July Wallis & Wallis, Sussex £17.
A late Victorian officers silver and gilt lance cap plate. GC.

1984 January Wallis & Wallis, Sussex £500.
A rare officers gilt & silvered plate of the *17th Light Dragoons (Lancers)* pre 1855 pattern. The Victorian Royal Arms above the skull and crossed bones. No battle honours. Plate measures 10" x 5 1/2". GC. (several fixing wires missing), the gilt good. Illus. One upper ray tip of plate missing.

1984 August Wallis & Wallis, Sussex £80.
An officers pattern pre 1876 lance cap plate, being without the letters "DCO" (Duke of Cambridge's Own), four battle honour scrolls to Sevastopol. GC. (few fixing wires missing). Illus. N.B. *See Fig: 95.* for an illustration of an other ranks plate of this particular pattern.

1990 October Wallis & Wallis, Sussex £105.
A Victorian officers gilt and silvered lance cap plate. Six battle honours, to '*South Africa 1879*'. GC. (small hole at base of plate, "D" in design missing) gilt rubbed. Illus. Presumably the 'D' referred to was from the "D.C.O" on the overlay. *See Fig: 96.* for an illustration of a similar pattern plate in very good condition.

1995 March Spink's, London £1400.
A very fine and rare crimean period officers chapka plate Circa 1850. The gilt plate with white metal Royal Arms, above a finely detailed white metal death's head and motto between sprays of laurel and oak leaves. Illus. Two upper ray tips as found, otherwise in VGC for age.

1995 March Spink's, London £360.
An officers fine gilt and silvered chapka plate Circa 1860.
The plate mounted with white metal ornamentation in the form of the Royal Arms, death's head, motto, and scrolls. *Four battle honours.* (top most point of plate slightly as found). Illus. The top tip was very much as found.

1998 February Bosleys, Buckinghamshire £625.
A fine & scarce 1856-1860 officers lance cap plate. The Royal Arms in silver, with the honours '*Alma*', '*Balaclava*', '*Inkerman*' and '*Sevastopol*'. The skull and crossed bones above a scroll bearing 'Or glory', beneath which is a two part scroll inscribed '*Seventeenth Lancers*'. An untouched example, the silver tarnished, the gilt fresh under age grime. Illus. Looked to be a nice plate.

1998 April Bosleys, Buckinghamshire £1000.
A fine and rare 1828-1837 example of an officers lance cap plate of the *17th Light Dragoons*. Triangular gilt metal plate mounted with the Hanoverian Royal Arms, beneath the arms, the skull and crossed bones in silvered metal, below which is a tri-part scroll bearing the motto "*Or glory*". Some ray tips slightly bent, tail of the 'supporter' lion detached, but present, some wear to gilt, silver nicely toned.

1999 October Bosleys, Buckinghamshire £95.
A post 1880 example of an other ranks lance cap plate. Six honours to '*South Africa 1879*'. Two screw studs to back of plate. VGC. *See Fig: 97.* for an illustration of a similar pattern plate.

21st (Empress of India's) Lancers

1970 July Wallis & Wallis, Sussex £16.
A Victorian officers silver and gilt lance cap plate of the 21st (Empress of India's) Lancers. 2nd pattern with the honour '*Khartoum*'. VGC.

1984 August Wallis & Wallis, Sussex £105.
A Victorian officers gilt and silvered lance cap plate. Plate of the 1st pattern without the battle honour '*Khartoum*', or the Imperial title. Near VGC. Illus. Top ray tip of plate slightly as found. N.B. *See Fig: 100.* for an illustration of a similar pattern plate in excellent condition.

1998 June Bosleys, Buckinghamshire £140.
A good scarce brass other ranks post 1898 example (2nd pattern). The plate with the battle honour '*Khartoum*' and '*VRI*' cypher. To the reverse are two screw studs. VGC. This plate with the title scroll 'Empress of India's Lancers'. N.B. *See Fig: 103.* for an illustration of a similar pattern plate in excellent condition.

1998 August Bosleys, Buckinghamshire £150.
A good scarce brass other ranks example C.1897-98 (1st pattern), being without the honour '*Khartoum*' and the VRI cypher. Two screw studs to reverse. VGC. N.B. *See Fig: 101.* for an illustration of a similar pattern plate, in what looks to be un-issued condition.

Reserve Regiment of Lancers

1985 July Wallis & Wallis, Sussex £24.
A Victorian helmet plate of HM Reserve Regiment of Lancers, Near VGC. Illus. N.B. *See Fig: 53A.* for an illustration of a similar pattern helmet plate.

1999 October Bosleys, Buckinghamshire £90.
A Victorian Reserve Regiment other ranks helmet plate. A good example, worn of the foreign service helmet. Two loops to reverse, top point to star with slight defect. GC. Illus.

1ST CITY OF LONDON YEOMANRY

1997 October Bosleys, Buckinghamshire £550.
An officers lance cap plate circa 1907. Gilt rayed plate with a sil-

vered oak wreath surmounted by a '*King's*' crown etc. The gilt fresh, the silver nicely toned. The silver overlay has been re-affixed to the back plate at some period, otherwise in VGC. N.B. *See Fig: 110.* for an illustration of a similar pattern plate.

1998 February Bosleys, Buckinghamshire £140.
A good circa 1907 example of an other ranks lance cap plate. Brass rayed plate with oak wreath surmounted by a crown, with below the wreath, a scroll bearing '*Rough Riders*'. At the base of the wreath a four part scroll bearing the regimental title, with to the left a scroll bearing '*South Africa*' and to the right a scroll with '*1900-02*'. Old strengthening repair to ray tip, one or two screw studs absent, otherwise GC. Illus. N.B. *See Fig: 111.* for an illustration of a similar pattern plate.

LINCOLNSHIRE IMPERIAL YEOMANRY

1980 July David Young, Paddington £200.
A good officers pattern lance cap plate. The plate was in VGC.

Replacement Plumes and Cap-Lines for the Lance Cap

For many collectors, an item of military head-dress without its plume is incomplete, for surely the plume enhances the appearance of most types of full dress head -dress, that certainly being the case with a lance cap.

Additionally the inclusion of a set of cap-lines complements a chapka, particularly when they are connected to a cap that is on display.

Genuine examples of either officers, or other ranks pattern plumes for lance caps of British regular cavalry regiments, are on rare occasions offered for sale at either auction salerooms, or at specialist militaria shops. Plumes for yeomanry lance caps however, rarely appear to be offered for sale, possibly because so few caps were made/worn.

On the infrequent occasions that a lance cap plume is offered for sale by auction, it is often accompanied by other various articles of militaria not related to a item of head -dress, and is sold as 'a lot'. The price realised for such a 'lot' obviously encompasses all the items included within the lot as a whole, which therefore makes it difficult to estimate the actual cost of the plume itself.

Notwithstanding the above, before concluding this particular chapter, we have assembled below a small selection of officers plumes, other ranks pattern plumes and cap-lines etc that have been offered for sale over a seventeen year period at the saleroom of Wallis and Wallis, together with one example from Christie's, South Kensington saleroom. N.B. The descriptions below are reproduced approximately as they appeared in the relevant sales catalogue.

Lance Cap Plumes

1980 November Wallis & Wallis, Sussex £50.
Thirteen various horsehair plumes for other ranks lance cap, including two with holders. GC.

1981 January Wallis & Wallis, Sussex £55.
An officers scarlet feather plume for the 12th Lancers in its tin case. QGC. (some wear and fading)

1981 May Wallis & Wallis, Sussex £18.
An officers black and white hair plume of the 9th Lancers with gilt socket. GC.

1982 April Wallis & Wallis, Sussex £18.
A 16th Lancers troopers black plume with holder, and red and yellow wool boss and button. GC.

1985 October Wallis & Wallis, Sussex £155.
A black over white feather plume for 9th Lancers cap. Good gilt socket, in its tin case (dented and worn). GC.

1986 October Wallis & Wallis, Sussex £5.
A wooden crimping block, with black and white other ranks plume in situ, and an army issue razor, Basically GC. Plume for the 9th Lancers.

1992 June Wallis & Wallis, Sussex £90.
A scarlet feather plume for 12th Lancers officers head-dress, with its gilt socket (minor moth), in its tin case (worn). GC.

1997 June Wallis & Wallis, Sussex £120.
A good green hair plume for 5th Lancers lance cap, gilt socket and band. VGC.

Lancer Cap-lines

1982 April Wallis & Wallis, Sussex £42.
An officers set of full dress cap-lines, and body belt of the 12th Lancers, together with a gilt waist-belt. GC.

1989 May Wallis & Wallis, Sussex £260.
A lancer officers set of gilt cap-lines with flounders and tassels; ditto in buff cord, and two yellow other ranks lines Average GC. This style of cap-lines was worn with the 1828 pattern lance cap.

1989 June Wallis & Wallis, Sussex £150.
A set of lancer officers gilt cap-lines, with acorns and sliders GC, and an early gilt lace girdle.

1990 January Christie's South Kensington £60.
A 17th Lancers officers set of gold cord cap-lines with white cotton

lining, and a pair of full dress sword slings (on web belt) for the same regiment. (2).

1997 July Wallis & Wallis, Sussex £180.
A set of officers gilt cap-lines for a lance cap. Near VGC (slight wear at clip, one slide replaced).

Sundry Lancer Head-Dress Items

1982 April Wallis & Wallis, Sussex £16.
A tin case for officers lance cap, containing seven various plumes of different sizes. Average GC. N.B. None of the plumes were for a lance cap.

1989 May Wallis & Wallis, Sussex £150.
Six officers gilt plume sockets: One for Albert shako, one for Quilted shako, two for Hussar busby, one for Lance cap, one for Light Dragoon (?); two small white metal, and one bronzed; one other ranks for busby and one for lance cap. (11). GC to VGC.

1990 March Wallis & Wallis, Sussex £70.
A square tin for officers lance cap, with brass name plate engraved "*HIH Prince Adolphus of Teck 17th Lancers*", with another tin. QGC (tins rusted).

[1] Regimentals (Islington) ceased trading from 70 Essex Road, Islington, London in May 2000, and are now offering their wide range of militaria on the internet.

Appendix IV

Past and Present Titles of the Regular Lancer Regiments

The following dates and previous titles of the lancer regiments, are with a few exceptions, those given in J.M. Brereton's most informative book on the regiments and corps of the British Army (9).

However, as we all know, few things in life are easy, and verifying dates and facts relating to the formation of, and past titles of army regiments is even less so. Our research into regimental histories and other sources of reference, has identified small anomalies regarding the recorded date certain regiments were raised and their past titles. Therefore in addition to the dates and titles shown in the aforementioned reference book, alternative dates/titles have also been listed, these entries being presented in italic text, followed by the relevant source reference number.

5th Lancers

1689 Wynne's Regiment of Enniskillen Dragoons
1704 The Royal Dragoons of Ireland
1751 5th (or Royal Irish) Regiment of Dragoons
1799 The above regiment disbanded
1858 Newly formed 5th (Royal Irish) Dragoon raised
1858 5th or Royal Irish (Light) Dragoons (Lancers) (4)
1861 5th (Royal Irish) Lancers
1920 5th Royal Irish Lancers (119)
1922 April 1922 amalgamated with the 16th The Queen's Lancers
16th/5th Lancers

9th Lancers

1715 Wynn's Dragoons
1751 9th Regiment of Dragoons
1783 9th Regiment of (Light) Dragoons
1816 9th Regiment of (Light) Dragoons (Lancers)
1830 9th (The Queen's Royal) Lancers
1830 9th (The Queen's Royal) Light Dragoons (Lancers) (12)
1861 9th (Queen's Royal) Lancers (12)
1920 9th Queen's Royal Lancers (119)
1960 September 1960 amalgamated with the 12th Royal Lancers (Prince of Wales's)
9th/12th Royal Lancers (Prince of Wales's)

9th/12th Lancers

1960 9th/12th Royal Lancers (Prince of Wales's)

12th Lancers

1715 Bowles's Dragoons
1751 12th Regiment of Dragoons
1768 12th (or The Prince of Wales's) Regiment of (Light) Dragoons
1816 12th (The Prince of Wales's) Lancers (12)
1817 12th (or The Prince of Wales's) Royal Regiment of Lancers
1817 12th or Prince of Wales's Royal Lancers (12)
1856 12th (Prince of Wales's Royal) Lancers
1920 12th Royal Lancers (Prince of Wales's) (12)
1960 September 1960 amalgamated with the 9th Queen's Royal Lancers
9th/12th Royal Lancers (Prince of Wales's)

16th Lancers

1759 16th Regiment of (Light) Dragoons, also known as Burgoyne's Light Horse
1766 2nd (or the Queen's) Regiment of (Light) Dragoons
1766 16th The Queen's Light Dragoons (8)
1769 16th (or The Queen's) Regiment of Light Dragoons
1816 16th (the Queen's) Light Dragoons (Lancers) (12)
1861 16th (The Queen's) Lancers (12)
1920 16th The Queen's Lancers (12)
1922 April 1922 amalgamated with the 5th Royal Irish Lancers
16th/5th Lancers

16th/5th Lancers

1922 16th/5th Lancers

1954 16th/5th The Queen's Royal Lancers

1993 25th June 1993 amalgamated with the 17th/21st Lancers
The Queen's Royal Lancers

17th Lancers

1759 18th Regiment of (Light) Dragoons

1763 17th Regiment of (Light) Dragoons

1765 3rd Light Dragoons (12)

1766 3rd Regiment of (Light) Dragoons

1769 17th Regiment of (Light) Dragoons

1823 17th Regiment of (Light) Dragoons (Lancers)

1861 17th (Light) Dragoons (Lancers), changing that same year to the 17th Lancers (119)

1876 17th (Duke of Cambridge's Own) Lancers

1920 17th Lancers (Duke of Cambridge's Own) (12)

1922 April 1922 amalgamated with the 21st Lancers (Empress of India's)
17th/21st Lancers

21st Lancers

1858 3rd Bengal European Light Cavalry (H.E.I.C.) (119)

1861 21st Light Dragoons (12)

1863 21st Hussars

1897 21st Lancers

1898 October 1898 renamed 21st (Empress of India's) Lancers (28)

1899 21st (Empress of India's) Lancers

1920 21st Lancers (Empress of India's) (12)

1922 April 1922 amalgamated with the 17th Lancers (Duke of Cambridge's Own)
17th/21st Lancers

17th/21st Lancers

1922 17th/21st Lancers

1993 25th June 1993 amalgamated with the 16th/5th The Queen's Royal Lancers
The Queen's Royal Lancers

1816: Cocks feather (12).

1822: Cock-tail feathers (111).

1826: Swan feathers, twelve inches long (112).

1828: Feather, nine inches rising from the cap, and falling sixteen inches (6).

1831: Cock-tail feathers, drooping sixteen inches in front, nine inches at back (rising from cap) (113).

1834: Cock-tail feathers, eight inches from the cap, and falling sixteen inches. Horse hair plumes allowed to be worn in India (6).

1846: Cock-tail feathers, fourteen inches long, and four inches on the mount. In India, horse hair of the same length (110).

1855: Horse hair plumes, feather allowed at levees (6).

1857: Cock-tail feathers, twelve inches long, standing four and a half inches above the top of the cap (107).

1874: Horse hair, twelve inches long, and rising four and a half inches above the top of the cap (108).

1875: Swan feathers, length fourteen inches, and seven inches behind from the bend of the feathers[5] (43).

1876: Cocks feathers permitted for levees and review order (6).

1934: Swan feathers, fourteen inches long in front, and seven inches behind from the bend of the feathers (114).

2000: Cockerel feathers (44).

NOTES

1. A coloured illustration of a painting of Captain William Barker, 16th Lancers, reproduced in *Regiment Magazine* issue No.20. gives the date of the painting as 1871, however Issue No.47. of the same magazine gives the date c.1877 for the identical painting.

2. A photograph on an officers of the 17th Lancers c.1858, and two separate photographs, each depicting an officer of the this regiment c.1860, that appeared in *Regiment Magazine* Issue No.20. all show a white horsehair plume to each officers lance cap.

3. The officers feather plume was virtually black, having only a hint of green to the feathers (14).

4. In *Regiment Magazine* Issue No.47., a photograph of an officer having a black plume in his cap gives the date as c.1869-1871, and an officer having a white plume as c.1872.

5. The sealed pattern date for this pattern of plume is given as 29th March 1875 (43).

Selected Bibliography

Suggestions For Further Reading

Angelsey The Marquess of: *A History of the British Cavalry 1816-1919* (eight volumes). London: Leo Cooper.,1973 -1997.

Barclay, Brigadier C.N. CBE. DSO.: *History of the 16th/5th The Queen's Royal Lancers 1925-1961*. Aldershot: Gale and Polden., 1963.

Barlow, L. & Smith, R. J.: *The Uniforms of the British Yeomanry Force 1794-1914. Volume: 1. The Sussex Yeomanry Cavalry*. Aldershot, Hampshire: Robert Ogilby Trust., C.1981

Brereton, J.A.M.: *A Guide to the Regiments and Corps of the British Army on the Regular Establishment*. London: Bodley Head., 1985.

Carman, William. Y.: *British Military Uniforms From Contemporary Pictures, Henry VII to the Present Day*. London: Leonard Hill (Books) Limited., 1957.

Carman, William. Y.: *Head Dresses of the British Army - Cavalry*. Surrey, England: Carman., 1968.

Carman, William. Y.: *Head Dresses of the British Army - Yeomanry*. Surrey, England: Carman., 1970.

Carman, William. Y.: *Richard Simkin's Uniforms of the British Army - The Cavalry Regiments*. Exeter, Devon: Webb & Bower., 1982.

Dawson, Malcolm: *Uniforms of the Royal Armoured Corps*. New Malden, Surrey: Almark Publishing., 1974.

French, The Hon E.G.: *Good-Bye to Boot and Saddle*. London: Hutchinson & Co (Publishers) Ltd., 1951.

Ffrench Blake, Lt Colonel R.L.V. DSO.: *A History of the 17th/21st Lancers 1922-1959*. London and New York: Macmillan & Co Ltd., 1962.

Graham, Colonel H: *History of The Sixteenth the Queen's Light Dragoons (Lancers) 1759-1912*. Published privately., 1912.

Harris, R.G.: *Yeomanry Drum Banners and Mounted Bands*. Aldershot, Hampshire: Robert Ogilby Trust., 1991.

Hobson, Lt Colonel G.W.: *Some XII Royal Lancers*. Shipston, England: King's Stone Press., 1936.

King, Hugh L. & Kipling, Arthur L.: *Head-Dress Badges of the British Army - Volume One*. London, Frederick Muller Limited., 1973, and republished Farnham, Surrey, England: Hugh King., 1995.

Langridge: *9th Queen's Royal Lancers, Dress Distinctions*. England: Langridge Military Publishing., 1962.

Langridge: *12th Royal Lancers, Dress Distinctions*. England: Langridge Military Publishing., 1960.

Lummis, Canon William Murrell M.C.: *Honour The Light Brigade*. London: J.B. Hayward and Sons., 1973.

Lunt, James: *The Scarlet Lancers, The Story of 16th/5th The Queen's Royal Lancers 1689-1992*. London: Leo Cooper Publishing., 1993.

Micholls, Major Gilbert: *A History of the 17th Lancers (Duke of Cambridge's Own) 1895-1924*. (two volumes). London: Macmillan & Co Ltd., C.1927.

Mileham, P.J.R.: *The Yeomanry Regiments - A Pictorial History*. Tunbridge Wells, Kent: Spellmount Limited., 1985.

Mollo, John. & Boris: *Into The Valley of Death, The British Cavalry Division at Balaclava 1854*. London: Windrow & Greene., 1991.

Rankin, Robert.H. Colonel: *A Pictorial History of Military Head-Dress 1660-1914*. London: Arms & Armour Press., 1976.

Renard, F.H.: *The Ninth (Queen's Royal) Lancers 1715-1903*. England: Blackwood., 1904.

Rowe, David J.J.: *Head Dress of the British Heavy Cavalry*. Atglen, U.S.A.: Schiffer Military History., 1999.

Sheppard, Major E.W. OBE. MC. psc.: *The Ninth Queen's Royal Lancers 1715-1936*. Aldershot, Hampshire: Gale & Polden Ltd., 1939.

Skilton, Wendy: *British Military Band Uniforms - Cavalry Regiments*. Leicester: Midland Publishing Limited., 1992.

Smith, R.J. & Harris, R.G.: *The Uniforms of the British Yeomanry force 1794-1914*. Volume:10. The Yeomanry Force at the 1911 Coronation. Aldershot, Hampshire: Robert Ogilby Trust., 1991.

Stewart, Captain P.F.: *The History of the XII Royal Lancers 1715-1945*. England: Oxford University Press., 1950.

Sumner, Ian. & Wilson, Roy: *Yeomanry of The East Riding*. East Yorkshire: Hutton Press., 1993.

Walton, P.S. Lieutenant Colonel: *Simkin's Soldiers, The British Army in 1900*, Volume One. Dorking, Surrey: The Victorian Military Society., 1981.

Warner, Philip: *The British Cavalry*. London: J.M. Dent & Sons Ltd., 1984.

Wilkinson, Frederick: *Militaria*. London and Sydney: Ward Lock & Company., 1969.

Wilkinson-Latham, Robert & Christopher: *Cavalry Uniforms of Britain and the Commonwealth including other Mounted Troops*. London: Blandford Press., 1969.

Regiment Magazine. Issue No. 5. The Yeomanry 1794 - 1994. November 1994. Issue No. 20. The Queen's Royal Lancers 1689-1997. Hemel Issue No. 47. British Army Lancer Regiments 1816-1914. June 2000. Swanley, Kent: Specialist Interests.

War Office: *Dress Regulations for The Officers of the Army (Including Militia) 1900*. H.M.S.O. Reprinted by Arms & Armour Press., 1969, with introduction by W.Y.Carman.

War Office: *Dress Regulations for The Officers of the Army 1934*. H.M.S.O. Wembley, Middlesex: Reprinted by Ray Westlake Books., 1986.

Source References

(1) Written correspondence from William Carman to David Rowe relating to the origins and early uniforms of the lancers. 23rd July 2000.

(2) Written correspondence from William Carman to David Rowe relating to the Ulans Britanniques, and early pattern lance cap plates. 25th June 2000.

(3) *Brassey's History of Uniforms - Napoleonic Wars, Napoleon's Army*. Rene Chartrand. 1996.

(4) *Good-bye to Boot and Saddle*. Lt Colonel Hon E.G. French D.S.O. Published 1951 by Hutchinson & Co, New York.

(5) Written correspondence from William Carman to David Rowe regarding the formation of British lancer regiments (31st July 2000), on the early pattern lance caps (6th August 2000), and the cap of the 17th Lancers (4th September 2000).

(6) *Head Dresses of The British Army - Cavalry.* W.Y. Carman. Privately published 1968.

(7) Royal Personages and Regimental Uniforms 1840-1939. Ronald G. Harris. Published in the Journal of the *Society For Army Historical Research.* No. 257., 1986.

(8) *The Scarlet Lancers, The Story of 16th/5th The Queen's Royal Lancers 1689-1992.* James Lunt. Published 1993 by Leo Cooper, London.

(9) *A Guide to the Regiment and Corps of the British Army on The Regular Establishment.* J.M. Brereton. 1985.

(10) The 16th/5th Lancers, part of a series of articles by Ronald G. Harris entitled 'Cavalry Mounted Bands, Drum Horses and Drum Banners'. Published in *Military Modelling Magazine*, June 1983.

(11) *The Regiment Journal.* Summer 1896.

(12) *Uniforms of the British Army - The Cavalry Regiments.* William Y. Carman.

(13) British Cavalry Regiments - 9th Lancers c.1820. Christopher Rothero. An article published in *Military Modelling Magazine*, May 1976.

(14) *Regiment Magazine.* Issue Forty-seven, entitled 'British Lancer Regiments 1816-1914'. June 2000.

(15) The 12th Lancers. *Journal of the Royal Armoured Corps.*

(16) *Regiment Magazine.* Issue Twenty, entitled 'The Queen's Royal Lancers 1689-1997'. March 1997.

(17) *In The Finest Tradition, The Royal Scots Dragoon Guards (Carabiniers & Greys).* Stephen Wood. Published 1988 by Mainstream Publishing Co, Edinburgh.

(18) Author's card index and filing systems.

(19) *Into The Valley of Death* (The British Cavalry Divison at Balaclava 1854). John & Boris Mollo. Published 1991 by Woodrow & Greene, London.

(20) *Honour The Light Brigade.* A record of the services of the officers, non-commissioned officers and other ranks of the five light cavalry regiments that comprised the Light Brigade on the 25th October 1854. Canon W.M. Lummis. M.C. Published 1988 by J.B. Hayward and Son, London.

(21) Written correspondence from Captain J.M. Holtby, Curator of The Queen's Royal Lancers Museum to the David Rowe regarding Lt Henry Wood, Sgt T. Lawrence, and the uniform of the Bandmaster of the 17th/21st Lancers. November 1999.

(22) *Who Was Who 1941-1950.* Published 1951 by Adam & Charles Black, London.

(23) *The British Empire Magazine*, Issue Fifty-six, entitled 'The Army at Ease', 1973.

(24) *Who Was Who 1897-1916.* Published by Adam & Charles Black, London.

(25) *Who Was Who 1916-1928.* Published 1929 by Adam & Charles Black, London.

(26) *British Military Uniforms from Contemporary Pictures (Henry VII to the Present Day).* William Y. Carman. 1957.

(27) Written correspondence from William Carman to David Rowe regarding the history and uniform of the 19th Lancers. 2nd August 2000.

(28) The Uniform of the 21st (Empress of India's) Lancers. Donald S. Fosten and Robert J. Marrion. Published in *Tradition Magazine* No.38., April 1970.

(29) One Hundred and Twenty Seconds in Hell. Peter Lewisham. Published in *Soldier Magazine (U.S.A.)* Vol.3. No.2., 1973.

(30) Forgotten Regiments - the 21st Hussars/Lancers. Bob Marrion & Doug Hagger. Published in *Military Modelling Magazine*, February 1994.

(31) Written correspondence from William Carman to David Rowe relating to the formation, lance cap and uniform of the 23rd Lancers. 23rd July 2000.
(32) *Harts Army List 1905.*
(33) *Who Was Who 1929-1940.* Published by Adam & Charles Black. London.
(34) *The Monthly Army List* for October 1897. Published by the War Office 30 September 1897.
(35) *Harts Army List 1909.*
(36) *Who Was Who 1961-1970.* Published by Adam & Charles Black, London.
(37) *The Happy Warrior - The Life Story of Sir Winston Churchill.* Hulton Press Ltd. 1958.
(38) *Head Dress of the British Heavy Cavalry.* David J.J. Rowe. Published 1999 by Schiffer Military History 1999.
(39) The 17th Lancers 1904. A. H. Bowling. Published in *Model-world Magazine*, March 1973.
(40) Other Ranks Dress for the Cavalry in 1899. Published in the Journal of the *Crown Imperial Society*, September 1982.
(41) *The Wonder Book of Soldiers.* c.1914 Published by Ward Lock & Co, London.
(42) Written correspondence from William Carman to David Rowe regarding the first pattern lance cap plate of the 16th Lancers (7th June 2000), and further information on the first pattern plate (2nd August 2000).
(43) *Dress Regulation for The Army 1900.*
(44) Interview with Louis Chalmers of 'The Plumery'. 19th May 2000.
(45) British Lance Caps. William Y. Carman. Published in *Antique Arms and Militaria Magazine*. Vol:1. No.3., December 1978.
(46) *Head-Dress Badges of the British Army.* Volume One. Arthur Kipling and Hugh King 1979.
(47) *Cavalry and Yeomanry Badges 1914.* F. Wilkinson.
(48) A letter by Walter Lambert that appeared on the correspondence page of the Journal of the *Crown Imperial Society* - Yeomanry Cavalry Issue, March 1983.
(49) Written correspondence from Walter Lambert to David Rowe regarding the Reserve Regiments. June 2000.
(50) Abbreviated details taken from of a copy of the Special Army Order of 29th May 1900, supplied by Geoff Frost A.M.S.
(51) The *Regimental Journal of the 17th/21st Lancers.* Volume: 42., January 1970.
(52) *Uniforms of The Royal Armoured Corps.* Malcolm Dawson. 1974.
(53) *The Scarlet and Green Journal.* 1980/81 Edition.
(54) The official programme of The Royal Tournament 1991.
(55) *British Military Band Uniforms - Cavalry Regiments.* Wendy Skilton. 1992.
(56) Telephone conversation with Captain Holtby, Curator of The Queen's Royal Lancers Museum regarding the regimental museum. April 2000.
(57) Telephone conversation with Captain J.M. Holtby QRL regarding the uniform worn by the band from amalgamation to the present day, also Director of Music. July 2000.
(58) *16th/5th The Queen's Royal Lancers Journal.* 1982.
(59) Written correspondence from William Carman to David Rowe relating to the Adlington Troop, Radbourne Troop and Duke of Cornwall's Yeomanry. 13th June 2000.
(60) Written correspondence from William Carman to David Rowe relating to the West Essex Yeomanry. 29th June 2000.
(61) 'Interesting Photograph Notes'. K.B. Hook. *Published in the Journal of the Crown Imperial Society*, March 1983.
(62) *The British Cavalry.* Philip Warner. 1984.
(63) *The Sunday Telegraph Newspaper.* 4th June 2000.
(64) *The V.C. and D.S.O.* Sir O'Moore Creagh V.C. G.C.B. G.C.S.I., and E.M. Humpries. c.1920.
(65) A series of articles by Major Roy Wilson entitled 'The Yeomanry Cavalry'. *Military Modelling Magazine*, 1985.
(66) Booklet entitled: *The Yeomanry Force at the 1911 Coronation.* Ronald G. Harris and Robert J. Smith. Robert Ogilby Trust., 1988.
(67) Booklet entitled: *Yeomanry Drum Banners and Mounted Bands.* R.G. Harris. Robert Ogilby Trust., 1991.
(68) *The Yeomanry Regiments - A Pictorial History.* P.J.R. Mileham 1985.
(69) Information based on an officers lance cap of the Bedfordshire Yeomanry in the Geoff Frost collection.
(70) *The Book of Public Arms.* Arthur Fox Davies 1915.
(71) *Fifty Years of Yeomanry Uniforms.* Ronald G. Harris 1972.
(72) Written correspondence from William Carman to David Rowe relating to the Lincolnshire Yeomanry. 8th July 2000.
(73) An article by David le Roi relating to the 1st City of London Yeomanry (Rough Riders). National Army Museum bin book No 95.
(74) *Head-Dresses of the British Army - Yeomanry.* William Y. Carman 1970.
(75) *Cavalry Uniforms of Britain and the Commonwealth including Other Mounted Troops.* Robert and Christopher Wilkinson-Latham 1969.
(76) *Yeomanry of the East Riding.* Ian Sumner and Roy Wilson. 1993.
(77) The East Riding Yeomanry (Wenlock's Horse) 1902-47. Major Roy Wilson. An article published in *Military Modelling Magazine*, April 1983.
(78) Photograph of an officers lance cap of the East Riding of Yorkshire Yeomanry. National Army Museum Accession No. 65094.
(79) Written correspondence from Major Roy Wilson to David Rowe, regarding the officers lance cap of the East Riding of Yorkshire Yeomanry. March 2000.
(80) *Records of the Lanarkshire Imperial Yeomanry.* Russell E. Wood. 1910.
(81) A contemporary newspaper account relating to the Lanarkshire Yeomanry.
(82) Written correspondence from William Carman to David Rowe relating to the Lanarkshire Yeomanry. 8th July 2000.
(83) Description based on an officers blue cloth helmet of the Lanarkshire Yeomanry sold at the saleroom of Wallis and Wallis. August 1988.

(84) Description based on an officers lance cap of the Lanarkshire Yeomanry that sold at a Buckinghamshire Auction House. December 1994.

(85) National Army Museum's bin book No 98. (Scottish Yeomanry). Within this album is a colour photograph of a dismounted officer and trooper in full dress uniform, though to have been taken prior to the outbreak of the Second World War.

(86) Description based on an officers full dress tunic that sold at the saleroom of Wallis and Wallis. January 1972.

(87) The Lincolnshire Yeomanry. R.J. Smith. Published in Military *Modelling Magazine*, May 1980.

(88) An article entitled the 'Lincolnshire Yeomanry' by Eric Dickinson. *Lincolnshire Life Magazine*, January 1987.

(89) Telephone conversation with Eric Dickinson regarding the cap of the Lincolnshire Yeomanry and the uniform worn. Also information relating to the colour of the velvet backing to the cypher on the lance cap that he formerly owned, and other matters relating to this cap. May and July 2000.

(90) Written correspondence from Robert J. Smith to David Rowe relating to the officers uniform of the Lincolnshire Yeomanry. February 2000.

(91) Written correspondence from William Carman to David Rowe relating to the Surrey Imperial Yeomanry and the uniform worn. 8th July 2000.

(92) Information (head-dress excepted) based on a colour illustration of a dismounted officer of the Surrey Yeomanry in full dress uniform, by the artist Robert J. Marrion. Published in *Military Modelling Magazine*, February 1977.

(93) Booklet entitled: *The Sussex Yeomanry Cavalry*. Leslie Barlow and Robert J. Smith. Robert Ogilby Trust. c.1981.

(94) The Royal Bucks Hussars. Ronald G. Harris. Published in *Military Modelling Magazine*. February 1979.

(95) Written correspondence from William Carman to David Rowe relating to the Taplow Lancers, their brief history and uniform. 8th July 2000.

(96) National Army Museum's bin book No 94. (Yeomanry A- H).

(97) *Berkshire Yeomanry Journal*. 1998-1999.

(98) Written correspondence from William Carman to David Rowe regarding the lance cap plate of the 16th Lancers c.1830, and a brief history of the Adlington Troop. 25th June 2000.

(99) The Volunteer Cavalry of Derbyshire. M.D. Brittain. Published in the Journal of the *Crown Imperial Society*, March 1983.

(100) *Regiment Magazine*. Issue Five, entitled 'The Yeomanry 1794-1994', December 1994.

(101) Booklet entitled: *3rd County of London (Sharpshooters)*. Leslie Barlow and Robert J. Smith. Robert Ogilby Trust. 1983.

(102) Booklet entitled: *North Somerset Yeomanry*. Leslie Barlow and Robert J. Smith. Robert Ogilby Trust. c.1982.

(103) *Harts Army List 1904*.

(104) *Harts Army List 1910*.

(105) National Army Museums bin book No.95. (K-L).

(106) *Soldier Magazine*. 15th/19th The King's Royal Hussars - 'Sabres of Keener Metal'. A article in the series 'Your Regiment' (No. 66).

(107) *Regulations for the Dress of General, Staff, and Regimental Officers of The Army 1857*.

(108) *Dress Regulations 1874*. (abbreviated title).

(109) *Dress Regulations 1883*. (abbreviated title).

(110) *Dress Regulations 1846*. (abbreviated title).

(111) *Dress Regulations 1822*. (abbreviated title)

(112) *Dress Regulations 1826*. (abbreviated title).

(113) *Dress Regulations 1831*. (Abbreviated title).

(114) *Dress Regulations for The Army 1934*.

(115) *A History of the 17th/21st Lancers*. Lt Colonel R.L.V. Ffrench-Blake D.S.O.

(116) Written correspondence from William Carman to David Rowe relating to the 1822 pattern officers undress cap, and the Reserve Regiment. 29th September 2000.

(117) *Who Was Who 1951-1960*. Published by Adam & Black, London.

(118) Written correspondence from the Scottish War Museum to William Carman relating to the Lanarkshire Yeomanry. November 2000.

(119) Written correspondence from William Carman to David Rowe relating to the past titles of the regular lancer regiments. 27th January 2001.

(120) Written correspondence from the Museum of Linclonshire Life to David Rowe relating to finite details of the Lincolnshire Yeomanry lance cap. 25th January 2001.

(121) *History of the 16th/5th The Queen's Royal Lancers 1925-1961*. Brigadier C.N. Barclay C.B.E. D.S.O. 1963.

(122) *A History of the 17th Lancers (Duke of Cambridge's Own) 1895-1924*. Major Gilbert Micholls. c.1927.

(123) Walter Lambert. A letter that appeared in the September 1981 issue of the Journal of the Crown Imperial Society.

Index

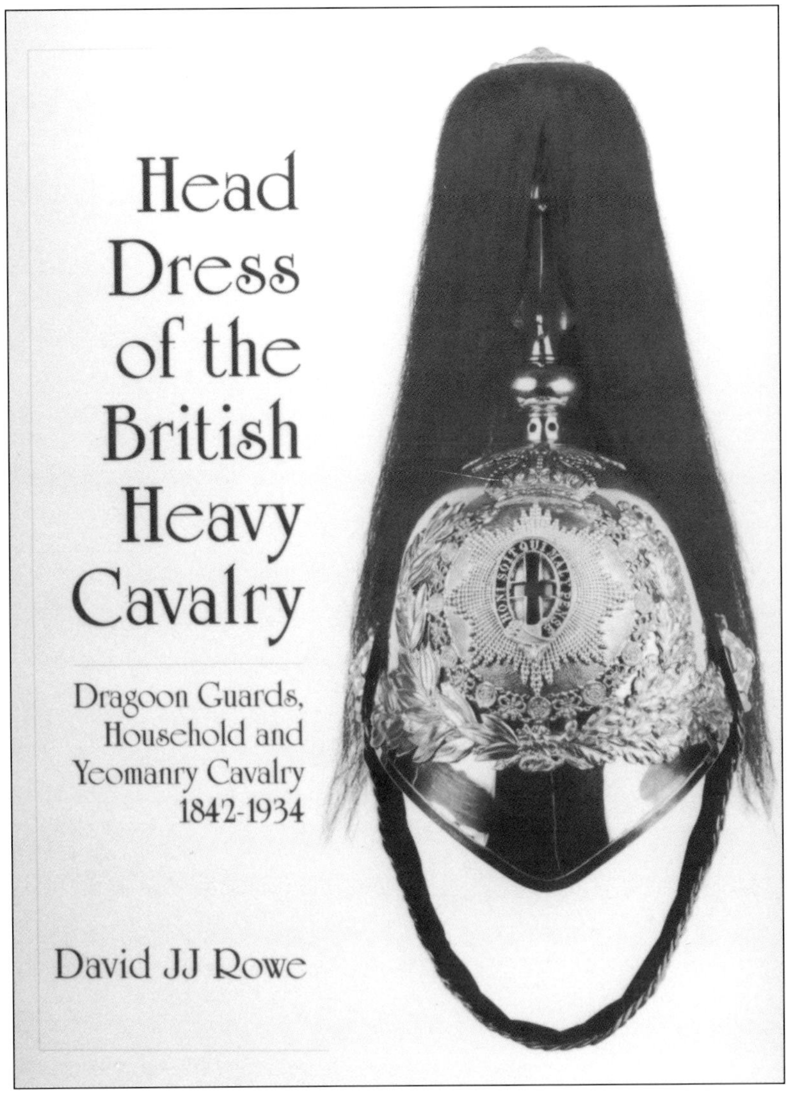

Head Dress of the British Heavy Cavalry
Dragoon Guards, Household, and Yeomanry Cavalry 1842-1934

David JJ Rowe

Here is a book dedicated to the head-dress worn by the British Heavy Cavalry of the period 1842 to the present day. It is lavishly illustrated with both colour and black and white photographs of helmets, most of which have never previously been published. This book is an essential source of reference for both the established, and new collectors, and to the student of cavalry full dress uniforms of the period c. 1850 to 1914.
Size: 9" x 12" • 135 color and b/w photographs • 256 pp.
ISBN: 0-7643-0957-9 • hard cover • $75.00